D0978923

The New York Times
DISUNION

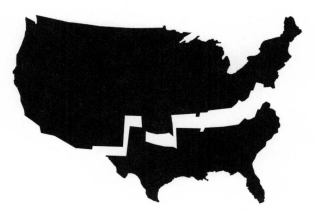

Widmer, Edward L.
The New York Times
disunion : 106 articles
c2013.
33305228747568
wo   10/17/13

rk Times

DISUNION

106 articles from
The New York Times Opinionator

MODERN HISTORIANS REVISIT AND RECONSIDER

THE CIVIL WAR

FROM LINCOLN'S ELECTION TO THE EMANCIPATION PROCLAMATION

EDITED BY TED WIDMER
WITH CLAY RISEN AND GEORGE KALOGERAKIS

BLACK DOG
& LEVENTHAL
PUBLISHERS
NEW YORK

Copyright © 2013 The New York Times

All rights reserved. No part of this book, either text or illustration, may be used or
reproduced in any form without prior written permission from the publisher.

Published by
Black Dog & Leventhal Publishers, Inc.
151 West 19th Street
New York, NY 10011

Distributed by
Workman Publishing Company
225 Varick Street
New York, NY 10014

Manufactured in the USA

Image Credits:
The Library of Congress: pp 6, 21, 38, 93, 105, 129, 142, 144, 153, 180, 203, 216, 241,
    247, 260, 335, 343, 402
Chicago Historical Society: p 49
Daniel Borris: p. 267
New York Public Library: p 71
The Museum of the Confederacy Richmond, Virginia Photography by Katherine
    Wetzel: p. 166
National Archive: p. 297
U.S. Games Systems: p. 375

Cover Design by Liz Driesbach
Interior Design by Sheila Hart

ISBN-13: 978-1-57912-928-6

h g f e d c b a

Library of Congress Cataloging-in-Publication Data on file

CONTENTS

Acknowledgements

vi

Introduction

vii

Chapter 1

SECESSION

1

Chapter 2

THE WAR BEGINS

99

Chapter 3

BULL RUN

159

Chapter 4

1862

233

Chapter 5

THE WAR EXPANDS

267

Chapter 6

TOWARD EMANCIPATION

389

List of Contributors

439

Index

445

ACKNOWLEDGEMENTS

Disunion began with Jamie Malanowski, who brought the kernel of the idea for the series to The New York Times Op-Ed staff in early 2010. For that, and for the many articles he later wrote for the series, some of which appear in this volume, we cannot thank him enough. Our gratitude goes as well to David Shipley, the Op-Ed editor who gave us the green light to proceed, and to his successor, Trish Hall, for continuing to back us. Behind and above all of this has been Andy Rosenthal, the Editorial Page editor and not-so-secret Civil War buff; without his support, none of this would have happened.

Though it is the writers' names that appear on the articles, and our names on the cover of the book, much of the hard work in producing the Disunion series was performed by our Web team—Snigdha Koirala, Whitney Dangerfield and Kari Haskell—our copy editors—John Guida, Kristie McClain and Roberta Zeff—and our indefatigable accounts payable experts, Inell Willis and Natalie Shutler.

Finally, our thanks to Alex Ward, who helped take this book from a vague idea to a concrete plan, and the folks at Black Dog and Leventhal—J.P. Leventhal, Lisa Tenaglia and Stephanie Sorensen—for taking that plan and turning it into the beautiful tome you now hold in your hands.

The Question of Disunion

BY TED WIDMER

"But what can I say of that prompt and splendid wrestling with secession slavery, the archenemy personified, the instant he unmistakably showed his face? The volcanic upheaval of the nation, after that firing on the flag at Charleston, proved for certain something which had been previously in great doubt, and at once substantially settled the question of disunion."

—Walt Whitman, *Specimen Days*

It is not easy to find a new way to write about a subject as well-reconnoitered as the Civil War. But 2013 seems a particularly appropriate year to take stock of our national epic. Historic anniversaries can pile up on themselves, and it requires concentration to celebrate the 150th anniversary of Gettysburg and the 50th anniversary of the March on Washington at the same time. Yet they are part of the same broad story, a rhyme that Dr. Martin Luther King Jr. appreciated, as he used Lincoln's temple to preach to the nation about the unfinished business of the Civil War. That business remains unfinished. For despite the peace that came, finally, at Appomattox, the Civil War remains a ghostly presence in American life. It will never vanish, as long as its principal monument, the United States of America, survives. Of course, the armies laid down their arms, and the soldiers came home to build new lives. Some tried desperately to forget the war. Then, inevitably, the prodigious act of remembrance began. Politicians waived their bloody shirts, generals wrote their memoirs, and, ever-dutiful, the veterans themselves reunited, on both sides, well into the 20th century. They decorated graves, they listened to speeches, sometimes they re-assembled on those original battlefields.

A century ago, in 1913, what was probably the most extraordinary Civil War reenactment of all took place at Gettysburg, played out by the former soldiers themselves, 53,407 of whom showed up, roughly a third of the number who had originally fought there. They were the same people, in the same place, but the Civil War had changed considerably since they last met there. A new Southern president, Woodrow Wilson, called it "a forgotten quarrel," when it was nothing of the sort. But reawakening the bitterness of the conflict was nowhere near the agenda in 1913, and the majority of speakers that day preferred to remember how, rather than why, they had fought.

Each generation reenacts the Civil War in its own way. Even after the demise of the warriors (the last known veteran, Albert Woolson, died in 1956), it has never lost its power to fascinate. Today's re-enactors are so numerous that one wonders if their swampy battlefields are, in fact, spawning grounds. The Union lives on, in all of the ways that its adherents hoped, and more than a few that they could not have anticipated. Nor is the Lost Cause lost—its acolytes populate State Houses and Southern rock songs, and even in Northern shrines like Gettysburg, Confederate memorabilia vastly outsells the less romantic souvenirs of the side that actually prevailed. On election night in November 2012, the map of red and blue states bore an uncomfortable similarity to a map of November 1862, an anniversary moment that no one had quite intended.

More than merely relevant, the Civil War remains essential. Each year, millions of students encounter it in the middle of year-long surveys of American history, halfway between the Revolution and the Atomic Age, when it interrupts our mostly happy national narrative with an explosive bang, just before the end of the fall semester. But its centrality stems from more than its timing. For the Civil War determined an enormous amount of the history that ensued, from the rise of mechanized conflict, so tragically a part of the 20th century, to the spread of multi-racial democracies, a happier chapter in recent history. It also permanently redefined the relationship between American citizens and their government. Ralph Waldo Emerson got it right when he said, "We are undergoing a huge Revolution." What Lincoln called a "new birth of freedom" often felt like a straitjacket to those who opposed it, and their legacy is still felt, in the many forms of opposition to the federal writ that we witness on a daily basis. But the important fact with Lincoln is not simply that he wrote well; it is that he won. His fuller vision for the United States triumphed, with ramifications for nearly every walk of American life.

Superlatives come quickly in any discussion of the war. It was our most lethal conflict, by far, and its list of casualties continues to rise, as our means of counting improves. The Battle of Gettysburg killed more Americans than the recent fighting in Iraq and Afghanistan. Historian and Harvard president Drew Gilpin Faust has reminded us that our dead in the Civil War exceeded those of the Korean War, the two world wars, the Spanish American War, the Mexican War, the War of 1812 and the American Revolution combined. Yet out of those terrible statistics, our greatest president emerged. Abraham Lincoln has never strayed far from the popular imagination, and in the wake of the 2012 film "Lincoln," his position as our most beloved president is secure for some time to come. Writing instructors like to say "keep your hero in trouble," and Lincoln was true to that injunction, frustrating generals, disappointing Senators, changing his stance on emancipation, appearing crude and indecisive to many, and nearly falling short in his bid for reelection. The worldwide adulation that he now commands never seemed possible, let alone likely, during much of his presidency. As he said, the Almighty has his own purposes.

American history continues to move forward, relentlessly, and one might expect the Civil War to fade into the past, and become more visibly antiquarian. Yet it shows no sign of doing so. Robert Penn Warren called it our most keenly "felt" history. Although the Vietnam War had not yet been fought when he wrote that in 1961, most would still agree. We don't need to refight it, but there is an intensity to our feelings about the Civil War that remains volatile and unfinished. (A bumper sticker I once saw in Tennessee read "North 1, South 0: Halftime Score.") As new malls threaten battle sites, and high school textbooks assert (or fail to assert) painful chapters from the past, we realize, all over again, just how much we care to get this story right.

That may be the most compelling reason we come back to the war. For more than a century after it was fought, as Dr. King reminded America in 1963, victory made little difference to African-Americans. The work of the historian David Blight has shown how narrowly Americans chose to remember the war, effectively removing slavery from the story. In the bitter aftermath of the fighting, that may have achieved the temporary expedient of reuniting the North and the South. But it did so at a cost, preventing the full story from being told.

The writing of history began as soon as the war commenced, as each side struggled to place its cause in a sympathetic light. The past, too, became a battlefield, with each side claiming the mantle of George Washington on important days like his birthday. But both governments found it difficult to compress the largeness of current events inside that older narrative. The South ultimately renounced the Declaration of Independence, which inconveniently promoted human rights, and even Lincoln, for all of his reverence toward the past, asked

Americans to "disenthrall" themselves from the past.

One significant result of the war was the federal government's recognition that it had a responsibility before the bar of history. In 1864, before the war had ended, the government committed to collect and publish a documentary history of the war, which appeared in seventy volumes, published between 1881 and 1901, as "The Official Records of the War of the Rebellion." The Navy Department undertook its own history, appearing in 30 volumes between 1894 and 1922 (the Navy was still writing its Civil War history as Theodore Roosevelt and then Franklin D. Roosevelt climbed the ladders of Navy bureaucracy, early in their careers). Other massive efforts were done privately, like the ten-volume "Photographic History of the Civil War" (1911), and the comprehensive papers issued by the Southern Historical Society from 1869 to 1959.

Of course, historians were far from alone in writing about the war. Nearly everyone did, in letters home, and in memoirs after the fact, and of course, in the newspapers, where the first draft of history was served up to a voracious reading public. There were no fewer than 3,700 of them publishing on the eve of war, clamoring and competing for attention. In his book on Civil War literature, "Patriotic Gore," Edmund Wilson asked, "has there ever been another historical crisis of the magnitude of 1861–65 in which so many people were so articulate?" Throughout the United States, observers recorded the story, from stay-at-home diarists to photographers to the armies themselves, which were filled with literate young men. The classicist Edward Everett is often ridiculed for having given a long and pedantic speech before Lincoln's jewel-like Gettysburg Address. Yet Everett's oration, filled with allusions to Greek antiquity, spoke eloquently to Americans, satisfying their sense that the United States had, at long last, an epic of its own.

The result, 150 years later, is a mountain of literature that will always exceed our ability to read it, and shows no sign of abating. In his preface to "Battle Cry of Freedom," the historian James McPherson estimated that more than 50,000 works had been written, and that was back in 1988. Year after year, new works add to our knowledge, and sometimes they overwhelm it. But if the Civil War is the best-known subject in American history, there remains much that we do not know and cannot know. To this day, it retains a beguiling capacity to surprise us. Each generation of historians finds new heroes and causes, and the work of challenging earlier interpretations will never cease.

That element of surprise was present from the beginning. In his second inaugural, Lincoln called the war "astounding," and it seems to have caught many Americans that way when it erupted in 1861, despite the fact that it had been predicted for some time. Each side looked for, in Lincoln's words, an "easier triumph" than the long, entrenched conflict that resulted. At the beginning, the idea of war was so new that there was little consensus how to refer to it. Walt Whitman called it "the Secession War," the United States government called it "the War of the Rebellion," and it was only with some hesitation that Lincoln came to use "civil war," the phrase we all now use. But he did so in lower case letters, as if hesitating to admit an inter-family split.

If the war's name was up for grabs, its causes were even more elusive. Over 150 years, many have tried to impose an overarching meaning on the great conflict, usually with mixed results. As usual, Lincoln brings us down to earth. In a letter to Senator Lot Morill of Maine, he wrote, "I don't know but that God has created some one man great enough to comprehend the whole of this stupendous crisis and transaction from end to end, and endowed him with sufficient wisdom to manage and direct it. I confess that I do not fully understand and foresee it all."

Many observers felt the same way. To most foreign visitors, the idea of a huge industrialized war breaking out in North America, so far from Europe's problems, and in a time of general prosperity, was inconceivable. Anthony Trollope, traveling in the United States as the war broke out, wrote of his shock that such a calamity had happened in a country whose politics seemed to be arranged around consensus. "It would seem that they could never be great at war; their very institutions forbid it, their enormous distances forbid it," he wrote. But Americans proved to be quick learners, and soon, the scale and efficiency of their violence stupefied the world. That is only one of the ways in which the United States changed, forever, during the crisis of disunion.

The war especially haunts us during a major anniversary. The centennial, from 1961 to 1965, coincided with an exciting new decade, and offered a chance for history to speak with great authority. The civil rights movement gave an electric charge to the memory of the war, and on occasion its leaders referred directly to it to remind Americans how old their quest for justice was. On May 17, 1962, Martin Luther King formally requested a national rededication to the Emancipation Proclamation, and as federal troops were again dispatched to Mississippi and Alabama, it was easy to remember the ghosts of Corinth, Vicksburg and Mobile Bay. But the official celebrations of the centennial largely muted any references to the civil rights agenda, and the result was a celebration longer on rhetoric than relevance.

Indeed, one could be excused for thinking, in the middle of the 1960s, that the Civil War had been catalogued enough. Did we really need thousands of new books on the best-covered terrain in our history? The answer, evidently, was yes. Asking some of the questions that the civil rights movement had asked, and which America's most beloved historians had failed to, a new generation of scholars brought a refreshing impatience into the profession. In the spirit of Martin Luther King Jr. they expanded our horizons, giving readers a far deeper knowledge of the African-American perspective on the war, and that of women and other groups underrepresented in the first century of scholarship. The arrival of number-crunching computers brought a democracy of their own, and allowed scholars greater command over the raw data of the experience. In countless other ways, as Internet access has become nearly a first amendment right of its own, and great libraries like the Library of Congress have put their holdings online, we have seen a dramatic rise in self-published writings about the war. One can't help feeling that the self-publisher who occupied the White House during those years would approve.

Furthermore, we continue to learn new things about the war. Documents turn up, and improved approaches to old information—for example, the death toll is now estimated around 750,000, twenty percent higher than before. Works of synthesis still remind us, in new language, why these old events remain important. Sometimes a book breaks through to a wide audience—McPherson's "Battle Cry of Freedom," or Doris Kearns Goodwin's "Team of Rivals," which perfectly anticipated the arrival of a president who asked his principal adversary to serve as his secretary of state. Occasionally, it is simply the fact of a new medium that brings the Civil War to a new audience. When Ken Burns aired his nine-part series, "The Civil War," on PBS in the fall of 1990, it became the most-watched program in the history of public television, and attracted forty million viewers, more than the population of the United States in 1860. In a different way, no less visceral, the 1977 television series "Roots" and the 1989 film "Glory" brought the war to life, finally offering wide audiences a glimpse of the African-American perspective.

With all of these thoughts in mind, The New York Times turned to the legacy of the Civil War in the fall of 2010, on the eve of its 150th anniversary. We asked ourselves how we might write a new history, in a new medium, that would express a multiplicity of perspectives. How could we display our respect for the past, and a restless spirit of innovation at the same time? We knew from the start that we wanted these online posts to be more dynamic than the elaborate arguments of academic journals. We wanted serious essays, but we also hoped for some of the snap, crackle and pop of lively online writing, with quick links, illustrations and a spirit of experimentation. Emerson almost seemed to predict our laptops and tablets when he wrote, "the war is a new glass to see all things through."

Most of all, we wanted readers to feel the same awe before the war that Lincoln confessed in his second inaugural. We wanted to get away from the sense, all too easily found in textbooks, that history is a foreordained conclusion. And we hoped to explore some of the lesser-known qualities of the war—its international impact, its broad geography and its huge range of different participants. As Tony Horwitz wrote in an early post,

"You find Rebel Choctaws and Union Kickapoos; Confederate rabbis and Arab camel-drivers; Californians in gray and Alabamans in blue; and in wondrous Louisiana, units called the Corps d'Afrique, the Creole Rebels, the Slavonian Rifles and the European Brigade. By war's end, black troops constituted over 10 percent of the Union Army and Navy. The roster of black sailors included men born in Zanzibar and Borneo."

If there is a 19th century figure who would have enjoyed the 21st century pleasure of posting discursive essays online, it is Walt Whitman. His 1882 book "Specimen Days" captured the essence of the Civil War memorably, with short blog-like essays, about his time in army hospitals and around Washington. Famously, he complained that "the real war will never get into the books," in a phrase often quoted by historians (more or less proving him right).

In the same book, Whitman advanced his hope that his memories of the "fervid atmosphere" of the Civil War would serve as a rejoinder to the "mushy influences of current times." True to that spirit, we sought something robust and alive in the American past. We wanted a multiplicity of perspectives, including those doing the fighting, the Native Americans who fought on both sides, the freedmen who were trying to join the fight, the huge numbers of foreigners who continued to arrive before, during and after the conflict, and Lincoln himself. Whitman called the Civil War a "many-threaded drama"; we hoped to follow some of those threads, including the long threads of reader responses that accompanied each piece.

As Disunion continued, through the winter and into 2011, we were faced with a problem—now that our experiment had succeeded, how and when would we kill it? None of us expected to cover the entirety of the war—four years!—yet the posts were so good, that we kept going. Now, past the two-year mark, it feels like an appropriate time to pause, publish and reflect. The sections of this book are divided into major topical categories, with short introductions by Disunion contributors. We hope, if you enjoy the essays, that you will consult the full roster of Disunion articles at the website that accompanies this publication.

At this stopping point, midway through Disunion's coverage, it is antithetical to the spirit of the series to close with a heavy-handed message. But readers willing to take the time to relive the agony of disunion will, I hope, come away with an appreciation for the privilege of Union. Our era is not especially civil; perhaps this front-row seat at the Civil War will make it more so. After all, Disunion will last but a while longer; the Union endures forever.

CHAPTER 1

Secession

On December 20, 1860, just 42 days after the election of Abraham Lincoln, South Carolina seceded from the United States. In the following months 10 more states would follow suit, eventually forming the Confederate States of America. Then, on April 12, 1861, Confederate forces under Gen. P.G.T. Beauregard, a former commandant at West Point, launched an attack on the Union soldiers at Fort Sumter, an artificial island in the harbor of Charleston, South Carolina, precipitating the Civil War. These two events seem, in retrospect, to follow one from the other. But did they?

Historians have long debated whether widespread secession and war were, in the long view, inevitable. There can be little doubt that Lincoln's election guaranteed that at least several slaveholding states would secede. Though Lincoln the candidate took pains to emphasize that he would not move against slavery where it already existed, and as president-elect remained studiously silent on the question, many Southerners believed that the man from Illinois and his new and newly empowered Republican Party would move aggressively to limit slavery's expansion, isolating the South and putting the institution on a short road to extinction.

But secession was not an immediate, sudden step for every state. Though six states—Mississippi, Florida, Alabama, Georgia, Louisiana and Texas—had joined South Carolina by the end of January 1861, the final four—Virginia, Arkansas, North Carolina and Tennessee—did not leave the Union until after the war began. Four more slave states—Delaware, Maryland, Kentucky and Missouri—remained in the Union. In reality, secession was a fractious, drawn-out process in most places, with degrees of pro-Union sentiment pushing back against secession advocates. In some parts of the Confederacy, primarily the Appalachian Mountain regions of Virginia and Tennessee, Unionist sentiment remained a force throughout the war, generating significant guerrilla activity. Western Virginia undertook a "reverse" secession as a result of the Wheeling

Conventions of May and June 1861, leading to the creation of the loyal state of West Virginia.

Though a war was not inevitable, Lincoln did everything he could to ignite one. He understood that the Union would be hobbled without the South's resources; more importantly, he understood that a successful secession over a political dispute would fatally undermine the core premise of American democracy as a system for working out political differences. And if the Union were to be re-formed, it had to happen quickly; should the South win diplomatic recognition, it would be nearly impossible to force it to rejoin without completely defeating it in battle. While that is precisely what it took to end secession, Lincoln was probably still correct in his calculation: allowing the South to gain diplomatic recognition might well have meant fighting not just Richmond, but London and even Paris as well.

It is harder to determine just how eager the Confederacy was for war. Certainly, many of its military and political leaders were keen to fight. But others cautioned against rushing into conflict, recognizing how ill prepared the new country was for a drawn-out war. Fatally, the South did not have the deliberative political structure, let alone the vibrant public sphere, to allow for such a discussion. Put simply, the same hotheads who pulled the South out of the Union were then able to dictate the speed with which it went to war. Rather than negotiate a deal over the Union installations on Confederate soil still held by Northern forces—most notably Fort Sumter—the Confederacy simply occupied them, or demanded their surrender. It was precisely the pretext that Lincoln was looking for to begin a fight, and he soon found it, in Charleston Harbor.

The Last Ordinary Day

By ADAM GOODHEART

Nov. 1, 1860

Seven score and 10 years ago, a little Pennsylvania town drowsed in the waning light of an Indian summer. Almost nothing had happened lately that the two local newspapers found worthy of more than a cursory mention. The fall harvest was in; grain prices held steady. A new ice cream parlor had opened in the Eagle Hotel on Chambersburg Street. Eight citizens had recently been married; eight others had died. It was an ordinary day in Gettysburg.

It was an ordinary day in America: one of the last such days for a very long time to come.

In dusty San Antonio, Colonel Robert E. Lee of the U.S. Army had just submitted a long report to Washington about recent skirmishes against marauding Comanches and Mexican banditti. In Louisiana, William Tecumseh Sherman was in the midst of a tedious week interviewing teenage applicants to the military academy where he served as superintendent. In Galena, Ill., passers-by might have seen a man in a shabby military greatcoat and slouch hat trudging to work that Thursday morning, as he did every weekday. He was Ulysses Grant, a middle-aged shop clerk in his family's leather-goods store.

Even the most talked-about man in America was, in a certain sense, almost invisible—or at least inaudible.

On Nov. 1, less than a week before Election Day, citizens of Springfield, Ill., were invited to view a new portrait of Abraham Lincoln, just completed by a visiting artist and hung in the statehouse's senate chamber. The likeness was said to be uncanny, but it was easy enough for viewers to reach their own conclusions, since the sitter could also be inspected in person in his office just across the hall. Politically, however, Lincoln was almost as inscrutable as the painted canvas. In keeping with longstanding tradition, he did not campaign at all that autumn; did not so much as deliver a single speech or grant a single interview to the press.

Instead, Lincoln held court each day in his borrowed statehouse office, behind a desk piled high with gifts and souvenirs that supporters had sent him—including countless wooden knicknacks carved from bits and pieces of fence rails he had supposedly split in his youth. He shook hands with visitors, told funny stories and answered mail. Only one modest public statement from him appeared in the Illinois State Journal that morning: a small front-page ad, sandwiched between those for a dentist and a saddle-maker, offering the services of Lincoln & Herndon, attorneys at law.

The future is always a tough thing to predict—and perhaps it was especially so on the first day of that eventful month. Take the oil painting of Lincoln, for example: it would be obsolete within weeks when its subject unexpectedly grew a beard. (The distraught portraitist tried to daub in whiskers after the fact, succeeding only in wrecking his masterpiece.) Or, on a grander scale, an article in the morning's New York Herald, using recent census data to project the country's growth over the next hundred years. By the late 20th century, it stated confidently, America's population would grow to 300 million (pretty close to accurate), including 50 million slaves (a bit off). But, asked the author, could a nation comprising so many different people and their opinions remain intact for that long? Impossible.

Writing about the past can be almost as tricky. Particularly so when the subject is the Civil War, that famously unfinished conflict, with each week bringing fresh reports of skirmishes between the ideological rear guards of the Union and Confederate armies, still going at it with gusto.

In many senses, though, the Civil War is a writer's—and reader's—dream. The 1860s were an unprecedented moment for documentation: for gathering and preserving the details of passing events and the texture of ordinary life. Starting just a few years before the war, America was photographed, lithographed, bound between the covers of mass-circulation magazines, and reported by the very first generation of professional journalists.

Half a century ago, as the nation commemorated the war's centennial, a scruffy young man from Minnesota walked into the New York Public Library and began scrolling through reels of old microfilm, reading newspapers published all over the country between 1855 and 1865. As Bob Dylan would recount in his memoir, "Chronicles:

Volume 1," he didn't know what he was looking for, much less what he would find. He just immersed himself in that time: the fiery oratory, the political cartoons, the "weird mind philosophies turned on their heads," the "epic, bearded characters." But much later, he swore that this journey deep into the Civil War past became "the all-encompassing template behind everything I would write."

Lincoln Wins. Now What?
By JAMIE MALANOWSKI

Nov. 7, 1860

Yesterday, the start of the most exciting day in the history of Springfield, Ill., could not wait for the sun. At 3 a.m., somebody got Election Day started with volleys of cannon fire, and after that there were incessant and spontaneous eruptions of cheering and singing all day long. A moment of delirium erupted in mid-afternoon, when the city's favorite citizen emerged from his law office and went to vote, taking care to slice his name off the top of the ballot so as to prevent accusations that he had voted for himself. After the sun went down, he joined other Republican stalwarts in the Capitol building, where they eagerly received the early returns that were trotted over from the telegraph office.

There were no surprises: the long-settled Yankees in Maine and New Hampshire and pioneering Germans of Michigan and Wisconsin delivered the expected victories. And then came news from Illinois: "We have stood fine. Victory has come." And then from Indiana: "Indiana over twenty thousand for honest Old Abe."

The throngs in the streets cheered every report, every step towards the electoral college number, but news from the big Eastern states was coming painfully slowly, and finally the candidate and his closest associates decamped the capitol and invaded the narrow offices of the Illinois and Mississippi Telegraph Company. The advisers paced the floorboards, jumping at every eruption of the rapid clacking of Morse's machine, while the nominee parked on the couch, seemingly at ease

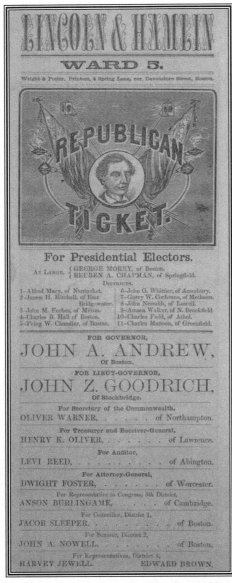

The Lincoln and Hamlin election ticket from 1860.

with either outcome awaiting him.

It wasn't until after 10 that reports of victory in Pennsylvania arrived in the form a telegram from the canny vote-counter Simon Cameron, the political boss of the Keystone State, who tucked within his state's tallies joyfully positive news about New York: "Hon. Abe Lincoln, Penna seventy thousand for you. New York safe. Glory enough."

Not until 2 a.m. did official results from New York arrive, and the expected close contest in the make-or-break state never appeared: the one-time rail-splitter won by 50,000 votes. His men cheered, and broke out into an impromptu rendition of "Ain't You Glad You Joined the Republicans?" Outside, pandemonium had been unleashed, but Abraham Lincoln partook of none it, and instead put on his hat and walked home to bed.

"The Republican pulse continues to beat high," exulted a correspondent for The New York Times. "Chanticleer is perched on the back of the American Eagle, and with flapping wings and a sonorous note proclaims his joy at the victory. The return for the first Napoleon from Elba did not create a greater excitement than the returns for the present election."

Well should he sing, for the days of song will end soon enough. Mr. Lincoln is indeed the president-elect, but barely by a whisker, and what exactly one means by "the United States" any more is apt to become a topic of some heated discussion. Lincoln won his parlay, taking 16 of the 17 Northern states that he set his sights upon, including the hard-fought New York, and most by a solid majority.

But there were states where he was more lucky than popular, like California, where all four candidates polled significant numbers. Lincoln won only 32.3 percent of the ballots, but managed to eke out a victory and capture the state's four electoral votes by the wafer-thin margin of 734 votes. A similar, if slightly less dramatic story played out in Oregon, where Lincoln's victory margin was fewer than 1,200 votes. In his home state of Illinois, facing Mr. Douglas, Mr. Lincoln won by fewer than 12,000 out of 350,000 votes cast, a clear win but hardly a romp.

The South, of course, presents a vastly different picture. In the states of Alabama, Arkansas, Florida, Georgia, Louisiana, Mississippi, North Carolina, Tennessee and Texas Mr. Lincoln received a combined total of no votes. None. True, his name wasn't even listed on the ballot, but that seems to be a mere technical oversight that would have had no great consequence. After all, in Virginia, the largest and wealthiest southern state, Mr. Lincoln was on the ballot, and there he tallied a total of 1,887 votes, or just 1.1 percent of the total cast. The results were even worse in Kentucky, his place of birth. One might have thought that sheer native pride should have earned him more than 1,364 of the 146,216 votes cast, but perhaps Kentuckians resented that he deserted them at such a tender age.

All told, Mr. Lincoln will assume the presidency in March on the strength of his muscular 180 electoral votes, and despite the puny 39.8 percent of the popular vote he accumulated.

The narrowness of this fragile mandate (if that word can even be used) naturally invites speculation about what might have been. The year began with Mr. Douglas standing, like Franklin Pierce and James Buchanan before him, as an electable anti-slavery Northerner who could be depended on to maintain southern prerogatives. But from the moment last April when fire-eating Southern Democrats made it clear that they would rather punish Mr. Douglas for his vote on the Kansas-Nebraska Act two years ago than win the White House in the fall, it was ordained that the Little Giant, so long touted as a certain president-to-be, was steering a doomed vessel.

Yet there were times when his campaign picked up speed, and at such moments Mr. Douglas seemed very close to capturing enough support to thwart Mr. Lincoln's northern sweep and deny him his electoral college majority. Had that happened, Mr. Douglas would be sitting solidly in second place. He would have demonstrated support both north and south, and he would offer the South preservation of the status quo. That might well have been enough to pacify the reckless Southern Democrats who shunned him in the spring, and to win their support in the House of Representatives.

But for every Douglas surge there was a Douglas blunder. Final tallies show that wherever Mr. Douglas actually campaigned in New York, he won more votes than President Buchanan took when he captured the state four years ago. But instead of investing his time in the Empire State, Mr. Douglas headed into the inhospitable South, where he did the seemingly impossible—he managed to make southern voters dislike him even more than they already did. Appearing before a crowd in Virginia, he was asked if the election of Mr. Lincoln would justify secession. A politician of Mr. Douglas's experience should have known how to handle this kind of question with finesse, but instead he offered the one answer certain to damage him. No, he told the crowd.

He might have stopped at that, but perhaps figuring that, having jumped the fence, he may as well have a picnic, he told the crowd, *It is the duty of the president of the United States to enforce the laws of the United States, and if Mr. Lincoln is the winner, I will do all in my power to help the government do so.* With that answer, Mr. Douglas dismissed the purported right to secede that the south so cherishes, and surrendered his claim as the only man who could be counted on to keep the union together.

Now that task falls to a president who received fewer than 4 votes in 10; a president who is purely the creature of only one section of the country; a president who, apart from one undistinguished term in the House of Representatives a decade ago (and a period in the state legislature), has no experience in public office; a president who comes from a Republican party that has been stitched together from various interests, who will be asked to work with a Congress whose two houses are controlled by Democrats.

The fire eaters in South Carolina have already announced that they will immediately introduce a bill of secession. But that has been something they have been itching to do for years; as any doctor or fireman will tell you, sometimes the best way to end a fever or a blaze is to just let the thing burn out. Not everyone in the South is a slave owner, and not every slave owner is a disunionist. If any of the firebrands would take the time to listen to what Mr. Lincoln has actually said, they would see that he is no raving abolitionist like Sen. William Seward and his ilk. (Indeed, anti-slavery activist Wendell Phillips sneeringly calls Mr. Lincoln a "huckster" and William Lloyd Garrison says he has "not one drop of anti-slavery blood in his veins.")

Mr. Lincoln has made his position clear: while he is against slavery and calls it evil, he would not do anything—more to the point, that he is powerless under the Constitution to do anything—to end slavery where the Constitution already permits it. The line that he has drawn is against an expansion of slavery in the territories, but look at a map: there are no more territories held by the United States in North America that are in dispute. On every other matter relating to slavery he has been silent. And ultimately, they ought to realize that Mr. Lincoln may not be an experienced politician, or have strong political support, but that by training and avocation, he is a lawyer, and a good one. And almost every lawyer will tell you that it is cheaper to settle a matter quietly than to fight it out in court.

The Civil War and Abraham Lincoln

By LOUIS P. MASUR

Few presidents have faced a more difficult road than Abraham Lincoln, a road that began even before he took office. Between his election in November 1860 and his inauguration the following March, his patience helped calm a frenzied nation. Seven Southern states had seceded. The president-elect said he would uphold the Constitution, declared he had no intention of attacking slavery where it existed and expressed his belief that all Americans were "united in one feeling for the Union." He also worked behind the scenes to prevent the adoption of compromise measures and he resisted entreaties to make conciliatory statements. In public he was typically self-deprecating: at the recommendation of an 11-year-old girl, who thought he "would look a great deal better" with whiskers, he grew a beard.

Over his first two years in office, Lincoln would be tested and he would grow. His previous national political experience had consisted of only one term in Congress over a decade before, but he soon proved deft at balancing competing pressures. Much to the consternation of opponents, he also greatly expanded executive power. Though he had no real military experience, he proved to be a quick study in military matters and asserted his authority as commander in chief. By Jan. 1, 1863, Lincoln had refashioned himself and the executive office to put himself firmly in control of developing policy and overseeing the war effort.

In his inaugural address, Lincoln beseeched his countrymen to "think calmly and well, upon this whole subject. Nothing can be lost by taking time." In the urgency of the moment, however, he never abandoned a deliberate decision-making process that often distressed supporters who accused him of being hesitant and slow. Lincoln would not be rushed. He would fully examine an issue, consider multiple points of view and then act. "I think it cannot be shown that when I have once taken a position, I have ever retreated from it," he said. While not literally true, Lincoln's assessment captures his self-confidence and tenaciousness once he did choose a path.

The president had much to study and many decisions to make. His immediate and ongoing concerns included developing national policy and military strategy, making certain that the four loyal slaves states — Delaware, Maryland, Kentucky and Missouri —remained in the Union, presiding over the unprecedented expansion of the Army, preventing foreign intervention, navigating relations with Congress, contending with threats to internal security at a time of rebellion and maintaining broad popular support for what he called "a people's contest."

Enthusiasm came easily in the spring of 1861 as Northerners rallied around the flag. With Richmond, Va., the Confederate capital, only 100 miles from Washington, and Union manpower and resources formidable, the hope, as Lincoln put it that July 4, was that the war would be "a short, and a decisive one."

It was not to be. In July, Confederates won at Bull Run, in October at Ball's Bluff, both easily within a day's ride of Washington. Moreover, Lincoln revoked an order from Gen. John C. Fremont that freed the slaves of disloyal masters in his department. But Lincoln shifted, too. In December 1861 the president told Congress that he would not employ "radical and extreme measures" and did not want the conflict to "degenerate into a violent and remorseless revolutionary struggle." In 1862, he changed his mind about the former statement and regretted the latter, even as he authorized measures that would remake the war into a revolution. "I shall not surrender this game leaving any available card unplayed," he said.

January 1862 found Lincoln at a low point. "The bottom is out of the tub. What shall I do?" he asked Montgomery Meigs, the quartermaster general. The emergence in the Western theater of Ulysses S. Grant offset for the moment the ineffectiveness in the East of George B. McClellan, whom Lincoln relieved of command in November. But the price of victory was steep. At Shiloh, combined casualties exceeded 20,000. In February, death came to the White House when Lincoln's son Willie succumbed to typhoid fever. Grieving, the president kept up his work through what one minister called "a dark shadow of affliction."

Seeing a hard struggle ahead, Lincoln began to move against slavery. He did so in multiple ways, offering financial aid to any border state that would adopt a plan to gradual abolition, and signing the two Confiscation Acts as well as an act abolishing slavery in the District of Columbia. But he also overturned another general's order that freed some slaves, stating that "I reserve to myself" the power to act.

Lincoln needed to figure out how to proclaim freedom without violating the Constitution, which protected slavery from federal meddling. In 1864 he would declare, "I am naturally anti-slavery. If slavery is not wrong, nothing is wrong. I can not remember when I did not so think, and feel. And yet I have never understood that the presidency conferred upon me an unrestricted right to act officially upon this judgment and feeling."

For months he considered the problem. He read widely and discussed the issues with political opponents as well as supporters. At last, he became convinced that as commander in chief he could legally justify a move against slavery by invoking the doctrine of military necessity. In July, he decided to act, but also to await a victory before doing so. On Sept. 22, five days after the Battle of Antietam, he issued the preliminary Emancipation Proclamation stating that he would sign a final decree on Jan. 1, 1863.

Over the next 100 days, Lincoln's position continued to evolve. He became less preoccupied with the border states. He considered the enlistment of black men in the Army, which he authorized in the final proclamation. He endured a political setback in the fall elections when his Republican Party lost 28 Congressional seats (even Lincoln's home district in Illinois went Democratic), but he refused to take the results as a referendum on emancipation. "I would rather die than take back a word of the Proclamation of Freedom," he told a visiting group of Kentucky unionists.

Other challenges remained. Military defeat continued to plague him. After the battle of Fredericksburg in December, Lincoln lamented, "If there is a worse place than hell, I am in it." He also faced a crisis in his Cabinet when the Republican senators sought the removal of Secretary of State William H. Seward, who was a rival of the Treasury secretary, Salmon P. Chase. By insisting that both men remain in the Cabinet after receiving their resignations, Lincoln dexterously defused the crisis and let the Republican Senate know he was firmly in charge.

Lincoln signed the Emancipation Proclamation on Jan. 1, 1863. It applied only to those slaves in Confederate areas still in rebellion, but there would be no turning back—preserving the union and abolishing slavery were now linked. "In *giving* freedom to the *slave*," Lincoln declared, "we *assure* freedom to the *free*." At the ceremony, he took his time. He signed slowly. When he was done, he smiled and said, "That will do."

Moses' Last Exodus

By ADAM GOODHEART

Wilmington, Del., Nov. 30, 1860

The knock came after dark. Hastening to answer it, the old Quaker found a familiar figure in the doorway: a tiny, dark-skinned woman, barely five feet tall, with a kerchief wrapped around her head. Someone who didn't know her might have taken her for an ordinary poor black woman begging alms—were it not for her eyes. Wide-set, deep-socketed and commanding, they were the eyes not of a pauper or slave, but of an Old Testament hero, a nemesis of pharaohs and kings.

> **FOR SALE.**
> A NEGRO WOMAN, a good Cook, Washer and Ironer, 34 years old and healthy, who has three children, one, four, and nine years old, all healthy and sound and slaves for life. Apply to the Editor. [apr 10-tf
>
> **NEGROES WANTED.**
> I AM still in the market, and will pay the highest CASH prices for any number of likely young Negroes that are slaves for life. Persons having such property to dispose of, will find it to their interests to see me before they sell. I can be found at the Brick Hotel in Easton.— Communications addressed to me, or information left with A. J Loveday, Esq., will be promptly attended to
> ma 29-3m   WM. HARKER.

Slave ads from a newspaper on the Eastern Shore of Maryland, 1859.

Five others followed her: a man and woman, two little girls and, cradled in a basket, the swaddled form of a tiny infant, uncannily silent and still. They had braved many dangers and hardships together to reach this place of safety, trusting their lives to the woman known as "the Moses of her people."

As politicians throughout the country debated secession and young men drilled for war, Harriet Tubman had been plotting a mission into the heart of slave territory. She did not know that it would be her last. Over the past 10 years, she had undertaken about a dozen clandestine journeys to the lower Eastern Shore of Maryland, the place from which she herself had escaped in 1849. She had managed to bring some six dozen people—most of them family and friends—across the Mason-Dixon Line into freedom, then across the Canadian border to safety. But Tubman had never managed to liberate several of her closest relatives: her younger sister Rachel and Rachel's two children, Ben and Angerine. In the autumn of 1860, she decided to rescue them.

Although it lay on the border between North and South and had few large plantations, the part of Maryland east of the Chesapeake

Bay was an especially hazardous place to be a slave. Soil depletion and economic stagnation had left many local planters with more field hands than they needed—as well as chronically short of cash. By the mid-19th century, the Eastern Shore had become known as one of the nation's principal "breeder" regions, where slaves were frequently sold to slave traders, speculators who sent them south to the burgeoning cotton and sugar plantations of the Gulf Coast. As a child, Tubman had seen two of her own sisters sold away, and heard her parents' anguished tales of others taken before her birth. Four of her remaining siblings had escaped, three of them helped by their sister Harriet. Only Rachel had remained.

By this time, Tubman was well connected to the nationwide abolitionist movement, and before departing, she raised money for the trip (and for possible bribes along the way) from Wendell Phillips and other activists. She set out from her home in Auburn, N.Y., and by mid-November she was in Maryland.

Tubman arrived to learn that her sister would never know freedom: Rachel had died a short time earlier. There were still the two children, her niece and nephew, to rescue. Here too, Tubman failed. She set a rendezvous point in the woods near the plantation where the two were held, but they failed to appear at the appointed time. Tubman waited all through that night and the following one, crouching behind a tree for shelter from the wind and driving snow. At last she gave up. Ben and Angerine's fate is unknown.

Tubman had, however, found another family that was ready to seek freedom: Stephen and Maria Ennals and their children, six-year-old Harriet, four-year-old Amanda and a three-month-old infant. (One or two other men may have joined them as well.) The fugitives made their way up the peninsula, traveling mostly by night. Once, they were pursued by slave patrollers alerted to their presence. The escapees hid on an island in the middle of a swamp, covering the baby in a basket. Eventually a lone white man appeared, strolling casually along the edge of the marsh, seemingly talking to himself. They realized he was an agent of the Underground Railroad, telling them how to reach a barn where they could take shelter.

As they continued on their journey, Tubman would go out each day in search of food while the Ennalses hid in the woods, their baby drugged with an opiate to keep it from crying. Returning at the end of the day, Tubman would softly sing a hymn until they heard her and reemerged:

Hail, oh hail, ye happy spirits,
Death no more shall make you fear,
Grief nor sorrow, pain nor anguish,
Shall no more distress you dere.

Even as the group approached Wilmington, it was not yet out of danger: Delaware was still officially a slave state. In fact, due to the Fugitive Slave Act of 1850, the escapees could have been recaptured anywhere in the North and returned to bondage. Tubman herself could have been re-enslaved, or—as an abettor of fugitives—sentenced to spend the rest of her life in a Maryland prison. But at last, on the night of Nov. 30, she reached the house of the elderly Quaker, Thomas Garrett, a leading Underground Railroad "conductor" who would smuggle the Ennals family to relative safety in Philadelphia.

Although the Underground Railroad had already become famous— and, for many Americans, infamous—only a tiny percentage of slaves managed to escape to the North: estimates have put the number at just a thousand or so each year out of a total enslaved population of some four million. Still, these fugitives were a major bone of contention for disgruntled Southerners. An adult field hand could cost as much as $2,000, the equivalent of a substantial house. To Southerners, then, anyone who helped a man or woman escape bondage was simply a thief. But more infuriating than the monetary loss it occasioned, the Underground Railroad was an affront to the slaveholders' pride— and a rebuke to those who insisted that black men and women were comfortable and contented in bondage.

In an 1860 speech, Senator Robert Toombs of Georgia thundered against Republicans "engaged in stealing our property" and thus "daily committing offences against the people and property of these States, which, by the laws of nations, are good and sufficient causes of war." As secession loomed, some Northerners attempted to soothe such fears. A New York Times editorial suggested not only that stronger efforts be made to enforce the Fugitive Slave Act, but that the federal government compensate slaveholders for their escaped "property."

Tubman was back in Auburn by Christmas Day, 1860, having conveyed the Ennals family safely to Canada. (Abolitionists often noted the irony of Americans fleeing the "land of liberty" to seek freedom under Queen Victoria's sheltering scepter.) Her secret missions ended with the approach of war.

But one night in the midst of the secession crisis, while staying at the house of another black leader, a vision came to Tubman in a dream that all of America's slaves were soon to be liberated—a vision so powerful that she rose from bed singing. Her host tried in vain to quiet her; perhaps their grandchildren would live to see the day of jubilee, he said, but they themselves surely would not. "I tell you, sir, you'll see it, and you'll see it soon," she retorted, and sang again: "My people are free! My people are free."

Misgivings
By TED WIDMER

Day after day, the ripples from Lincoln's election continued to wash over Americans in different ways. Some proclaimed an ardent zeal for separation, and if necessary, war; most expressed abhorrence at the thought. And in one poetical soul, at least, there was an attempt to resolve these tensions. Isn't that what poetry is for?

Herman Melville was not, at first glance, the writer most likely to achieve precision or economy in his poetry. Or, for that matter, to write poetry at all. The author of sprawling works like "Moby-Dick," Melville had no problem generating language, but he was having trouble getting people to read what he had written. It had not been a good decade—"Moby-Dick" belly-flopped upon its release in 1851, and his sequel, "Pierre," fared even worse. By the end of the 1850s, he was no longer able to support his wife and four children. In 1860, to restore his physical and mental equilibrium, Melville went on a long cruise to the Pacific, on a ship commanded by his brother Tom.

But the poet was in there. Melville had often inserted bits of verse inside his long romances (including "Moby-Dick"), and as the countercurrents of 1860 swirled around the United States, they swirled inside him as well. The grandson of Revolutionary heroes, he felt deeply about the Union—many have argued that "Moby-Dick" is an allegory about a nation that has lost its course. There are 30 sailors on board the Pequod, "federated along one keel," just as there were 30 states at the time of writing. Like so many Americans, he was feeling elegiac in the fall of 1860, missing something that seemed to have vanished, even before secession made it official. Lincoln was elected on Nov. 6. On Nov. 8, while still at sea, he read these lines of Schiller, about love, but also descriptive of the fraternal bonds that had once united the states:

> Can those sweet longing hopes, which make
> Love's essence, thus decay?
> Can that be love which doth forsake?—
> That love—which fades away?

He sailed into New York harbor on Nov. 13, and rejoined his family in the Berkshires. There he began to pour out his feelings into sharp and concise poems that captured the somber mood of a moment trapped between eras, with the original Republic dying, and something new struggling to be born. The declining light of November and December, the cold and the grim news all merged into a vision quite unlike anything that he had ever written—or what we associate with Herman Melville, the spinner of yarns.

One poem, "The Conflict of Convictions," seemed to express his vexation at Buchanan ("he who rules is old"), and with Tea Party-like urgency, regretted what seemed like the final failure of the bold American experiment. ("But the Founders dream shall flee./Age after age shall be/As age after age has been.") A footnote he added (who writes a footnote to a poem?) read, "The gloomy lull of the early part of the winter of 1860–1, seeming big with final disaster to our institutions, affected some minds that believed them to constitute one of the great hopes of mankind . . ." The weather was not good inside Melville's poems; a blustery wind served as a perfect metaphor for the angry speeches on all sides, rending the Union: "I know a wind in purpose strong—it spins against the way it drives."

(Continuing on that wintry theme, "Apathy and Enthusiasm" complained of "the clammy cold November," and compared the news that fall and winter to "the thunder-cracks of mass ice/in intensity of frost-/Bursting one upon another/through the horror of the calm.)

A simple poem, "Misgivings," was among the most powerful he wrote that winter. It says everything about the plight of the good man, caught between his hope for what America once promised, and his dread before what she now demanded.

Misgivings (1860)
When ocean-clouds over inland hills
Sweep storming in late autumn brown,
And horror the sodden valley fills,
And the spire falls crashing in the town,
I muse upon my country's ills—
The tempest bursting from the waste of Time
On the world's fairest hope linked with
    man's foulest crime.

Nature's dark side is heeded now—
(Ah! Optimist-cheer disheartened flown)—
A child may read the moody brow
Of yon black mountain lone.
With shouts the torrents down the gorges go,
And storms are formed behind the storm we feel:
The hemlock shakes in the rafter; the oak in
    the driving keel.

The months that followed were hard for Melville. He tried valiantly to secure appointment as a U.S. consul in Florence, Italy, but never stood a chance. In March, he even traveled to Washington to advance his cause, and waited in a very long line to shake the hands of the new president. He was possibly the worst self-promoter of all time, and said nothing to Lincoln, though he admired him ("Old Abe is much better looking [than] I expected & younger looking. He shook hands like a good fellow—working hard at it like a man sawing wood at so much per cord"). Later in the visit, he sat in the park opposite the White House, "sunning myself on a seat," and noticed that the shrubbery was starting to bud. Then he tried to get into the Washington Monument and failed. He was a middle-aged man, next to a half-finished obelisk, with no idea where he or his country were headed.

Unsurprisingly, this office-seeker was rebuffed in his quest to secure the consulship. Instead, he found far less glamorous form of government employment: the man who may have been America's greatest writer settled into a long and depressing career as Customs Inspector 75, monitoring Manhattan's docks to make sure no contraband was smuggled in.

Eventually, his poems on the war combined into a book, "Battle-Pieces," which came out in 1866, after all the excitement had ended. It tanked instantly. But with the exception of Whitman, no poet ever wrote more piercingly about what happened, or what it felt like as it was happening. And who is to say that Herman Melville had no influence, even watching from the wings? After the Emancipation Proclamation, Lincoln remarked, "We are like whalers who have been on a long chase. We have at last got the harpoon into the monster, but we must now look how we steer, or with one flop of his tail he will send us all into eternity."

Visualizing Slavery
By SUSAN SCHULTEN

The 1860 Census was the last time the federal government took a count of the South's vast slave population. Several months later, the United States Coast Survey—arguably the most important scientific agency in the nation at the time—issued two maps of slavery that drew on the Census data, the first of Virginia and the second of Southern states as a whole. Though many Americans knew that dependence on slave labor varied throughout the South, these maps uniquely captured the complexity of the institution and struck a chord with a public hungry for information about the rebellion.

The map uses what was then a new technique in statistical cartography: Each county not only displays its slave population numerically, but is shaded (the darker the shading, the higher the number of slaves) to visualize the concentration of slavery across the region. The counties along the Mississippi River and in coastal South Carolina are almost black, while Kentucky and the Appalachians are nearly white.

The map reaffirmed the belief of many in the Union that secession was driven not by a notion of "state rights," but by the defense of a labor system. A table at the lower edge of the map measured each state's slave population, and contemporaries would have immediately noticed that this corresponded closely to the order of secession. South Carolina, which led the rebellion, was one of two states which enslaved a majority of its population, a fact starkly represented on the map.

Conversely, the map illustrated the degree to which entire regions —like eastern Tennessee and western Virginia—were virtually devoid of slavery, and thus potential sources of resistance to secession. Such a map might have reinforced President Abraham Lincoln's belief that secession was animated by a minority and could be reversed if Southern Unionists were given sufficient time and support.

The map quickly caught the public's attention, and was reproduced throughout the war. Its banner headline, "for the benefit of the sick and wounded soldiers," also became the slogan of the Union's most important homefront organization, the United States Sanitary Commission. The map gave a clear picture of what the Union was up against, and allowed Northerners to follow the progress of the war and the liberation of slave populations.

We don't know when Lincoln first encountered the Coast Survey's map of slavery. But he became so taken with it that Francis Bicknell Carpenter included it in the lower right corner of his painting, "President Lincoln Reading the Emancipation Proclamation to His Cabinet." Carpenter spent the first six months of 1864 in the White House preparing the portrait, and on more than one occasion found Lincoln poring over the map. Though the president had abundant maps at his disposal, only this one allowed him to focus on the Confederacy's greatest asset: its labor system. After January 1, 1863—when the Emancipation Proclamation became law—the president could use the

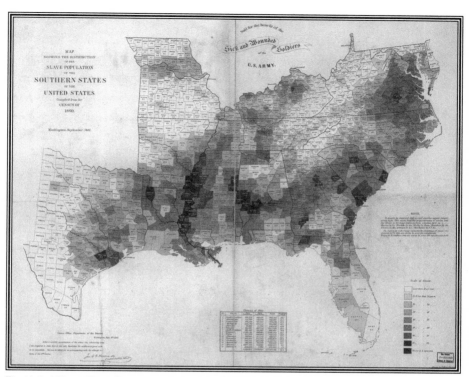

The United States Coast Survey's map of the slaveholding states, which clearly illustrates the varying concentrations of slaves across the South.

map to follow Union troops as they liberated slaves and destabilized the rebellion. Lincoln was enthusiastic about Carpenter's finished portrait, and singled out the map as one of its most notable details.

(Slavery also informed the painting in another way. Carpenter arranged the Cabinet according to his perception of their sentiment regarding emancipation: its two leading proponents, Secretary of the Treasury Salmon P. Chase (standing) and Secretary of War Edwin Stanton, are to Lincoln's right, while Secretary of State Seward sits in the foreground. To Lincoln's immediate left are the secretary of the navy, the secretary of the interior and the postmaster general standing to the rear, while Attorney General Edward Bates sits at the far right of the portrait. Lincoln sits at the center, as Carpenter wrote, "nearest that representing the radical, but the uniting point of both." A copy of the anti-slavery New York Tribune lies at Stanton's feet, while a portrait of Simon Cameron—the prior secretary of war who urged emancipation early in the conflic—is visible beyond Stanton's head. The map lying across the table behind Seward is the Coast Survey's 1863 "Map of the State of Virginia," which included both population statistics and concentric rings around Richmond to guide Union strategy.)

It may seem odd that the Coast Survey—originally responsible for detailing the nation's coastlines and rivers—produced a map of slavery in the south. Yet over the preceding two decades its superintendent, Alexander Dallas Bache, had skillfully widened the Survey's work and made it a hub of mapmaking innovation. The Survey experimented with several new methods of cartographic representation, including the use of shading to represent the human population. As early as 1858 Bache had directed the Survey to produce maps of the rivers and coasts of the South, in anticipation of a conflict. But the 1861 map was in a class by itself: a landmark cartographic achievement, a popular propaganda tool, and an eminently practical instrument of military policy. No wonder Lincoln liked it.

Fear and Doubt in Cleveland
By JOHN STAUFFER

Lucy Bagby was cautiously hopeful on Election Day in 1860. A pretty, 28-year-old fugitive slave from Virginia, and pregnant with her first child, she lived in Cleveland, a hotbed of abolition sentiment, and worked as a maid for a Republican politician.

Two months later Lucy's world was turned upside down. Her master, William Goshorn, arrived in Cleveland looking for his property, and within days he had her arrested and jailed. Goshorn was purportedly worth $300,000 (about $22 million in today's dollars), so he did not need to recover Lucy for her monetary value. Amid the secession crisis, Goshorn came as a representative of Virginia, which was still in the Union, in order to test whether or not Lincoln's Republican Party would uphold its platform of respecting slavery where it existed by enforcing the Fugitive Slave Act and affirming its "fidelity to law and order."

Cleveland's activists had long been proud of their success at undermining the draconian Fugitive Slave Act of 1850, which suspended habeas corpus and required all citizens to assist in hunting down suspected fugitives. In 1859 one local paper had even declared that "the Fugitive Slave Act is at an end" here, owing to residents' resistance to it.

But in January 1861, when Lucy Bagby was arrested, five states had already seceded, citing northerners' unwillingness to enforce the act as a primary reason. In the hopes of restoring the Union, Cleveland's white citizens responded by vowing to uphold the law. "Let us in this instance testify to the country that we are a law-abiding as well as liberty-loving community," declared a judge in the case.

Cleveland's blacks felt differently. They kept vigil outside Lucy's jail cell, and when a federal marshal led her to the courthouse where her fate would be decided, some 60 black men tried to free her, though they were beaten back by police armed with clubs.

On Jan. 23 the court remanded Lucy to her master. In a final effort to free her, black activists tried to hijack the train carrying her back into slavery. But their efforts were in vain. Back in Virginia she was "severely punished," and her baby was born into slavery like herself. Lucy Bagby's ordeal reflected the general sentiment of Northern blacks toward Lincoln during the election of 1860: initially enthusiastic that an antislavery candidate had been elected, they were driven to despair by Inauguration Day.

Few of the 500,000 Northern blacks had supported Lincoln's nomination. They knew that the Republican platform, while seeking to prevent slavery's spread, did not threaten it in the states, and that it favored colonization as a means of ridding the nation of free blacks. Those who did support Republicans had preferred William Seward or Salmon Chase as presidential candidates, both of whom called for resisting and repealing the fugitive slave law, arguing that it was unconstitutional. Lincoln, by contrast, consistently defended it.

Northern blacks had been especially outraged at Lincoln's defense of a law that made even legally free blacks vulnerable to enslavement, sparking an exodus of some 15,000 to Canada. The Chicago black leader H. Ford Douglas captured Northern black sentiment in early 1860 when he called Lincoln "simply a Henry Clay Whig" and "odious to the antislavery cause." As everyone knew, Clay, the slaveholding leader of the Whig Party, had orchestrated the passage of the fugitive slave law and had been Lincoln's hero.

In fact, Northern blacks felt far more comfortable with the political views of the tiny Radical Abolition Party and its presidential candidate Gerrit Smith. One of the most progressive parties in American history, Radical Abolitionists advocated immediate emancipation and equality before the law for all persons; vigorous resistance to the fugitive slave law; full suffrage for all men and women (at a time when women and most black men were denied the vote); and the redistribution of land to prevent extreme disparities of wealth.

But if Northern blacks were cool toward Lincoln, they hated his four chief contenders for president even more. By calling slavery evil and vowing to prohibit its spread, Lincoln appeared far more progressive than Stephen Douglas, John Bell and John Breckinridge. And blacks were heartened by the fact that Southerners despised Lincoln. "I love everything the South hates," black abolitionist H. Ford Douglas said a few days before the election, "and since they have evidenced their dislike of Mr. Lincoln, I am bound to love you Republicans with all your faults." And so when Lincoln was elected, blacks responded with tempered enthusiasm. His victory was a blow to the growing power of slaveowners. And it was the first time since John Quincy Adams's election in 1824 that an antislavery candidate had been elected president.

But as southern states began seceding, Northern whites blamed the secession crisis on blacks and abolitionists. The backlash against Northern blacks was severe: the four months between election and inauguration marked a high point of mob violence against them and a rigorous defense of the fugitive slave law. In Chicago more than 100 blacks boarded a train for Canada to avoid violent confrontations. Black leaders were attacked throughout the North. Several state legislatures repealed laws that had protected fugitives from slave-catchers. Even Harriet Tubman, hailed as one of the "bravest persons on the continent," lost her nerve and left for Canada. As one Northern journalist observed, "Public sentiment is more intense against the colored man than at any previous period."

Like in Cleveland, whites throughout the North sought to appease Southerners and reverse the tide of secession. Many Republicans even called for repealing their platform preventing slavery's spread. Although Lincoln notably refused to endorse such a repeal, during the transition he made virtually no public speeches and did nothing to check the upsurge of violence against blacks.

Congress, too, sought to appease Southerners. Two days before Lincoln's inauguration, in the hope of wooing secessionists back into the Union, it passed a 13th Amendment. Although it was never ratified, this "first" 13th Amendment was the opposite of the actual one that abolished slavery in 1865: it forever prohibited Congress from interfering with slavery in the slave states.

During these tense, violent days, Northern blacks anxiously awaited Lincoln's inaugural address. No group was more disappointed by it than they were. Lincoln vowed to vigorously uphold the Fugitive Slave Act, suppress slave insurrections and never interfere with slavery in the slave states. He even supported the new 13th Amendment guaranteeing slavery in the states. Frederick Douglass spoke for most Northern blacks when he said that Lincoln's inaugural "is little better than our worst fears." In the days that followed, thousands more blacks began making plans to emigrate to another country.

Perhaps the most unusual response to Lincoln's election came from a free black woman who considered casting her lot with the South. Elizabeth Keckley, a former slave from Missouri, had purchased her freedom years earlier and moved to Washington, D.C., where she owned one of the country's most successful dressmaking shops. One of her best patrons was Varina Davis, the wife of Jefferson Davis, a Mississippi senator and the future president of the Confederacy.

In the weeks after the election Davis kept Keckley busy making dresses for herself and an extravagant bathrobe for her husband. After Mississippi seceded, she warned Keckley of war, which she felt certain the South would win. Davis even invited Keckley to come south with her. "I will take good care of you," she said. She predicted that "when the war breaks out, the colored people will suffer in the North. The Northern people will look upon them as the cause of the war, and in their exasperation they will be inclined to treat you harshly."

Perhaps in despair over the course of the new administration's position on slavery, Keckley felt tempted to accept Davis's invitation. "Her reasoning seemed plausible," she said. But after thinking it over and comparing the two sections, she decided to "cast my lot among the people of the North." Though few Northern blacks likely faced a similar conundrum, in the months after Lincoln's election, they would have surely understood her dilemma.

Ghosts of a Christmas Past
By ADAM GOODHEART

Macon, Ga., Dec. 24, 1860

The city was preparing itself for the holiday. In the pages of the Macon Daily Telegraph, ads touted toys and sweets, books and jewelry, all at bargain prices. In a large front-page ad, the store of H.N. Ells & Co., on Mulberry Street, reminded readers that "Old Santa-Clauz" was coming to town, and urged upon them such last-minute stocking stuffers as apples, figs, candy and firecrackers.

On the next page of that Christmas Eve newspaper was a more discreet advertisement, this one just five lines of small print:

> FOR SALE.
> A NEGRO WOMAN 21 years old, and her daughter about
> six years old. The woman is a good house servant, plain
> cook, and good washer and Ironer. Warranted sound.
> Terms cash.

Men, women and children were for sale throughout the much of the United States during that last holiday season before the Civil War, exactly a century and a half ago. In Easton, Md., "Negro Henry, Aged about 26 years, and Negro George, aged about 19 years," were "offered at private sale until the 25th inst."—that is, until Christmas Day. In Washington, D.C., just a few blocks from the White House, one owner advertised "a servant girl, seventeen years of age—a slave for life." In the Christmas morning edition of the Augusta (Ga.) Chronicle, the local sheriff announced the upcoming sale of a "Mulatto Boy slave named Charles, about 14 years of age." The lad, who had been seized from his mistress to satisfy debts, was to be put up for public auction in the town market on New Year's Day.

The last weeks of each December were a strange and frightening time to be a slave in America. (Was there ever a normal time, however?) In the antebellum period, the end of the calendar year was—as it is now—a busy period for financial transactions. Assets were liquidated, debts settled, taxes paid, balance sheets scrutinized. Any of these might lead a slaveholder to divest himself of some human property. Based on the evidence in contemporary newspapers, New Year's Day slave auctions like the one in Augusta were common.

The estimated 5 to 10 percent of American slaves who were rented from one master to another (in some regions the figure was more than 60 percent) had their own reasons to be terrified. Jan. 1 was when old rental contracts expired and slaves' services were auctioned off for the year ahead, sending them to different, often far-flung, plantations. One former bondsman would recall how each New Year's Day, "the cries and tears of brothers, sisters, wives and husbands were heard in the streets" as black families were separated—at least for twelve months, but possibly forever.

At the same time, surreally enough, Christmas was a time when many masters encouraged their slaves to eat, drink and be merry. Field hands were commonly given the entire week as a holiday— their only one of the year. South Carolina Senator James Henry Hammond—who did not hesitate to rape female slaves and to lash servants with his own hand—distributed gifts throughout the quarters, and noted in his journal that on Christmas, "a barbecue is given, beef, mutton, and pork, coffee and bread being bountifully provided." On the morning of Dec. 25, right after opening presents and emptying stockings, masters would bring their families down to the slave cabins to watch blacks perform dances and songs that had been handed down from Africa.

Frederick Douglass, remembering boyhood Christmases on the Eastern Shore of Maryland, wrote:

> From what I know of the effect of these holidays upon the
> slave, I believe them to be among the most effective means

in the hands of the slaveholder in keeping down the spirit of insurrection. These holidays serve as conductors, or safety-valves, to carry off the rebellious spirit of enslaved humanity. But for these, the slave would be forced up to the wildest desperation; and woe betide the slaveholder, the day he ventures to remove or hinder the operation of those conductors! I warn him that, in such an event, a spirit will go forth in their midst, more to be dreaded than the most appalling earthquake.

The holidays are part and parcel of the gross fraud, wrong and inhumanity of slavery. They are professedly a custom established by the benevolence of the slaveholders; but I undertake to say, it is the result of selfishness, and one of the grossest frauds committed upon the down-trodden slave.

The Yuletide season was an unquiet time throughout the nation on the brink of the Civil War—and not just among black Americans. Judging from period newspapers, Christmas 150 years ago was just as politicized as it is now, if not more so. With the nation splitting in half (South Carolina had seceded on Dec. 20), each side of the Mason-Dixon Line tried to claim the holiday as its own.

In the South, the Augusta Chronicle accused the Yankee Puritans of being joyless Christmas-haters: "Our broad Union is divided between the descendant of the Norman Cavalier reverencing Christmas, and the descendant of the Saxon Puritan repudiating it ... Let us hear no more of a 'Cotton Confederation' but let us have instead (what may sound like a jest, but which has something of seriousness in it) a Confederation of the Christmas States."

Meanwhile, several hundred miles closer to the North Pole, the same day's Philadelphia Inquirer called Christmas a "good old Yankee custom" and added: "If Charleston growls and, playing the Scrooge, would curse our Christmas carol, let us hope that the Marley's Ghost of her old patriotism will soften her by and by."

Culturally, Christmas in 1860 was also at a strange transition point. In many parts of America, it was still celebrated as a riotous old pagan Saturnalia: working-class revelers known as "callithumpians" paraded through the streets in drag or blackface (sometimes both), firing off guns and starting street brawls, defying annual attempts by the city fathers to ban Christmas, as it were. A few years earlier, the Grinch-like Horace Greeley had complained that the day was simply an excuse for New York's "young men and boys" to drink themselves silly: "As early as 10 o'clock we saw, in Broadway, between the Park and Broome-st., about a dozen parties of boys, each numbering from four to ten persons, nearly every one grossly drunk, and [some] being dragged along by the neck and heels by their hardly less drunk companions."

But commercialized, mass-market Yule was already coming into its own. An article in the New York Herald analyzed Christmas retail trends much as a newspaper today might do. (Candy sales were up compared to the previous December, while jewelry sales were down: consumers, anxious about the political news, were economizing on gifts.)

American Christmases in the mid-19th century do not seem to have had much religious significance—neither for the callithumpians, nor the proto-shopaholics, nor anyone else. Many, if not most, Protestant churches did not even have Christmas services, though some staged holiday parties, pageants and "entertainments." The New-York Tribune remarked in 1860 that only gradually was the festival starting to become as widely observed as more important national celebrations like the Fourth of July, Thanksgiving and New Year's Day.

Very soon, however, Christmas more or less as we know it today would emerge. A young magazine sketch artist, Thomas Nast, was on his way home from covering Garibaldi's conquest of southern Italy; two years later, in the pages of Harper's Weekly, he began publishing his iconic images of Santa Claus. In Galena, Ill., the middle-aged shop clerk Ulysses S. Grant was busy attending to his customers' last-minute demands. Ten years later, as president of the United States, he would sign into law a bill declaring Christmas a national holiday.

As for the slaves Henry and George, the teenage Charles and the nameless mother and daughter, it is not known how they spent future Christmases. Perhaps they survived that bitter December to celebrate in freedom.

Cup of Wrath and Fire
By DAVID W. BLIGHT

F
ew people in the North welcomed South Carolina's secession in December 1860, but Frederick Douglass, America's most prominent former slave and African-American abolitionist, was one of them. From his editorial desk in Rochester, N.Y., Douglass heaped scorn on the Palmetto State's rash act, but he also relished it as an opportunity. He all but thanked the secessionists for "preferring to be a large piece of nothing, to being any longer a small piece of something."

To Douglass, secessionists provided what he initially hoped would be the long-awaited opening for the antislavery cause: disunion, political crisis and some form of sanctioned military action against slavery and the South. He would get his wish, but only after the tremendous confusion and fear of the secession winter of 1860 and '61.

Douglass's reactions to secession represented nearly 20 years of pent-up personal travail and abolitionist struggle as slavery had grown across the cotton kingdom and into the American West, and as the antislavery cause seemingly failed in electoral politics, the Supreme Court and public opinion. Douglass and many of his fellow abolitionists had long yearned for a politics of disorder that might force the nation to confront, willingly or not, its future over slavery vs. freedom in a rapidly expanding republic. Was that prospect now at hand?

"Her people [South Carolina's]," Douglass declared with anxious glee in his Douglass Monthly, "(except those of them held in slavery, which are more than half her population) have hailed the event as another and far more glorious Fourth of July, and are celebrating it with plenty of gunpowder and bad brandy, but as yet no balls, except those where perfumed ladies and gentlemen move their feet to the inspiring notes of the fiddle." With no veiled intent, Douglass wished for a fight. "Other balls may yet come," he wrote, "and unless South Carolina shall retreat, or the Federal Government shall abdicate its functions, they must come." And he lampooned what South Carolinians imagined as "peaceful secession," celebrated by "bonfires, pyrotechnics . . . music and dancing." He cautioned Carolinians over their confidence about "a thing as easily done," so he maintained they believed, "as the leaving of a society of Odd Fellows, or bidding good night to a spiritual circle."

Not that Douglass believed that South Carolina had a right to secede. The state, he wrote within a week of its actions, was "out of the Union" only "on paper" and in "resolutions and telegrams." Governments, he continued, "rest not upon paper, but upon power. They do not solicit obedience as a favor, but compel it as a duty." Douglass acknowledged the "right of revolution" for a state or a political group, but no constitutional "right of secession."

As a result, he believed, conflict was inevitable: "But revolution in this country is rebellion," he maintained, "and rebellion is treason, and treason is levying war against the United States, with something more than paper resolutions . . . there must be swords, guns, powder, balls and men behind them to use them." Secession, therefore, was no abstract debate over federalism or states' rights, but a matter of power and guns. "The right of South Carolina to secede," declared the abolitionist, "depends upon her ability to do so, and to stay so."

Douglass's sentiments were those of an antislavery activist who insisted that secession was intimately about slavery. He believed, as many reasonable Americans have ever since, that the significance of any exercise of states' rights doctrine is in the issue for which it is employed. The prospect of civil war frightened him, but by January and February 1861, he cast the dreaded prospect in positive and apocalyptic language: The "God in history everywhere pronouncing the doom of those nations which frame mischief by law," he declared, had caused a "concussion . . . against slavery which would now rock the land." National will and institutions had not solved the problem. "If there is not wisdom and virtue enough in the land to rid the country of slavery," he claimed, "then the next best thing is to let the South go . . . and be made to drink the wine cup of wrath and fire, which her long career of cruelty, barbarism and blood shall call down upon her guilty head."

From the snowy isolation of upstate New York, Douglass could not easily define the course of disorder he sought as he watched several more Deep South states follow South Carolina out of the Union by Feb. 1. His own confusion was not unlike the indecision, even incredulity, of many Northern Republicans that winter. He had himself encountered the rage of a white mob on Dec. 3 at Tremont Temple in Boston. At a gathering to commemorate the first anniversary of John Brown's execution, Douglass fought, according to one reporter, "like a trained pugilist" against those who shouted down and forcefully disrupted the antislavery gathering. For many, even in Boston, abolitionists had become easy scapegoats for the fear of disunion, disruption of the intersectional American economy, and the potential of war.

Above all, Douglass feared that the crisis would be resolved in yet further concessions to the South and slaveholders' interests. For a former slave, and now famous orator and editor—whose political consciousness had awakened with the Mexican War and the Compromise of 1850, who had seen the fate of slaves bandied about in one political crisis after another, who had struggled to preserve hope of freedom and citizenship in the face of the Dred Scott decision's egregious denials—a resolute stand by the North against secession and the "Slave Power" was hardly a sure thing. The best hopes for blacks, Douglass said in an editorial that winter, had always been dashed by the "old medicine of compromise."

He feared the same would be true in the latest crisis. As he watched Congress offer resolutions and conventions intended to settle the crisis, Douglass complained that South Carolina and her Northern enablers had "filled the air with whines of compromise." As March and the inauguration of Abraham Lincoln approached, Douglass, like so many Americans, felt powerless before the mercy of events. Would Lincoln and the Republicans cave into Southern demands and rebellion, or would they take a stand to defend federal authority and property?

Although it seemed unrealistic, what Douglass most desired was federal power marshaled for an organized war against the South and slavery. The necessity of a response to disunion might force Republicans into radical directions they would never take solely by their own accord. He wanted what Southerners most adamantly rejected: coercion against secession, even by force of arms.

But he warned about the tradition of compromise, feared Northerners had lost their "moral sense," lacked confidence in Lincoln's resolve and worried that the abolition movement was about to be eclipsed by desire for a "peaceful disunion." In near despair in late February 1861, and employing his only weapon (a newspaperman's angry pen), Douglass envisioned a future where abolitionists would attack slavery in a foreign country by increasingly revolutionary means. "So much for the moral movement against slavery," he declared. "Hereafter, opposition to slavery will take a new form . . . Slaves will run away, and humane men and women will help them; slaves will plot and conspire, and wise and brave men will help them. Abolition may be postponed, but it cannot be prevented. If it comes not from enlightenment . . . it will come from the fears of tyrants no longer able to hold down their rising slaves."

These sentiments and images of near race war are all the more interesting given the startling turn of events caused by the bombardment of one island fort in Charleston harbor. Nothing explodes painful uncertainty like the awful clarity of war.

Rethinking the Old Public Functionary
By RUSSELL MCCLINTOCK

By late December 1860, President James Buchanan was easily the most despised man in America, and particularly in the North. "The President," one supporter observed glumly, "seems to be execrated now by four fifths of the people of all parties"—and this in New York City, the center of the cotton trade and the most pro-Southern city in the free states.

In his own time and ever since, the 15th president has been castigated as worse than useless; his purported failure to act resolutely in the face of secession is often cast as a leading factor in the country's descent into war. Certainly the "Old Public Functionary," as he was known, deserves his place in the bottom rank of chief executives. But there are also historical considerations that make his actions during the secession crisis a bit more understandable.

Northerners' loathing for Buchanan was nothing new. Early on his administration's zealously pro-Southern policies and corruption scandals had alienated both Republicans and free-state members of his own Democratic Party; the latter was especially disgruntled by his vicious patronage war against Stephen A. Douglas, a popular Democratic senator from Illinois.

But condemnation of "Old Buck" reached new depths in December 1860. Buchanan's assertion, in a speech early in the month, that although no state had the right to secede, the federal government had no authority to coerce a state into remaining provoked general scorn. His cabinet was disintegrating. General-in-Chief Winfield Scott publicly lambasted the administration for not taking the strong stand that he insisted would deter disunion. Secretary of the Interior Jacob Thompson of Mississippi traversed the Lower South as one of numerous state agents negotiating a multi-state secession. The administration's official organ, the Washington Constitution, openly favored disunion. And within days of South Carolina's formal secession on Dec. 20, a scandal erupted over the War Department's freewheeling use of Indian trust-fund money—followed almost immediately by Secretary of War John B. Floyd's astonishingly ill-advised decision to order the transfer of heavy artillery from a Pittsburgh foundry to Deep South forts.

The public response was almost universally negative. When rumors reached Springfield, Ill., that Buchanan had negotiated the surrender of Deep South federal forts, President-elect Abraham Lincoln said, "If that is true, they ought to hang him," and then wrote to Republican leaders assuring them that, upon assuming office, he would act to retake lost federal possessions. Northerners of both parties weighed in on whether the president was "imbecile, and not competent to the emergency; or has so far committed himself to the authors of the evils that are now upon us"—that is, the secessionists—"that he is either tacitly acquiescing, or secretly promoting their aims and ends."

One imaginative Massachusetts Democrat opined that "the best thing that could now be done for the Country would be to Send down to Washington a delegation of Old Women, armed with Six pieces of diaper to clout Mr. Buchanan, double and triplicate and to pin them on his posteriors with a wooden skure instead of a diaper pin for he has evidently got the bowel complaint."

Few historians share the suspicion of some contemporaries that Buchanan was colluding with the secessionists, but most concur with one senator's characterization of the 15th president as "feeble, vacillating & irresolute." Yet it is unrealistic to think that in 1860 the White House could have been occupied by a chief executive willing to take a sufficiently bold stand.

That's in part because of party politics. Four years earlier the Democratic Party was in grave danger of succumbing to the sectional hostility that had already consumed the Whig Party and given birth to the openly anti-Southern Republicans. If the party was to retain the loyalty of both its Northern and Southern wings in the 1856 election, selection of a presidential candidate with strong convictions— someone like the controversial Stephen Douglas—was impossible. So the party chose a Northern candidate with traditional Democratic views on the limited nature of federal power and a history of sharing Southern views regarding property rights in slavery. And those, of course, are precisely the convictions Buchanan displayed in the winter of 1860–61.

Bolstering Buchanan's natural caution and conservatism was his sense of history: the United States, he knew, had been faced with numerous sectional crises over slavery before, and each one had been resolved through compromise. As far back as 1787, threats of Deep South delegates not to ratify the new constitution had forced Convention delegates in Philadelphia to find middle ground on such thorny issues as congressional power to ban slave imports, the counting of slaves in apportioning each states' representation in Congress and the right to retrieve fugitive slaves who had escaped across state lines. A generation later, in 1820 and '21, Congress had resolved the first great threat of disunion, over whether Missouri should be added as a slave state, with mutual concessions that became known as the Missouri Compromise.

Then, in 1833, as President Andrew Jackson prepared to start a civil war by marching troops into South Carolina to enforce federal law, congressional leaders again struck a bargain that prevented hostilities. And as recently as 1850, when the country had nearly torn itself apart over the spread of slavery into the vast new territories conquered from Mexico, a complex congressional settlement had yet again averted secession.

Given this long history of compromise, Buchanan was confident that Congress would settle this crisis, too, if given the chance. Thus his chief role, as he saw it, was to guarantee the peace long enough for Congress to do its work.

Indeed, Buchanan was doing all he could to encourage congressional negotiations. Not only did he offer his own compromise proposal—a constitutional amendment designed, naturally, to protect slaveholders' property rights from meddling Northern radicals—but, he quietly sent Duff Green, once a member of Andrew Jackson's notorious "kitchen cabinet," to speak with Lincoln in Springfield, Ill. Recognizing that compromise was impossible without the support of congressional Republicans, he hoped that Green could persuade the president-elect to join him in publicly advocating compromise.

Meanwhile, Buchanan declared (paraphrasing Job) that he would "come between the factions as a daysman, with one hand on the head of each, counseling peace." In practical terms, this meant he would bend over backward not to goad secessionists even as he tried to maintain the Union. On the one hand, he sent an emissary to the South Carolina secession convention in a vain effort to counsel calm and reason, permitted Secretary Thompson to travel the Deep South (wrongly believing that he was discouraging disunion) and pronounced Jan. 4 a day of national fasting and prayer. On the other hand, he publicly rejected both the right and the wisdom of secession and refused (according to his own account, at least) to commit himself to a formal truce with South Carolina representatives.

The president also declined to reinforce the federal forts in the Deep South, fearing that doing so would ignite hostilities, and he replaced the garrison commander at the most dangerous of these, Fort Moultrie in Charleston Harbor, with a man whose Southern background, he believed, would help mollify the Carolinians: Maj. Robert Anderson of Kentucky. Buchanan wasn't selling out to the South, though: He authorized Anderson to take whatever action he deemed necessary to defend his command, and he readied the warship Brooklyn to carry reinforcements to Charleston should Anderson need them.

But by late 1860, compromise was an increasingly unlikely outcome, and Buchanan's efforts came across as naïve, weak and possibly traitorous, an image that has stuck ever since. Yet few of the men who have occupied the White House could have stood up to the challenge of the moment. Was Buchanan the strong, vigorous leader his contemporaries believed the times demanded? No. But neither was he the feeble, unprincipled caricature in which history has cast him.

Seceding from Secession
By ADAM GOODHEART

Parkersburg, Va., Jan. 1, 1861

The small Southern courthouse was packed to bursting. On this first afternoon of the new year, the Commonwealth of Virginia was preparing to chart her path forward—with the Union or apart from it—and the people of Wood County had gathered to make their voices heard.

Presiding over the meeting was a local squire named B.H. Foley, a conservative Democrat described by one attendee as "a large slave owner." Seated near him were the two John J. Jacksons—grave, bearded worthies, father and son—whose cousin, not yet known as Stonewall, would soon link their family name indelibly with the Confederate cause.

But these Virginian patriarchs had not come to lend their support to the rebellion. They intended, rather, to denounce it as folly, as criminality—perhaps even as treason.

Wood County lay across the Blue Ridge Mountains from the plantations of Tidewater Virginia, far from the Chesapeake shores where black children were considered a cash crop. Slaves here—despite the holdings of a few men like Foley—totaled less than 2 percent of the population. Fortunes were made instead from the steamboats and barges that plied the nearby Ohio River, carrying Pennsylvania iron and coal through Parkersburg on their way down to Cincinnati, Louisville and beyond. A few farsighted entrepreneurs were beginning to see potential in the local "rock oil"—also known as petroleum—that had long been a nuisance to people drilling wells for drinking water.

If the Old Dominion seceded, the far side of the river—the state of Ohio—would, overnight, become a foreign country, perhaps even enemy territory. And in that event, one politician warned, places like Wood County would bear the brunt of "sacrifices in battle, and raids, and reprisals, and destruction of every kind." Others pointed out that slaveholders would pay an especially heavy price: their human "property" could escape across an international border, beyond the reach of legal restitution. Slavery would be far more secure within the Union than without it, many Virginians argued.

And so the hills of western Virginia echoed with the thunder of cannons during that first week of 1861—but not the din of battle. Instead, it was the local "Union Men" firing "one hundred guns in honor of Major Anderson for the gallant stand he is taking in defence of Fort Sumpter."

"Life In Eastern Virginia: The Home of the Planter" (1845).

At the Parkersburg meeting, citizens quickly found a common voice. The elder of Stonewall Jackson's cousins—a grizzled general in the Virginia state militia—was chosen to draft a series of resolutions. "In the judgment of this meeting, 'secession is revolution,'" declared the document's first paragraph, quoting Daniel Webster. It continued:

> We are deeply impressed with the conviction that our national prosperity, our hopes of happiness and future security, depend on preserving the Union as it is, and we see nothing in the election of Abraham Lincoln to the Presidency of the United States—as much as we may have desired the election of another—as affording any just or reasonable cause for the abandonment of what we regard as the best Government ever yet devised by the wisdom and patriotism of men.

By acclamation, the assemblage endorsed these resolutions, among others, with near-perfect unanimity. (Just one or two shouts of nay were heard in the hall, witnesses would remember.)

Similar calls for resistance to secession were being heard throughout much of Virginia as a special session of the state legislature prepared to confront the national crisis. Even in Richmond, the slaveholder and former congressman John Minor Botts was decrying South Carolina's "headlong impetuosity" and "disloyalty and treachery" that had pitched the nation toward catastrophe.

But nowhere did such cries resound louder than among the Appalachians. In Wheeling, 80 miles up the Ohio River from Parkersburg, a large gathering of "workingmen" condemned the "fanatics who with unholy zeal would plunge their country, their brothers, and kindred into the dark and fearful abyss of disunion and civil war. Patriots of Virginia, resist it unto the bitter end!" And when a band struck up "Yankee Doodle" and "The Star-Spangled Banner," the sturdy laborers "stood up, swinging their hats and cheering with the wildest enthusiasm," according to a report in the Wheeling Daily Intelligencer.

Perhaps no newspaper in the slave states—and almost none, indeed, in the entire country—was fiercer in its Unionism than the Intelligencer. In an editorial that ran alongside its report on the Parkersburg meeting, the paper savaged the "traitor" President James Buchanan in astonishing terms: "If he suffers Maj. Anderson and his gallant little band to be massacred by the blood thirsty traitors, [Buchanan's] life will not be safe a single hourafterwards. Not an hour."

The Intelligencer's editors were among the Virginians who had begun advocating disunion of a different kind. A front-page headline on Jan. 1 proclaimed: "A WARNING TO THE SECESSION TRAITORS IN OUR MIDST. Western Virginia will Secede from Eastern Virginia, if she Secedes from the Union."

Perhaps in deference to the occasion, however, the editorial page struck a gentler, more hopeful note that New Year's Day. Gazing a year ahead, into the uncertain future, the editors wrote: "We hope that if 1862 comes to us all, it may come amidst different scenes from those which we are now beholding throughout the country.—That it may see no miserable rattlesnake flag substituted in any section of the Union for the glorious stars and stripes."

But this New Year's wish was destined to be unfulfilled. The year 1862 would open upon a divided nation and a divided commonwealth.

Before long, one of the orators at the Parkersburg meeting—a promising young Wood County attorney—would be sworn in as governor of a brand-new state. And Stonewall Jackson's cousin would become West Virginia's first federal judge, appointed to the bench by Abraham Lincoln.

The Transatlantic Slave Trade and the Civil War

By DAVID ELTIS and DAVID RICHARDSON

The conclusion of the historian David Brion Davis's most recent book, "Inhuman Bondage," traces the significance of the United States Civil War in the ending of slavery elsewhere. It implicitly poses the question: What if the Confederacy had won recognition from Britain in 1862 and had survived the war? Our rather frightening answer is that the three great centers of slavery in the Americas, the United States South, Cuba and Brazil—plus the smaller plantation economy of Dutch Suriname—would not have abolished slavery when they did.

That the Civil War and the subsequent Thirteenth Amendment ended slavery in the United States is self-evident. What's less well known is that the Civil War also had immense significance for the ending of slavery elsewhere, especially in the Americas. Indeed, few people recognize that it took a war to finally bring the brutal transatlantic slave trade to a close. In all likelihood, without a Union victory, slavery would have remained a central institution underpinning global economic growth until possibly the present day.

It's true that only a small share—about 4 percent—of the total slaves carried off from Africa landed on the North American mainland. And an even smaller share of those destined for slavery in the rest of the Americas completed their voyage in vessels flying the United States flag, or set sail from mainland ports.

Yet small as the United States role was, there is no doubt that the federal government effectively protected transatlantic slave traders in the half-century before 1861 and that the outbreak of the Civil War just as effectively removed that protection. Indeed, thanks to America's role, almost one-quarter of the total transatlantic slave trade occurred after the government banned American participation in the slave trade in 1807.

How was it possible for such a minor player to have such a large impact? The answer turns on the nature of the nascent system of international law that had emerged by the early 19th century, and the fact that the transatlantic slave trade was perhaps the most thoroughly multinational business of the early modern era.

For one thing, Denmark, the United States and Britain, the first nations to take action against the trade, might have banned their own citizens from participating and forbid the entry of slaves into their own territories, but without negotiating international treaties, they could do nothing to stop foreign nationals carrying on the slave trade elsewhere—including the high seas.

After 1807, the British constructed an elaborate, costly but ultimately ineffective network of treaties that allowed their cruisers to stop suspected slave vessels flying the flags of other nations. But it didn't cover all countries, and in these years slave ships sailed under the colors of Mexico, Russia, Sardinia and Argentina, among many others, solely because these flags prevented British intervention. And as long as a single nation allowed its flag to be used in this way, and as long as Brazil and Cuba remained open to new arrivals from Africa, the transatlantic slave trade would continue.

Moreover, France and the United States never allowed the British to stop and search their own merchant vessels. Instead, they undertook to patrol the Atlantic themselves. The French at one stage assigned more than 40 warships to anti-slave trade duties. The American fleet, on the other hand, never exceeded six warships and for years at a time the country deployed none at all. And neither nation sought permission to stop and search suspected slave ships operating under another flag. As a consequence, the British navy accounted for almost 80 percent of the nearly 2,000 slave vessels detained in Atlantic waters in the era of suppression; the United States detained just 68.

Why such a half-hearted effort? The answer is simple. American administrations were often stocked with Southerners in key positions like secretary of state, secretary of the navy and president, and they refused to take serious action against the foreign slave trade. Thus they tacitly allowed the Stars and Stripes to be used as a cover. In the absence of a treaty the British were reluctant to interfere with American shipping; only American naval ships could stop this practice, and even when they acted officers would usually detain a ship only if slaves were on board (thus ships heading to Africa, even if they were obviously slavers, were let go).

But an unwillingness to enforce the law was just part of the story. American shipbuilders also sent a steady stream of fast sailing vessels into the slave trade after 1830. The premium on speed had partly to do with voyage mortality risks and the high-value nature of the cargo—by the 1860s, 500 slaves could fetch close to half a million dollars in Cuba. The design of the slave vessel changed radically between 1800 and the mid-1830s, and the duration of the middle passage to Cuba declined by one third between the 1790s and 1850s. Many of these fast slavers were yachts or clippers made in the United States: Baltimore, in particular, developed a reputation for constructing fast sailing vessels. In all, about one-third of the slave ships sailing after 1810 were built in American ports.

Second, the use of the United States flag by slave traders escalated after 1835. In the early years of suppression, the Cuban trade was conducted under the Spanish flag, the traffic to the French Americas under the French flag and the traffic to Brazil under the Portuguese and Brazilian flags. Only a few of these vessels were American, with an American master and crew. But this situation began to change in 1835 when Great Britain and Spain signed a treaty that for the first time specified a range of equipment that could provide grounds for detention. In other words, slavers without slaves on board could be detained. The immediate effect was that slave traders abandoned the Spanish flag, and began to register their vessels as Portuguese, though a growing number sought registration under American colors.

The British introduced other measures in 1839 and 1845 that extended the so-called equipment clause to Brazilian and Portuguese slave traders, thus increasing reliance on the American flag even further. For a few years a weird set of flags appeared on the African coast, with vessels frequently carrying more than one set of papers, each to be used as required. Many ships flew no flag at all.

The use of the American flag ended only after the Civil War began. In 1862, with Southern politicians finally gone from national politics, the United States at last signed a treaty with the British providing for mutual right of search on the high seas, an equipment clause and joint Anglo-American joint courts (called Courts of Mixed Commission) for adjudicating detentions. The fact that those courts never heard a single case detracts not at all from their impact.

True, the slave trade continued for another five years, but at decreasing annual volumes. More importantly, there were only three recorded voyages under the United States flag after the 1862 convention—and, we should add, after the execution that same year of Nathaniel Gordon, the only individual to suffer the full penalty of the 1820 Act that made slave trading a capital offense. Compare this to 123 such voyages documented in the five years preceding the 1862 treaty. Secession, and a Union victory in the war that precluded any renewed trading under the Confederate aegis, made all the difference.

Dr. Smith's Back Room

By CARLA L. PETERSON

My family has deep roots in New York City, and a number of my relatives kept written accounts of the events and people around them. My great-grand-aunt Maritcha Lyons, for example, reminisced in her memoir about a particularly popular meeting place for politically active blacks in the 19th century. "The store had a back room which was a rallying center," she wrote, "it had a library and in there were held discussions and debates on all the topics of the day. The visitors had public spirit which had much to do in bringing about a more favorable state of things affecting the colored people of the state."

The store in question was the medical office and pharmacy of James McCune Smith, located at 93 West Broadway in what is now the Tribeca neighborhood. Overshadowed today by Frederick Douglass, Smith was the most important black leader in antebellum New York City. Born a slave to a slave woman and a white man, he gained his freedom with the state's 1827 Emancipation Act. Smith attended the New York's Manumission Society Mulberry Street School, where he was a star student; after graduation, he left for Europe to attend the University of Glasgow medical school, finishing at the top of his class. He returned to New York in the late 1830s, set up shop on West Broadway, and plunged into political activism.

The decades leading up to the Civil War provided New York's black leaders with a severe schooling in political activism: they moved from local to national politics, from establishing all-black organizations to participating in interracial societies, from avoidance of party politics to full involvement. When the Civil War broke out, they were ready to make their voices heard.

Although unfamiliar to many of us today, the men who crowded into Smith's backroom were significant political actors in mid-19th-century New York. Among them were restaurateurs Thomas Downing and his son George; reverends Henry Highland Garnet and James Pennington; William Powell and Maritcha's father Albro

Lyons, co-owners of the Colored Sailors' Home; newspaper editor Charles Ray; and the two Reason brothers, Patrick, an engraver, and Charles, a teacher.

Their long conversations centered on two goals. The first, close to home, was the restitution of black male suffrage, severely restricted by the 1821 New York state constitution, which had raised the property requirement for black voters to $250. The second was the abolition of the southern slave system. True, the South was a faraway place, but slavery in New York was a recent memory and its legacy had a stranglehold on the city. Throughout the antebellum years, leaders constantly worried about the precarious legal position of members of the black community. After the passage of the Fugitive Slave Law in 1850, they banded together to prevent escaped slaves from being kidnapped and remanded into slavery. Following the Supreme Court's 1857 Dred Scott decision, they mounted an all-out campaign in support of the 1860 state amendment repealing the property qualification (not surprisingly, the referendum failed).

It was strategy, not goals, that were debated in Smith's back room, concerns that would continue to reverberate for decades after the war. "So far as we think it good policy to have separate institutions," one man insisted, "we can, and we intend to support our moral, literary and domestic establishments." A second good policy was participation in broader and better-financed interracial organizations, especially the American Anti-Slavery Society, run by William Lloyd Garrison, the white abolitionist.

Smith's back room witnessed a gradual shift in these positions. Many black leaders became increasingly disenchanted with Garrison's aims. They accused his society of limiting its activism to the antislavery cause while ignoring the ultimate goal of full social equality; men like Garnet challenged Garrison's principle of nonviolence; Smith and others took issue with his stance that the Constitution was a pro-slavery document and hence that party politics should be avoided at all costs.

It was only a matter of time before black leaders in New York and elsewhere recognized the necessity of moving beyond theoretical positions and engaging in electoral politics, in part to gain influence but also as an assertion of citizenship, or what they called "manhood rights." Early on, a number of prominent New York blacks affiliated with the Whig party created in the early 1830s in opposition to Jacksonian Democrats. In Illinois, the party gained the support of young Abraham Lincoln; in New York, it attracted descendants of old Federalist families and Manumission Society members. As tradesmen aspiring to professional status, black leaders were drawn to the old-fashioned Whig values of austerity and virtue as well as to the party's more recent liberal ideas of individualism and capitalism and its pro-business orientation.

By 1850, however, slavery had split Whigs along sectional lines. Lincoln withdrew. Black leaders began looking elsewhere too. Many had already abandoned the American Anti-Slavery Society to affiliate with Arthur and Lewis Tappans' American and Foreign Anti-Slavery Society and the Liberty Party—which, in dramatic contrast to Garrison, held that the Constitution was an antislavery document and electoral politics a necessity. In addition to white abolitionists like the Tappans and Gerrit Smith, the Liberty Party drew black men like Henry Highland Garnet, Samuel Ward and Frederick Douglass.

James McCune Smith, however, withheld his support. He was suspicious of the party's commitment to blacks as well as of its presidential nominees, especially James Birney, a former slaveholder from Kentucky. But when a group of white and black abolitionists split off from the Liberty Party to form the Radical Abolition Party, he quickly joined up. Their radicalism lay in a vision of a new, inclusive American nation, and they insisted on revising the Constitution's meaning of "men" to include all men, demanded immediate emancipation and acknowledged the necessity of violent action (John Brown was a party member). Anticipating 20th-century rainbow coalitions, in 1856 the Radical Abolitionists nominated Gerrit Smith as their presidential candidate and James McCune Smith as his running mate, the first black man on a national ticket.

Health problems curtailed McCune Smith's activism in the late 1850s. His place was taken by Henry Highland Garnet, a Presbyterian minister whose family had fled slavery in Maryland and come to New York in the mid-1820s. The two men had been friends since their days at the Mulberry Street School. Unlike Smith, however, Garnet was inconsistent in his politics. He was an early and fervent supporter of the Liberty Party, yet in the mid-1850s he was absent from Smith's back room and apparently never attended Radical Abolitionist meetings. Garnet, it seemed, had abandoned hope of black Americans ever achieving full citizenship. He formed the African Civilization Society to promote emigration to other countries of the diaspora, notably Haiti and Liberia; he himself left for Jamaica to work as a missionary. Yet on the eve of the Civil War, he was back in the city ready to assume a leadership role.

New York's political scene was an ugly place. It was dominated by Peace Democrats, wealthy white men with last names like Astor, Havemeyer, Belmont and Tilden, who, recognizing where their economic interests lay, lined up solidly behind the South. They preached conciliation but insisted that if conflict was inevitable they would side with their race. They hailed Fernando Wood's election as mayor in 1859, as well as his proposal for New York to secede from the state and country and become an independent city-state.

On the other end of the spectrum, New York's white liberals were a more varied lot, many of them refugees from defunct political parties. Some, like Henry Ward Beecher, had been Free Soilers and had become early, enthusiastic supporters of Lincoln. Others, like New York Tribune editor Horace Greeley, were cautious former Whigs. Although conservative whites deemed Greeley a firebrand radical, black New Yorkers were dubious: Greeley, they knew, had steered clear of the abolitionist agitation of the Tappans, equivocated on the Fugitive Slave Law, dragged his heels on the issue of slavery and endorsed conservative Whigs for president. Holding back, he pronounced for Lincoln only after the Illinoisan won the Republican presidential nomination.

With the rapid deterioration of national political conditions in the late 1850s, black leaders needed to decide which party to support. They were skeptical of Democrats and Republicans alike. Democrats, they knew, were unabashed proslavery men. But summing up the opinion of many, Thomas Hamilton, editor of the Anglo-African Magazine, argued that Republicans were not much better and in fact might be worse because they were hypocritical and cowardly. "Their opposition to slavery," he asserted, "means opposition to the black man—nothing else. Where it is clearly in their power to do anything for the oppressed colored man, why then they are too nice, too conservative, to do it." Lincoln was not exempt from such criticism: blacks were well aware that he had refused to condemn the Fugitive Slave Law, avoided defending John Brown's raid, speculated that southern slavery could wither away without conflict and suggested that it would be best for all if blacks left the country and colonized themselves in South America.

Once Lincoln declared war, however, black New Yorkers threw him their full support. And when the president issued the Emancipation Proclamation on Jan. 1, 1863, they were jubilant. Accompanied by white activists, they came by the thousands to a mass meeting in the great hall of the Cooper Institute. Garnet presided over the gathering and, after reading the Proclamation aloud, addressed the assembly. "With his eyes set on the God of Justice," he proclaimed, "the President had now fulfilled his promise of emancipation." The men from Smith's back room now had a new challenge: convincing the Lincoln administration to allow blacks to fight in the Civil War, and thus to prove their loyalty to the nation, their courage, their capacity for citizenship, their manhood.

Lincoln's Other Mother

By TED WIDMER

On the evening of Jan. 30, 1861, a slow freight train chugged into the small hamlet of Charleston, Ill., having completed a 12-mile run from Mattoon. Or nearly 12 miles—the train didn't quite make it all the way to the station. A few people straggled out of the caboose and trudged through slush and ice toward the depot, where a gaggle of townsfolk loitered. To their astonishment, they realized that the tall man coming toward them, wearing a shawl, was Abraham Lincoln.

He did not seem very presidential. He had been traveling all day to cover the 120 miles from Springfield, and had missed the last passenger train to Charleston—hence the ignominious arrival by freight. According to an observer, he wore "a faded hat, innocent of a nap, and his coat was extremely short, more like a sailor's pea-jacket than any other describable garment. A well-worn carpet-bag, quite collapsed, comprised his baggage." He had no bodyguard.

Across the country, people were saying goodbye as the new world shaped by secession came into focus. Some did it loudly—the grandiloquent farewell speeches of Southern senators and still-serving cabinet members—but most did it quietly, inside the family. As Lincoln wrapped up his affairs in

Sarah Bush Johnston Lincoln, Abraham Lincoln's stepmother.

Springfield, he realized that he needed to say a special goodbye to someone who had arguably done more to shape him than any other. And so on the morning of the 30th, this most closely observed person slipped away from it all and boarded a train in Springfield to the southeast. We know that it departed at 9:50—the United States was beginning to acquire the railroad precision for which it would become famous. But that precision was not yet universal, and Lincoln did not make all of his planned transfers. He handled it the way he usually did—fellow passengers that day remembered that he told an endless succession of droll stories, punctuated by his own hearty laughter.

Lincoln spent the night of the 30th in Charleston, and the next morning began the final phase of his journey, to reach the secluded farmhouse where he found a 72-year-old woman, his father's widow, Sarah Bush Lincoln.

"Stepmother" can be a fraught phrase in the telling of childhood stories—one thinks of Cinderella and the well-named Brothers

Grimm—yet it was a very good day for Lincoln when she came into his life. His mother, Nancy Hanks, had died when he was nine years old, and we don't have to look far for the sources of his legendary melancholia. In 1844, as a rising local politician, he returned to the Indiana of his boyhood and was so moved by the experience of being near the graves of his mother and sister that he wrote an uncharacteristically emotional poem about it. It began:

> My childhood home I see again,
> And gladden with the view;
> And still as mem'ries crowd my brain,
> There's sadness in it too—

Sarah Bush Lincoln had known sadness, too—a difficult marriage to an improvident husband—but after her husband died, Thomas Lincoln came to Kentucky and proposed to her on the spot (they knew each other from childhood). She accepted, on condition that her late husband's debts be paid, and together they came to the Pigeon Creek settlement in Indiana, with her three children and all of her worldly possessions. Although she was illiterate, these possessions included several books, including "Aesop's Fables," "Robinson Crusoe," Bunyan's "Pilgrim's Progress" and "Sinbad the Sailor." We are today so cosseted by technology that it is difficult to imagine the impact that these world-expanding devices—the iPads of their day—must have had on the young Lincoln. Years later, she remembered that moment, and remarked that she instantly set to work to help Abe and his sister become "more human"—implying that, like Robinson Crusoe, she had discovered young savages in the wilderness.

Under her guidance, Lincoln made rapid progress. "He read all the books he could get his hands on," she recalled, and was already practicing writing and speaking at a young age, eager to get at the exact meaning of words. After hearing sermons by a local preacher, he would sometimes stand on a stump, gather the children around, and "almost repeat it word for word."

She obviously was behind this progress—she remembered, "His mind and mine, what little I had, seemed to run together, more in the same channel." She added other information, vital to future biographers—that he cared little for clothes, or food, but a great deal for ideas. Also, tucked away in her memories, the surprising physical fact that young Lincoln was "more fleshy in Indiana than ever in Illinois."

As his star rose, he saw her less and less, and did not attend his father's funeral in 1851, which has led scholars to speculate about what may or may not have been a difficult relationship. But there is no doubt about the closeness of stepmother and stepson. On Jan. 3, as Lincoln was preparing his cabinet, he received a letter from a kinsman, saying that "she is getting somewhat childish and is very uneasy about you fearing some of your political opponents will kill you. She is very anxious to see you once more." And so he went.

It was quite a reunion. Local folk remembered it for decades. Word got out quickly to neighboring farms, and families came over to celebrate, bringing turkey, chicken and pie. The local school released the children for the day, and Lincoln laughed with them (he told them he'd rather be in their place than his). Some of them walked in his shoes, to feel what it must be like to be president. One youngster there, a six-year-old named Buck Best, lived until 1947, and never tired of reliving the day.

That evening Lincoln gave a speech in Charleston's town hall, one of many we do not have recorded. It's a pity, because he spoke about his boyhood that night. Lincoln rarely went into autobiographical territory, to put it mildly. Unlike today's politicians, for whom every childhood challenge is an opportunity for publicity, Lincoln was reticent to a fault about the traumas of his youth. He had conquered all that—why go back there?

And yet, he did go back there, this one time. Charleston was a typical community in 1861, split like many others between pro- and anti-slavery families (though in Illinois, it was founded by Southerners). Surprisingly, Lincoln had argued a legal case there in 1847, Matson v. Ashmore, defending the rights of slaveowners to have their runaway slaves returned. Three years after Lincoln's visit, in 1864, a riot broke out in Charleston when marauding Confederate sympathizers attacked half-drunk Union soldiers preparing to return to their regiment. But that night in late January, the town turned out as one to hear a son honor his mother. He told a resident, "she had been his best friend in this world and that no son could love a mother more than he loved her."

There are several versions of their final goodbye, which each probably knew would be their last. Like him, she was haunted by visions of the future. A letter written by one of her kinsmen recorded the scene, complete with grammatical inexactitudes: "She embraced him when they parted and said she would never be permitted to see him again that she felt his enemies would assassinate him. He replied no no Mama (he always called her Mama) they will not do that. Trust in the Lord and all will be well We will see each other again."

They did not, but today we can see her thanks to a single daguerreotype taken near the end of her time on earth, a striking likeness of an old lady who had a more than ordinary brush with greatness.

Four years later, after her premonition came true, another lawyer from Springfield made the pilgrimage to Coles County. William Herndon, Lincoln's former law partner, was in mourning like the rest of the country in 1865, and undertook to find everyone he could who had known Lincoln, and to record their impressions. Long before the phrase "oral history" existed, he was undertaking one of the most important efforts to recapture the past yet attempted in the United States. Nearly every story we know of the young Lincoln is traceable to these researches. Herndon found Sarah Lincoln feeble and breathing with difficulty, but by asking her simple questions about her life, he breathed new life into her.

After she died in 1869, she was buried in a black dress Lincoln gave her on this visit—as if they were both already in mourning. She then lay in an unmarked grave until 1924, when a local Lions Club erected a stone marker for her. That seems appropriate—for if Lincoln saved the Union, she saved him, and for that alone she's entitled to a decent respect. Measured by the usual yardsticks of wealth and distinction, her own life may not have made much of a dent in the historical record. But at just the right moment, she encountered a small motherless boy, and helped him to become Abraham Lincoln.

The Civil War and Politics

By ADAM I.P. SMITH

Both sides went to war in 1861 to preserve what they saw as the principles of democracy. Northerners of all parties were outraged that the rebels were breaking up the Union because they did not like the outcome of a freely conducted election—"the essence of anarchy," in Abraham Lincoln's words.

Southerners, however, saw secession as the will of the people. A state legislator from North Carolina, Jonathan Worth, joined the Confederate Army once his state had voted for secession even though he had opposed it. "I leave the flag of the Union," he explained, "because I am subjected and forced to submit to my master—democracy."

But if they were fighting for democracy, most Americans would, at the same time, also have conceded that the outbreak of war indicated that something was rotten in the political process. Republicans thought an aristocracy of slaveholders was corrupting the republic. Secessionists asked how a fanatical antislavery party had come to power in the 1860 election, when slavery was, they believed, enshrined in the Constitution. And in the view of northern Democrats, extremists on both sides had agitated sectional tension for their own political ends.

What these different perspectives shared was the sense that "politics as usual" had exacerbated the crisis, perhaps even, as The New York Times put it, had "brought the nation to this state of Armageddon." Politics as usual essentially meant *parties*—those organizations seemingly so crucial for the organization of American political life and yet simultaneously so mistrusted. George Washington had warned of the curse of "faction" and, even as party organization developed in the 1830s and 40s, an important strain of antipartisanship persisted in American political culture. It was often, in fact, partisans themselves who used antiparty rhetoric, presenting their opponents as "slavish partisans" and themselves as the antidote—offering candidates who were, in the idiom of the day, "fresh from the loins of the people."

On the brink of Civil War, newspaper editors who unashamedly promoted the interests of one or the other slate of candidates could be found denouncing "the licentiousness of modern partisan politics," the corruption of office-seekers, and the sinister influence of "wire-pullers" (the 19th-century term for spin doctors). Popular songs celebrated the virtue of non-partisanship in wartime with lines like "No party nor clan shall divide us/ the Union we'll place above all." An Ohio newspaper editor agreed that it seemed unpatriotic to "plot for partisan ends" at a time when citizens were sinking their differences and joining together to defend the republic. A group of Pennsylvania citizens assured Lincoln that they "knew no division of parties" in their state.

In the capital of the new Confederacy, The Richmond Whig concluded likewise that "we should profit by the failure [of parties] for our future guidance." And in 1863, The New York Times expressed its hope that "one of the great providential ends secured by this terrible strife" shall be that "the old party corruptions shall in some good measure cease; that the public soul, in its renewed patriotism, shall realize, as it has not before, what deadly agencies they are and no more tolerate them."

Yet if there was a near consensus that party politics should be abandoned in wartime, it was far less clear what the alternative organizing principle might be.

Confederates took pride in creating a republic that, true to the spirit of Washington, was free from the "stain" of party. In the first Confederate congressional elections in November 1861, candidates ran without reference to party identity. Most, in fact, were former Democrats and many had past records that were well known, but the non-partisan tone of the elections—and even the relatively large number of non-contested races—were taken to be a sign of political health. It soon became clear, however, that an absence of party labels did not mean an absence of political conflict. President Jefferson Davis faced challenges from Congress, from state governors and even from his own vice president.

In the North, elections in 1861 saw the creation of "Union parties" with candidates appealing to voters to put aside party differences. The rhetoric of these organizations reflected the mood that partisanship must give way to patriotism. "The mousing politicians who rattle the dry bones of dead parties, can make no headway," declared one newspaper with satisfaction. Another hailed an effort by New York State Democrats to present themselves under a new label as an "anti-politician" movement.

In some places these Union parties were little more than the old Republican organization in new garb. But often they were more than that. In Ohio and Pennsylvania, an important faction of Democrats joined Republicans in creating a Union party, and some prominent Democratic leaders abandoned their old party decisively. One such figure was Edwin M. Stanton, who had served in Buchanan's cabinet and served as Lincoln's second secretary of war. In California and Rhode Island it was Democrats who took the lead in creating Union parties. In Massachusetts, former Whigs and Know Nothings joined with some Democrats to form an avowedly non-partisan "People's party," in opposition to the radicalism of the Republicans in that state. And in the border slave states, the old pattern of party politics was utterly disrupted as all those opposed to secession identified themselves as Unionists.

Precisely because Union parties usually involved cooperation with former partisan enemies and therefore compromise on principles, some Democrats and Republican radicals denounced the Union party movement and insisted on maintaining party "regularity." They rejected the message sent out by Union parties—whoever had taken the lead in organizing them—that they were the embodiment of patriotism and that the loyalty of those opposing them must necessarily be suspect.

Nevertheless, when a political group lost control of the language of Union, they generally lost the election. This happened to the Republicans in the New York gubernatorial election in 1862. Democrats successfully portrayed the Republican nominee as a dangerous radical and their own man, Horatio Seymour, despite being a long-time party stalwart, as a patriotic figure who transcended partisanship (this was an effort that unravelled the following year when Seymour appeared to sympathize with the New York City draft rioters).

Whatever semblance of non-party unity each section managed in the first year or so of the war had crumbled by 1863. In the North, the Emancipation Proclamation created bitter divisions over whether it was a legitimate tool to crush the rebellion or a usurpation of the proper aim of the war by a fanatical party. Lincoln's emancipation policy probably had a unifying effect within the Confederacy, at least temporarily, but as battles and territory were lost, the South began to face its own internal battles over the administration's conduct of the war. So there, too, the early promise of non-partisan politics began to look hollow.

Despite this, the basic dynamic of wartime politics in both sections remained unchanged. It was a battle over who defined loyalty and who most represented the ideals of the republic or the founding fathers. Even while politicians behaved in an increasingly "partisan" way, "partisanship" remained a dirty word. Neither section resolved the basic paradox of fighting a war to preserve democratic ideals while mistrusting the most characteristic forms that democratic politics took.

Mark Twain and the Fortune-Teller

By ADAM GOODHEART

Cairo, Ill., Feb. 6, 1861

At the age of 25, Sam Clemens had every reason to feel pleased with himself. He was already one of the "aristocrats of the river"—a Mississippi steamboat pilot earning the princely sum of $250 a month. His job gave him the leisure to continue his process of self-education during slow stretches aboard, as he dipped into the works of Darwin and Macaulay, Suetonius and Shakespeare. The income gave him the wherewithal to live like a prince: in the finest New Orleans restaurants, the youth from Hannibal, Mo., dined on shrimp and oysters, washed them down with good brandy, smoked the very best cigars, and bought his brother Orion a splendid $12 pair of alligator-skin boots.

On this particular day, he had just finished a voyage aboard the side-wheeler steamboat Alonzo Child, bringing her safely 500 miles upriver from New Orleans. But apparently his mind still dwelt upon something that happened just before his departure. When he sat down to write Orion a long letter, he said nothing about the journey, but a great deal about a curious encounter in the Crescent City a week or two earlier: a visit to a psychic. That Feb. 6, 1861, letter is one of few detailed ones to survive from a pivotal time in Sam Clemens's life. It casts a strange—perhaps even unearthly—light on the complicated young man who would soon be Mark Twain.

He had known about the fortune-teller for a long time; the only reason he finally went to see her—as he assured his brother, a bit too emphatically to be wholly convincing—was that he was bored. Madame Caprell's advertisements and handbills, which she distributed liberally throughout New Orleans, touted her gifts as a "clairvoyant" and "seeress."

More unusually, the ads also called her a "spiritual physician" who "locates all invisible diseases, and prescribes the proper remedies therefor." Her gifts, she assured the public, were not supernatural, but scientific. One suspects that later generations might have had a different term for her profession. (In distant Vienna, a lad named Sigismund Schlomo Freud was not yet five years old.)

Madame Caprell's fee was $2; her address, 37 Conti Street. Perhaps Clemens was nervous; he rang the wrong doorbell. Then he found the right one—and a few moments later, he told Orion, "stood in the Awful Presence":

> She is a very pleasant little lady—rather pretty—about
> 28—say 5 feet 2 ¼—would weigh 116—has black eyes
> and hair—is polite and intelligent—uses good language,
> and talks much faster than I do.

> She invited me into the little back parlor, closed the door;
> and we were—alone. We sat down facing each other. Then
> she asked my age. And then she put her hand before her
> eyes a moment, and commenced talking as if she had a
> good deal to say, and not much time to say it in.

The conversation that followed made such an impression on Clemens that he wrote it all down almost word for word. In classic fashion, Madame Caprell began with a few easy hits. "You gain your livelihood on the water," she said—as must have been obvious from the young man's attire and his upriver accent. "You use entirely too much tobacco"—perhaps his breath told her this. She continued on a more flattering note: "There is more unswerving strength of will, & set purpose, and determination and energy in you than in all the balance of your family put together"—exactly what any precociously successful twenty-something would want to hear.

Scientifically based though they may have been, Madame Caprell's prophecies were far from infallible. She told her client that he would marry twice. (He only married once.) She said he would have 10 children, a forecast that made him recoil in mock horror: "You must think I am fond of children." "And you are," she replied, "although you pretend the contrary." (She was right, but he would have only four.) She said he would die at the age of 28, 31, 34, 47 or 65—or possibly 86, but only if he quit smoking. (He never did, and died of heart failure and respiratory disease at 74.) In at least one prediction, however, the seeress was eerily prescient. "You have written a great deal," she said, "you write well—but you are rather out of practice; no matter—you will be in practice some day."

In fact, although he did not know it yet, Sam Clemens stood on the brink of great life changes as 1861 began—changes that probably would never have come to pass without the Civil War. As the Union fell to pieces around him, he seemed to have no strong views on the matter one way or the other. On Jan. 26, the day that Louisiana seceded, he wrote in his journal only: "Great rejoicing. Flags, Dixie, soldiers." Like many border-state Missourians at the start of the war, he vacillated. On one occasion, he distributed pro-secession cockades to a group of boys parading behind the Confederate flag. But shortly afterward, when he saw some other youths preparing to burn the Stars and Stripes, he rushed in to save it.

His views on slavery were similarly conventional. On the surface, at least, the young Clemens was a typical man of his place and time. He railed against "the infernal abolitionists" (even after Orion declared himself one). On a visit to New York, described the "mulat-toes, quadroons, Chinese," blacks and poor whites as a "mass of human vermin." (He referred to the blacks using an epithet for which he remains controversial.)

In later years, as Mark Twain, he would profess to have harbored deep doubts. He would recount an episode when, as a boy in Hanni-bal, he was horrified to see a white man "throw a lump of iron-ore at a slave-man in anger, for merely doing something awkwardly—he was dead in an hour." On another occasion, he wrote he saw "a dozen black men and women chained to one another awaiting ship-ment to the Southern slave market." The incident, Twain implied, had shocked him. (The story is oddly similar to one that Abraham Lincoln told, about seeing 12 chained slaves on a steamboat "strung together precisely like so many fish on a trot line.")

Yet these were all stories that he told only long after the war— at a time when he had befriended Frederick Douglass, put several black students through Yale Law School, and emerged as one of the nation's fiercest white opponents of lynching. And something about them rings hollow. Although he professed shock at once seeing slaves chained together, this was something he would have witnessed almost daily along the New Orleans wharves, where the slave trade was con-ducted on a massive scale.

This is not to say that the young riverboat pilot's inner moral qualms were not real. But one suspects that in his days on the Mississippi, he cruised a bit too easily between North and South, between free states and slave ones. As it would be for Huck and Jim, the river was his escape route—but in a different, and perhaps less flattering, sense.

All that would change very suddenly, not long after his visit to Madame Caprell. In May 1861, while Clemens was traveling up the Mississippi aboard the steamer Nebraska, a Union artillery battery blockading the river fired a warning shot across her bow. When the vessel failed to stop, a second shot smashed through her smokestack. The Nebraska was the last steamship to attempt such a voyage until the war's end. The Mississippi River that Sam Clemens had known suddenly existed no longer.

Not even the fortune-teller could have fully predicted what came next. After a brief, unhappy stint as a Confederate soldier, Clemens left his old life behind and lit out for the territories, following Orion to Nevada. Instead of a Northerner or Southerner, he became a Westerner. Instead of a riverboat pilot, he became a writer. And instead of Sam Clemens, he became Mark Twain.

The Strange Victory of the Palmetto State

By MANISHA SINHA

L ess than two months separated South Carolina's decision to secede from the United States and the creation of a new country, the Confederate States of America. In that time six other states, comprising the entire Deep South—Mississippi, Florida, Alabama, Georgia, Louisiana and Texas—had followed.

While each state had its share of secessionist fire-eaters, observers on all sides laid the blame firmly at the feet of the Palmetto State. Reverend R.J. Breckinridge of Kentucky, the pro-Union uncle of the southern rights Democratic candidate in the 1860 presidential elections, blamed secession fever on "the chronic hatred of South Carolina to the national Union." Edmund Ruffin, an ardent Virginia secessionist, argued that it was natural for South Carolina to lead the secession movement because "the people of S.Ca. have been schooled and in training for 30 years in their political doctrines." Republican party newspapers like The New York Times went so far as to call the seceded Lower South states the "Calhoun states" of America.

Though actual secession occurred quickly, South Carolinian leaders had indeed been pushing the idea for decades, without success. Criticized widely for its political distemper throughout the antebellum period, South Carolina remained immune to the charms of Jacksonian democracy and guided by the stern proslavery constitutional logic of John C. Calhoun. The state had gone to the brink in the 1830s, but the rest of the South held back; regional unity proved too thin to justify swift action. That changed over the next three decades, though—and in 1861, after nearly 30 years of resisting the siren call of secession from South Carolina, the cotton states followed its lead. What had changed?

Above all was a new sense of regional unity. When South Carolina seceded, emissaries from Alabama and Mississippi were on hand to commend the decision. There was also an element of strategy: immediately after it seceded, South Carolina sent secession commissioners to the other Lower South states, urging disunion. It cleverly assigned fire-eating secessionists like Leonidas W. Spratt, father of the southern movement to reopen the African slave trade; A.P. Calhoun, the son of John C. Calhoun; and Milledge Luke Bonham, later replaced by fellow Congressman Armistead Burt, to the more radicalized states of Florida, Alabama and Mississippi. But it sent the more moderate, Democratic politicians James L. Orr and John L. Manning to Georgia and Louisiana, respectively, where Unionist sentiment still ran high. Many of these men had either lived in the states they were sent to or, like Manning and Calhoun, owned plantations there.

The Carolinian commissioners urged the speedy creation of a southern nation and conveyed a united message in their speeches to the secession conventions of the cotton states. The North and the Republicans stood for "the social principle that equality is the right of man," according to Spratt, but the slave South embodied the "social principle that equality is not the right of man, but the right of equals only." Similarly, John McQueen, the state's commissioner to Texas, argued that the "policy" of the "Black Republicans" was "the elevation of our own slaves to an equality with ourselves and our children."

As in South Carolina, most of these conventions were elected with large secessionist majorities. Only in Texas was the decision to secede ratified post facto in a statewide referendum. Following South Carolina's prompting, representatives of the seceded states met in Montgomery, Ala., on Feb. 4, and they adopted a provisional constitution that explicitly recognized racial slavery on Feb. 8.

Another factor contributing to regional unity under South Carolina's leadership was the changing nature of North-South politics. A faction of South Carolinian planter-politicians had been crying secession at least since the Nullification Crisis of 1828 to 1832. Under Calhoun's political tutelage, they argued that tariff laws formed a precedent for the federal government to interfere with the South's "domestick institution" of slavery, and threatened to leave the Union unless they were allowed to "nullify" federal laws within the state.

But the rest of the South wasn't convinced the Union was a bad deal for the region. After all, the long national ascendance of Virginia's revolutionary dynasty of Washington, Jefferson, Madison and Monroe, as well as the resounding victory of Tennessee's Andrew Jackson in the 1828 presidential election, showed the South could exert significant power over national affairs. Moreover, Jackson's presence in the White House during the Nullification Crisis pulled many Southern states into the Unionist orbit and away from South Carolina.

Change was already afoot, however. With the rise of the abolition movement in the 1830s and the sectional controversy over the expansion of slavery in the aftermath of the Mexican War, South Carolinians began to appear more in the garb of far-seeing prophets than fringe radicals to proslavery advocates in the rest of the region.

During the debates over the Compromise of 1850, a fairly strong secession movement arose not just in South Carolina but also in Alabama, Mississippi and Georgia. Invoking and simultaneously subverting Patrick Henry's famous revolutionary slogan, the South Carolinian Edward Bryan proclaimed, "Give us slavery or give us death!" But a new split emerged, one between single-state secessionists, who believed in Calhoun's notion of absolute sovereignty that would allow any individual state to secede from the Union, and cooperationists, who argued that the South should secede as a whole. The latter won in 1850 and secession talk abated; 10 years later, the former won the day.

Why the flip? The Lower South states, with their large slave and slaveholding populations, started resembling South Carolina in more ways than one during the 1850s: with the demise of the Whig Party, they became one-party states and breeding grounds for Southern extremism. Slaveholders in those states became more receptive to radical ideas, like the Carolina-led movement to reopen the African slave trade. And they agreed with the contention by South Carolina's leaders that the opposition by newly formed Republican Party to the extension of slavery was the first step towards general emancipation.

South Carolina not only inspired its fellow Lower South states to follow suit, but those states in turn worked on getting the Upper South to fall in line. Mississippi and Alabama dispatched emissaries to North Carolina, Maryland, Kentucky and Missouri urging secession, though they took particular aim at Virginia. On Feb. 13, three commissioners from South Carolina, Georgia and Mississippi arrived simultaneously in that state. South Carolina's John S. Preston, who had earlier argued, "Slavery is our King—Slavery is our Truth—Slavery is our Divine Right," now told Virginians that the election of Lincoln meant the "annihilation" of Southern whites. But what had worked elsewhere failed here, and Virginians voted to stay within the Union.

But only for the moment. Indeed, it was hardly a coincidence that a military showdown on Carolinian soil precipitated the secession of four Upper South states. South Carolina had already fired the first shot of the Civil War in January 1861, when artillery gunners opened fire on the ship Star of the West, sent to reinforce federal forces marooned at Fort Sumter, forcing it to turn back. When Confederate forces commenced bombardment of the fort on April 12, 1861, the Upper South had to choose sides. Virginia, Tennessee, Arkansas and North Carolina rapidly seceded.

Despite their central role in fomenting secession, South Carolinian politicians did not dominate the Confederate government; in fact, Virginia, though it entered the Confederacy late, soon became home to its capital. Nevertheless, the Palmetto State had fulfilled the historical mission it had been rehearsing for years. As the unionist Reverend James W. Hunnicutt said of his native state, "The honor, the imperishable glory, of secession and inaugurating Civil War was reserved for South Carolina!"

What Lincoln Meant to the Slaves

By STEVEN HAHN

The enormous excitement and anticipation of the 1860 presidential election campaign spread into unexpected corners of the United States. Indeed, during the months surrounding the contest, and especially after Americans learned of Abraham Lincoln's victory, reports circulated across the Southern states of political attentiveness and restlessness among the slaves.

Southern newspapers noted the slaves' attraction to "every political speech" and their disposition to "linger around" the hustings or courthouse square "and hear what the orators had to say." But even more significantly, witnesses told of elevated hopes and expectations among the slaves that Lincoln intended "to set them all free." And once Lincoln assumed office and fighting erupted between the Union and Confederacy, hopes and expectations seemed to inspire actions. Slaves' response to the election of 1860 and their ideas about Lincoln's intentions suggest that they, too, were important actors in the country's drama of secession and war, and that they may have had an unappreciated influence on its outcome.

Scholars and the interested public have long debated Lincoln's views on slavery and how they influenced his policies as president. How committed was he to abolition? What was he prepared to do? Could he imagine a world in which white and black people lived together in peace and freedom? For many slaves, at least at first, the answer was clear: Lincoln's election meant emancipation.

On one Virginia plantation, a group of slaves celebrated Lincoln's inauguration by proclaiming their freedom and marching off their owner's estate. In Alabama, some slaves had come to believe that "Lincoln is soon going to free them all," and had begun "making preparations to aid him when he makes his appearance," according to local whites. A runaway slave in Louisiana told his captors in late May 1861 that "the North was fighting for the Negroes now and that he was as free as his master." Shortly thereafter, a nearby planter conceded that "the Negroes have gotten a confused idea of Lincoln's Congress meeting and of the war; they think it is all to help them and they expected for 'something to turn up.'"

The slaves, of course, had no civil or political standing in American society on the eve of the Civil War; they were chattel property subject to the power and domination of their owners, and effectively "outside" formal politics. But they were unwilling to accept their assignment to political oblivion. Relying on scattered literacy, limited mobility and communication networks they constructed over many years, slaves had been learning important lessons about the political history of the United States and Western Hemisphere. They heard about the Haitian Revolution and the abolition of slavery in the British West Indies; they knew of a developing antislavery movement in the Northern states and of slaves escaping there; and they heard of a new Republican Party, apparently committed to ending their captivity.

Some slaves discovered that John C. Fremont was the first Republican candidate for president in 1856 and, like William Webb, a slave in Kentucky and Mississippi, held clandestine meetings to consider what might come of it. But it was Lincoln, four years later, who riveted their imaginations. Even as a candidate he was the topic of news and debate on countless plantations. In the view of one slaveholder, slaves simply "know too much about Lincoln . . . for our own safety and peace of mind." News spread quickly, recalled Booker T. Washington, who grew up in western Virginia: "During the campaign when Lincoln was first a candidate for the presidency, the slaves on our far-off plantation, miles from any railroad or large city or daily newspaper, knew what the issues involved were."

Of course, the slaves' expectations that Lincoln and the Republicans were intent on abolishing slavery were for the most part misplaced. Lincoln's policy in 1860 and 1861 was to restrict the expansion of slavery into the federal territories of the West but also to concede that slavery in the states was a local institution, beyond the reach of the federal government. At the very time that slaves were imagining Lincoln as their ally, Lincoln was assuring slaveholders that he would uphold the Constitution and the Fugitive Slave Law and make no moves against them and their property.

Yet slaves were fortified in their beliefs by the dire predictions many slaveholders were making and by the secessionist movement that led to the creation of the Confederacy. They knew as well as anyone else in the country that the likelihood of civil war was growing and, by sharing information and interpreting the course of political events, they readied themselves to act—not only to escape their bonds, but to do their part to make the war about their freedom, whether the North wanted it that way or not.

Thus the case of Harry Jarvis. Born a slave on the eastern shore of Virginia, Jarvis took to the woods for several weeks after the Civil War began, where he survived owing to fellow slaves who brought him news and food. Then, seizing an opportunity, Jarvis headed to Fort Monroe, 35 miles away, where Union troops were stationed, and asked commanding General Benjamin Butler "to let me enlist." Although Butler rebuffed Jarvis and told him "it wasn't a black man's war," Jarvis stood his political ground: "I told him it would be a black man's war before they got through."

Like many other politicized slaves, Jarvis seems to have understood the stakes of the Civil War far better than the combatants themselves. And by testing their expectations, they began to reshape federal policy. By the time of the first Battle of Bull Run, General Butler had declared fugitive slaves within Union lines to be "contrabands of war," and the Congress soon confirmed him. Before too much longer, as Northern armies moved into the densely populated slave plantation districts of South Carolina and the lower Mississippi Valley, slaves crossed the Northern lines by the thousands, at once depriving the Confederacy of needed labor and forcing the Lincoln administration to reevaluate its position on slavery.

By the early fall of 1862, Lincoln had decided to issue an Emancipation Proclamation and enroll African Americans in the Union Army and Navy. Bold initiatives these were, revolutionary in effect, and wholly unimagined when the war began: except by the slaves whose actions helped bring them about. Lincoln's political sensibilities had finally caught up to theirs.

The Ashen Ruin

By ADAM GOODHEART

Washington, D.C., Feb. 16, 1861

His was a quintessential Virginian face: refined, hawkish, melancholy. It was now slightly diminished, to be sure; the cheeks sunken, the lips pinched, the gray curls retreating from the high forehead. But it was hardly fair to call him, as certain radical Northern papers did that winter, a "tottering ashen ruin," a relic of some "antediluvian" age. The much blunter epithet that would soon be applied to him—traitor—is still a matter of debate.

John Tyler, the former president, had, in any event, lately shown a surprising burst of energy. "Who would have thought the old man had so much blood in him?" asked the editor of the Richmond Examiner, quoting "Macbeth" to good effect. Perhaps Tyler's vitality should never have been in question: he had fathered no fewer than 15 children, the latest one at age 70, no small achievement in the pre-Viagra era. (That child, a daughter, lived until 1947; two of Tyler's grandsons, Lyon and Harrison, were still alive in 2011, remarkably enough, 221 years after his birth.)

Now Tyler had taken on a different sort of paternal role: that of founding father. Or, rather, re-founding father. Since early February 1861, he had been presiding over the Peace Conference, a gathering of elder statesmen making a last-ditch attempt to rescue the Union as it pitched toward civil war.

The meeting was taking place, appropriately enough, at Willard's Hotel, a Washington institution where, according to many insiders, more government business was enacted than anywhere else in the capital. (Its anteroom, where patronage-seekers mingled with political bosses, is said to have inspired the word lobbyist.) Since its founding as a small inn in 1818, Willard's had come to occupy almost an entire block. Rather than demolishing the buildings that stood in its path, it strangled them like some relentless jungle vine, sending out shoots and tendrils of faux marble, carved oak and polished brass until the unfortunate structures were wholly engulfed. Most recently, it had swallowed up God himself in the form of a handsome little Greek Revival church whose Presbyterian congregation had hastily vacated, paying due reverence to the superior claims of America's nascent hospitality industry.

That sanctuary had been reconsecrated as a conference room. Three figures from American history—George Washington, Andrew Jackson and Henry Clay—were installed in lithographic form at its altar end. A fourth, Tyler, was installed beneath them in the flesh.

In several respects he had a great deal in common with those other heroes. Like Washington, Jackson and Clay, Tyler owned slaves (43 of them, according to the last census). Like them, he was a border state man—in his case, a Virginian, a scion of the Cavaliers, not one of those swaggering Gulf Coast parvenus who had lately led the drive to secession. And like them, Tyler loved the Union—at least for the time being. On the basis of these claims, the last one especially, he had been selected as the conference's president by unanimous acclamation.

The other delegates were among the most distinguished men America had to offer: not merely an ex-president, but senators, congressmen, former ambassadors, war heroes and railroad owners. They were also, as many observers noted, disproportionately elderly, in some cases actually decrepit. One man, 77-year-old John C. Wright of Ohio, was feeble and nearly blind—and, having vowed to sacrifice his life for the Union, made good that pledge by dying eight days into the convention.

Many, like Tyler himself, had been born in the 18th century; their cherished nation's revolutionary founding was hardly ancient history to them. The ex-president was speaking quite literally when he exhorted his fellow delegates on the second day: "Our godlike fathers created, we have to preserve." The post-revolutionary generation of Americans would now finally have its shot at undying glory. Tyler continued:

> [Our fathers] built up, through their wisdom and patriotism, monuments which have eternized their names. You have before you, gentlemen, a task equally grand, equally sublime, quite as full of glory and immortality. If you reach the height of this great occasion, your children's children will rise up and call you blessed.

Conservative newspapers throughout the country praised Tyler's oration: The Washington Star went so far as to call it "one of the most affecting and eloquent efforts ever spoken in this country." (Even the staunchly Republican New York Times offered plaudits.) Others were not so complimentary. One Ohio paper called Tyler "a man who is more cordially despised by honest men than any man who ever occupied the presidential chair." The 22-year-old Henry Adams saw Tyler at a ball hosted by Senator and Mrs. Stephen A. Douglas:

> A crowd of admiring devotees surrounded the ancient
> buffer Tyler. Ye Gods, what are we, when mortals no
> bigger—no, damn it, not so big as—ourselves, are looked
> up to as though their thunder spoke from the real original
> Olympus. Here is an old Virginia politician, of whom by
> good rights, no one ought ever to have heard, reappearing
> in the ancient cerements of his forgotten grave—politi-
> cal and social—and men look up to him as they would at
> Solomon, if he could be made the subject of a resurrection.

Indeed, Tyler had been controversial ever since, two decades earlier, he had unexpectedly become chief executive after the sudden death of President William Henry Harrison. Many Americans in 1841 believed that the Constitution did not mandate that the vice president actually assume the highest office in the land, but merely that he execute its powers while retaining his title. So when Tyler asserted that he was actually president, he was condemned as a usurper and ridiculed as "His Accidency." The following year he became the target of the first congressional impeachment attempt in American history. Northerners believed that his actions as president—especially his appointment of an almost wholly Southern cabinet and his push to annex Texas as a slave state—had done much to deepen fissures in the Union.

Tyler remained a staunch advocate not just of slavery's existence but of its expansion. The week after Abraham Lincoln's election in November 1860, he wrote to an old friend:

> On one thing I think you may rely, that [Virginia] will never
> consent to have her blacks cribbed and confined within pro-
> scribed and specified limits—and thus be involved in all the
> consequences of a war of the races in some 20 or 30 years.

> She must have expansion, and if she cannot obtain for her-
> self and sisters that expansion in the Union, she may sooner
> or later look to Mexico, the West India Islands, and Central
> America as the ultimate reservations of the African race.

In 1861, many Northerners had little faith that Tyler could truly serve as a neutral arbiter of the secession crisis. Several state legislatures even refused to send delegates to the Peace Conference. Among radical Republicans, the assembly became an object of derision; Horace Greeley's New-York Tribune consistently referred to it as "the old gentlemen's convention."

At any rate, the proceedings at Willard's went steadily downhill after Tyler's opening address. The problem, indeed, was that the delegates were too eloquent: hour after hour, they declaimed on the urgent necessity of saving the Union—invoking Washington, Franklin, Bunker Hill and Yorktown—while making precious little headway toward actually doing anything about it. On the morning of Feb. 16, a delegate proposed that speeches be limited to no more than 30 minutes each—and the body then proceeded to spend almost the entire day debating this, to no conclusive result. Henry Adams predicted: "I suppose they will potter ahead until no one feels any more interest in them, and then they may die."

Tyler and his colleagues pottered ahead, but they did not die quite yet. On Feb. 23, the conference became even more surreal when the man whose recent victory had caused the Union's split—President-elect Lincoln—arrived in Washington and checked into a suite at the hotel, just upstairs. Tyler and other delegates visited him that evening. One convention member warned that unless Lincoln placated the South, the nation's economy would crumble: "It is for you, sir, to say whether grass shall grow in the streets of our commercial cities." Lincoln replied: "If it depends upon me, the grass will not grow anywhere but in the fields and the meadows."

Several days later, the conference adjourned after approving a set of proposed constitutional amendments that stood little hope of mollifying either North or South—and even less of being passed by Congress. Tyler returned to his home in Richmond, Va., on Feb. 28. That evening, a group of admirers came to serenade him on the veranda of the Exchange Hotel. He replied with a speech denouncing the conference, assailing its proposed compromise as a "miserable rickety affair" that did little to protect Southern slaveholders, and calling for Virginia to secede immediately as the only means of preserving its sovereignty.

Later that spring, Tyler cast a vote for Virginia's secession and personally drafted a document placing the state's militia force under Jefferson Davis's direct control. His son Robert, then a lawyer in Philadelphia, narrowly escaped a lynch mob as he fled southward; his neighbors satisfied their fury by burning him in effigy in his own front yard.

In November 1861, John Tyler was elected to the Confederate Congress—becoming the only former American president ever to win office in a foreign country. Arriving in Richmond in January for the opening session, he took a room once again at the Exchange Hotel. Two days later, he had a sudden attack of the chills and nausea, then collapsed unconscious onto a sofa. Less than a week later, he was dead, having never taken his seat in the rebel government.

Back in Washington—the city where he had once presided as chief executive, now an enemy capital—Tyler was subjected to a final indignity when his portrait was removed from its place of honor in the Capitol and exiled to deep storage. But the passage of 150 years has effected a rehabilitation: that painting now hangs in the Blue Room of the White House.

Like a Thief in the Night
By HAROLD HOLZER

In February 2009, President-elect Barack Obama staged the final leg of his pre-inaugural journey by boarding a train in Baltimore for a very public rally at the Amtrak station, followed by a leisurely rail journey to Washington, where the media and a large and exuberant crowd welcomed the future president and his wife. Preceding as it did Mr. Obama's "new birth of freedom" inauguration, billed as a tribute to his hero, Abraham Lincoln, there was little doubt that the carefully

An 1863 cartoon lampooning Lincoln's secret trip from Baltimore to Washington. The president-elect peers out of the rail car in fright at a hissing cat. The writing near the bottom-right of the car door reads: "freight Bones" and "Cap[acit]y 000."

crafted trip from Baltimore was meant as a symbolic prelude. Lincoln, too, had traveled from Baltimore to Washington on the final sprint of his own so-called journey to greatness.

But most Americans overlooked a critical historical irony. Whereas Obama was greeted by a cheering crowd, Lincoln was met by a single friend—no one else in the capital even knew he was arriving. Following 11 days and more than 2,000 miles of travel on 20 different railroad lines, after making 100 speeches and appearing at dozens of parades, receptions, dinners and church services, Lincoln made the final leg of his journey in total secrecy, in the dead of night, disguised to avoid detection and at one point sleeping near a woman who was not his wife.

The bizarre episode began in Philadelphia, toward the end of what Lincoln called his "meandering" journey from Illinois. There he received a chilling report from detective Allan Pinkerton that assassins planned to kill him in Baltimore when he changed trains to continue his journey south. (At the time track lines didn't connect, even in large cities, so he would have to go from one depot to another to reach southbound tracks.)

The story sounded credible to Lincoln. Baltimore was the first southern, slaveholding city on Lincoln's itinerary, and as such inherently dangerous territory. Walking from his train platform out into the street, no doubt wearing his signature stovepipe hat, the looming president-elect would have made a plum target. When warned that even Baltimore's local police force might betray him in a pinch, Lincoln chose to abort his published schedule. Living to take office was more important than appearing in public in a city where only one or two percent of voters had supported him.

Bravely, Lincoln did insist on continuing his itinerary in Pennsylvania. He was feted in Philadelphia, then his train headed west to Harrisburg, where he had promised to appear with the state's recently elected Republican governor, Andrew Curtin. But that night, in the midst of a supper in his honor, Lincoln slipped outside, donned a soft, wide-brimmed hat and long overcoat ("I was not the same man," he later crowed) and raced off in a waiting carriage, accompanied only by Pinkerton and the president-elect's physically imposing friend and bodyguard, Ward Hill Lamon. Pinkerton ordered telegraph wires severed to prevent leaks. (Oddly, Lincoln left behind the largest security retinue ever assigned to protect an incoming or sitting president.)

Arriving in Philadelphia around 10 p.m., Lincoln rode a carriage to the next depot and there boarded a sleeping car under an assumed name, with Pinkerton agent Kate Warne, posing as his sister, occupying a nearby bunk. After its arrival in Baltimore at 3:30 a.m., horses drew the sleeper from the Calvert Street to the Camden Street station and coupled it to a southbound locomotive. Pinkerton later insisted, as if to emphasize the danger, that he heard strains of the incendiary new pro-South song "Maryland My Maryland" wafting through the darkened streets.

Lincoln finally arrived in Washington at 6 a.m. on Feb. 23. Following a week and a half of loud and boisterous welcomes, the silence there must have seemed eerily portentous. No music played. Not a soul shouted his name. One old friend who spotted him on the lonely platform—Rep. Elihu Washburne of Illinois—did try to approach. But so tense was the situation (the capital abounded with hostile slaveholders, several of whom had vowed Lincoln would not live to be sworn in) that when Washburne neared, Pinkerton tried to strike him.

News of Lincoln's premature and clandestine arrival quickly found its way into the newspapers, and it shocked the country. Yet the incident might have been quickly forgotten had it not been for The New York Times. Its embedded inaugural journey reporter, Joseph Howard, no doubt incensed that he had been left behind in Harrisburg, reported that Lincoln had passed through Baltimore disguised in a "Scotch cap and military cloak." Though Lincoln had worn no such garb, the calumny spread rapidly. (He likely intended his slur to hold meaning only for the president's closest friends, for his claims could be read as coded messages. A scotch cap sounded just like a "scotch cop"—and the Glasgow-born Pinkerton was certainly that. Lamon had only recently been named an honorary colonel to validate his credentials as Lincoln's protector—engendering much teasing—and he may have been Howard's idea of a "military cloak.")

Within days, editorials assailed him. Cartoons showing "The Flight of Abraham" poured off the presses depicting him in the Howard-invented masquerade, running for his life and cowering in fear. Frederick Douglass compared Lincoln to a "poor, hunted fugitive slave," reaching his designation "in concealment, evading pursuers by the underground railroad crawling and dodging under the sable wing of night." Other observers were even less charitable. To the pro-secession Charleston Mercury, the country was "disgusted at his cowardly and undignified entry." Even The New York Herald conceded that Lincoln had "crept into Washington" like "a thief in the night."

Lincoln supposedly later confided that his Baltimore escapade was a mistake. And for years, artists who wanted to cast him in a negative light would draw him in a beribboned Scottish tam. But in hindsight, was his decision unwise? Was the plot authentic? Was the most bizarre presidential journey in American history justified? It's hard to know. Lincoln did not object to having his official traveling party—including his wife and sons —enter Baltimore later, as scheduled. Reportedly they were harassed but never really threatened.

What about Pinkerton's report? Today he is best remembered not as a lifesaver but a chronic worry wart and exaggerator; his wildly inflated estimates of Confederate troop strength in 1862 scared Union General George B. McClellan into virtual paralysis. And he certainly did not hear "Maryland My Maryland" in Baltimore, because it had yet to be written. So there is reason to doubt the solidity of his evidence concerning an assassination plot.

On the other hand, just weeks after Lincoln evaded Baltimore, rioters there attacked a train bearing Massachusetts soldiers en route to Washington. Blood was spilled in the streets, inspiring a frightened mayor to rush to the White House and demand that the new president order future regiments to bypass his city.

If a Baltimore Plot existed at all, it was at most ad hoc, poorly organized and probably destined to fail. But as Lincoln's private secretaries later insisted, "the fate of the government" required him to "shun all possible and unnecessary peril." Lincoln had to reach Washington to rule there.

And until the end of his days, Lincoln's bodyguard defended the evasion. Lamon insisted that, "there never was a moment from the day he crossed the Maryland line, right up to the time of his assassination, that he was not in danger of death by violence." And when Lincoln did die at the hands of an assassin in 1865, the killer hailed from Maryland.

The Other Emancipation Proclamation

By ADAM GOODHEART

St. Petersburg, Russia, March 3, 1861

Four thousand miles from where President-elect Abraham Lincoln was counting down the final hours before his inauguration, the leader of a very different nation prepared for the most momentous day of his reign. Czar Alexander II rose before dawn and, dressed in his favorite cherry-red dressing gown, stood contemplatively by the window, watching the pale light grow in the square outside the Winter Palace. This morning he would set 23 million of his subjects free.

The tall, bewhiskered Russian emperor differed in many respects from the tall, bewhiskered Illinois lawyer. He had been born not into frontier obscurity, but amid the salutes of cannons and the festive tolling of the Kremlin's bells. The two men would never meet, although they would exchange a number of letters, which they would sign "Your good friend, Alexander" and "Your good friend, A. Lincoln."

Yet when Alexander signed his emancipation decree on the eve of Lincoln's inauguration, 150 years ago today, the coincidence of timing hinted at deeper connections. In fact, the czar's liberation of Russia's serfs may even have lent momentum to the forces that would soon liberate America's slaves.

Comparisons between the two systems were already familiar to

Americans of every region and party. In 1858 the Georgia proslavery apologist Thomas Cobb listed certain alleged similarities between Russian serfs and American blacks: "They are contented with their lot and seek no change. They are indolent, constitutionally. They are filthy in their persons, and in their rude huts; exhibiting, in all their handiworks, the ignorance of a savage and the stupidity of a dolt." A Virginia writer, George Fitzhugh, wrote of the "cheerfulness" of the serfs and noted approvingly that Russia was, along with the American South, "the only conservative section of civilized christendom," since it too kept its inferior classes in bondage. (He condemned all other Western nations, and the free states, as "socialist.")

Northern leaders, on the other hand, pointed with shame to the fact that the world's greatest democracy and its most infamous autocracy stood alone among major Western powers in retaining slavery. In 1850, no less a politician than William Seward, condemning Russia as "the most arbitrary Despotism, and most barbarous State in Europe," asked rhetorically, "Shall we select our institutions from the dominions of the Czar?" Five years later, Lincoln himself wrote to his old friend Joshua Speed:

> Our progress in degeneracy appears to me to be pretty rapid. As a nation, we began by declaring that "all men are created equal." We now practically read it "all men are created equal, except negroes." When the Know-Nothings get control, it will read 'all men are created equal, except negroes, and foreigners, and catholics.' When it comes to this I should prefer emigrating to some country where they make no pretence of loving liberty—to Russia, for instance, where despotism can be taken pure, and without the base alloy of hypocracy.

There were both similarities and differences between the two versions of servitude. Russia's serfs were bought and sold, although never on anything like the scale of America's domestic slave trade. And serfs, too, were viciously flogged and sexually exploited; had few legal rights; and could make hardly any important decisions without their masters' permission.

On the other hand, serfs were customarily required to labor for their masters only three days a week; the rest of the time they were free to work for their own benefit; Russian law even mandated certain minimum allotments of land for each family. (Unlike American slaves, they could also own real estate with their masters' consent.) Serfs had not, of course, been kidnapped from their native country and thrust into the horrors of the Middle Passage. And the relatively static nature of Russia's economy and society meant that serf families were far less vulnerable to sudden, arbitrary separations and dislocations.

Perhaps the most significant difference was that by the 1850s, America's slave system was growing more and more rigid and confining while Russia's was swiftly dissolving. Back in the 1780s, Catherine the Great—like Thomas Jefferson and James Madison—had admitted that serfdom was wrong but done little to curtail it. But her 19th-century successors forbade the sale of serfs apart from the land on which they resided and made various other decrees protecting them from abuse (although these often went unenforced). By midcentury, fewer than half of Russia's peasants lived as serfs.

No one was terribly surprised in 1856 when, barely a year into his reign, Alexander II announced to an assembly of noblemen, "I've decided to do it, gentlemen. If we don't give the peasants freedom from above, they will take it from below." After five more years of bureaucratic dithering among various commissions and committees, he finally determined to abolish serfdom the old-fashioned way: by imperial fiat.

Alexander chose Sunday, March 3, 1861, for his epochal act. (Under Russia's antiquated Julian calendar, the date was reckoned as Feb. 19.) That morning, he prayed alone in the chapel of the Winter Palace, then attended a grand cathedral mass with his family. After breakfast, he went into his private study—separated by a curtain from his bedchamber—and sat down at a desk piled high with papers. Atop this heap lay the historic manifesto that would grant the serfs their freedom in two years' time. The czar crossed himself, dipped his pen in an inkwell and signed.

He waited another couple of weeks to announce this decree to the nation and the world. Some of Alexander's advisors predicted that the serfs, emboldened by the news, would stage a revolution. Others feared that the serf-holding aristocrats would try to overthrow him. Civil wars had been fought in Russia over far less. Wisely, though, the czar had decided to grant land to the newly freed families and reparations to the aristocrats (many of whom promptly decamped with their windfall to live the good life in Paris or Biarritz). In the end, calm prevailed.

Across the Atlantic, however, the news from Russia made waves in an already turbulent political sea. Just a few days before the Confederate attack on Fort Sumter, Horace Greeley wrote in The New-York Tribune:

> The Manifesto of the Czar is throughout in most strik-
> ing contrast to the recent Manifestoes of the leaders of
> the rebel slaveholders in this country. [The Confeder-
> ates] with brutal coolness doom a whole race to eternal
> bondage. The Russian autocrat, on the other hand, admits
> that man has certain rights. The whole world and all suc-
> ceeding ages will applaud the Emperor Alexander for the
> abolition of Slavery in Russia. But what does the world
> think, what will future generations think, of the attempt
> to make Slavery perpetual in America?

Despite the two nations' vast cultural and political differences, some of the same forces were operating in both. Like the United States, 19th-century Russia was expanding aggressively across a continent, building railroads and telegraph lines as fast as it could, and guzzling foreign capital in the process. Those same new technologies had also broken down the geographic isolation of both countries. What the rest of the world thought—especially regarding slavery and serfdom—suddenly mattered more than ever.

In the months that followed Alexander's decree, Americans watched intently to see what the reaction within Russia would be. Eventually news came of certain scattered disturbances among the peasants, who were impatient with the two-year delay of their freedom. In November 1861, Greeley's Tribune suggested that this proved "how delicate a business is partial emancipation." Overall, the paper concluded, it showed that nothing less than instantaneous and total emancipation would suffice in America: "In dealing with our own problem, it concerns us to consider alike the encouragement and the warning of [Russia's] example."

As for the czar, he too was peering across the ocean. In July, his foreign minister sent a communiqué to the Russian envoy in Washington, expressing the strongest support of the Union cause yet offered by any European power:

> For the more than 80 years that it has existed, the American Union owes its independence, its towering rise, and its progress, to the concord of its members, consecrated, under the auspices of its illustrious founder, by institutions which have been able to reconcile union with liberty. In all cases, the American Union may count on the most heart-felt sympathy on the part of the [czar] in the course of the serious crisis which the Union is currently going through.

To this document Alexander added a notation in his own hand: "So be it."

The modern-day Russian historian Edvard Radzinsky, an admirer of Alexander, has called him "a reformer for a new kind for Russia— a two-faced Janus, one head looking forward while the other looked back longingly." In this respect, Radzinsky has suggested, the czar resembled Mikhail Gorbachev. He might also have compared Alexander to Lincoln. Like the emperor, the president looked backward (toward America's founding principles) as well as forward (toward a new birth of freedom). He used radical methods (freeing the slaves) to achieve conservative goals (preserving the Union).

When, more than a year after Alexander's, Lincoln issued his own Emancipation Proclamation, it too was handed down as an executive decree from on high. (The president's opponents assailed him as an "autocrat," an "American Czar.") It too proclaimed only partial freedom. And perhaps unwisely, Lincoln—unlike his Russian counterpart—provided neither compensation to the slaveholders nor land to the freedmen.

The czar outlived the president, but he too would fall by the hand of an assassin. On March 1, 1881—nearly 20 years to the day after freeing the serfs—Alexander was riding through St. Petersburg in a closed carriage when two young radicals hurled bombs. The emperor, his legs torn to shreds and stomach ripped open, was carried back to his bedroom-study in the Winter Palace. Alexander died just a few feet from the spot where he had signed his decree of liberation.

What Would Jefferson Do?

By WILLIAM W. FREEHLING

During the secession crisis, no Americans were more trapped between secession and Union, between slavery and emancipation, than middle-of-the-road Virginians. And no Virginia family was more torn than Thomas Jefferson's clan.

The Jeffersons, going back to the patriarch, embodied all the contradictions of Upper South slaveholders. The author of the Declaration of Independence was also a founding father of procrastination on slavery. At times Jefferson seemed a determined proponent of abolition. He termed slavery an "assemblage of horrors." He called "nothing . . . more certainly written in the book of fate than that these people are to be freed." Otherwise, he feared that "his people" would free themselves in a slave revolt. He thus winced that "if something is not done, and done soon, we shall be the murderers of our own children."

But he found emancipating slaves without removing freedmen from the country even more frightening than risking black insurrectionists. In his climactic proposal to effect safe emancipation, presented in 1824, Jefferson suggested a constitutional amendment authorizing the use of profits from federal land sales to free slaves born in the future—and then deport them. But he never urged this plan of delayed emancipation publicly, and he privately shuddered that "we have the wolf by the ears, and we can neither hold him, or safely let him go."

Five years after the patriarch's death, the 1831 Nat Turner revolt impelled his executor and eldest grandson, Thomas Jefferson Randolph, to urge his grandfather's allegedly safe alternative in the Virginia legislature. Randolph's bill would have emancipated slaves born eight years hence, after they became adults, and then deported them. This racist species of antislavery would have left Virginia enslaved for at least 80 years. After spending two nervous weeks debating the compromised scheme and listening to non-slaveholders from western Virginia cheer for Randolph, the legislators voted 71-54 against an even more watered-down antislavery proposal. (Yet the state had hardly united behind permanent slavery: forty-three percent of the delegates had voted to seek some sort of legislative end to slavery.)

But Thomas Jefferson Randolph wasn't the family's only scion to join the debate: In late 1860 and early 1861, after the Lower South had seceded, Jefferson's youngest grandson, emerged as a vociferous skeptic of slavery—and, surprisingly, Unionism. During this latest and worst Virginia antebellum crisis, George Wythe Randolph, 26 years younger than Thomas Jefferson Randolph, scorned more than his eldest brother's (and his grandfather's) slavery apologetics and tremulous antislavery proposals. He also loathed the pointless debating that occupied the Virginia secession convention, which met for two months before reaching a consensus.

During what seemed to him the convention's interminable talk, George Wythe Randolph suffered through other delegates' unending predictions, usually absurd to him, about where the spinning world might stop. Would Abraham Lincoln let the South secede? Would Lower South seceders return to the Union? It was useless, he said in a March 16 speech, to debate whether the Lower South should have seceded or not. The Confederacy now existed as a cold fact, good or bad, and the old Union was no more. "We are not assembled to consider," he emphasized, "whether we will remain as we were," in a Union with 15 slave states, "but whether we shall rest in the new and perilous" Union "in which we now find ourselves," with only eight slave states. In other words, once the Lower South states had seceded, the only issue for the Upper South, which republic should we join? (Or, as the question evolved after Fort Sumter, whose soldiers should we kill?)

Randolph considered these non-choices. He trembled over Virginia's fate if the convention chose the new federal Union. He scoffed at the fantasy, held by many of the state's Unionists, that Southerners would bring the "Northern people . . . right after a while" on slavery's blessings. "Sir, they are much more likely to make us wrong than we are to bring them right. Their anti-slavery is as old as slavery itself. . . . It has all the signs of a great mental movement. The opposite sentiment with us . . . is comparatively a thing of yesterday—it has not been inculcated in early life. . . . It has hardly had time to be understood and appreciated. . . . To dash it now against the iron-bound fanaticism of the North would be the height of folly."

Randolph winced that the North's previously "merely speculative" opinion against slavery now came armed with "power" for "energetic action," which would require "separation from the North" even "if they had not otherwise injured us." Lincoln, an antislavery president, "will wield all the patronage of the government." With an ideological enemy dispensing "honors and fortune" inside a mere eight states (four of them Border States where slavery was waning, the rest Middle South states where Jeffersonian apologetics were waxing!) "the odds against us . . . will be tremendous."

The roots of Randolph's complex perspective were in part economic. Although born (and later buried) on his grandfather's Monticello plantation, he had rejected Jefferson's qualms about cities no less than about slavery. Where the grandfather had called urban spaces sores on the body politic and Thomas Jefferson Randolph presided over a plantation near Monticello, George Wythe Randolph had become an important Richmond lawyer.

In the Virginia convention, this urbanite denied "that there is an irrepressible conflict between white and slave labor." Instead, "the true competitors of our laboring whites are the gigantic corporations of the North." Northern industrialists had used their high tariffs and head start to crush Richmond manufacturers and their white employees. The problem would worsen in the new federal Union. But in the new Southern Confederacy, with its underdeveloped industries and its "protection from Northern industry," secession will stimulate a vast takeoff in demand for Richmond industrial products. Even the rural and nonslaveholding western Virginians, he added, after receiving "protection from Northern industry" would become "what they ought to be—the manufacturers and miners of a great nation." These and other economic emphases consumed more pages than Randolph's warnings about Lincoln's immediate menace, a fact that should give pause to oversimplifiers who think that *only* the very important fears about slavery impelled disunion.

What most provoked Randolph's impatience was the lack of a firm decision. Like capitalists throughout the nation, he could hardly bear a moment more of this counterproductive delay, this killing uncertainty. "Are we to stand for an indefinite period," he agonized, "with our industry paralyzed, our people feverish and impatient, our manufacturers ready to emigrate?"

With his certitude that secession alone could be viable, and his conviction that this latest procrastination was as destructive as his family's long paralysis had been, Randolph stood ready to join other frustrated spirits in extralegal action if a chance arose, even before a convention vote took place. He did not know that in exactly a month, events would unleash his and his compatriots' lethal exasperation.

Divorce, Antebellum Style
By ADAM GOODHEART

The end of a marriage: it seemed an almost perfect metaphor to the worldly Mary Boykin Chesnut. As she surveyed the Union (uppercase) splitting apart, with North and South hurling bitter recriminations at each other, they reminded her of nothing so much as a long-married, long-quarreling husband and wife whose union (lowercase) had finally gone asunder.

"We separated North and South because of incompatibility of temper," the South Carolina diarist wrote in March 1861. "We are divorced because we have hated each other so. If we could only separate, a 'separation à l'agréable,' as the French say it, and not have a horrid fight for divorce."

Chesnut was not the only American to whom such comparisons occurred during the early months of 1861. The New York journalist John O'Sullivan likewise compared the sectional crisis to a "divorce for incompatibility of temper and interests" in which "it will be better to part in peace" than to launch a bloody civil war. A Unionist orator, on the other hand, compared the disagreements between North and South to "occasional bickerings between husband and wife, which ought not to lead to an immediate divorce."

Even Abraham Lincoln took up the comparison. In February, on the first day of his train journey to the capital, the president-elect gave a speech in which he accused secessionists of viewing the bond between states as "no regular marriage, but a sort of free love arrangement, to be maintained [merely] by passional attraction." This public allusion to Southerners as sexual profligates was criticized, even among some Republicans, as being off-color—certainly beneath the dignity of the nation's chief executive. (Lincoln's closest associates, on the other hand, knew that he was capable of much bawdier humor than this.)

Yet divorce was no mere metaphor on the eve of the Civil War. In fact, it was a volatile political issue, one that occasionally seemed to divide the nation as sharply as the slavery question did. In early 1861, the question of when—or even whether—a man and woman should be permitted to end their marriage was being hotly debated by many of the same legislators, journalists and activists who were also arguing over national disunion. Like slavery and secession, divorce was an issue involving civil rights, moral responsibilities and conflicts over state and federal authority. It was a controversy that, in many ways, foreshadowed present-day debates over marriage laws and rights.

American divorce laws in the mid-19th century were a complicated patchwork that varied widely—and, it seemed to many people, unjustly and illogically—from state to state. Was sexual infidelity sufficient reason for divorce? (And should adulterous husbands be penalized the same as unfaithful wives?) What about physical abuse? (And how severely must a husband beat his wife before the law could intervene?) It often seemed that no two courts or legislatures agreed on such matters.

In most states in the early 19th century, an act of the legislature was required to end a marriage—and the process of obtaining one could be long, expensive and publicly humiliating, which discouraged all but the most desperately unhappy spouses. But by the 1850s, this was beginning to change, and in some states, divorces could be obtained unobtrusively in court.

During the 1850s, Indiana was widely condemned as a Midwestern Sodom for its relatively lax statutes. Couples there obtained divorces on any grounds that a judge ruled "proper"—attracting a flood of applicants from out of state. The editor Horace Greeley lambasted the Hoosier State as "the paradise of free-lovers" whose example would soon lead to "a general profligacy and corruption such as this country has never known." (In 1859, its legislature finally voted to require a year's residency before allowing a divorce suit to be heard.)

South Carolina stood at the other extreme. Since the Revolution, the Palmetto State had refused to permit divorce for any reason whatsoever. Although a court might, very rarely, grant an annulment, most disgruntled spouses had no recourse except to abandon each other. (In fact, South Carolina did not pass its first divorce statute until 1949.) In many states, including New York, divorce was often only granted on condition that neither spouse could remarry—which was supposed to safeguard public morality by ensuring that no one could trade in an old partner for a new one. In North Carolina, the "guilty party" was forbidden to remarry during the lifetime of the "innocent party."

On March 14, 1861, The New York Times' editors considered these nationwide discrepancies in the fresh light of the secession crisis. In an editorial entitled "Is Democracy a Failure?", they asked whether "our Government has, after all, ever been a Republic? We have laws as different in our States as in the various countries of Europe. The mere subject of divorce, with its contradictions, has more than once been pointed out by writers as entirely inconsistent with the idea of a stable and harmonious Government."

Indeed, the paper's news columns offered almost daily examples of such legal capriciousness. On Jan. 19, 1861, a New York City judge refused to grant a divorce to a wife whose husband had beaten her unconscious in an argument over letting the family dog sleep on the bed—and, on a later occasion, tried to strike her with a wooden stick. The judge admonished the couple that a mere "one or two acts of cruel treatment" were not proper grounds for divorce, and that "the wife should not seek on slight provocation to dissolve that sacred tie which binds her to her husband for life, for better or worse." The Times, quoting the New Testament, headlined its article "Wives be Obedient Unto Your Husbands." The following month, another headline asked flippantly, "Is a Black Eye Sufficient Ground for Divorce?" (The article also mentioned that the husband had tried to cut his wife's throat with a knife.)

Often, indeed, the paper's editors played spousal abuse for laughs. An article on Feb. 12, 1861, was headlined "Action for Divorce—No

Happiness Without Beefsteak," and suggested that a wife had filed for divorce because her husband had failed to supply her with sufficient luxuries, like red meat. Only farther down in the story did it emerge that the he had also "used personal violence to the plaintiff on a number of occasions."

Such stories were no laughing matter to activists like Elizabeth Cady Stanton. For her and others, the American legal system's unjust treatment of women was inextricably entwined with its oppression of African-American slaves.

In February 1861, in fact, Stanton traveled to Albany, N.Y., to fight for the twin causes of abolitionism and liberalized divorce. Early that month, she arrived in the capital to take part in a statewide antislavery convention. That same week, she was allowed to testify before the New York State Senate's judiciary committee on behalf of a bill that would—very slightly—relax the state's stringent divorce code. Similar legislative debates were held that winter and spring in Ohio, Massachusetts, and elsewhere.

Some months earlier, in the pages of the abolitionist magazine The Liberator, Stanton had compared the struggle over divorce law to the struggle over slavery. "We decide the whole question of slavery by settling the sacred rights of the individual," she wrote. Surely, marriage and divorce also involved fundamental questions of individual liberties, human rights and free will.

Not all abolitionists—even those sympathetic to women's rights—agreed with Stanton. Wendell Phillips, the antislavery leader, admonished her that it was politically "premature and unwise" to take on such a controversial issue. Stanton reminded him that only a few decades earlier, most people had said the same thing about slavery.

A few women went even further than Stanton, however. In another issue of The Liberator, in December 1860, the "free love" advocate Caroline Hinckley wrote: "Persons should be left free to unite as they please—to themselves decide what is and is not marriage—to marry permanently or temporarily—and to separate when they themselves feel called upon thus to do."

It then occurred to Hinckley that her argument had certain logical implications that went beyond literal marriage into other, even more contentious debates. "I see not why a State or an individual who desires to withdraw from a compact should not have the right to do so," she concluded. "So I say to-day to Alabama, South Carolina, Georgia, Florida, if you don't like the Union, peaceably leave it."

From San Marino, With Love

By DON H. DOYLE

Hundreds of letters congratulating Abraham Lincoln on his inauguration poured in from all over the world in the spring of 1861, but one in particular caught the eye of Secretary of State William Henry Seward: it was from the oldest surviving republic in the world, "the Most Serene Republic of San Marino," addressed to the new president of a much younger and most troubled republic facing secession and civil war.

Seward brought it to Lincoln's attention. Though it took several weeks for him to respond, Lincoln was greatly moved by the letter. It stirred him to see the national calamity now facing his own country as part of a much grander question: what future, if any, did republican democracy have in a world beset by slavery and tyranny?

Perched high in the Apennine Mountains on the Adriatic side of the Italian peninsula, San Marino occupied (and continues to occupy) about 24 square miles of rocky escarpments. Less than a thousand families inhabited the land, most of them clustered inside San Marino's city walls or in scattered villages.

San Marino's history as an asylum from persecution and despotism stretched back to its very founding in 301 A.D., when a Christian named Marinus fled the persecution of the Romans to seek refuge in the mountainous enclave. Eventually a small colony of Christians formed, taking its name from their founder, later to become Saint Marinus. Thanks in part to their country's formidable geography and in part to their consistent political neutrality, the San Marinese were able to resist conquest by aggressive neighbors for centuries: the Duke of Montefeltro next door in Urbino, the Pope in Rome, French armies under Napoleon I and, in 1861, the newly united Kingdom of Italy.

But an even more striking aspect of the country's history was its political structure. Since about 1300, San Marino had been governed by the same body of elected representatives, the Capitani Regenti. In 1600 San Marino promulgated a written constitution that codified its institutions and laws, a document still in force in the 21st century. San Marino remains the oldest constitutional republic in the world, almost twice as old as the runner up, the United States.

San Marino and the United States were members of a very small club: in the mid-19th century republics were an endangered species. Amid the ruins of dozens of revolutionary republican movements that erupted in Europe between the French Revolution in 1789 and the revolutions of 1848, few genuine republics endured, and the tide of democracy was giving way to the imperialist ambitions of kings and emperors. Only Switzerland, a federated republic modeled after the United States, and tiny San Marino upheld the republican ideal in Europe. Across the Atlantic, most of the Spanish American republics had either fallen under the despotic rule of military caudillos or were torn by warring factions of conservative landowners and clergy against liberal republicans.

But much more so than San Marino, since its founding the United States had been admired among liberals in Europe and elsewhere as a pioneer in the "republican experiment," a model—imperfect and unfinished, to be sure—but nonetheless a working example of how a free, self-governing people might live. Now it was descending into a fratricidal war that threatened to prove the whole experiment in self-government a failure, a risk that its leaders were all too aware of. In his Inaugural Address earlier that March, Lincoln argued against the abstract principle of secession as a threat to the fundamental workings of a self-governing republic; to allow aggrieved minorities to secede every time they did not like the outcome of an election or some act of government was "the essence of anarchy" and the ruin of a self-governing society. And he knew what that failure would mean in the international arena: America stood as one of the few lonely beacons of the republican ideal, the "last best hope of earth" as Lincoln would later put it.

It's no surprise, then, that both Seward and Lincoln took interest in the letter from the Regent Captains of San Marino. The letter had two columns, with perfect Italian on one side, and imperfect but clear English on the other. "We have wished to write to you in our own hand and in English, although we have little knowledge and no practice in the language," the regents explained. "It is a some while since the Republic of San Marino wishes to make alliance with the United States of America in that manner as it is possible between a great Potency and a very small country."

Indeed, the two countries faced similar political straits as well. San Marino's recent troubles went back to 1849, when it offered asylum to Giuseppe Garibaldi and his army of Red Shirts who were fleeing from French and Austrian troops after the fall of the revolutionary Republic of Rome. Pope Pius IX controlled the Papal States surrounding San Marino and the Austrian Empire controlled Venice to its north. To the Pope and the Hapsburgs, Garibaldi and his "red republicans" were akin to revolutionary terrorists. Somehow Garibaldi then escaped San Marino, leaving Austrian soldiers to kick in doors looking for men and arms left behind.

By 1861 the Austrians still controlled Venice, but the realm of the Papal States had shrunk to the area immediately surrounding Rome. The previous year Garibaldi and his Red Shirts conquered much of the area to the South of San Marino in the name of King Victor Emanuel II. San Marino became surrounded by a newly united kingdom that proclaimed its existence as a nation in March 1861, precisely as the regents wrote to Lincoln proposing an "alliance" between fellow republicans in a perilous world. Whether the new monarch would appreciate San Marino's role in protecting Garibaldi, let alone respect its right to exist as an independent republic, was unsure—hence the plea to Lincoln. "As we think not extention of territories but conformity of opinions to procure friendly relations," the regents wrote, "so we are sure you will be glad to shake hands with a people who in its smallness and poverty can exhibit to you an antiquity from fourteen centuries of its free government."

"Now we must inform you," the letter to Lincoln continued, "that to give to the United States of America a mark of high consideration and sincere fraternity the Sovereign Counsel on our motion decreed in its sitting of 25th October that the citizenship of the Republic of San Marino was conferred for ever to the President pro tempore of the United States of America and we are very happy to send you the diploma of it."

The regents then alluded to the recent difficulties of their sister republic across the sea: "We are acquainted from newspapers with political griefs, w[h]ich you are now suffering therefore we pray to God to grant you a peaceful solution of your questions. Nevertheless we hope our letter will not reach you disagreeable, and we shall expect anxiously an answer which proves us your kind acceptance."

The letter from San Marino was addressed to Lincoln in New York, which the Regent Captains must have assumed was the capital of the United States. It probably arrived in Washington in mid-April, when Lincoln was about to experience even more "political griefs." But on May 7, amid all the turmoil, Lincoln and Seward (both signed the letter) found time to graciously accept the "honor of citizenship" from San Marino.

"Great and Good Friends," the reply to San Marino began, "Although your dominion is small, your State is nevertheless one of the most honored, in all history. It has by its experience demonstrated the truth, so full of encouragement to the friends of Humanity, that Government founded on Republican principles is capable of being so administered as to be secure and enduring."

Lincoln's letter then turned to America's troubles: "You have kindly adverted to the trial through which this Republic is now passing. It is one of deep import. It involves the question whether a Representative republic, extended and aggrandized so much as to be safe against foreign enemies can save itself from the dangers of domestic faction. I have faith in a good result"—a thought the president would place at the center of his Gettysburg Address, still two and a half years in the future.

Bats, Balls and Bullets

By GEORGE B. KIRSCH

In late March and early April 1861, ballplayers in dozens of American towns looked forward to another season of play. But they were not highly paid professionals whose teams traveled to Florida or Arizona for spring training. Rather, they were amateur members of private organizations founded by men whose social standing ranged from the working class through the upper-middle ranks of society. There were no formal leagues or fixed schedules of games, although there were regional associations of clubs that drew up and enforced rules for each type of bat and ball game. Contests between the best teams attracted large crowds (including many gamblers), and reporters from daily newspapers and weekly sporting magazines wrote detailed accounts of the games.

The English national game of cricket was the first modern team sport in the United States. During the 1850s, an estimated 10,000 English immigrants and native-born men and boys founded about 500 clubs in at least 22 states in the Union. By 1861, Philadelphia had become the cricketing capital of the nation, boasting the most organizations and the largest contingent of proficient, American-born players. But cricket also faced major challenges from two upstart versions of baseball that had recently exploded in popularity. "The Massachusetts game" reigned supreme in Boston and most of New England, while "the New York game" ruled Manhattan, Brooklyn and New Jersey.

The Massachusetts game matched sides of 8 to 15 men on a square field with bases or tall stakes (up to five feet high) at each corner, generally 60 feet apart. The batsman stood midway between first and fourth base and tried to hit a ball thrown swiftly overhand by a pitcher who stood in the middle of the square, often only about 30 feet away. The batter could strike the ball in any direction, since there was no foul territory. After swatting the ball, the batsman ran around the bases until he was put out or remained safely at a base. Generally he tallied a run each time he arrived safely at a base, but in some matches a run counted only when a runner arrived safely at home. The batter could be put out if he missed three pitched balls, or if a ball he hit was fielded on the fly, or if he was struck by a ball thrown at him by a fielder while he was between bases. One out usually ended an inning, and the first team to score a fixed number of runs (sometimes as many as 100) won the game.

The origins of the New York game dated back to the mid-1840s, when members of the New York Knickerbocker Base Ball Club experimented with new regulations to govern their play. During the late 1850s, several conventions of New York City ballplayers modified the original Knickerbocker rules. The newest code mandated a diamond instead of a square for the bases, which were placed 90 feet apart. The batsman stood at home plate, at the bottom point of the diamond. The pitcher delivered the ball to the batter underhand from a distance of 45 feet. A ball knocked outside lines drawn from home to first and third bases (and extending beyond each base) was declared foul and out of play. A striker was put out when a fielder caught a hit ball on the fly or the first bounce, or if a fielder held the ball on a base before a runner arrived, or if a fielder touched a runner with the ball while he was between bases. Throwing the ball at base runners was prohibited, three outs retired the side and nine innings decided the outcome of the match, provided that the teams had an equal number of outs.

Cricket and the two types of baseball received a mixed reception south of the Mason-Dixon line. Southern plantation owners showed little interest in ballgames, which they dismissed as Yankee imports that were antithetical to their culture. Many southern towns were equally indifferent. Richmond, Va., is a prime example.

Henry Chadwick was a cricket enthusiast and pioneer sporting journalist who later earned fame as "the father of baseball." In 1848 he married a young lady from Richmond, and for the next dozen years he tried to stir up interest in both cricket and baseball in that city, especially because of its good fields and abundance of young men of leisure. In late March 1861, The New York Clipper published a notice that advised any interested young men of Richmond to contact "H.C." at the journal's office. Chadwick still hoped that a baseball nine might be organized by mid-April. But a few weeks later the firing on Fort Sumter and the ensuing war spoiled Chadwick's campaign to initiate baseball in the city that soon became the Confederate capital.

Union prisoners playing ball in Salisbury, N.C., ca. 1863.

But in the upper and lower South cricket and both the New England and New York City versions of baseball gained followers, especially in those cities that had strong commercial ties with northern business and financial firms. Cricketers founded clubs in Baltimore, Savannah and New Orleans. A visit by the famed Brooklyn Excelsiors sparked the creation of several baseball clubs in Baltimore, while Washington, D.C., inaugurated the Potomac and National clubs. In 1859 a baseball boom in New Orleans produced seven teams, with two more added the following year. In the southwest. St. Louis had five baseball nines. Most teams initially observed the Massachusetts rules, but by 1860 all had switched to the New York version. Publicity provided by New York sporting magazines and active promotion by New York City-based merchants and bankers boosted the New York game over its New England rival.

As military action between the North and the South loomed, sportswriters highlighted the analogy between America's first team sports and warfare. Yet they were also aware of the crucial differences between play and mortal combat. In March 1861, The New York Clipper anticipated the impending crisis:

> God forbid that any balls but those of the Cricket and
> Baseball field may be caught either on the fly or first
> bound, and we trust that no arms but those of the flesh
> may be used to impel them, or stumps, but those of the
> wickets, injured by them.

But three months later sober realism replaced wishful thinking. A Clipper editor remarked:

> Cricket and Baseball clubs are now enlisted in a different
> sort of exercise, the rifle or gun taking the place of the
> bat, while the play ball gives place to the leaden messen-
> ger of death. Men who have heretofore made their mark
> in friendly strife for superiority in various games, are now
> beating off the rebels who would dismember this glorious
> "Union of States."

Thousands of members of northern cricket and baseball clubs volunteered for service in the Union Army, while a handful chose the Confederate side. In Cincinnati, Abraham G. Mills, a future president of the National League, packed a bat and ball with his Army gear before reporting for military duty. In late May Wilkes' Spirit of the Times reported that the pitcher of St. Louis' Union club planned to resign from his team to accept a commission in the Second Missouri Artillery after leading his team to victory in a city championship match. According to that paper, his fans hoped that "the balls he will pitch at the foes of his country's flag, may be as successful in putting down their insolent presumption, as were those pitched against his civil opponents yesterday," the former champions of St. Louis.

In New York City, where a stunning patriotic outburst reversed that metropolis' strong antebellum pro-southern sentiment, many sportsmen put ethnic and political divisions aside to rally to the flag. The Clipper enthusiastically backed Lincoln's call for troops, and published the names of enlistees, including ballplayers. It praised those who had signed up, and urged others who were slower to act to follow their example. "Better join in boys," it advised the slackers, "than be loafing the streets or hanging around bar-rooms, and thus show the people you have some noble traits that atone for whatever bad ones you get credit for." Otto W. Parisen, a member of the Knickerbockers, received a commission in July as Captain in Company C and Quartermaster of the Ninth Infantry Regiment, New York Volunteers. He survived the Battle of Antietam, was honorably discharged, and was commissioned again as first Lieutenant, Company F in the

122nd Infantry Regiment, New York Volunteers. He served for the duration of the war, mustering out in June 1865.

Over the course of the war a steady stream of members of northern baseball clubs joined the Union Army. But in one notorious case, midway in the war, the Brooklyn Excelsiors' star first baseman defected to the Confederate Army. While 91 members of the Excelsiors volunteered to fight to preserve the Union, A.T. ("Aleck") Pearsall, a successful physician, slipped out of Brooklyn sometime during the winter of 1862–63. He reappeared in Richmond as a brigade surgeon. There he treated a few Union prisoners, including some former teammates from the Excelsior Club. When word of his current position and whereabouts reached Brooklyn, the Excelsiors promptly expelled him.

Rural southerners who enjoyed playing informal forms of early baseball enlisted in the ranks of the Confederacy, as did a few members of baseball clubs in New Orleans. As Johnny Reb and Billy Yank prepared themselves for battle in army camps, they sought distraction and diversion on cricket or baseball grounds. Time and good luck would determine the outcome of the rebellion, and who would live to a ripe old age, and which form of ballplaying would defeat its rivals during four years of sectional strife and emerge as America's national pastime.

Partners in Iniquity
By SVEN BECKERT and SETH ROCKMAN

Both professional historians and the general public have long explained America's descent into civil war as the result of the economic divergence between an industrial North and an agrarian South.

Southern planters accumulated untold riches from the labor of their slaves, declared cotton king and boldly embraced aggressive policies culminating in secession. Northerners had wisely abolished slavery, so the story runs, and found prosperity by allowing free farmers and laborers to compete in the marketplace. Nearly four decades of debate over national tariff policy—with Northerners pushing for higher tariffs to protect domestic industry, and Southerners for lower tariffs to promote cotton exports—attested to the fundamental antagonism of these two sectional economies. Only after the forces of industrial modernity had destroyed the archaic system of human bondage could the United States achieve its true economic potential.

Told this way, the Civil War seems a fait accompli, the inevitable outcome of the economic incompatibility of slavery and capitalism. Moreover, such an account has allowed Northerners to hold themselves blameless for the crime of American slavery: the South was, in this telling, practically a different country.

Yet historians increasingly understand that slavery was not just important to one region of the United States, but to the economic development of the United States as a whole. This realization changes everything: by recognizing the economic interdependence of North and South and slavery's centrality to American capitalism itself, it becomes possible to see the outbreak of the Civil War as more surprising than predictable.

What's strange is that these ties were hardly secret at the time. The North's investment in slavery had been a favorite polemical theme for abolitionists and proslavery ideologues alike. During the Missouri statehood debate in 1820, Southern Congressmen catalogued the Rhode Island fleet that delivered African slaves to South Carolina. Opponents of protective tariffs denounced the transfer of Southern wealth into Northern pockets, and planters regularly lamented their dependence on New England manufacturers. As one Alabama polemicist wrote at the end of the 1840s, "our slaves are clothed with Northern manufactured goods, have Northern hats and shoes, work with Northern hoes, ploughs, and other implements, are chastised with Northern made whips, and are working for Northern more than Southern profit."

Likewise, abolitionists targeted Northern complicity in slavery. William Lloyd Garrison declared the North "a partner in iniquity." As cotton prices plunged during the Panic of 1837, Garrison joked that New York businessmen were too busy counting their losses to partake in their usual anti-abolitionist mobbing. A decade later, Charles Sumner decried "the unholy alliance of the lords of the lash and the lords of the loom"—a damning acknowledgment of the impossibility of New England's industrial revolution without access to slave-grown cotton.

In fact, many saw the economic marriage of North and South as a solution to escalating sectional tensions at the end of the 1850s. Thomas Prentice Kettell, an American political economist, published his book "Southern Wealth and Northern Profits" in the spring of 1860 in hopes of revealing "the great profits derived from sectional intercourse, harmony, and dependence." An essayist for national business publications like Hunt's Merchant Magazine and Debow's Review, Kettell warned that the North was on the brink of economic suicide by antagonizing the South out of the Union.

Kettell marshaled remarkable statistics: over $100 million in northern merchandise vended in the South annually, perhaps one-third of which was in shoes alone. Tallying up the receipts of cotton bales moving through New York City and the ancillary value accruing to brokers, insurers, shippers and carters, Kettell estimated interregional trade at $1 billion a year. Kettell's analysis in turn gave Southern politicians confidence that the North, if only from the standpoint of self-interest, would eventually accede to new constitutional protections for slaveholding.

No group supported such compromises more than the merchants and bankers of New York City. The early months of 1861 brought unprecedented volatility to the city's financial markets, with stocks rising and falling on rumors swirling around Virginia's secession debate. A delegation of 30 New York businessmen traveled to Washington at the end of January with a petition for compromise with the signatures of some 40,000 merchants, clerks and scriveners.

At the Congressional peace talks that February, William E. Dodge spoke "as a plain merchant" sent at the urging of the New York Chamber of Commerce. "I am a business man, and I take a business view of this subject," Dodge said. From his point of view, "the whole country is upon the eve of such a financial crisis as it has never seen." Dodge had voted for Lincoln, but actively supported constitutional amendments to protect slavery. Told that New Englanders would never brook such overt protection for slavery, he scoffed: "they are true Yankees; they know how to get the dollars and how to hold on to them when they have got them."

Many voices echoed Dodge's claim that self-interest would prevent the outbreak of violence. As a New York group calling itself the American Society for Promoting National Unity pointed out, a war might serve the needs of politicians and agitators in both sections, but it would jeopardize the prospects of businessmen everywhere. Writing in The New York Times, businessman Daniel Lord contended that South Carolinians would not "any more than Yankeedom, refuse a good bargain because driven with parties of different politics." In turn, William Gregg, one of the South's leading manufacturers, predicted that war "will be death to every branch of business." A few days after the bombardment of Fort Sumter, Gregg wrote to a Massachusetts associate, "I trust that you business men of the North will see the necessity of putting a stop to a war."

By that time, however, many of the same Northern business leaders who had earlier argued for concessions to the South now rallied to the Union cause. Prominent merchants in New York, along with Mayor Fernando Wood, abandoned their own secessionist fantasies of a no-tariff "free city" at the mouth of the Hudson and instead raised funds to mobilize the Union army. Some realized that war was now the only way to bring the South back into the Union, and that to let the Confederacy go would have allowed Southerners to default on the $125 million they still owed New York firms.

Others represented a new class of industrialists, men whose investments were not primarily linked to slavery and whose political demands on the federal government increasingly diverged from those of Southern slaveholders and their Northern allies. They demanded higher tariffs, not free trade, and they hoped for the expansion of free labor agriculture in the West, not slave plantations.

Of course, the dire predictions did not come to pass. The northern economy did not collapse without access to Southern markets, a monopoly on cotton did not make the Confederacy invulnerable and economic self-interest did not forestall a bloody conflict. Yet by reminding us of slavery's importance to the nation as a whole, these prognostications suggest that the Civil War was hardly the result of the inherent hostility of capitalism to slavery. The intertwining of those two economies over the previous decades yielded a Civil War more surprising and singular than our histories have yet recovered.

CHAPTER 2

The War Begins

In his poem "First Songs for a Prelude," Walt Whitman captured the electric current that ran through Manhattan on the evening of April 12, 1861. As news of the attack on Fort Sumter spread across New York, he could feel in its very wake a sudden martial energy. "How you sprang," he wrote of the crowds he encountered that night, "how you threw off the costumes of peace with indifferent hand; How your soft opera-music changed, and the drum and fife were heard in their stead."

A similar eagerness for war erupted in towns large and small, North and South. After Lincoln called for 75,000 volunteers on April 15, thousands rushed off to join a Union Army that was barely able to outfit and command a skeleton force of soldiers along the Western borders, and a Confederate Army that, for all intents and purposes, did not yet exist. Armies can't form overnight, and the lack of preparation on both sides explains much of the war's course for the first year.

Why did so many join the fray? For some, perhaps most at first, it was in part the thrill of the fight. For many in the South, it was to defend against an ill-defined threat to their way of life (better defined for those who owned slaves; less so for the majority, who did not). Many in the North went to war to defend a political value, "Union," the legacy of the founding fathers and the beacon of freedom, however dimmed by political discrimination, for the rest of the world. On April 20, some 100,000 people massed in New York's Union Square to hear Robert Anderson, the former Union commander at Fort Sumter, deliver a rousing call to arms against the seceding states.

What these men did not go to fight over was slavery, at least not in the main, and especially not in 1861. Though the war was certainly "about" slavery, for the men involved it was much more complicated. To the extent that most Northerners cared about slavery, they cared about the threat it posed to them: the political power it gave Southerners, the economic power it held over free labor. They did not, by and large, think about slaves themselves. That was to change, but in April 1861, the war for these men was not to end slavery, but to end secession.

At the tip of the Virginia Peninsula, Fortress Monroe, one of the last federal installations on Southern soil still in Union hands, saw a curious development: first a trickle, and then a wave of runaway slaves poured into the installation. The commander, Benjamin Butler, refused to return these "contraband." If the Union was yet unwilling to use the war to end slavery, then slaves would use the war as a means to end their own servitude.

Fighting did not begin all of a sudden. Skirmishes were reported here and there, particularly in Missouri, where Confederate partisans hoped to bring their state over to the South. A pro-South mob in Baltimore attacked Union troops headed south to defend Washington. Early fighting wasn't confined to the newly uniformed, either: in the wooded mountainsides of Tennessee and other Appalachian states, Union and Confederate sympathizers, often neighbors and sometimes from the same family, attacked one another, setting off a bloody series of reprisals that would run through the war.

But for the first few months of the war, there was very little actual war: with the two capitals just a few days' march apart, both sides expected a single, set-piece battle to determine the entire conflict, and neither wanted to engage until it was ready, or until patience wore too thin.

A Conflict's Acoustic Shadows

By KEN BURNS

More than once during the Civil War, newspapers reported a strange phenomenon. From only a few miles away, a battle sometimes made no sound—despite the flash and smoke of cannon and the fact that more distant observers could hear it clearly.

These eerie silences were called "acoustic shadows."

On the 150th anniversary of the Civil War, we ask again whether in our supposedly post-racial, globalized, 21st-century world those now seemingly distant battles of the mid-19th century still have any relevance. But it is clear that the further we get from those four horrible years in our national existence—when, paradoxically, in order to become one we tore ourselves in two—the more central and defining that war becomes.

In our less civil society of this moment we are reminded of the full consequences of our failure to compromise in that moment.

In our smug insistence that race is no longer a factor in our society, we are continually brought up short by the old code words and disguised prejudice of a tribalism beneath the thin surface of our "civilized" selves.

And in our dialectically preoccupied media culture, where everything is pigeonholed into categories—red state/blue state, black/white, North/South, young/old, gay/straight—we are confronted again with more nuanced realities and the complicated leadership of that hero of all American heroes, Abraham Lincoln. He was at once an infuriatingly pragmatic politician, tardy on the issue of slavery, and at the same time a transcendent figure—poetic, resonant, appealing to better angels we 21st-century Americans still find painfully hard to invoke.

The acoustic shadows of the Civil War remind us that the more it recedes, the more important it becomes. Its lessons are as fresh today as they were for those young men who were simply trying to survive its daily horrors.

And horrors there were: 620,000 Americans, more than 2 percent of our population, died of gunshot and disease, starvation and massacre in places like Shiloh and Antietam and Cold Harbor, Fort Pillow and Fort Wagner and Palmito Ranch, Andersonville and Chickamauga and Ford's Theater.

Yet in the years immediately after the South's surrender at Appomattox we conspired to cloak the Civil War in bloodless, gallant myth, obscuring its causes and its great ennobling outcome—the survival of the union and the freeing of four million Americans and their descendants from bondage. We struggled, in our addiction to the idea of American exceptionalism, to rewrite our history to emphasize the gallantry of the war's top-down heroes, while ignoring the equally important bottom-up stories of privates and slaves. We changed the irredeemable, as the historian David Blight argues, into positive, inspiring stories.

The result has been to blur the reality that slavery was at the heart of the matter, ignore the baser realities of the brutal fighting, romanticize our own home-grown terrorist organization, the Ku Klux Klan, and distort the consequences of the Civil War that still intrude on our national life.

The centennial of the Civil War in 1961 was for many of us a wholly unsatisfying experience. It preferred, as the nation reluctantly embraced a new, long-deferred civil rights movement, to excavate only the dry dates and facts and events of that past; we were drawn back then, it seemed, more to regiments and battle flags, Minié balls and Gatling guns, sentimentality and nostalgia and mythology, than to anything that suggested the harsh realities of the real war.

Subsequently, our hunger for something more substantial materialized in James McPherson's remarkable "Battle Cry of Freedom" and many other superb histories, in the popular Hollywood movie "Glory," and in my brother Ric's and my 1990 documentary series "The Civil War."

It was an emotional archaeology we were all after, less concerned with troop movements than with trying to represent the full fury of that war; we were attracted to its psychological disturbances and conflicted personalities, its persistent dissonance as well as its inspirational moments. We wanted to tell a more accurate story of African-Americans, not as the passive bystanders of conventional wisdom, but as active soldiers in an intensely personal drama of self-liberation.

We wished to tell bottom-up stories of so-called ordinary soldiers, North as well as South, to note women's changing roles, to understand the Radical Republicans in Congress, to revel in the inconvenient truths of nearly every aspect of the Civil War.

Today, the war's centrality in American history seems both assured and tenuous. Each generation, the social critic Lewis Mumford once said, re-examines and re-interprets that part of the past that gives the present new meanings and new possibilities. That also means that for a time an event, any event, even one as perpetually important as the Civil War, can face the specter being out of historical fashion.

But in the end, it seems that the War of the Rebellion, the formal name our government once gave to the struggle, always invades our consciousness like the childhood traumatic event it was—and still is.

Maybe Walt Whitman, the poet and sometime journalist who had worked as a nurse in the appalling Union hospitals, understood and saw it best. "Future years," he said, "will never know the seething hell, the black infernal background of the countless minor scenes and interiors . . . of the Secession War, and it is best they should not.

"The real war," Whitman admonished us, "will never get in the books." We are, nonetheless, obligated to try.

The Defenders

By ADAM GOODHEART

Charleston Harbor, S.C., April 12, 1861

Among the private papers of Maj. Robert Anderson, commander of the Union garrison at Fort Sumter, is a single elegant sheet of faded lavender-blue notepaper, neatly creased where it was once folded between the gloved fingers of a Confederate adjutant. The note, preserved today in the Library of Congress, reads:

Fort Sumter, S.C.
April 12, 1861. 3:20 a.m.
Major Robert Anderson

U.S. Army
Comdg Fort Sumter

Sir

By authority of Brig General Beauregard commanding
the provisional forces of the Confederate States we have
the honor to notify you that he will open the fire of his
Batteries on Fort Sumter in one hour from this time.

We have the honor to be

Very Respectfully
Yr. obt. servts.,
James Chesnut Jr., Aide de Camp
Stephen D. Lee, Capt., S.C. Army, Aide de Camp

The two aides handed this note to Anderson with a gentlemanly
bow. He escorted them hospitably to Sumter's wharf, where their
longboat awaited with its slave oarsmen. Before the Confederates
stepped into the launch, Anderson shook each man's hand and bade
them all farewell: "If we never meet in this world again, God grant
that we may meet in the next."

Returning to his officers and men, Anderson hinted that all except
the sentries should return to their bunks and try to get some sleep. It
was clear that Sumter's defenders could accomplish little until sunrise, since the garrison had no lights; the fort's lamp oil and candles
had long since run out, along with all provisions save a little hardtack
and some half-rancid pork. After breakfast, such as it might be, they
would begin to return fire. The only other order he gave was to raise
the fort's flag, which was duly run up its staff, disappearing into the
blackness above. But most of the officers and soldiers waited expec-
tantly to see the war begin.

One of those on the ramparts peering out into the night was a blue-
eyed, dark-haired young Irishman named John Thompson, a private, who
left what may be the only surviving description of the battle by a rank-
and-file soldier: a long letter that he sent two weeks later to his father
back in County Derry, Ireland. Even though he planned to return home

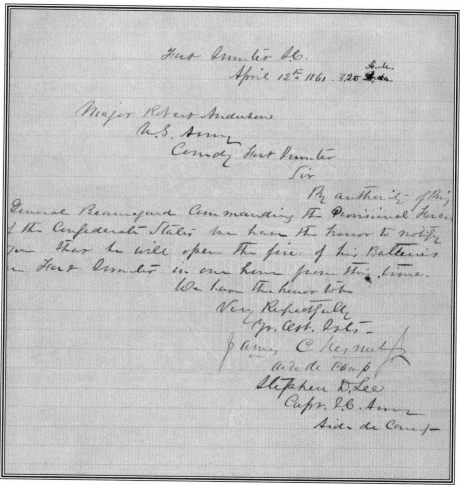

The note that began the Civil War, 3:20 a.m., April 12, 1861.

to the old country as soon as his enlistment expired in a few months' time, Thompson felt a surge of pride as "we hoisted our colors the glorious 'Star Spangled Banner' and quietly awaited the enemies fire."

As an immigrant who, on his enlistment form, described his occupation as "laborer," Thompson was typical of the men who were now about to risk their lives in defense of Fort Sumter. Some two-thirds of the men in the Union Army in the antebellum years were foreigners, mostly German and Irish. Officers often complained of soldiers who could not understand commands in English, and a significant share of recruits were unable to sign their own names to the enlistment form, let alone pen a letter. (Thompson's missive to his father may well have been dictated to a better-educated superior.)

Sumter's garrison was even more heavily foreign-born than average: of the 73 enlisted men whose birthplaces are known, just 13 were from the United States. The roster of privates reads like the roll call in an old World War II movie: Murphy, Schmidt, Onorato, Klein, Wishnowski. Their names, unlike those of Sumter's officers, are almost forgotten today—a simple bronze tablet at the site records them— and were equally unknown to most Americans in 1861, despite the intense public interest in Sumter and the exhaustive newspaper coverage of every new development at the fort. Such men were considered mere ciphers, certainly not likely to become heroes.

At those rare moments when the entire nation went to war—1775, 1812, 1846—soldiering suddenly became a noble calling for patriotic Americans of every class and condition. So it would become again soon in 1861. But the peacetime Army that garrisoned Sumter and other forts as the war began was a different matter. Service in its ranks was considered a last resort for men who couldn't get by otherwise in the merciless economy of 19th-century America—or the first resort of immigrants with no resources or connections. "Uncle Sam"—a figure known even to those newcomers—provided a roof over their heads (even if it was often one made of canvas), shoddy woolen uniforms and food consisting mainly of bread and coffee, with occasional salt pork.

A British traveler, while expressing his esteem for the American officer corps, disdained common soldiers as a "rag-tag-and-bobtail herd the scum of the population of the older States, or the worthless German, English, or Irish immigrants." Enlisted men existed in a different world than their superiors, even in such unusually close confines as Sumter's: the officers' letters and memoirs almost never mention soldiers as individuals, much less by name, and as provisions dwindled, everyone took it for granted that officers would get the last of the salt pork, while privates enjoyed their one daily biscuit apiece.

Enlisted men even looked physically different from their superiors. Although several of Sumter's officers—including Capt. Abner

Doubleday and Surgeon Samuel W. Crawford—were over six feet tall, not a single private was, according to their enlistment records. The average height of the garrison's foreign-born privates was only 5 feet 5-and-three-quarters inches tall, fully three inches shorter than the average native-born male of the mid-19th century. This was almost certainly a result of poor nutrition in childhood. The average age of Sumter's enlisted men was 29—four years older than the typical later Civil War serviceman—with several of the men in their 40s.

It might seem inevitable that the months of tension and uncertainty, crowded and makeshift quarters, and sparse rations, these enlisted men would have been driven to quarrels, brawls or worse. Throughout the winter of 1861, newspapers in both the North and South buzzed with rumors of soldiers at Sumter being shot for mutiny. Yet the reports from inside the fort show quite the opposite case: the longer the siege lasted, the more tightly the group knit itself together. Thompson told his father of his fellow privates' scorn for the "rash folly" of the rebels: "They no doubt expected that we would surrender without a blow, but they were never more mistaken in their lives."

Even the snobbish Crawford wrote often in his diary and letters of the men's high spirits, and said that when the final battle loomed, "it increased their enthusiasm to the highest pitch." If anything, the common soldiers' morale was higher than their officers'. Although it is often said today that half the Army resigned in 1861 to join the Confederacy, this is untrue. Only 26 privates out of all 15,000 ended up defecting to the rebels—compared to more than 300 out of the 1,000 or so men in the officer corps. (Indeed, one of Sumter's Union lieutenants would end up fighting, and dying, for the Confederacy.)

Very few, if any, of the enlisted men who stood on the battlements at Sumter awaiting the first shot of the war had ever been on the receiving end of an artillery barrage. Until just days earlier, all of them had fully expected to be evacuated to safety at any moment by orders of President Abraham Lincoln. (So had their officers; Sumter's chief engineer had busied himself making arrangements to return a borrowed mustard spoon to a Charleston friend now serving with the rebels.) It must have seemed surreal that they now had to defend themselves against fire from what had just recently been friendly territory—including even from their own former fort. They knew that militarily, Sumter was almost worthless to the Union. They were being asked to die for a symbol.Yet they were ready to do so.

"At 4 1/2 a.m., the first shell came hissing through the air and burst right over our heads," Thompson would tell his father. "The thrill that ran through our veins at this time was indescribable, none were afraid, the stern defiant look on each man's countenance plainly told that fear was no part of his constitution, but something like an expression of awe crept over the features of everyone."

Out across the water, all around the harbor, unseen cannons were being carefully adjusted and aimed. And then the full barrage began.

'How Manhattan Drum-Taps Led'
By TOM CHAFFIN

On the evening of April 12, 1861, Walt Whitman attended a performance of Gaetano Donizetti's opera "Linda di Chamounix" at the Academy of Music, on 14th Street and Irving Place in Manhattan. Just before midnight he was walking down the west side of Broadway, toward the Fulton Ferry to return to his home, in Brooklyn. Suddenly, he later recalled, he "heard in the distance the loud cries of the newsboys, who came presently tearing and yelling up the street, rushing from side to side more furiously than usual."

Whitman bought a paper and, near Prince Street, crossed Broadway, where he found a crowd reading the papers under the gas lamps of the Metropolitan Hotel. Fort Sumter, they reported, had been shelled in the wee hours of that same day. "For the benefit of some who had no papers, one of us read the telegram aloud, while all listen'd silently and attentively," he wrote. "No remark was made by any of the crowd, which had increas'd from thirty or forty, but all stood a minute or two, I remember, before they dispers'd."

In the coming days, the news from Charleston unified skeptics in the North behind a belief that "secession slavery" constituted a palpable evil that had to be confronted. But perhaps no one more so than Whitman: "The volcanic upheaval of the nation, after that firing on the flag at Fort Sumter, proved for certain something which had been previously in great doubt." Indeed, the beginning of the war would mark the end of his bohemian days and set him on another, more purposeful course.

Despite enthusiastic reviews that greeted his 1855 book "Leaves of Grass" and expanded editions of the book in 1856 and 1860, Whitman remained a struggling writer through the second half of the 1850s. By then in his 30s and early 40s, Whitman was often professionally and personally adrift.

Though by all accounts not much of a drinker, Whitman became a regular at Pfaff's, a now long-vanished bar at 647 Broadway, just north of Bleecker Street. The cramped and smoky watering hole, in the vaulted basement of a (still standing) five-story building, was operated by Charles Ignatius Pfaff, a native of either Switzerland or southwest Germany.

Beyond its connection to Whitman, Pfaff's is best remembered for introducing New York and America to the then new milieu of "bohemianism"—today a general term, but in the mid-19th-century a definable counterculture, and one with which Whitman became associated. The term's origins remain murky, but bohemianism is generally believed to have arisen from a misconception by Parisians that "gypsies"—or, more specifically, the Romani people, associated in France with a life of poverty and wandering—came from Central Europe's Bohemia region. The term was popularized by French author Henri Murger's 1845 short story collection "Scénes de la Vie de Bohème" ("Scenes of Bohemian Life"), which celebrated Paris's outlier artists. Among its other reverberations, the book later became the basis for Puccini's opera "La bohème." Bohemianism thus became associated with artists, journalists, performers, intellectuals and others who lived—or who thought of themselves as living—unconventional lives on the margins of urban society.

With the exception of Whitman, the other artists and intellectuals drawn to Pfaff's are now largely forgotten—including the painter

Elihu Vedder, actresses Ada Clare and Adah Isaacs Menken, and writers George Arnold, Bayard Taylor, Fitz Hugh Ludlow, John Brougham and Henry Clapp Jr.

Though Clapp's name is now obscure, he was a seminal figure of his day, when the Bleecker Street area was New York's theater and literary center. Clapp edited the Saturday Press, a weekly journal devoted to opinion, fiction and poetry, that ran from 1858 to 1860 and 1865 to 1866. Whitman often wrote for the Saturday Press, and Clapp, through the paper, fervently promoted "Leaves of Grass." Though its sales were disappointing, "Leaves" established Whitman as an important new voice in American poetry—among the nation's first poets to repudiate the anti-urban prejudices of English and American poetry and to romanticize the nation's teeming cities.

Over the years Clapp, a New Englander, promoted free love, temperance, Fourier socialism, abolitionism and other reformist ideologies; he also had lived in Paris and had become enthralled with that city's first blush of bohemianism. Clapp dominated the gatherings at Pfaff's—and he left his mark on Whitman and his poetry: "You will have to know something about Henry Clapp if you want to know all about me," Whitman asserted years later.

By the late 1850s, Pfaff's had joined Barnum's Museum, Tammany Hall and Castle Garden as essential New York stops for visitors to the city. Not that the cellar itself held any physical allure. "It was not an attractive looking place, for it was on the floor beneath the street level, and was fitted up in a plain quaint fashion," according to The New York Times; but then again, tourists did "get a look at the lions of Bohemia."

Whitman, reading aloud, occasionally tried out new poems at Pfaff's; to gawking tourists, he reigned as the subterranean den's alpha lion. But the poet himself never saw it that way: "My own greatest pleasure at Pfaff's was to look on—to see, talk little, absorb. I was never a great discusser." More specifically, Whitman recalled, "There was a long table extending the length of this cave; and as soon as the Bohemians put in an appearance, Henry Clapp would take a seat at the head of the table. I think there was as good talk around that table as took place anywhere in the world. Clapp was a very witty man."

In "The Two Vaults," Whitman's unfinished poem about Pfaff's, he captured the ambience: "Drink on drinkers!/ Bandy and jest!/Toss the theme from one to another!"

Indeed, guided by Clapp, the bohemians embraced a carefree, jaded view of the world—a vantage often aloof from real-world political distinctions. Typifying that perspective was Clapp's reaction, in November 1860, to Lincoln's election as president: "We are opposed to slavery of every kind," he wrote, "but we are more opposed to what is stupidly called antislavery, for the simple reason that it has no distinct aim or purpose, and consists of nothing but a series of noisy and unmeaning howls." Lincoln, Clapp charged, "has merely used the negro as a stepping-stone to power, and is now ready to kick him aside, and let him go to the devil."

During the presidential campaign, Whitman, then 41 years old, had expressed similar misgivings. On Feb. 19, 1861, however, during Lincoln's passage through New York en route to Washington, the poet began to see a different man. Watching the president-elect emerge from a carriage and enter the Astor House hotel as a crowd of 30,000 looked on in silence, it occurred to Whitman that there might be more to Lincoln than he had earlier thought. If nothing else, this man seemed to possess an unexpected dignity, a quiet sense of resolve.

And courage: Lincoln, after all, had won only 35 percent of New York's popular vote in November. And in the wake of his election, Mayor Fernando Wood had whipped up anti-Union sentiments by calling for the City's own secession from the Union. Against that background, Whitman reasonably feared that among the throngs that day, "many an assassin's knife and pistol lurk'd in hip or breast-pocket there, ready, as soon as break and riot came."

Over the next several months Whitman's passion for the Union cause and fascination with the war would take him in a far different direction than his Bohemian habits might have predicted. In "Drum-Taps," Whitman's 1865 collection of Civil War poems, one work in particular—later given the title "First O Songs for a Prelude"—captured that evening of April 12, the city's quickening martial spirit and the poet's pride in the volunteers from New York who soon swelled the Union Army's ranks:

How you sprang! how you threw off the costumes of
    peace with indifferent hand;
How your soft opera-music changed, and the drum and
    fife were heard in their stead;
How you led to the war, (that shall serve for our prelude,
    songs of soldiers,)
How Manhattan drum-taps led.

Whitman wasn't alone in feeling his life shaken by the outbreak of war. By April 1861 bohemianism in its first New York incarnation—the spirit that had brightened Pfaff's dark cellar—was in full retreat. Young men set off to war in droves. In December 1860, Henry Clapp had suspended publication of the Saturday Press. Pfaff's hung on until 1876, when Charles Pfaff closed the bar that Whitman had haunted and moved the business uptown, to 24th Street. By the late 1880s, after several lean years, he closed those doors too.

In December 1862, Whitman himself would leave Brooklyn, never—except for six months in 1864—to live in New York again. In departing, concerns guided him far different than any he could have imagined on that April night when he stopped, under gaslights, to read the latest news from faraway South Carolina.

Nick Biddle and the First Defenders

By RONALD S. CODDINGTON

On the afternoon of April 19, 1861, Nick Biddle was quietly helping his unit, the Washington Artillery from Pottsville, Pa., set up camp inside the north wing of the Capitol building. The day before, he was almost killed.

Biddle was a black servant to Capt. James Wren, who oversaw the company of about 100 men. On April 18 the Washington Artillery had been one of several Army outfits, totaling about 475 men, heading through Baltimore en route to Washington, D.C., in response to

President Lincoln's call for 75,000 troops to put down the Southern rebellion.

Thousands of pro-Confederate Baltimoreans turned out to meet them at the city's northern train station. (Another group, 45 regular Army soldiers from the Fourth Artillery en route from St. Paul, Minn., to Fort McHenry, also disembarked.) The crowd expressed disappointment in the non-military look of some of the volunteers, who hailed from eastern Pennsylvania coal-mining country. They "were not more than half uniformed and armed, and presented some as hard-looking specimens of humanity as could be found anywhere," reported The Baltimore Sun. Most of the men carried their own revolvers, while a few toted antiquated flintlocks. A select group carried state-issued modern muskets, but had no gunpowder for them.

Captain Wren, Biddle and the others were aware of Baltimore's pro-secession sentiment and expected trouble. One volunteer reportedly asked Biddle if he was afraid to face rowdy "plug-uglies" and jokingly warned, "They may catch you and sell you down in Georgia." Biddle replied in dead earnest that he was going to Washington trusting in the Lord, and that he wouldn't be scared away by the devil himself—or a bunch of thugs.

The Pennsylvanians formed a line and prepared to march through Baltimore to another station, where they could catch a Washington-bound train. The regulars would lead the way. The line started and moved rapidly, shielded from the abusive mobs by policemen stretched 10 paces apart. A private recalled the "Roughs and toughs, 'longshoremen, gamblers, floaters, idlers, red-hot secessionists, as well as men ordinarily sober and steady, crowded upon, pushed and hustled the little band and made every effort to break the thin line."

The mob derided the volunteers and cheered for Jefferson Davis and the Confederacy. Some aimed their abuse at Biddle. Capt. Wren remembered, "The crowd raised the cry, 'Nigger in uniform!' and poor old Nick had to take it."

Around the halfway point of the journey, the regular troops split off and marched to Fort McHenry, leaving the Pennsylvanians alone. "At this juncture the mob were excited to a perfect frenzy, breaking the line of the police and pushing through the files of men, in an attempt to break the column," wrote one historian. The boldest in the crowd spit, kicked, punched and grabbed at the coattails of the volunteers.

As the Pennsylvanians neared the station, rioters chucked cobblestones and jagged pieces of broken brick. The bombardment intensified as the volunteers arrived at the station and began to board the cars. Suddenly a chunk of brick struck Biddle in the head and left a deep, profusely bleeding cut. He managed to get on the train as the mob climbed on top of the cars and jumped up and down on the roofs. Biddle found a comfortable spot, wrapped his head in a handkerchief, and then pulled his fatigue cap close over the wound.

When the Pennsylvanians finally arrived in Washington that evening, they received a very different reception, as enthusiastic crowds welcomed them as saviors. They occupied temporary barracks in the north wing of the Capitol. One officer remembered that, when Biddle entered the rotunda of the building, "He looked up and around as if he felt that he had reached a place of safety, and then took his cap and the bloody handkerchief from his head and carried them in his hand. The blood dropped as he passed through the rotunda on the stone pavement."

A grateful President Lincoln later greeted the Pennsylvanians. He reportedly shook hands with Biddle and encouraged him to seek medical attention. But Biddle refused. He preferred to remain with the company. At the time some considered Biddle's blood the first shed in hostility during the Civil War.

The House of Representatives later passed a resolution thanking the Pennsylvanians for their role in defense of the capital. The volunteers came to be known as the "First Defenders" in honor of their early response to Lincoln's call to arms.

The Washington Artillery remained in the capital area until their 90-day enlistment expired, and then returned to Pottsville; Biddle led the company as it marched through town. (Many in the unit re-enlisted and formed Company B of the 48th Pennsylvania Infantry, a regiment remembered for its role in digging and detonating the mine along the frontlines of Petersburg, Va., that prompted the July 1864 Battle of the Crater.)

But Biddle remained in Pottsville for the rest of the war, becoming something of a local celebrity. He soon sat for his carte de visite, a popular photographic format from France that became all the rage in America coincident with the rise of hostilities. "Nick himself sold thousands of these photographs," remembered one veteran, who added, "to this day a photographic album is not considered complete in Pottsville without the picture of the man whose blood was first spilled in the beginning of the war."

Biddle died destitute in 1876. His First Defender comrades paid his final expenses and attended his funeral en masse along with a large crowd that gathered at his home. Biddle's body lay in an open casket in the front yard. "A pretty floral cross rested upon the old man's breast. Except that the marks of death were visible in the attenuated look, there was but little change in the face," noted a local newspaper. Also visible was a deep scar left by the Baltimore mob. According to a biographer, Biddle had considered it "his military badge and brand of patriotism."

The General in His Study
By ELIZABETH BROWN PRYOR

The writing is blurred and the paper nearly translucent, but the scene it portrays is vivid. In a recently discovered letter, Mary Custis Lee, the eldest daughter of Robert E. Lee, describes how her father wrestled with the decision to resign his commission in the United States Army and side with the South. The letter, found in a folder of fragments at the Virginia Historical Society, was written in 1871 to Charles Marshall, Lee's former aide-to-camp, as he prepared to write a biography of the great general.

It provides the most reliable information currently available to historians, overshadowing the questionable second-hand accounts that scholars once had to rely on. Not only was Mary Custis Lee an eyewitness to the scene, but her letter was written just a few years after the war, whereas the traditional depictions did not appear until decades later.

And her words fundamentally alter the story of Lee's fateful choice. Lee biographers have long claimed that his decision to leave

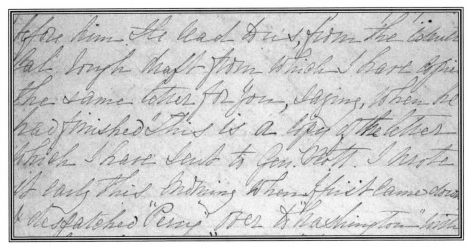

An excerpt from Mary Custis Lee's letter.

the Army was an inevitable one, driven by the pull of relatives, state and tradition. However, as his daughter shows us, in the end the decision was highly personal, made in spite of family differences and the military conventions he revered.

Lee's decision to give up his 35-year Army career came after a week of cataclysmic events: the southern capture of Fort Sumter, Lincoln's call for 75,000 troops to protect federal property and, on April 17, the secession of Virginia.

The days had been personally traumatic as well. Like many border-state families, the Lees and their friends were sharply divided on the issues. When Lee consulted his brothers, sister and local clergymen, he found that most leaned toward the Union. At a grim dinner with two close cousins, Lee was told that they also intended to uphold their military oaths. (Samuel Phillips Lee would become an important admiral in the Union navy; John Fitzgerald Lee retained his position as judge advocate of the Army.) Sister Anne Lee Marshall unhesitatingly chose the northern side, and her son outfitted himself in blue uniform. Robert's favorite brother, Smith Lee, a naval officer, resisted leaving his much-loved berth, and Smith's wife spurned her relatives to support the Union cause. At the same time, many of the clan's young men, such as nephew Fitzhugh Lee, were anxious to make their mark for the South in the coming conflict, creating a distinct generational fault line.

Matters became more complicated when, on April 18, presidential adviser Francis P. Blair unofficially offered Lee the command of the thousands of soldiers being called up to protect Washington. Fearing that such a post might require him to invade the South, Lee immediately turned down the job. Agitated, he went to tell his mentor, Gen. Winfield Scott, the Army's commander in chief. Another dramatic scene followed. Scott, though a proud Virginian, had dismissed as an insult any hint that he himself would turn from the United States. When Lee offered to sit out the troubles at his home, Arlington, the general told him bluntly: "I have no place in my army for equivocal men." Greatly distressed, Lee returned to Arlington to contemplate his options.

Although his wife called it "the severest struggle of his life," historians have long trivialized Lee's decision. It was "the answer he was born to make," biographer Douglas Southall Freeman put it. "A no-brainer," said another. But daughter Mary's letter, along with other previously unknown documents written by his close family and associates, belies such easy assessments. These newly found sources underscore just how complex and painful a choice it was to make.

The conventional wisdom holds, for example, that Lee disdained secession, but once his state took that step he was duty bound to follow. But these documents show that he was not actually opposed to disunion in principle. He simply wanted to exhaust all peaceful means of redress first, remarking in January 1861 that then "we can with a clear conscience separate."

Nor was he against the pro-slavery policies of the secessionists, despite postwar portraits of the general as something of an abolitionist. He complained to a son in December 1860 about new territories being closed to slaveholders, and supported the Crittenden Compromise, which would have forbidden the abolition of slavery. "That deserves the support of every patriot," he noted in a Jan. 29, 1861, letter to his daughter Agnes. Even at the moment he reportedly told Francis Blair that if "he owned all the negroes in the South, he would be willing to give them up to save the Union," he was actually fighting a court case to keep the slaves under his control in bondage "indefinitely," though they had been promised freedom in his father-in-law's will.

The decision was made yet more difficult by Lee's pacifism. Haunted by the prospect of prolonged and bloody warfare, he warned of it repeatedly at a time when few others were anticipating a lengthy conflict. He saw destruction and possible ignominy in the future, not the glory anticipated by the Southern masses.

He was "worn and harassed," Mary Custis Lee tells us, yet she recalls that he remained calm, and counseled others to do so. This is at odds with conventional stories which portray Lee melodramatically pacing and praying as he weighed his future. Instead, her father made the fateful choice alone in his office, without fanfare. Before breakfast on April 20, he quietly entrusted his resignation letter to a slave, for delivery at the War Department.

"I have been unable to make up my mind to raise my hand against my native state, my relations, my children and my home," Lee wrote to a kinsman, only minutes after he penned his resignation. With minor variations, this was his lifelong mantra, elegantly extricating him from the more uncomfortable aspects of decision. Yet even as he wrote it he must have known that no matter what he decided he would be in conflict with some relation. Moreover, the Army, which another daughter called Lee's "home and country," was also divided: forty percent of Virginian officers would remain with the Union forces.

But what is most astonishing about Mary Custis Lee's letter is that it shows how Lee made his decision despite the feelings of his own wife and children. Lee at first did not tell his immediate circle that he had resigned, and when the announcement finally came, he apologized. "I suppose you will all think I have done very wrong," he lamented. Noting that she was the sole secessionist in the group, and that her mother's allegiance to the Union was particularly strong, Mary described how the words left them stunned and speechless. Lee then remarked that he did not believe Virginia had reason to secede—at least not yet. But after refusing command there was no military role for him, and now, he acknowledged, "it had come to this and after my last interview with Gen. Scott I thought I ought to wait no longer."

The turmoil Lee's resignation caused at home was mirrored within the Army. Mary Custis Lee describes how a cousin on Scott's staff rode over to Arlington, informing the family of the disarray at the War Department. Several other officers had quickly followed Lee's example, and Scott had taken the news hard: "He laid on his sofa, refusing to see anyone and mourning, as if for the loss of a son. To some one who rather lightly alluded to the fact, he said with great emotion, 'don't mention Robert Lee's name to me again, I cannot bear it.'"

These are riveting details. But what is most striking about this description is the loneliness of Lee's decision. For the stunning message of Mary Custis Lee's account is that that there was no pressure from kin or colleagues for Lee to give up the allegiances of a lifetime. Some would later become dedicated Confederates, but in April 1861 their feelings were with the Union. If even his wife, and most of his children, did not support his stand, Robert E. Lee must personally have wanted very much to take this path. This was not an answer he was compelled by home and heritage to make. It was a choice—and it was his alone.

The Civil War and Geography

By SUSAN SCHULTEN

It was, of course, not just a civil war but a geographical one, where location determined both one's identity and side in the conflict. Likewise, the shape of the land carved the shape of the war.

As the historian James McPherson has noted, Southern geographical advantages included superior knowledge of the terrain and proximity to the battlefields. Moreover, the Eastern Theater of the war centered on a mountain range and rivers that flowed from west to east, both of which offered the Confederacy natural lines of defense. Yet in the West the Cumberland and Tennessee Rivers became "highways of invasion" for the Union Army, while the Mississippi River—completely under northern control by July 1863—effectively bisected the Confederacy. Topography did not determine the outcome of the conflict, but it set many of its parameters.

To preserve the Union required the conquest of the Confederacy, and thus much of the long war was fought on Southern soil, devastating its landscape and infrastructure. The fighting seemed to have the opposite effect in the Northern states and territories, advancing industrialization and strengthening trade, communication and transportation networks.

By focusing on the heat of battle, our histories tend to overlook this development, but President Lincoln captured some of this trajectory in his annual address to Congress in December 1862. The president emphasized, as he had since the formation of the Confederacy, that secession was impossible, for the nation was indivisible not just politically but physically. The proximity of the two regions compounded this difficulty, for "there is no line, straight or crooked, suitable for a national boundary," and any imagined line was easily crossable and in many cases already populated on both sides. Steam power and the telegraph had integrated the nation even further, making disunion a completely inappropriate remedy for sectional strife.

Perhaps the greatest of these obstacles, Lincoln wrote, was not in the North or South, but in the West, for the nation's future rested in the "great interior region" bounded by the Alleghenies in the east, the Rocky Mountains in the West, the Canadian border to the north and "the line along which the culture of corn and cotton meets" along the south. Lincoln predicted that this region of one million square miles, which encompassed the Great Plains, the Midwest and even parts of the South, would be home to 50 million people within 50 years. In his eyes, the interior would soon form not just the geographical but the economic core of the nation, "the great body of the republic."

This interior held natural and extractive resources that had only begun to be tapped and exploited, yet it bordered no ocean or natural port. Secession—and the subsequent formation of a separate Southern nation—would cut off this interior to trade. Anywhere a line was imposed within the United States would similarly stifle growth and suffocate this "Egypt of the West." But as the geographer Donald Meinig reminds us, there was no law that guaranteed the United States would extend across the continent, or that it would endure as a single entity. Such a nation was preserved through military force, not geographic inevitability.

Lincoln's reflections on American geography came just as the nation was turning its attention westward. Decades of military reconnaissance had produced far more accurate knowledge of the region, which was sought more intensely after the discovery of gold and other minerals in California and the Rocky Mountains. These mineral rushes raised expectations for the west for the president, who wanted these resources "to be developed as rapidly as possible."

That development was affected profoundly by secession, which left the fate of the West largely in the hands of a Republican Congress. In June 1862 Congress abolished slavery in the territories, with little fanfare and no opposition. The greatest cause of the sectional crisis—the very real possibility of slavery's expansion westward—was eliminated overnight. Then, advancing that template further, Lincoln signed several bills that established a plan for the transcontinental railroad and the distribution of land grants. The vision of a nation open for development and free from slavery is symbolically captured by the coincidence that Lincoln signed the Emancipation Proclamation on the same day that the Homestead Act went into effect, Jan. 1, 1863.

Thus the war remade North and South, but also to a great extent the American West. Even the political construction of the West owes much to the war: from 1861 to 1865 Congress organized six new territories and retained many more, all of which allowed the president, through executive appointments, to nurture the power of the Republican Party in a region that was still in its political infancy.

This relationship between geography and political power reminds us how deeply the conflict subsumed complex regions into "Northern" and "Southern" identities. The ongoing sectional crisis began to harden these identities long before the war, but they were entrenched further by the military stage of the conflict. And while Lincoln repeatedly insisted that the Union would persevere, the war ultimately defined the deep regional identity that governed the American South for more than a century to come, one imbued with a sense of loss, nostalgia and racial division.

Ms. Dix Comes to Washington

By JUDITH GIESBERG

Hundreds of thousands of Northerners were mobilizing for war in April 1861, but few with the speed and initiative of Dorothea Dix. When news of President Lincoln's call for three-month volunteers reached her home in Trenton, the middle-aged reformer set out immediately for Washington. She arrived in Philadelphia just in time to catch the last train through Baltimore before the bridges north of the city were burned, cutting off Washington and temporarily suspending travel to the capital from points north. Undeterred by what must certainly have been a harrowing ride, Dix arrived in Washington on April 19th and headed straight for the White House.

Dix met briefly with Lincoln and volunteered to organize a corps of women nurses. Four days later she received authorization from Secretary of War Simon Cameron to organize and equip hospitals and appoint nurses. By June, Dix had been appointed superintendent of Women Nurses, the first woman to serve in a federal-level executive position. Dix didn't tread lightly, either: unsatisfied with merely managing nurses, she quickly began pushing for improvements in the military medical establishment, "thorning the side of army doctors," as one observer put it. Among the hundreds of women Dix would place as nurses, there were those who called Dix "General," but never to her face. Dorothea Dix was the organizing force behind the enormous wartime nursing effort, an initiative that not only saved the lives of thousands of Union soldiers but also helped open the door for women to work as nurses in postwar civilian life. But if she is less well known today, it is because within two years she had been pushed aside by men who wanted to limit the role of women in the war effort. Her story demonstrates the opportunities opened to women during the Civil War—as well as the obstacles that awaited them in the male-dominated field of professional medicine.

Though the first major battle was still several weeks away, Dix was in the right place. The capital was ill-prepared to welcome the first regiments arriving in Washington and was caught off guard by the Baltimore attacks. Mary Livermore, a Civil War nurse who worked with Dix, described the capital as "a great camp. Hospitals were hastily organized and filled with sick, while there were few to nurse them. Everywhere was confusion and disorder, lack of discipline and executive ability."

So when the tall and ethereal Dix picked her way through the men stretched out for the night in and around the White House and offered to bring some order to the chaos, she was well received. For Lincoln's secretary John Nicolay, at least, the relief was immediate. "[W]e have been much more impressed with the conditions surrounding us by the arrival this evening of Miss Dix," he reported late that same night.

A seasoned advocate for hospital reform and the humane incarceration of the mentally ill, Dix was in her element in the confused environment of Washington. "The sun shines fair today," Dix reported on the morning of April 20, in a voice that brimmed with optimism, "the sky is blue and cloudless." Here was Dix's Crimea, her chance to become the Lady with the Lamp, the American Florence Nightingale. A popular hero among American women who had read about her nursing work during the Crimean War, Nightingale was celebrated by the British press because she provided a positive image during an extended and increasingly unpopular war, where disease and inadequate medical care claimed more lives than did battle. "She is a 'ministering angel' without any exaggeration in these hospitals," wrote The Times, with much enthusiasm and, yes, some exaggeration:

> And as her slender form glides quietly along each corridor,
> every poor fellow's face softens with gratitude at the sight
> of her. When all the medical officers have retired for the

night and silence and darkness have settled down upon
those miles of prostrate sick, she may be observed alone,
with a little lamp in her hand, making her solitary rounds.

Now Dorothea Dix stood ready with a lamp of her own. Dix had long been an admirer of Nightingale and tried unsuccessfully to meet her on a recent trip to London. The popular women's magazine Godey's Lady's Book, encouraged the comparison when it featured Dix alongside Nightingale on the cover of the January 1861 issue.

As flattered as Dix must have been by the dual billing, she might have winced at the premature epitaph that followed Godey's account of her advocacy work; it read "[Dix's] name will always be remembered as an earnest philanthropist." At the age of 58, Dix—like Nightingale—was very much alive and not yet content with her life's work.

Her house on 15th street, around the corner from the White House, quickly became the nerve center for volunteer work and a depot for supplies that arrived from voluntary societies throughout the North. Women who arrived in the capital hoping to volunteer as nurses were ordered to report to Dix.

Indeed, in the early months of the war Dix seemed to be everywhere. She toured the hospitals in the city where the wounded from Baltimore, and then from the Battle of Bull Run in July, were treated. She needled army surgeons about the lack of order and discipline, strategically placed protégés where they could make sure her orders were carried out, and routinely went over the heads of army regulars on matters relating to the care of wounded and ill soldiers. In September Dix reported for duty in St. Louis, where she organized the delivery of medical care to the wounded from the Battle of Wilson's Creek. And the following spring, Dix set up headquarters near Yorktown, Va., in advance of George McClellan's Peninsula Campaign.

Dix's prewar activism smoothed the way for her when she first arrived in Washington, but her personality and work habits did little to endear her to her colleagues. Dix's combativeness resulted, in part, from the inhospitable treatment she and other women nurses received from army regulars who saw them as interlopers. During the Civil War, most army nurses were men, often soldiers recovering from an illness or injury. Army surgeons resented the presence of female nurses, particularly those who clashed with them about how best to care for the men.

Concerns about introducing women into the male environment of army medical care were reflected in the original orders Dix received from Secretary Cameron, prohibiting women from residing in army camps and accepting applications only from women who could produce certificates proving their good moral standing. Wary of these concerns, Dix would only consider women over 30 years old and those whom she described as "very plain looking." Furthermore, Dix wanted her nurses to dress plainly, in brown or black dresses, "with no bows, no curls, or jewelry, and no hoop skirts." Like Catholic school girls, Dix's nurses were supposed to turn in early and resist the many temptations of wartime Washington.

Caught up by the same enthusiasm that led Dix to board the last train to Washington, women eager to nurse found Dix's rules unfair and arbitrary, and Dix alienated more than a few of them. Livermore expressed the sentiments of many when she characterized Dix's nurses as "plain almost to repulsion in dress, and devoid of personal attractions." Thirty-year-old Louisa May Alcott, the author of "Little Women" who nursed at Union Hospital in Washington, admired Dix but steered clear of her personally, admitting that "no one likes her and I don't wonder." Elizabeth Blackwell, the physician in charge of training nurses, referred to Dix as the army's "medler [sic] general." When Dix reproached 28-year-old Georgeanna Woolsey for some minor infraction, her sister advised Georgeanna to "outflank the Dix." And that is what most women who became Civil War nurses did—they found alternative routes to the Civil War hospital and went around her.

As rapid as was Dorothea Dix's rise through the ranks, her fall was even faster. In a series of orders in the summer and fall of 1863, the army restricted the number of women nurses that could be placed in army hospitals and stripped Dix of her authority to place them. Frederick Law Olmsted, a hospital volunteer, compared Dix to George McClellan. "Both are popular heroes," explained Olmsted, "both are great at beginnings and in promises and hopes." And Olmsted went further, adding "but I am sure that [McClellan] is no more to be compared with such men as Rosecrans and Grant, for handling an army in the wilderness of the South than Miss Dix is to be compared with Miss Nightingale in the work of reforming military hospitals."

Although mean-spirited, perhaps, and a little self-serving—Olmsted was actively engaged in a program of hospital reform when he so readily dismissed Dix—Olmsted's comparison effectively captured Dix's fall from wartime grace. Instead of Dix, it is Clara Barton who is most often remembered as the standard bearer for Civil War nursing, as the closest thing to an American Nightingale that the war produced.

When the war began, Barton was a painfully shy clerk in the Patent Office in Washington. Ignoring orders directing women nurses to stay safely in Washington, Barton outflanked Dix and showed up on the field at nearly every major engagement in the eastern theater, beginning with the Second Battle of Bull Run in August 1862. With no medical training, Barton was resourceful and fearless, combing the battlefield alongside army surgeons looking for survivors, performing triage under fire and helping evacuate the wounded. Barton wisely stayed out of Washington, coming in only to take on supplies before returning to the field. And Barton remained in the field long after the war was over, identifying missing soldiers and marking the graves of the dead at Andersonville. If Dix was the McClellan of army nurses, then Barton became nursing's Grant.

Shots Heard 'Round the World

By MAYA JASANOFF and ADAM GOODHEART

Three hearses, flag-draped and drawn by horses, rolled through the colonial streets of Boston on May 1. The men of the Sixth Massachusetts—the "noble sons who have given their life's blood in defense of the laws and maintenance of their country's honor," in the words of the next morning's newspaper—had come home. The cortège, accompanied by Gov. John A. Andrew and by militia cadets marching with their muskets reversed, drew up at last before the staid 18th-century portico of King's Chapel on Tremont

Street. Slowly, the chapel's great bell, cast long ago in bronze by Paul Revere himself, tolled a dirge.

It was appropriate that the fallen soldiers had been brought to a place literally resonant with history. The first combat fatalities of the Civil War, they had been killed two weeks earlier in the streets of Baltimore, struck down by an angry pro-Southern mob that hurled bricks and stones, then fired pistols at the Union soldiers in the streets. The first man to die—the first of all the 620,000 who would perish in the four years to come—was a 17-year-old farmboy named Luther C. Ladd. He was said to have gone down gasping his own epitaph: "All hail to the Stars and Stripes!"

But most resonant of all to the silent throngs of Bostonians watching the funeral procession was the date on which the men had died: April 19. On that same day 86 years earlier, in 1775, the first patriot martyrs of the American Revolution had been killed at nearby Lexington.

This remarkable coincidence attracted comment across both the Union and the Confederacy. "The First Blood of the First and Last Revolution," the Albany Journal headlined the news from Baltimore. "The same scenes—on a larger scale—were re-acted on the 19th of April, 1861, which were acted on the 19th of April, 1775, in Massachusetts."

Governor Andrew had lost no time in noting "the parallel the day and the event suggest with the 19th of April, 1775, and the immortal memories which cluster around the men of Lexington and Concord." Other Unionists confidently declared that "the blood that flowed at Baltimore will be no less surely avenged than that which consecrated Lexington to liberty." For what had the American Revolution been if not the foundation of that very Union that the north now fought to preserve?

Southerners had their own interpretation: hadn't the American Revolution been a struggle in which a secessionist group of rebels sought to break away from established authority? "It is the old Revolutionary fight over—a fight between the people and a strong Government," one pro-Southern journalist declared.

A Virginia newspaper shrewdly observed that George Washington had been branded a rebel and a traitor by the British, while the New Orleans Daily Picayune recalled how the British officer who confronted the minutemen at Lexington had cried out "throw down your arms, you rebels, and disperse" in much the way Lincoln demanded that the Confederate States put down their own weapons. Further developing the parallel, the paper compared the way patriots stopped the British march on Concord "for the purpose of crippling the liberties of the American colonies," just as the Baltimore mob blocked the Union soldiers "summoned for the purpose of aiding in suppressing the rights of a unanimous people to independence. It reads like a rehearsal of the Past—another battle of Lexington—another immolation of life for the purposes of another war upon Freedom."

Historical analogies can be tricky things, as is evident in Currier and Ives's pro-Union lithograph "The Lexington of 1861," issued shortly after the combat in Baltimore. It portrays the mob scene in all its torrid, smoky mess, and its visual cues are equally confused. As in 1775, the "enemy" in the print wears red, probably meant to suggest the shirts of volunteer firemen, often in the front ranks of urban mobs. But then the markers break down. At Lexington, the British had been the ones who—like the Union men now—were orderly, uniformed and well armed, in contrast to the haphazardly organized patriots. The lithograph's depiction of troops advancing head-on against the civilian mob might have suggested strength and rectitude to Union sympathizers, but the image also bears an uncanny resemblance to a notorious indictment of just such organized force from the American Revolutionary era, Revere's woodcut of the Boston Massacre.

Such ambiguities did not prevent Bostonians from harking back across eight decades to find parallels to the present. The renowned poet Oliver Wendell Holmes Sr. visited the tree near Harvard's campus beneath whose branches Washington was supposed to have taken command of the Continental Army. His resulting composition, entitled "Under the Washington Elm, Cambridge, April 27, 1861," began:

Eighty years have passed, and more,
Since under the brave old tree
Our fathers gathered in arms, and swore
They would follow the sign their banners bore,
And fight till the land was free.

"The Lexington of 1861," depicting the Baltimore riots, print by Currier & Ives.

Half of their work was done,
Half is left to do,—
Cambridge, and Concord, and Lexington!
When the battle is fought and won,
What shall be told of you?

And on May 1, the same day on which the fallen Massachusetts soldiers' remains were brought to King's Chapel, another patriotic gathering was held at nearby Old South Church, a sanctuary even more closely associated with Revolutionary history. Here Unionists raised a large American flag inscribed with the motto "True to Our Revolutionary Principles." Orators invoked Franklin and Adams, the Boston Massacre and the Tea Party, encouraging listeners to recall "the glorious history of which we should all be proud."

Yet one orator at the old church, amid his own litany of historic icons, also struck a different, forward-looking note. Like Holmes, the Rev. J.M. Manning suggested that the revolutionary struggle of 1861 was not just about honoring the legacy of 1775, but also about enlarging it. The clergyman was more explicit than the poet. "The African, out of his ages of bondage, is peering, with a strange thrill of joy, at these Stars and Stripes," Manning said. "To him, they are an auroral vision—the early twilight, with its streak of flame, telling him that the day of redemption draweth nigh. Into this shadow flock those who would honor the mighty past, and secure a mightier future."

Lincoln, Douglass and the 'Double-Tongued Document'

By DAVID W. BLIGHT

The two months following Lincoln's inauguration found Frederick Douglass struggling to understand and bitterly demoralized by the president's policies, but also exhilarated by the outbreak of war at Fort Sumter. He had no interest in the new president's oratorical olive branches to the seceded South, his poetry about the "mystic chords of memory" or the "better angels of our nature." Indeed, Douglass despised the olive branches, calling the speech "little better than our worst fears," and a "double-tongued document, capable of two constructions," concealing rather than declaring a "definite policy."

In his brutal critique of Lincoln's address, published in late March in his Monthly newspaper, Douglass had drawn from his own deep well of radical antislavery arguments. The frustrated abolitionist, like many in his camp, wanted a full-throated denunciation of Southern secessionists and, in effect, a declaration of war on slavery and slaveholders. That, of course, Lincoln would not and could not do at that point in time; rather, he spent the weeks after his inauguration reaching out to unionist sentiment in the South, appealing to what he mistakenly hoped were cool heads in the seceded states to consider some conciliatory measures that might hold the nation together.

True, Lincoln firmly rejected secession as unlawful, and he promised that the "Union will constitutionally defend, and maintain itself." But, to Douglass's dismay, he also vowed to enforce all the laws, including the fugitive slave clause of the Constitution. Lincoln quoted the Constitution itself, saying that runaway slaves "shall be delivered up." He even implied that the only legitimate controversy on this issue was whether federal or state authority should be exercised to seize and return runaway slaves.

These efforts of Lincoln's to assuage Southern fears of Republicans deeply disturbed Douglass, a former fugitive slave who wore the runaway's travail on his body and in his soul. On this question Douglass had no sympathy with Lincoln's sensitive plight nor his constitutionalism; all morality was on the side of the human rights of the fugitive slave. Equally disappointing was Lincoln's reiteration of his oft-repeated intention to "have no purpose, directly or indirectly, to interfere with the institution of slavery in the States where it exists." Douglass knew that this was a political and legal stance by the president, and he grasped, at least tentatively, that Lincoln viewed slavery as morally wrong. But what mattered now in this late stage of the secession crisis, and with the looming test over whether Fort Sumter in Charleston Harbor would be defended, was, in the abolitionist's view, the resolve to fight rather than kowtow to the wishes of the Slave Power. Douglass had wanted a war-maker's inaugural, not a negotiator's diplomatic appeal for calm and mystic unity.

Initially, Douglass blistered Lincoln with both satire and contempt. He lampooned the secretive, quiet way Lincoln had arrived in Washington, likening the scene to the way the "poor, hunted fugitive slave reaches the North, in disguise evading pursuers, by the underground railroad crawling and dodging under the sable wing of night." Douglass wondered how "galling" it must have been to the president-elect to feel like "a fugitive slave, with a nation howling on his track." But Douglass's anger became fiercer yet. Lincoln's acknowledgment of the South's "right of property" in slaves seemed to this former slave only "weakness and conciliation towards the tyrants and traitors." Douglass demanded "rebuke" and not "palliations." The embittered editor imagined Lincoln on bended knee to slaveholders, performing as an "excellent slave hound" and the "most dangerous advocate of slave-hunting and slave-catching in the land."

It is too easy to simply conclude that the black activist was out of touch with the president's dire situation and the necessity of pragmatic overtures for peace. At this point, his was indeed a higher law than the Constitution. Without blinking, Douglass compared slavery itself, and especially any effort to return fugitive slaves to bondage, to "murder." In the rhetoric of the lecture platform, where Douglass had few peers, he proclaimed: "Your money or your life, says the pirate; your liberty or your life, says the slaveholder. And where is the difference between the pirate and the slaveholder?"

In those last weeks of peace Douglass begged his readers to see the impending crisis in such stark terms and to prepare to treat secessionists and all who would follow them as thieves and murderers operating in the dark. To this abolitionist, the secession movement was an attempt to destroy the United States, and to permanently extinguish any humane future for him or his people. All who would abet or even negotiate with that cause were partners with injustice and on the wrong side of history.

There were elements of Lincoln's address from which Douglass took a "slight gleam of relief." Lincoln did embrace "safeguards" against free blacks being captured and enslaved as fugitives. Douglass acknowledged this, however backhandedly, as a recognition that blacks possessed some human rights and that slavery itself was inhumane. But in his close reading of Lincoln's address, Douglass could only conclude with fear and distress that it simply "remains to be seen whether the Federal Government" would be "powerless for liberty, and only powerful for slavery." On that note of near despair Douglass rested his uneasy case against, as well as to some extent for, "our first modern antislavery President."

So uncertain of the future was Douglass that in early April, just before the firing on Fort Sumter, he wrote an article in his paper announcing "A Trip to Haiti." He had booked passage for himself and his daughter, Rosetta, on a steamer out of New Haven to visit the island nation and to observe the emigration project there led by the American abolitionist James Redpath.

Douglass waxed romantic about both the legacy of the Haitian Revolution and the black republic that resulted, as well as the "beams of a tropical sun," and his desire to inhale the "fragrance of tropical breezes." Worry over the current crisis and fear that blacks might have no future in the United States, Douglass said he spoke for many of his black countrymen in wishing for a "place of retreat, an asylum from the apprehended storm which is about to beat pitilessly upon them."

So, even he, a long opponent of black emigration schemes that would remove his people from their native North America, declared his personal interest in a "tour of observation" and potential exile. But just before going to press with his April edition, he added a postscript declaring that since the article was "put in type," recent events—namely, the assault on Fort Sumter—had wrought "a tremendous revolution in all things pertaining to the possible future of the colored people of the United States." His long anticipated war was on. "This," he announced, "is no time for us to leave the country."

The Union's 'Shoddy' Aristocracy
By RON SOODALTER

With the Pentagon budget up two-thirds over the last decade, it's no surprise that charges of war profiteering make for regular front-page fodder. But for sheer scale and audacity, nothing beats the corruption that surrounded the Union war effort—and, thanks to the horrendously poor quality of the resulting equipment, did much to undermine it.

From the very beginning, government representatives awarded contracts based not on the best product, or the fairest price, but on the highest bribe. As the war progressed, the problem became epidemic: during one week alone in November 1861, contractors in New York generated nearly $3 million in revenues from military deals. It would be easy to excuse a little corruption, or even a lot, if the result was high-quality equipment. But much of the contractors' profit came from cutting corners. And with the government representatives more concerned with lining their own pockets than establishing a system of standards, there was little quality control over the goods that went into the field.

Take the clothing sector, where companies made fortunes responding to the demands of a suddenly vast army. Brooks Brothers, for example, was awarded an initial contract for the fabrication of 12,000 uniforms just two weeks after war was declared; in 1861 alone, it filled 36,000 orders. The company had obtained the contract through questionable means, and proceeded to fill the order in much the same way: turned out in a matter of weeks, the uniforms were so ill-fitting—many lacking buttons and button holes—that the New York Volunteers who wore them suffered humiliation from other outfits. Even worse, the soldiers were responsible for paying for their own uniforms out of their clothing allowance, so they took a double hit.

But this was not the worst of it: facing a paucity of wool, Brooks Brothers glued together shredded, often decaying rags, pressed them into a semblance of cloth, and sewed the pieces into uniforms. Far from protecting the soldiers from inclement weather, these uniforms would fall apart in the first rain. The New York State Legislature eventually spent $45,000—about $10.8 million in current dollars—to replace the uniforms. The company stonewalled; when asked why he did not lower his prices for using lesser materials, one of the proprietors, Elisha Brooks, responded, "I think that I cannot ascertain the difference without spending more time than I can now devote to that purpose."

Nor did the Brooks Brothers scandal stop the states from engaging with war profiteers. Soon, wool mills sprang up all over the North, operating at outlandish profit margins and brazenly cheating the government. Some of the uniforms were made from cloth of non-regulation color, which sometimes resulted in soldiers firing upon their own comrades by mistake. When the administration looked abroad for its cloth, the Northern mill owners and contractors cried foul in the name of patriotism. Other manufacturers learned to cut corners as well, producing cheap knapsacks, blankets and hats. Some made shoe soles of glued-together wood chips, which would fall apart after just a half hour of marching.

None of this was a secret; in fact, the poor quality of the soldiers' equipment gave a new word to the English language: "shoddy." The term, according to a Harper's Weekly article, described "a villainous compound, the refuse stuff and sweepings of the shop, pounded,

rolled, glued, and smoothed to the external form and gloss of cloth."
One writer for The New York Tribune painted an equally graphic
picture: "Shoddy" was, he wrote,

> poor sleezy stuff, woven open enough for seives [sic],
> and then filled with shearman's dust. Soldiers, on the first
> day's march or in the earliest storm, found their clothes,
> overcoats, and blanket, scattering to the wind in rags or
> dissolving into their primitive elements of dust under the
> pelting rain.

The same story played out in practically every corner of the war-
contracting business. So-called victuallers made huge profits by providing spoiled meat, and hostlers sold old, blind and spavined horses
to the government at usurious prices.

Sadly, the practice of over-pricing under-quality goods continued from the firing on Fort Sumter to the surrender at Appomattox,
and made fortunes for many New York businessmen. In 1860, when
the war was nothing more than a strong rumor, there were only a
few dozen millionaires in all of New York City; by the end of the
war, they numbered in the hundreds. True, some made their fortunes
fairly, but not for nothing were they known popularly as the "Shoddy
Aristocracy." The New York Herald complained,

> The world has seen its silver age, its golden age. This is
> the age of shoddy. The new brown-stone palaces on Fifth
> Avenue, the new equipages at the Park, the new diamonds
> which dazzle unaccustomed eyes the new people who
> live in the palaces, and ride in the carriages, and wear the
> diamonds and silks—all are shoddy. Six days in the week
> they are shoddy businessmen. On the seventh day they are
> shoddy Christians.

One of the most conspicuous offenders, the merchant George
Opdyke, was elected mayor of New York in 1862. During his campaign, prominent New York attorney John H. White referred to the
candidate as "a faithful public servant, a sincere philanthropist and
an honest man." Actually, as the city's largest clothing manufacturer,

Opdyke made a good deal of his money before the war by producing cheap clothes for Southern planters to give to their slaves. And shortly before the mayoral election, it was Opdyke himself, in his capacity as clothing inspector, who approved the shoddy uniforms produced by Brooks Brothers. Before the war ended, a noted statesman observed that Opdyke "had made more money out of the war by secret partnerships and contracts for army clothing, than any fifty sharpers in New York." His unflagging support of the Lincoln administration, however, and his efforts in raising troops for the cause, did much to mask his unsavory activities.

As with war profiteers in other conflicts, not a single member of the shoddy aristocracy was shot or hanged for treason; the more opulent the transgressor, it seemed, the more socially acceptable. As the Herald wrote, "The individual who makes the most money—no matter how—and spends the most money—no matter for what—is considered the greatest man."

Black or White?

By DANIEL J. SHARFSTEIN

In February 1861, just weeks after Louisiana seceded from the Union, Randall Lee Gibson enlisted as a private in a state army regiment. The son of a wealthy sugar planter and valedictorian of Yale's Class of 1853, Gibson had long supported secession. Conflict was inevitable, he believed, not because of states' rights or the propriety or necessity of slavery. Rather, a war would be fought over the inexorable gulf between whites and blacks, or what he called "the most enlightened race" and "the most degraded of all the races of men." Because Northern abolitionists were forcing the South to recognize "the political, civil, and social equality of all the races of men," Gibson wrote, the South was compelled to enjoy "independence out of the Union." (Read Randall Lee Gibson's article, "Our Federal Union.")

The notion that war turned on a question of black and white as opposed to slavery and freedom was hardly an intuitive position for

Gibson or for the South. Although Southern society was premised on slavery, the line between black and white had always been permeable. Since the 17th century, people descended from African slaves had been assimilating into white communities. It was a great migration that was covered up even as it was happening, its reach extending into the most unlikely corners of the South: although Randall Gibson was committed to a hardline ideology of racial difference, this secret narrative of the American experience was his family's story.

Gibson's siblings proudly traced their ancestry to a prosperous farmer in the South Carolina backcountry named Gideon Gibson. What they didn't know was that when he first arrived in the colony in the 1730s, he was a free man of color. At the time the legislature thought he had come there to plot a slave revolt. The governor demanded a personal audience with him and learned that he was a skilled tradesman, had a white wife and had owned land and slaves in Virginia and North Carolina. Declaring the Gibsons to be "not Negroes nor Slaves but Free people," the governor granted them hundreds of acres of land. The Gibsons soon married into their Welsh and Scots-Irish community along the frontier separating South Carolina's coastal plantations from Indian country. It did not matter if the Gibsons were black or white—they were planters.

The Gibsons were hardly alone in their journey from black to white. Hundreds of families of color had gained their freedom in the colonial era because they had English mothers, and within a generation or two, they could claim to be white. Their claims were supported by law, which never drew the color line at "one drop" of African ancestry in the antebellum era. Most Southern states followed a one-quarter or one-eighth rule: anyone with a black grandparent or great-grandparent was legally black, and those with more remote ancestry were legally white. Antebellum South Carolina, though, never had a legal definition of race. "It may be well and proper," a state judge and leading defender of slavery wrote in 1835, "that a man of worth, honesty, industry and respectability, should have the rank of a white man, while a vagabond of the same degree of blood should be confined to the inferior caste." Preserving the institution of slavery mattered far more than preserving the purity of white "blood." As long as people who claimed to be white were productive members of society—in effect, supporting the prevailing order—it made little sense to mandate a stricter measure of race.

When the Gibsons moved west in the 1790s, they had money and land and slaves, but professed to know very little about their history, explaining a tendency towards dark complexion with vague accounts of Gypsy or Portuguese roots. They soon epitomized the manners and attitudes of the planter aristocracy. Randall Gibson grew up shuttling between a family mansion in Lexington, Ky., where his mother was from, and Live Oak, a sugar plantation in Terrebonne Parish, La., where his father had sought his fortune. He knew the family's slaves well and often asked after them in his letters home from Yale, referring to them always as "servants." Gibson's father, a Whig and longtime supporter of "the Great Compromiser" Henry Clay, gave significant responsibility to his slaves, hiring no outside overseers. Indeed, Tobias Gibson repeatedly expressed dismay at the institution. "I am in conscience opposed to slavery," he wrote. "I don't like it and the older I get the worse it seems." Such sentiment provided an easy way for him to feel virtuous about his way of life—disliking slavery made him an enlightened master.

Enlisting in the Louisiana army represented a humbling new start for Randall Gibson. At Yale he had been lionized by his classmates, the flower of a select group of Southerners walking in the footsteps of John C. Calhoun and Judah P. Benjamin. Gibson had thought of himself and his peers as the nation's great hope, an educated brotherhood that could guide the country through sectional crisis. The years that followed his graduation, however, were full of disappointment. He studied law, only to decide that he did not wish to practice. After traveling around Europe, he bought a sugar cane plantation near his father's land southwest of New Orleans, but could not make a profit and found the neighbors distasteful.

Almost as soon as Gibson returned to Louisiana from Yale, he embraced an uncompromising Southern position on slavery, declaring his opinions to be "as decided as if I were a member of Congress." This was a predictable stance: without a fortune or connections to the primarily Northern-born merchant elite in New Orleans, Gibson could not afford to take an unpopular political stance. At the same time, he became convinced that "Southern society is based, its life and soul are staked, upon the inequality of the races, not only its aims, its expansion and progress, but its very existence."

Gibson's position that war was necessary to preserve white supremacy reveals how racism flourished at the prospect of abolition. When slavery served as a broad proxy of black and white, there was little need to dwell on the purity of "white blood" and the finer points of racial difference. Only freedom required a hard line on race, to preserve the existing order. As the abolitionist chorus swelled in the generation leading up to secession, Southerners responded, in one Virginian's words, by "rising up to promulgate the philosophical, sociological, and ethical excellence of slavery." In 1857, the Louisiana Senate considered a bill for the "prevention of marriages where one of the parties has a taint of African blood."

Had the bill passed, the racial status of countless whites would have been put in jeopardy. That it was proposed at all reveals a society that could not imagine such consequences. The South's traditional flexibility on questions of race—the ease with which families like the Gibsons were able to assimilate into white communities and the security that most people living as white had in their racial status—actually enabled white Southerners to embrace the idea of absolute, blood-borne racial difference.

If Gibson's ideology demanded secession, more practical considerations motivated him to enlist in the army. Well before the presidential election of 1860, Gibson expressed doubts that the Union would survive and urged the South to "prepare for every emergency," but his views did not bring the success that he craved. He ran for a seat at the state convention that would determine whether Louisiana would stay in the Union, but placed third out of four candidates. He had failed in business and politics. War seemed the only path left to a world that was bigger than cane fields and river levees. Ironically, when army life forced Gibson to confront the gap between his theories about race and how Southerners experienced it every day, the opportunity to serve trumped his ideology.

Soon after enlisting, Gibson was promoted to captain of an artillery company and then elected a colonel in the 13th Louisiana Volunteer Infantry Regiment, 10 companies totaling 830 men, mostly from New Orleans. They were, according to an aide, "as cosmopolitan a body of soldiers as there existed upon the face of God's earth. There were Frenchmen, Spaniards, Mexicans, Dagoes, Germans, Chinese, Irishmen, and, in fact, persons of every clime known to geographers or travellers of that day." They wore "jaunty zouave uniform[s]," drilled in English and French, sang songs in their native languages, speculated on their regiment's unlucky number and lived a continuous "saturnalia" of gambling and drink.

Rather than dwell upon his recruits' racial origins, Gibson focused on turning them into soldiers. As he worked with his officers in camp, he refused to subscribe to the gentlemanly romance of war. While many in his regiment predicted a glorious Confederate victory before they had finished their training, Gibson devoted himself to the study of military tactics. Without any experience in war, he knew that the army's true weakness was a lack of "military men by education," "scientific officers" and "West Pointers."

By late autumn, the regiment was leaving Louisiana for the war's western front, marching as a band played "The Girl I Left Behind Me." They reached Kentucky on the last day in November. Shrouded in snow and sleet, they camped on frozen ground and waited for the fight.

Lincoln Captured!

By TED WIDMER

Despite recent rumors to the contrary, Lincoln displayed no vampiric powers in his early presidency. But it is true that he could appear many places at the same time, thanks to a chemical process that seemed to borrow as much from the dark arts as from science.

Photography was a fluid technique in 1861, in every sense. It had made rapid strides since the first inchoate smudges of a backyard in France were captured in 1826, the year that Jefferson and Adams died.

Improvements followed fast and furious; the daguerreotype in 1839; the ambrotype in 1851; the tintype in 1856. The United States had no shortage of tinkerers, and like characters in Hawthorne short story, these wizards drew from science, experimenting with bits of silver, iodine and even egg whites to cheat nature out of her secrets. Hawthorne placed a daguerreotypist in "The House of the Seven Gables," and like many other writers, believed that there was something supernatural about creating perfect portraits—"ghosts," in his words—that would live on long after death. Who needs vampires?

The process of creating ghosts was messy and slow. Photographers were artists as well as scientists, and many of the earliest pioneers, like Samuel F. B. Morse, were painters, deeply enamored with the human form. An early student of Morse's, a failed painter with terrible vision named Mathew Brady, borrowed from both science and art as he established a thriving photography business in New York and Washington.

For Lincoln, this dark technology was a godsend. Despite his penchant for making fun of his appearance, Lincoln knew that his "phiz" was instantly recognizable, all the more so after hair began to appear on it. And recognizability was an asset when all known facts relating to the government of the United States were up for grabs. Presidents have to be everywhere and nowhere at the same time; highly visible to the public on certain stage-managed occasions, and then quite invisible when there is work to be done. (It is still the same in 2011, when there is always an effervescent "Photo of the Day" on the White House Web site.) In the early months of his presidency, Lincoln more than tolerated his photographers; he intuitively understood that they were helping him a great deal as he tried to give the Union a face—his own.

Over the spring of 1861, as the new government came into focus, so did Lincoln. It was natural that he would be drawn to Mathew Brady, the self-made man whose studio was just down Pennsylvania Avenue from the White House. Lincoln said, "Brady and the Cooper Institute made me president." For on the same day that he gave the great Cooper Union address, in February 1860, he did something just as significant when he stopped at Brady's New York studio for a likeness.

Brady, the former painter, was not averse to certain forms of retouching (he made Lincoln's neck less scrawny by artificially

141

enlarging his collar), and the result was a surprisingly normal-looking candidate. Not a savage from the wilds of Illinois, or a baboon, as he was often called, but a reasonable facsimile of a human being. That image was widely disseminated during the tumultuous campaign, as Americans by the thousands bought small buttons with his tintyped image affixed to them.

But that was then, in the distant antebellum. Now that war had broken out, Americans needed to see their president as he actually looked that spring. In an age that was tiring of romantic clichés and simply wanted facts, the photograph was emerging as the portrait of choice. So Lincoln came to Brady. Repeatedly. He did so as soon as he arrived in Washington in late February, taking a photograph just after the wild train journey that brought him to the White House. That image was widely disseminated in Harper's Weekly on April 27. And he did so again in May, most likely on May 16, thanks to recent research. In 2003, Thomas F. Schwartz discovered that an artist named Arthur Lumley had drawn Lincoln in the act of being photographed (one form of art capturing another), and had written the date "May 16/61" at the bottom of the page.

The images that resulted from that session, his first serious sitting as president, are striking. This is not a teller of jokes, or an escapee from the back woods. What the English journalist William Howard Russell called his "wild republican hair" has been subdued and rests in place. He sits regally in an elegant chair—a chair, in fact, that Lincoln had given to Brady, after having rescued it from the House of Representatives. It was likely his former chair when he was a representative. The mood is somber, serious, and intense at times. He is no longer a mere politician—this is the president of the United States.

One striking image shows him deep in thought, seated like the Rodin sculpture "The Thinker," which would not be cast until 1902. He was perhaps reflecting on the great message to the American people that he was in the act of writing, which would be released on July 4. It is impossible to know, precisely, which problem he was thinking about—he had more than his share.

In these photographs, there is one trait that dominates. There is no equivocation. The Lincoln that emerges from the shadows is a force of nature, who looks like he could break an assailant in half. John Hay wrote of his ability to overwhelm a visitor: "He looked through the man to the buttons on the back of his coat." We feel that force in these images, particularly in the photograph that is broken, almost as if by the strain of trying to capture him. In so many other portraits, Lincoln displays the passive body language of a man of peace, responding to events rather than initiating them. Here he leans forward, taut, belligerent. This is no spectator.

Of course, he was never captured entirely. Many contemporaries wrote of the inadequacy of his portraits. John Nicolay said it perfectly:

> Graphic art was powerless before a face that moved
> through a thousand delicate gradations of line and con-
> tour, light and shade, sparkle of the eye and curve of the
> lip, in the long gamut of expression from grave to gay,
> and back again from the rollicking jollity of laughter to
> that serious, far-away look that with prophetic intuitions
> beheld the awful panorama of war, and heard the cry
> of oppression and suffering. There are many pictures of
> Lincoln; there is no portrait of him.

Walt Whitman wrote something similar:

> Probably the reader has seen physiognomies (often old
> farmers, sea captains, and such) that, behind their homeli-
> ness, or even ugliness, held superior points so subtle, yet
> so palpable, making the real life of their faces almost
> as impossible to depict as a wild perfume or fruit taste,
> or a passionate tone of the living voice—and such was
> Lincoln's face, the peculiar color, the lines of it, the eyes,
> mouth expression. Of technical beauty it had nothing—
> but to the eye of a great artist it furnished a rare study, a
> feast and fascination. The current portraits are all fail-
> ures—most of them caricatures.

But on this May day in 1861, he came closer than usual. Between the
White House and the Capitol, Lincoln and Brady advanced the idea of
representative democracy in their own way, by representing the leader
of the government to the American people. In so doing, they created six
indelible images of a nation girding itself for the struggle to come.

Blue, Gray and Everything in Between

By MICHAEL O. VARHOLA

While the colors blue and gray are almost iconically associated with the opposing ground forces of the Civil War,
early in the conflict many regiments reporting for duty
on either side were much more colorfully attired. Some rebel troops
wore blue, some northern troops wore gray, units on both sides
sported every shade of red, green, black, white or even tartan, and
uniform patterns were almost completely non-standardized.

This discordant variety of military garb reflected not just diverse
aesthetic sensibilities but, in some cases, ideological ones as well, and
was a virtual barometer for the lack of strong central organization

Members of the Garibaldi Guard parade past President Lincoln.

in either the Confederate or Federal camps. Uniforms for volunteer units were produced not according to the specifications of national war departments but to those of state militia authorities or even units themselves, and were issued not from central quartermaster depots but from local storehouses—or even ordered from tailors by individuals.

These disparate supply systems were not well suited to clothing the many troops that would ultimately be called into service for the war or to supplying them for the extended period it would last. And even the centralized mechanisms that were in place early in the conflict did not reflect the organization that would be required to outfit the two great military machines that eventually faced each other.

As late as April 1861, for example, the Confederate Quartermaster General was placing orders for regular army uniforms that included blue battle tunics. And the Confederate system of "commutation," in which the government reimbursed volunteers for providing their own uniforms, ensured that many troops wore civilian clothes, in whole or in part, the first year or two of the war.

Some of the most familiar of the exotic uniforms, of course, were those worn by zouaves—light infantrymen clad in baggy pantaloons, gaiters, braided jackets, sashes and tasseled fezzes or turbans, clothing more typical of North Africa than North America. Such uniforms were, in fact, inspired by those first worn by French colonial troops in Algeria in the decade before the U.S. Civil War, and both the Union and Confederacy had units that wore them.

While the zouaves' colorful uniforms are well known, they were not unique in their diversity, and atypical uniforms, many with an ethnic emphasis, were used by units on both sides. Some were patterned on those worn by various European troop types, especially skirmishers (e.g., French chasseurs, German jaegers).

The 79th New York Volunteer Infantry, the "Highland Guard," provides a particularly colorful example. Formed under the auspices of state militia authorities in 1858, it was essentially a Scottish-American tribute unit that took its numerical designation and the tartan for its uniforms from the British military's 79th Regiment of Foot, the "Cameron Highlanders" (it was even backed in part by the brother of Secretary of War Simon Cameron). Beyond these cosmetic commonalities, however, it had no actual connection to the original Scottish unit and was more or less a privately funded social club.

Official uniform for the New York Highland Guard's soldiers included wool trousers patterned with the chiefly red-and-black plaid tartan of the Scottish 79th; a dark blue jacket with red cording and red cuffs, and collars with white piping; a dark blue boat-shaped Scottish cap called a glengarry, complemented with a plaid band; and low-quarter leather shoes with false buckles.

New York State Militia guidelines precluded unit members from wearing kilts, but they ignored these provisions and did so anyway when on parade, wearing non-standard civilian-pattern versions in the same tartan as their trousers, holding them up with suspenders. They paired these with red and white diced hose and sporrans—pouches worn with kilts that took the place of pockets—made of nappy white horsehide and accented with black tassels.

Another New York unit distinguished by its couture was the 39th New York Volunteer Infantry Regiment, colloquially known as the

"Garibaldi Guard" or the "Italian Legion." Many of its members were, in fact, already combat veterans, followers of revolutionary leader Giuseppe Garibaldi during the Second Italian War of Independence. They showed their commitment to Garibaldi's ideals by adopting blousy red shirts similar to those they had worn as soldiers in Italy. (There was also, interestingly, a Louisiana-based "Garibaldi Legion" of Italians that fought for the Confederacy and wore red jackets.)

Southern militia and volunteer units were just as likely to have atypical uniforms as their northern counterparts, and also included both zouaves and other sorts of troops. A notable example of the former was "Wheat's Special Battalion," a Louisiana infantry outfit made up of largely of immigrants, street thugs, dockworkers and military adventurers.

At the other end of the social spectrum stood the Washington Artillery, a New Orleans militia battalion that had been formed in 1838, fought in the Mexican-American War of 1846–48 and functioned as an exclusive men's club. Prospective members had to apply, pay a fee and be accepted by an examination committee.

The Washington Artillery dress uniform included a dark blue frock coat with red collar, sky-blue trousers (with a gold stripe along the outer seam for officers and a red one for enlisted men), and a red kepi with a blue band and a brass device consisting of crossed cannons and the letters "WA" (augmented with a pelican for officers); enlisted men's uniforms also had red cuffs. Brass buttons, belt buckles and epaulettes (gold for officers)—emblazoned with various forms of pelican or the letters "WA" or "NO" as appropriate—buff white leather accoutrements (black for officers), and white gloves and gaiters completed the ensemble.

The Clinch Rifles of Augusta, Ga., was another unit formed by the social elite of its community and, when the War Between the States began, its uniform was patterned after the newest U.S. Army infantry uniform. Following the European tradition for infantrymen, however, the frock coat and trousers were forest green in color with gold braid trim, as was the forage cap, or kepi, worn by such troops even for dress purposes (and generally only in the field by regular units).

Soon after the first shots of the Civil War were fired, the exotic uniforms began to disappear and, as the war escalated and then ground on for months, then years, these colorful outfits became increasingly rare. Many of them were not practical for combat, were too expensive or logistically difficult to maintain or replace, or were too easily confused with enemy uniforms (as was the case with the uniforms of the Washington Artillery).

Some units did maintain muted versions or elements of their original uniforms, especially those organized as zouaves, whose uniforms had the benefit of being generally well-suited to hot weather and rough terrain. Predominantly, however, the realities of supplying great armies dictated that the opposing central governments overseeing the war efforts issue clothing in the uniform styles and colors that are most often associated with them. Countless patterns converged into a much narrower range dominated by standardized frock coats, jackets, trousers and forage caps, and the broad palette of colors was reduced, for the most part, to just two.

And so the festive diversity of uniforms largely vanished, leaving the opposing ground forces clad primarily in the two familiar and iconic colors. And with the colorful pageantry went the idea that the war was a grand adventure, displaced by the brutal realization that it was something far more grim and industrialized, fought not by individuals but by monolithic forces of blue and gray.

Lincoln's Rhetorical Fireworks

By HAROLD HOLZER

When the Confederacy opened fire on Fort Sumter in April 1861, Abraham Lincoln responded within hours, ordering a naval blockade of Southern ports and calling for 75,000 volunteers to "maintain the honor, the integrity, and the existence of our National Union." But in a 19th-century precursor to President Obama's decision to act alone against Libya, Lincoln made no effort to win immediate Congressional approval—much less appropriations to pay for his orders. The reason seemed simple enough: Congress was out of session and out of town.

Lincoln was fully aware that House and Senate support was required, if only to rubber-stamp the emergency measures he took during their recess. So he made one of the most audacious political decisions of his entire presidency: he called Congress back into special session. And with symbolic panache, he ordered it to re-convene on a sacred holiday—the Fourth of July—as if to recapture the ideals of independence and revolution for the North before they could be misappropriated by the South. There, amid the Independence Day celebrations, he sent Congress the text of (presidents rarely addressed Congress directly) one of the best and most overlooked statements of his presidency, a stirring and politically savvy call to arms against the Confederacy.

Enemies of the administration had predictably bristled at Lincoln's exercise in executive power in the wake of Fort Sumter. New Orleans' Daily Picayune denounced Lincoln as a "military dictator grasping at the power of a despot." And the New York Evening Day-Book likened his threat to "save the Union" with "the bayonet" as no less inhumane than the repressive actions against his own people by the French dictator, Louis Napoleon.

Lincoln might have avoided such attacks by summoning Congress back to Washington sooner (even though some seats were still up for grabs in springtime House races). Railroad and steamboat travel made the capital far more accessible than it had been in the days when Congressional sessions were preceded by weeks of exhausting travel. Instead, he gambled that once he had ordered resources into the fray, none would be recalled, not even by a Congress filled with dubious Democrats. Perhaps Lincoln could even suppress the rebellion and re-unite the country on his own.

On that score, Lincoln miscalculated. In the 10 weeks between April 18 and July 4, Southern resistance hardened, Upper South states seceded, and federal troops filled the capital. (Lincoln responded by acting alone once again, on April 27, to suspend the writ of habeas corpus between Philadelphia and Washington.)

Lincoln largely avoided the harsh judgment of history by deploying the most effective weapon in his personal arsenal: words. For at least two weeks in June, during which time he saw few visitors and focused intently on writing, he crafted a lengthy, deceptively simple, yet ingenious message for the special session. Though his final text did ramble, it combined lawyerly logic with evangelical zeal to accomplish several daunting but essential goals.

For one thing, it reminded Congress and the public that the South had been the original aggressors, not the North: "They have brought many good men to a willingness to take up arms against the government." Lincoln also used the message to defend his initial response to hostilities. He had acted alone with "the deepest regret," he claimed almost apologetically, only because "no choice was left but to call out the war power to resist force, employed for its destruction, by force, for its preservation." It had been a further duty, he argued, to suspend the hallowed writ. After all, he asked, "are all the laws, but one, to go unexecuted, and the government itself go to pieces, lest that one be violated?" He "could but perform this duty, or surrender the existence of the government."

The message then deftly recruited Congress as a partner in the impending war by requesting 400,000 men and $400 million in financing: "The material for the work is abundant, and needs only the hand of legislation to give it practical shape and efficiency." When read aloud, this passage reportedly elicited cheers from the House galleries.

Perhaps most importantly, Lincoln rallied the entire North by using appeals to both history and hope in words designed for "plain people" to understand (he even said so in his text). Today we would call them "sound bites." The idea that any state held supremacy over the entire Union he termed a "sophism." Secession was patently illegal, its defenders absurd, their arguments "sugar-coated" (a phrase he proudly retained even when a government printer suggested it was too coarse). Its supporters were the enemies not just of the Union, but of the entire concept of popular government.

In one particularly sublime passage, he dubbed the approaching war nothing less than "a people's contest," one that presented "to the whole family of man, the question, whether a government of the people, by the same people—can, or cannot, maintain its territorial integrity, against its own domestic foes." More than a fight for national preservation, it was "a struggle for maintaining in the world, that form, and substance of government, whose leading object is to elevate the conditions of men—to lift artificial weights from all shoulders—to afford all, an unfettered start, and a fair chance, in the race of life."

Reaction to this bravura declaration was predictably mixed. Even though Border State legislators chafed, Congress rallied behind the president. Friendly Republican newspapers heaped lavish praise. To the pro-Lincoln New York Times, it was nothing less than the most "careful" and "important" message ever transmitted to Congress. But a French journal warned that Lincoln was about to plunge his country into debt (some issues are perennial). And to one Baltimore paper, the message showed that the president was either "a disgusting fool" or "the equal, in despotic wickedness, of Nero or any of the other tyrants who have polluted this earth." But Lincoln meant business; the army soon shut that paper down. As he had ominously warned in the message: "Such will be a great lesson of peace, teaching men that what they cannot take by an election, neither can they take it by a war—teaching all, the folly of being the beginners of a war."

Lincoln himself never uttered a word of his greatest Congressional message. By tradition, he simply sent it to Capitol Hill to be read aloud by clerks; it was then sent to newspapers for wider distribution. In fact, the so-called July 4th message was not actually read until July 5th, and even then its first telegraphic transmissions were garbled.

Lincoln had brilliantly defined the coming struggle in words ordinary Americans could understand, appreciate and support. He could now count on public and Congressional support for his burgeoning war effort. No president before ever used the power of words more deftly. "And," as Lincoln sadly recalled four years later, "the war came." Had his Independence Day message failed, history—and this nation—might have been far different.

The Dogs (and Bears, and Camels) of War

By CATE LINEBERRY

As Union and Confederate soldiers left the comforts of home for the grim realities of war, many brought along family pets or adopted stray or wild animals, which quickly took on semi-official roles. Regiments from the North and the South kept dogs, cats, horses, squirrels and raccoons as mascots. Some chose more unusual animals, including bears, badgers, eagles, wildcats, even a camel.

Not only did these mascots provide comfort and entertainment to lonely and bored soldiers in camp and on marches, but they often became companions in battle, suffering alongside their regiments. When Union troops captured Company B of the Second Kentucky Infantry Regiment at the battle of Fort Donelson, Tenn., they also detained the company's canine mascot, Frank. The men and the dog were imprisoned for six months at Indiana's Camp Morton until they were exchanged for Union prisoners of war (though there's no record of whether a captured Union dog went free in exchange for Frank).

Most of these mascots began unofficially, often as the pets of conscripted soldiers, but were readily accepted by officers on both sides. They understood the bond between soldiers and mascots and the extraordinary power these animals had to unite the men. Perhaps the most famous mascot was a bald eagle named Old Abe. Lt. James McGuire of the newly formed Company C of the Eighth Wisconsin Regiment received permission from his commanding officer, Capt. John E. Perkins, to purchase the eagle from a Wisconsin couple who in turn had bought it from a local Native American tribe. The eagle was welcomed by the men, who changed their nickname from the Eau Claire Badgers to the Eau Claire Eagles. As they made their way to Camp Randall in Madison to meet the rest of the Eighth Regiment, Captain Perkins, whose lanky frame and bearded face resembled that of Lincoln, named the new mascot Old Abe in honor of the president.

Old Abe, eagle mascot of Company C of the Eighth Wisconsin Regiment.

The company reached Camp Randall in early September and readied themselves for battle. As the men obtained intensive training in weaponry and various formations, Old Abe was assigned to the color guard and received a new perch that consisted of a shield-shaped plate with a crossbar he could roost on. Decorated with stars and stripes, the plate connected to a five-foot long pole, which was carried by the men into battle.

A month later Old Abe and his regiment boarded a train and began their journey to the front. When they stopped in Chicago, the crowds and the newspapers couldn't get enough of Old Abe. Priv. John Williams wrote, "The eagle is more important than the [Eau Claire] Eagles." Despite the fanfare, the regiment pressed on, making its way through St. Louis where Southern sympathizers taunted the men with cries of "Yankee crow!" and "Wild goose!" Agitated by the noise, Old Abe briefly broke free, causing havoc within the ranks as the men chased after him.

Old Abe was almost killed twice. At the Battle of Corinth, in Mississippi, a minie ball cut the leather cord connecting him to his perch. As he flew down the Union lines of the battlefield, Confederates tried to shoot him. Confederate Gen. Sterling Price offered a bounty to his men, adding that he would rather get the eagle than a whole regiment. After someone in the regiment cropped Old Abe's tail and wing feathers to prevent him from flying away again, his outraged bearer, David McLain, resigned his post. Old Abe's other near miss occurred during the siege of Vicksburg in 1863 when a Confederate minie ball grazed his neck and chest, taking off the feathers in its path and damaging his left wing.

By the summer of 1864 the men decided that Old Abe had seen enough war. After much discussion of where he should go, the entire regiment voted to give him to the state of Wisconsin. Old Abe became the property of the state and was officially deemed a war relic. Thousands of people came to see him in his new home in the state Capitol; he appeared at fundraising events across the country where he autographed photos of himself by punching a hole in them with his beak. The showman P. T. Barnum offered to buy him for $20,000, but the state turned him down.

When a fire broke out in the Capitol in February 1881, Old Abe inhaled a large amount of smoke, and he died a month later while being held by his caretaker. Veterans throughout Wisconsin volunteered to be pallbearers at his funeral. For years, crowds came to see Old Abe's preserved body in the rotunda of the Capitol building, but a 1904 fire destroyed his remains.

Old Abe was lucky; indeed, countless mascots lost their lives in the fighting. As smoke cleared at Gettysburg, a small dog thought to be with the First Maryland Regiment limped on three legs through the dead. Union Brigadier General Thomas Kane wrote, "He licked someone's hand after being perfectly riddled with bullets. Regarding him as the only Christian-minded being on either side, I ordered him to be honorably buried." Other mascots died while trying to protect their companions. When the Baltimore American reported a scene from the battle of Antietam, it wrote, "Upon one dead body was found a large black dog, dead also from some chance shot which had struck him while stretched upon his master's corpse caressingly, his fore-paws across the man's breast."

Even President Lincoln wasn't immune to the solace provided by animals during the war. When Mary Todd Lincoln was asked if her husband had a hobby, she replied, "cats."

Evangelicals, Republicans and the Civil War
By DAVID GOLDFIELD

We often hear the phrase "the party of Lincoln" ascribed to the Republican Party. The image conjures a political movement dedicated to the abolition or restriction of slavery and to saving the Union. A less well-known feature of the party's early years was its grounding in the evangelical Christianity of the Second Great Awakening.

Not all evangelicals were Republicans, nor were all Republicans evangelicals. But many of its adherents brought a messianic zeal to the political issues of the day, particularly immigration and the extension of slavery into the western territories. The Republican positions on these political issues derived in great part from their belief that America was God's Chosen Nation and before His blessing could be fulfilled, the nation must be cleansed of its sins. The nature of that cleansing is known as the American Civil War.

The first national Republican convention occurred in Philadelphia in July 1856. It was a time of great agitation on the slavery issue as well as mounting concerns about immigration, often expressed in violent clashes between Catholics and Protestants in the nation's growing cities.

A participant reported that the gathering resembled a "Methodist conference rather than a political convention," and another characterized the party platform as "God's revealed Word." The delegates framed a platform condemning the "twin relics of barbarism"—slavery and polygamy. There was no pending national epidemic of individuals selecting multiple marriage partners. "Polygamy" was a code word for "Mormon," another despised religious group in the party's pantheon of proscribed faiths.

The ubiquity of religious rhetoric and imagery in the Republican campaign further polarized an already divided Union. One minister depicted the upcoming election as "a decisive struggle . . . between freedom and Slavery, truth and falsehood, justice and oppression, God and the devil." If our political system depends upon moderation and compromise, these were not promising sentiments in an increasingly torn nation.

The Republicans did not invent evangelical politics; they were, however, the most successful political organization to merge faith and policy. Party faithful were heirs (and, in some cases, members) of earlier short-lived political anti-slavery and anti-Catholic parties like the Liberty Party, which, during its 1844 presidential run, urged citizens "to vote the Liberty ticket as a religious duty." One of its leaders asserted, "The Liberty Party, unlike any other in history, was founded on moral principles—on the Bible, originating a contest not only against slavery but against atheistic politics from which Divine law was excluded."

Like the Liberty Party, the Free Soilers tapped into the evangelical spirit in the North, staging a revival-style convention in Buffalo in August 1848. Speakers called for a "great moral revolution" founded on "the idea of right and justice and the truth of God." The themes of spiritual rebirth and national rededication resonated throughout the hall. "God had determined to make the convention," one speaker assured the assemblage, "the medium of reviving . . . throughout this great . . .

Nation, the pure principles of Free Government . . . ; and by founding here a real . . . Republic, to diffuse its light and truth to all Nations, until every member of the great human family shall know and rejoice in this great Salvation." Though ostensibly against slavery, they were most concerned, as were the later Republicans, with keeping the territories white.

Messianic politics received a significant boost in 1850 from a speech by New York Senator William H. Seward, who would later join the Republican Party. In appealing to a "higher law" overriding the Constitution, Seward was, in effect, rhetorically transforming a nation of laws into a theocratic state. While the courts interpret the Constitution, each citizen can interpret the Bible. The result, I would argue, is intolerance and chaos.

By 1853, another evangelical party emerged, the Know Nothings. Less concerned with slavery than their predecessors, the new party focused on the dangers of immigration, especially of Irish Roman Catholics. One evangelical adherent called for the "extermination" of Catholics.

But none of these parties were as successful as the Republicans, who combined anti-Catholic and anti-slavery sentiment into a winning evangelical politics. During the 1856 presidential campaign, one Republican newspaper, blending anti-slavery and nativist rhetoric, alleged that "Roman Catholics, whose consciences are enslaved . . . regard the King of Rome—the Pope—as the depository of all authority." Republicans distilled the Democrats to an unholy trinity of "the Pope, a whisky barrel, and a nigger driver."

With Abraham Lincoln (who denounced religious bigotry) as its standard-bearer in the 1860 presidential contest, Republican rallies exuded an evangelical fervor that blended religious and military pageantry. The "Wide-Awakes," the party's shock troops of younger voters, 400,000 strong by one estimate, paraded in black oilcloth capes and red shirts after the fashion of the Paris revolutionaries of 1848. Even into the Democratic stronghold of New York City they marched, holding their torches high through the narrow streets of lower Manhattan preceded by booming military bands, and cheered on by thousands of partisan onlookers who sang out the "Freedom Battle Hymn," entreating citizens to march "On for freedom, God, our country, and the right." The rally culminated at Broadway and 10th Street at midnight in a shower of Roman candles. Wherever the Wide-Awakes went during that campaign season, their parades and the accompanying din of music and fireworks lent an impression of an inexorable tide changing the political landscape of America for all time. Here was not merely a political rally; here was a movement.

We all know the rest of the story: Lincoln was elected president; the lower South seceded; the Confederates opened fire on Fort Sumter on April 12 and the Civil War began. Yes, slavery was a major cause of the war. But evangelical politics polarized and poisoned a political process that works best with compromise and moderation. Politicians in the 1850s posed, postured and waved Bibles, but they did not resolve the major issues, until there was no longer any chance they ever could.

Harriet Beecher Stowe, whose best-selling novel, "Uncle Tom's Cabin," became an anti-slavery Bible in its own right, summarized the evangelical response to Fort Sumter. To Stowe, the Civil War, now underway, was a millennial war, "the last struggle for liberty" that would precede the coming of the Lord. "God's just wrath shall be wreaked on a giant wrong." Her brother, the nation's most popular evangelical preacher, Henry Ward Beecher, related the familiar story of Exodus to his congregation, how Moses led the children of Israel out of Egypt to the Red Sea, and how the sea parted and allowed the Chosen People to escape while burying their pursuers. "And now our turn has come," he exclaimed. "Right before us lies the Red Sea of War." And God was ready; foretelling Julia Ward Howe's famous lines, "that awful wine-press of the Wrath of Almighty God" would come down from the heavens and bury the South.

The war that followed buried 620,000 men. That war should teach us that self-righteousness and religious certitude are more likely to lead to violent rather than to peaceful resolution, and that even a good cause—the abolition of slavery—may be served better by peace than by war. We will never know that, of course, but the struggle of African-Americans to attain full citizenship for a century after the war should motivate us to at least speculate on a different outcome. Let us commemorate this war and honor the men who died. But it would have been a greater tribute to our nation had they lived.

CHAPTER 3

Bull Run

Like many conflicts, the Civil War began twice: the first, bloodless shots at Fort Sumter may have touched off the conflict, but the death and destruction did not start in earnest until July 21—over three months later—at the First Battle of Bull Run. There some 80,000 soldiers, numbers never before seen on a North American battlefield, fought over a wide swatch of Northern Virginia countryside just 25 miles west of Washington. At the end of the battle almost a thousand men were dead and another 4,000 wounded, captured or missing in a Union rout that sent Federal soldiers fleeing back to the capital. The Confederate commanders, however, failed to follow them, leaving the battle a strategic draw.

The casualties were small compared with later battles, but they were unlike anything either side had imagined possible. The Union public had expected a quick defeat of the South—"On to Richmond!" exhorted the New York editor Horace Greeley, shortly before the battle. The South had likewise expected a short fight, followed by a suit for peace by Washington. But the message from Bull Run, though a Confederate victory, was a shock to both sides: the war would not be short or bloodless. How long, and how bloody, they still could not imagine.

After the fighting, both sides pulled back to recuperate and reconsider strategy. One result of the fighting was the recognition by the Union of how valuable slave labor had been to the Southern fighting machine. On August 6, President Lincoln signed the First Confiscation Act, which allowed Union forces to confiscate slaves from owners who used them in the war effort. The bill's easy passage also signaled a political change afoot—as the war's horizon grew more distant, moderate Republicans, who had supported the conflict as a means of reuniting the country as it had been, began to see the need for more extreme steps to undermine the Confederacy, as well as the possibility of radical changes in the war's aims, including the end of slavery itself.

On August 30, Maj. Gen. John C. Frémont, the St. Louis-based commander of the Union's Western Department, issued an order confiscating all slaves owned by "all persons in the State of Missouri, who shall take up arms against the United States." Though Lincoln quickly rescinded the order, it was yet another critical step, however uncoordinated, in the Union's stumble toward emancipation as a central war aim. Lincoln was, however, moving quickly toward an emancipation agenda of his own: in November he drafted a bill to essentially buy out Delaware's 1,800 slaves.

Another massive battle would not occur until well into 1862, but the post-Bull Run period was hardly peaceful. Fighting continued across Missouri, along the Carolina Coast, and on the far western frontier, where Confederate forces undertook a star-crossed campaign to capture Southern California. The war literally came home for the Union in late October, when the Battle of Ball's Bluff took place just a few miles up the Potomac from the capital. In the wake of the Confederate victory, bloated bodies of fallen Union soldiers were seen bobbing in the water past Georgetown.

Nor were the war's machinations limited to American soil. The Union tightened its naval blockade of Southern ports, while a small but dangerous number of Confederate raiding ships brought havoc to Northern shipping. In Europe, Southern diplomats and spies worked assiduously to win over British, French and Italian politicians in the hopes of gaining recognition—and possibly assistance. The December arrest of two of those diplomats, James Mason and John Slidell, aboard a British ship, the Trent, led to an international incident that nearly set off a war with Britain.

The year ended in relative silence, though a storm was brewing in the West. Union forces, having solidified control of Missouri and Kentucky, were working their way south under the command of an as-yet-unknown officer named Ulysses S. Grant, aimed at Nashville and points south. Perceptive observers north and south knew that the worst was yet to come, and soon.

The Meaning of Bull Run

By EDWARD L. AYERS

O n a hot July morning, exactly 150 years ago, the armies of the barely born Confederacy and the badly shaken United States surrounded the town of Manassas, not far from a creek called Bull Run, for miles around, in every direction. It was a Sunday. Some people thought one major battle would be the very war itself, the beginning and the end, the resolution of decades of arguing over the place of slavery in the future of the United States.

Surely, Confederates thought, their new enemies would see the impossibility of defeating a people so committed to their independence; the United States would be forced to acknowledge the Confederacy's claims to nationhood. Surely, the Northerners thought, their new enemies would realize they could not overcome so vast and wealthy a nation as the United States and would rejoin the union they had helped create. A decisive battle would kill the rebellion in its infancy.

We know now, of course, how wrong both sides were. After all, how could they have imagined what lay before them, the four years and 620,000 American lives, the equivalent of six million lives today? How, too, could they have imagined that the war they began in earnest that day would become a war that would end perpetual bondage for four million people?

Such a profound consequence was far from the minds of people on either side that day, for such a consequence seemed impossible. But had the Civil War turned out differently, American slavery, never stronger than it was in 1861, might have lived on for generations, its survival changing the paths of world history. The significance of this battle, in other words, radiates far beyond the boundaries of the battlefield and far beyond the limits of the single day.

The land itself seemed destined for conflict. Part of it was a farm owned by a free black man, James Robinson. Susan Gaskins, with whom he raised a family even though she was enslaved, bore eight children with James and, as Virginia law dictated, the children took the mother's status as slaves. Susan and her daughters were freed at the death of her owner, and James was able to earn enough money to buy two of their sons, but two other sons were sold to the Lower South by Susan's owner.

Another part of this land was owned by a widow, Judith Carter Henry, who had left much of the farm fallow after her husband's death a few years earlier; it had grown up in cedar and pine. She was 85 years old, an invalid tended by her son, daughter and a young enslaved woman, Lucy Griffith, whom Mrs. Henry hired from a neighboring minister.

Those two families embodied some of the vast and tangled history of slavery in Virginia. Even in Manassas, located in Prince William County and only a few dozen miles to the Mason-Dixon Line, slavery showed no sign of fading away in July 1861. Virginia, despite the sale and exportation of so many thousands of enslaved people to the other Southern states over the preceding generations, remained the largest slave state in the United States, and thus the Confederacy. Prince William County held over a quarter of its population in slavery. In the nearby farms, growing wheat and corn, over 2,000 people lived in slavery, along with about 500 free black men and women. While most of those enslaved people were scattered in ones and twos among the farms here, 68 slaveholders owned more than 10 people each.

But Manassas was more than just a symbol of national strife; Manassas mattered because it was Manassas Junction, where crucial railroads met, connecting northern Virginia with the Shenandoah Valley, the rich Piedmont and the new Confederate capital in Richmond. Railroads, a recent arrival on the American landscape, would become the very sinews of the Civil War. Time and again, battles would rage to seize or protect or destroy a railroad. Trains brought the vast supplies that tens of thousands of men needed to live in the field for months at a time. And trains could bring the reinforcements that could turn a battle when it seemed lost.

The First Battle of Bull Run would also see the first use of a system of semaphore flags to send the equivalent of a Morse code, to transmit complex information across miles; one such message played a critical role in the battle, alerting the Confederates to a surprise Union maneuver. News of the battle—much of it incorrect or wildly exaggerated in one dimension or another—would flash across the continent almost immediately, carried over the new telegraph lines that wove places together just in time to carry news of the country's crisis and bloodshed. In this place, too, the United States would make the first use of balloon reconnaissance, providing a glimpse of the breadth and complexity of the scenes playing out below.

It was a place for other, non-technological firsts as well. Soldiers first heard the rebel yell. The most famous nickname in all American military history would emerge: "Stonewall." And on this battlefield the Confederates would realize they must have a distinctive battle flag, for the first flag of the Confederacy bore too strong a resemblance to the American flag in the confusion of the fighting.

Here, too, people would first see the devastating effects of war on civilians. The Henry house proved to be no shelter at all for the ailing widow Judith Henry, unable to be moved, killed by a shell in her bed, her daughter hiding in the chimney and her hired slave beneath her. That house would be one of countless places destroyed by war. Women would be critical participants in the war, becoming nurses, community leaders, spies and even soldiers as the war consumed one community after another.

But all of that lay ahead on the morning of July 21, 1861. That morning, some of the soldiers were praying, some were boasting. Some were hoping for a fight, some dreading the idea of either shooting or being shot. We need to imagine, if we can, a vast array of men, gathered from all over the country, in the army for only weeks, wearing uniforms that were anything but uniform, enlisting for months rather than years, stretched out for miles, with no way to communicate quickly or effectively. We need to imagine the soldiers as young, their average age 21. We need to imagine a place of unbelievable noise, with the cannon roaring and biting and killing for hour upon hour, with men and horses screaming, with smoke obscuring every line of vision, with the relentless musket fire making it sound as if the woods were burning all around them. "The bursting of shells, the shrieking of cannon balls, the crashing as they splintered the trees . . . would have filled the soul of a warrior with ecstasy," remembered one Virginian. "Not being a warrior but a plain citizen, I saw nothing especially entertaining in such a hubbub. We lay as flat as flounders."

We need to imagine immense confusion, with mistakes and failures and brilliance and bravery all swirled together. On this apparently gentle landscape, small creeks with slippery banks, and rutted roads with narrow bridges presented vast obstacles when thousands of men had to drag wagons and cannon and horses and mules and supplies across them.

In its most general outlines, a sketch of the fighting here is relatively simple. The United States army tried to slide around the Confederate forces to the west, to the ridge right behind us, and then move south to take this flank. Although the United States had greater numbers, they were not coordinated effectively and the Confederates were able to push them back away from Henry Hill. In the afternoon, the final reinforcements arrived, via railroad, from the Shenandoah Valley to your right, and overran the Union forces near here. The first guns fired around dawn and by 4 o'clock in the afternoon had fallen silent as the Union army retreated to Washington. The retreat began in an orderly way, but broke down into chaos as the soldiers struggled to cross Cub Run with massive guns to move and Confederate artillery shells bursting above them. About 50 civilian spectators, members of the Washington elite, male and female, were engulfed by the retreat and the pursuing Confederates. One Congressman from New York was captured and sent to a Richmond prison.

At the time, this battle was understood north and south as a United States defeat, though the two sides lost roughly equal numbers of men—about 5,000 total killed, wounded or missing. The United States was humiliated by the loss and the ragged retreat, but Abraham Lincoln, in office for only a few months, issued calls within the next week for a million men to join the Union cause, this time for three years rather than merely 90 days. Rallied by this defeat, Union men flooded the enlistment offices.

While people far from the battlefield might romanticize the fighting to come, those who were here saw what this war would be. The farms were covered with dead and dying. The stench of fallen horses and men filled the air. Houses and churches and schools for many miles around were turned into desperate hospitals where doctors had few ways to relieve pain or save lives.

A letter from Cpl. Sam Payne of Danville, Va., to his cousin Mollie Woodson, preserved at the Museum of the Confederacy, tells a story that could have been repeated in many variations:

> I can assure you we had a right scarry time of it, the ball[s] whistling around our heads just like a swarm of bees. I expected every minute for one to hit me, but as God would have it not one touched me at all, but several were right at me, my nearest man was shot. . . .

> I went over the field the next day and it was the most horifying sight I ever beheld, numbers were lying wounded on the field some with arms legs & hands shot off all beg[g]ing for help. I gave several of them some water and laid them in the shade. They at first thought that I was going to kill them, but when they found out that I intended to do them no harm, they seemed very much relieved.

One Union soldier had joined to help support his wife and two children, but, Payne wrote, "poor fellow he will never be able to do much now. He had both of his hands shot entirely off by a cannon ball oh the sight was sickening. I hope I shall never again see such a sight."

But Sam Payne would see such sights again, for this battle, the largest the continent had ever witnessed, was soon engulfed by others even more horrible. The young corporal himself would be killed less than a year later as the United States army tried to take Richmond in the Peninsula Campaign. The war brought the armies back to this very place only 13 months after they fought here. The year of 1862 would also witness Shiloh and Antietam, the bloodiest days in a war of many blood-soaked days.

During the year after this battle, Lincoln and some members of his party came to realize that destroying slavery would be essential to defeating the Confederacy. The determined efforts by enslaved people to flee to Union lines—efforts at escape that began even before this battle, in May at Fort Monroe, Va.—revealed their desperate longing for freedom. Slowly, some came to realize that uprooting slavery might help redeem the slaughter of the war and the history of a nation that had so long been built on slavery. Eventually, as black men fought and died for the Union, some would even come to believe in something like equality for African-Americans.

But that was many battles, many lives, many defeats, many victories, in the future. Bull Run. The brief Civil War imagined in 1861 would stretch on longer than people thought they could bear, bringing consequences greater than they could have imagined on that hot July morning 150 years ago. We have inherited the national unity and the end of slavery that war eventually brought. We are all fortunate that the battle fought there did not, as so many hoped and expected, begin and end the American Civil War.

The Southern Cross
By TERRY L. JONES

onfederate Gen. G.T. Beauregard was worried. It was the afternoon of July 21, 1861, and fighting had raged since daylight after General Irwin McDowell's Union army attacked Beauregard from across the small Virginia stream known as Bull Run. The battle seesawed throughout the day, but fresh troops rushed in from the Shenandoah Valley had finally given Beauregard the advantage. Now, just as victory seemed certain, he spied a heavy column of troops more than a mile away maneuvering on his flank.

Beauregard later explained, "At their head waved a flag which I could not distinguish. Even by a strong glass I was

First National Flag of the Confederacy.

unable to determine whether it was the United States flag or the Confederate flag. At this moment I received a dispatch from Capt. [Porter] Alexander, in charge of the signal station, warning me to look out for the left; that a large column was approaching in that direction, and that it was supposed to be Gen. [Robert] Patterson's command coming to reinforce McDowell. At this moment, I must confess, my heart failed me."

Beauregard knew his exhausted men could not withstand a determined flank attack. "I came, reluctantly, to the conclusion that after all our efforts, we should at last be compelled to yield to the enemy the hard fought and bloody field." Beauregard turned to an officer and instructed him to go to the rear and tell Gen. Joseph E. Johnston to prepare the reserves to support the retreat he was about to order. As the officer began to leave, Beauregard had second thoughts and told him to wait a minute so they could make sure that it actually was Yankees bearing down upon them.

It proved to be a fortuitous decision. "I took the glass and again examined the flag. . . . A sudden gust of wind shook out its folds, and I recognized the stars and bars of the Confederate banner."

The mysterious flag turned out to be the Confederacy's First National Flag, which resembled the United States flag in both color and design. It was carried at the head of Col. Harry T. Hays's Seventh Louisiana Volunteers, one of the lead regiments in Col. Jubal Early's brigade that was launching an attack on the Union flank. Hays's second-in-command, Lt. Col. Charles de Choiseul, wrote home after the battle that the regiment happened to carry the national colors that day instead of its blue regimental flag, but he did not explain why. Early's bold attack helped turn the tide, and the First Battle of Bull Run ended in a complete Confederate victory. Few people knew how close Beauregard had come to throwing that victory away simply because he could not identify one of his own side's flags.

As it turned out, Beauregard was not the first person to mistake the Seventh Louisiana for the enemy at Bull Run. In his memoirs, Early wrote that earlier in the day Confederate Gen. David R. Jones saw Hays's regiment approaching his position and he, too, thought it might be the enemy. Early galloped over to confer with Jones and found him scrutinizing the Louisianians through his binoculars and preparing his men to fire on them. Fortunately, Early got there in time to clear up the confusion.

Early also experienced a moment of uncertainty when he prepared to make his flank attack that afternoon. An officer came up to warn him that a Virginia regiment was on the other side of the hill in his front and not to fire on it. Early was sure there were no friendly forces in that position, but he rode ahead to check and saw soldiers dressed in what appeared to be Confederate uniforms. They, too, carried a flag but it lay limp in the dead air, and Early could not tell whether the troops were friend or foe. It was not until Jeb Stuart's horse artillery opened fire on the men and they retreated that Early saw it was a United States flag.

Determined to avoid such cases of mistaken identity on future battlefields, General Beauregard decided the Confederates needed a distinctive national flag. It just so happened that William Porcher Miles, a South Carolina congressman, was serving on Beauregard's staff at the time, and Miles had considerable experience dealing with flag issues.

As chairman of the confederate Committee on the Flag and Seal, Miles had overseen the adoption of the First National Flag a few months earlier. During the committee's deliberations, it became apparent that opinions were split between those who wanted a flag that was similar to the United States because of fond feelings for the old Union and those who wanted something completely different to mark a new beginning. Miles was among the latter, and he submitted a flag design containing a blue St. Andrew's Cross on a red background, with white stars on the cross to represent the Confederate states.

Miles's pattern was based on a South Carolina secession flag that displayed a traditional, or upright, St. George's Cross. However, a Southern Jew objected to the cross and requested of Miles that such a specific religious symbol not be made into a national symbol. Miles agreed to change the design to a St. Andrew's Cross: "It avoided the religious objection about the cross (from the Jews & many Protestant sects), because it did not stand out so conspicuously as if the cross had been placed upright thus."

In the end, the committee rejected Miles's entry and chose a design that was similar to the United States flag. The Confederates' First National Flag would have red and white bars, rather than stripes, and in the upper corner seven white stars (representing the Confederate states at the time) on a blue background. The flag, which became known as the "Stars and Bars," somewhat resembled the original United States flag used during the Revolutionary War.

When, after the Battle of Bull Run, Beauregard mentioned to Miles his desire for a distinctive national flag, Miles told him of his rejected design. Then, acting on behalf of Beauregard, Miles suggested to the Committee on the Flag and Seal that a new national flag be adopted in order to avoid confusion on the battlefield. When the committee refused by a vote of four to one, Beauregard decided there should be two flags.

Beauregard (who by then had embraced the St. Andrew's cross) wrote Gen. Joseph E. Johnston that he had recommended to Miles "that we should have two flags—a peace or parade flag, and a war flag to be used only on the field of battle—but congress having adjourned no action will be taken on the matter—How would it do for us to address the War Dept. on the subject for a supply of Regimental or badge flags made of red with two blue bars crossing each other diagonally on which shall be introduced the stars. . . . We would then on the field of battle know our friends from our Enemies."

Johnston agreed and suggested the battle flag be square instead of rectangular so as to be better proportioned. Beauregard introduced the new banner to his officers at a dinner party on Nov. 27, 1861. A reporter for the Richmond Daily Dispatch attended the event and wrote a detailed account for his readers. After telling the story of the confusion at First Bull Run, Beauregard brought the new flag out. The reporter was impressed and wrote, "The flag itself is a beautiful banner, which, I am sure, before this campaign is over, will be consecrated forever in the affections of the people of the Confederate States."

The next day, the new flags were officially issued to the Virginia army with great ceremony. Shortly afterward, Beauregard was transferred to the Western Theater and the new battle flag took root there as well.

The Southern Cross, as it is sometimes known, was never an official flag of the Confederate government, and it never flew over public buildings, despite what Hollywood might have one believe. Instead, it was simply a military banner that was carried by troops in the field. Nonetheless, it became more popular than the Stars and Bars and was incorporated into the Confederacy's Second and Third National Flags. For 150 years, the Southern Cross has been the symbol of the Rebel cause.

Up in the Air
By RON SOODALTER

The first manned balloon flight took place in France during the early 1780s and, not surprisingly, people began thinking of how to turn the balloon into an implement of war. Within a few years, the French army was using observation balloons in battle, and Benjamin Franklin even suggested that balloons might actually be used to convey soldiers into the fray. In 1849 the Austrian high command sent some 200 unmanned balloons, laden with timed explosives, over Venice. Unfortunately, the wind shifted, carrying them back over the hapless Austrians.

Ballooning caught on in the United States as well, and by the beginning of the Civil War there were several budding "aeronauts," as the balloonists styled themselves, anxious to place their crafts and skill at the disposal of the Federal forces, including an ambitious and highly capable young New Englander named Thaddeus Sobieski Constantine Lowe.

A self-educated former magician's assistant, Lowe had relatively little experience with balloons when the war began, having only built his first craft in 1858. Three years later, he set out to make history by navigating the first manned transatlantic balloon flight. He lifted off in Cincinnati in late April 1861, and made it as far as South Carolina, where the vagaries of wind forced him down—smack in the heart of the newly minted Confederacy. Lowe was immediately arrested by surprised rebels, but they released him when they determined—falsely, as events would prove—that he posed no threat.

Lowe realized the value of what he'd seen from above of rebel troop preparations. Through political connections, he finessed a June 11 meeting with President Lincoln and offered the chief executive a demonstration. Six days later, Lincoln watched as Lowe, in the company of officials from the American Telegraph Company, soared to some 500 feet above Washington's Columbia Armory in the hydrogen-filled balloon Enterprise. Lowe, ever the showman, had rigged the balloon with a telegraph key, and wired the president from aloft, "I have pleasure in sending you this first dispatch ever telegraphed from an aerial station "

Lincoln, a lifelong fan of new technology and desperately seeking an advantage over the enemy, was sold. In a subsequent introductory letter to Winfield Scott, commander of the army, he wrote, "General, this is my friend Professor Lowe who is organizing an aeronautics corps and who is to be its chief. I wish you would facilitate his work in every way." Lincoln authorized the creation of the Balloon Corps, which was staffed by civilians, and attached to the Army's Corps of Topographical Engineers. Lowe was placed in charge at a salary of $10 a day. Lowe went to work on Aug. 2, 1861, eventually constructing seven hydrogen balloons of cord-wrapped and varnished silk cloth. He also designed and built portable hydrogen gas generators for service in the field, making his balloons highly mobile.

Lowe, however, was not the only man who wanted to be the Union's chief aeronaut. One of the first orders for a military balloon went to an experienced Pennsylvania-born pilot, John Wise. For his first—and as it turned out, last—assignment, Wise was charged with observing the enemy at the Battle of First Bull Run. Unfortunately, his craft caught in tree branches en route to Manassas, rendering it useless. By this time, it was too late to contribute to the Union effort during the battle, but perhaps to show off his superior ballooning skills, Lowe went aloft after the fray, impressing the Union brass with his observations of the victorious rebels' troop movements.

At Arlington on Sept. 24, Lowe ascended in the balloon Union to over 1,000 feet, marked enemy troop movements in Falls Church (some three miles away) and relayed the information to the ground by telegraph. The ensuing Union barrage represented the first time in military history that artillery had been accurately used against an unseen enemy. Lowe also devised a method of launching a balloon from the water, by rigging a "flight deck" on a converted coal barge—thus creating the world's first aircraft carrier. He successfully used this system on rivers during the entire Peninsula Campaign. Reportedly, the Yankee aeronauts were so successful in marking rebel activities that some Confederate units banned campfires at night and created dummy camps to deceive the pilots.

Throughout the war, debate raged among aeronauts as to whether balloons should remain in a fixed position, or allowed to float on favorable winds. One of Lowe's competitors, a brassy young New York State native named John La Mountain (or La Montain), floated his balloon directly over enemy positions near Ft. Monroe, Va., sketched what he saw and caught an air current back to the Union lines. Generally, however, balloons were kept tethered—or "captive"—when sent aloft, held earthbound by rows of straining soldiers.

The reasoning was simple: besides providing an irresistible target for enemy (and, in some cases, friendly) fire, an unattached balloon was at the mercy of the winds, and, as Lowe himself had found, wind currents were neither predictable nor fully understood at the time. The Confederates discovered this for themselves when they created a much-abridged version of Lowe's Balloon Corps. Using multi-colored silk that, according to legend, had been designated for the manufacture of women's attire, the rebels constructed two hot-air "silk dress balloons." One escaped its tether, floated directly to the Yankees, and was captured. (The other was taken by the enemy as well, when the rebel tugboat that was towing it ran aground.)

While serving with the Topographical Engineers, the Balloon Corps was also invaluable in creating maps of the local terrain. The importance, and lack, of accurate maps during the Civil War cannot be exaggerated. When the war began, neither side had current or reliable information on the terrain—a problem that was neither easily nor speedily resolved. In 1862, Gen. George McClellan observed, "Correct local maps were not to be found, and the country, though known in its general features, we found to be inaccurately described in essential particulars." Frequently, both armies relied almost exclusively on the intelligence gathered by scouts—and no terrestrial observer could come close to the intelligence available to the Balloon Corps.

Despite the Balloon Corps' many contributions throughout numerous battles and campaigns, Army officers always viewed it with ambivalence. Despite the active support and encouragement of such highly placed generals as McClellan and Irvin McDowell, a large number of officers—often far from the front and unfamiliar with the workings of the Corps—tended to see the balloons as useless, and the pilots as a gaggle of unruly, overpaid civilians. The military didn't know how best to use the crafts, or, for that matter, where to house them.

The Army transferred the balloons to the Army Corps of Engineers in early 1863 and placed a non-aeronaut, Capt. Cyrus B. Comstock, in charge. He had no use for Lowe or his creations, and wasted no time in cutting the Corps' budget and drastically reducing Lowe's salary. Lowe quit in disgust in May, and by early August, bereft of both adequate funding and Lowe's inspired leadership, the Balloon Corps itself was no more.

The reappearance of observation balloons in American warfare would have to wait until World War I, during which the United States military created the Aeronaut Badge, to be worn by balloon pilots. The insignia, which would in time become known as the Balloon Pilot Badge, featured a winged balloon, across which were embossed the letters, "U.S." Thaddeus Lowe would have been pleased.

How to Lose Allies and Alienate People
By AMANDA FOREMAN

One of the more common misconceptions about the Civil War is that the world (meaning Europe and, in particular, Britain) favored a Southern victory because of its dependence on cotton. The economic data appears to provide incontrovertible evidence: the livelihood of one in five Britons was connected in some way to the textile trade.

But, while admittedly a powerful motivator in foreign reactions to the war, cotton was not king. In fact, during the first four months of the conflict, when Britain's response to secession was still maturing, the South's threat to withhold cotton until its independence was recognized caused far less anxiety than the bellicose threats emanating from the Union's secretary of state, William Henry Seward. One of the great tragedies of the Civil War is that Secretary Seward's crass resort to "spread eagle nationalism" at the beginning of the conflict turned Britain from being potentially decisive ally into a hostile neutral.

In April 1861 it was well known among the expatriate circles in Washington that the British minister, Lord Lyons, was "strong for the Union." But at that moment, Seward could not or would not see the signals. Tormented by his declining political influence over President Lincoln, Seward became obsessed with reasserting his once legendary authority in Washington. One byproduct of the Secretary's inner turmoil was a bizarre memorandum delivered to Lincoln's office on April 1, which argued that a foreign war was the only salvation for the Union. Seward proposed to reunite the country by creating an external threat—in his words, to "change the question before the Public from one upon Slavery . . . to one of Patriotism or Union."

Lincoln dismissed the proposal, but somehow its broad contents became known to the diplomatic community. Worse was to follow. The Republican-dominated Congress had just passed a series of highly punitive import taxes on European goods, known as the Morrill Act, with no thought about how such economic warfare would be regarded abroad. Soon after came the Confederate attack on Fort Sumter, and Lincoln's declaration that all Southern ports were under a federal blockade.

Both these developments required careful handling by the State Department. But instead of reassuring the diplomatic community, Seward was aggressively dismissive about the Morrill Act, and careless to the point of fatally negligent with regard to the legalities of the blockade. Neither the American legations abroad, for example, nor the diplomatic community in Washington was given advance warning of its implementation. Ministers who called at the State Department to discuss the situation met with threats and insults from Seward. Lord Lyons was told that if he wished to maintain peace with America he must refrain from describing Southern secession as a civil war. Diplomats were left wondering who was the real target of Washington's aggression.

The French minister, Henri Mercier, urged his colleagues to ignore the blockade, but Lyons vigorously lobbied against the idea, pointing out that such a blatant act would "entail utter ruin upon the [Northern] Administration and their supporters." Lyons wished he could have gone further; however, after another blistering confrontation with Seward, he wrote on May 6: "I confess I can see no better policy for us than a strict impartiality for the present The sympathies of an Englishman are naturally inclined towards the North—but I am afraid we should find that anything like a quasi-alliance with the men in office here, would place us in a position which would soon become untenable . . . my feeling against Slavery might lead me to desire to co-operate with them. But I conceive all chance of this to be gone for ever."

If Seward does not "pick a quarrel with us," wrote Lyons on another occasion, it would not be because "of the insanity which doing so at this crisis . . . would seem to indicate." He thought Seward had no intention of "conciliating the European Powers or at all events of not forcing them into hostility." British newspapers reached the same conclusion after Seward allowed William Howard Russell, a correspondent for the London Times, to see his latest message to the British foreign secretary: "The tone of the paper was hostile," reported Russell, "there was an undercurrent of menace through it, and it contained insinuations that Great Britain would interfere to split up the Republic, if she could, and was pleased at the prospect of the dangers which threatened it."

When these developments became known in England, even pro-Northern journals like the Spectator magazine complained, "The Americans are, for the moment, transported beyond the influence of common sense. With all of England sympathising, more or less heartily, with the North, they persist in regarding her as an enemy, and seem positively anxious to change an ally . . . into an open and dangerous foe." The pro-Northern journalist and social reformer Harriet Martineau blamed Seward for having allowed the passage of the Morrill tariff, since the bill was practically "inviting the world to support the Confederate cause." The New York banker August Belmont heard the complaints first-hand; during an unsuccessful visit to England to drum up interest in Union bonds, he was repeatedly asked to justify Congress's attack on British trade. Prime Minister Lord Palmerston told him at a private meeting: "We do not like slavery, but we want cotton, and we dislike very much your Morrill tariff."

Seward's discovery that his actions had led to British reluctance to do business with the North, let alone provide military or moral support, came as a rude shock to him. Two days before the Battle of Bull Run, on July 19, the secretary paid a private visit to the British legation. He "proceeded, with some hesitation," reported Lord Lyons, "and with an injunction to me to be secret," to explain "that he had used strong language in his earlier communications to Foreign Powers . . . from the necessity of making them clearly understand the state of Public Feeling here." Seward added that his only motive had been to prevent disunion, not begin a foreign war. "I was not altogether unprepared for the change in Mr Seward's tone," Lyons admitted, having heard from the French legation that Seward had made a similar speech to Mercier a few hours earlier.

The change in Seward's approach did not long survive the Confederate victory at Bull Run. In September, Lyon informed London that Seward was once again whipping up a public storm against Britain. "If he is in his present mood, he will be glad to find a pretext for performing other half-violent acts." But, Lyons added despondently, "this cannot go on forever." Some incident, he predicted, would push the war of words into a war of arms. Two months later Capt. Charles Wilkes instigated such an incident when he dragged two Confederate envoys off the Trent, a British mail boat bound for England, and took them back to Boston. London issued an ultimatum: the Confederates' release, or war.

It is important to stress that as the Civil War progressed, myriad factors affected the North's relationship with Britain. Moreover, Seward transformed over the four years to become the single most important instrument for peace between the two countries. But his early mistakes cost the Union dear. The trajectory of the war would have been quite different if, from the outset, Washington and London had been allied and agreed on a joint policy to prevent the South from using British ports, credit and war materiel. In the early months, as Charles Francis Adams Jr., the son of the American minister to London, later wrote, Seward had "found himself fairly beyond his depth; and he plunged! The foreign-war panacea took possession of him; and he yielded to it."

The Civil War and Literature

By CYNTHIA WACHTELL

Who among us has sent an unsolicited war poem to The New York Times? Yet unsolicited poetry flooded into the newspapers of the Civil War era in such abundance that one cash-strapped Southern paper threatened to charge the same rate to publish the verse that it charged to publish obituaries. Poetry held currency during the Civil War, even if that currency was calculated in soon-to-be-worthless Confederate dollars.

It is hard for modern readers to understan d the centrality of war poetry to Civil War literature. Our recent wars in Iraq and Afghanistan have sparked no popular songs nor filled our newspapers with verse. But in the age before newspaper photography, newsreels, radio, television and the Internet, the couplet, quatrain and octet held great sway.

The passion for verse wasn't limited to newsprint. Collections of war poetry began to appear soon after the conflict began. In June 1861, a mere two months after the start of fighting, "Chimes of Freedom and Union: A Collection of Poems for the Times" was published in Boston, with contributions by literary luminaries like Harriet Beecher Stowe, Oliver Wendell Holmes Sr. and John Greenleaf Whittier. Once the war was over, the editor of "The Southern Amaranth"—a 648-page anthology of Confederate war verse, honoring "the memories of the brave men who perished in

the late ineffectual effort for SOUTHERN INDEPENDENCE"—
expressed her deep "regret that a vast number of beautiful and
worthy productions are compelled for want of space to be crowded
out of this volume."

War literature, especially poetry, written during the Civil War
was highly romantic. Soldiers marched gallantly into the fray. They
fell as brave heroes. They were buried in tidy graves and remembered as valiant martyrs. In popular war poetry, the conflict was
presented in terms that admitted no moral ambiguity, no cynicism,
no doubt. Whether written by a Northerner or Southerner, the verse
of the era made clear that God was on "our" side. The cause of
righteousness was being served.

Literary realism had not yet gained traction in America, and the
irony, anger and dark humor that would come to define popular war
literature in the 20th century still lay far in the future. "Catch-22"
was as yet unwritten, and the only Battle of Verdun known to the
Civil War generation was the one fought in 1792 between French
Revolutionary forces and the Prussian Army.

Instead, the poetry of the Civil War served to allay the fears
and doubts of those left at home and of those who had headed off
to battle. Writers painted an image of war that was at once orderly,
inspiring and embellished. They imparted profound meaning to
each death, each family's sacrifice. The deaths of favorite generals
invited tremendous poetic outpourings, but even the deaths of less
loved leaders received poetic flourish.

Consider a representation of Gen. Albert Sidney Johnston's
death that appears in "The Southern Amaranth." Johnston, the
ranking field general in the Confederate Army, died on April 6,
1862, from a wound received while leading a charge on horseback
during the Battle of Shiloh. (He was struck on the back of his knee,
quite possibly by "friendly fire," and bled to death.) The poem
"General Albert Sidney Johnston," by the amateur poet James L.
Bowen of Virginia, reads in part:

> He sank upon the battle field,
> To take the warrior's final rest!

As ebbed his life-blood on the plain
The martyr cast one parting glance

Upon his comrades in the fight,
And cried, "Brave men once more advance!"

Note the use of the verb "sank" to describe the general's death. Boats sink. Hopes sink. But men killed in combat? The word—like so many others used by the Civil War era poets—tidily evades the raw reality of battlefield deaths. The description of Johnston as a "martyr" is also especially interesting, given that Johnston had been accused of incompetency and harshly assailed in Southern newspapers, following the fall of Fort Donelson and Fort Henry, in the weeks preceding his death.

In Civil War poetry all men are given good deaths and allowed to speak fine final words. No men are disemboweled, shot in the genitals, or otherwise immodestly mangled. No men suffer alone in agony on the battlefield or in the field hospital.

When Walt Whitman arrived in Fredericksburg, Va., in late December 1862, soon after approximately 12,500 Union fighters had been injured or killed in battle there, he came upon a horrific sight. As he confided in his journal, "A heap of feet, legs, arms, and human fragments, cut, bloody, black and blue, swelled and sickening" lay bleakly beneath a tree in front of an improvised field hospital. As he later assessed, the pile would have made "a full load for a one-horse cart."

It is a scene that lays bare the awful consequences of the war. And it is a scene not all that unlike one that appears in the recent Steven Spielberg film "Lincoln." Home from Harvard and eager to join the army, Robert Lincoln, the president's oldest son, is aghast to see a wheelbarrow full of severed limbs unceremoniously dumped outside a military hospital.

No piles of severed limbs—whether by the cartful or barrowful—appear in the popular literature of the Civil War. The era's writers shared a common inclination to spare readers the worst aspects of the conflict. Through a tacit understanding, they avoided depicting scenes of gore and instead presented scenes of determination, resilience and glory. Indeed, the fact that a barrowful of gore made it into Mr. Spielberg's film but not into the popular literature of the war era speaks volumes to how the aesthetic sensibility of the Civil War generation differs from our own.

Squeezing the South into Submission
By MICHAEL O. VARHOLA

Though the Union army was still getting its war footing, by August 1861 the Northern blockade of Southern ports and waterways was almost complete. That month federal ships closed the Mississippi River to commerce between loyal and secessionist states, while naval squadrons were in place off the coast of most Southern cities, from south Texas to the Chesapeake. President Lincoln had approved the blockade, known as the "Anaconda Plan," in April. At first it was widely derided in the North and dismissed in the South—the American navy, people said, was in no shape to clamp down on thousands and thousands of miles of coastline. Nevertheless, this massive operation had an immediate impact on the Confederate economy and, as it tightened its grip on the Southern coastline, began to choke the South into submission.

That is not to say that the blockade was perfect; in fact, scholars since have pointed to the seemingly large number of blockade runners who managed to slip past the Union ships. But the relevant data point is not how many ships evaded capture, but how many ships never sailed that, undeterred, otherwise would have. From that point of view, the blockade was an unimpeachable success: blockade runners only accounted for about five percent of the regular incoming and outbound trade that would have otherwise been conducted.

Moreover, these were commercial ventures, unguided by some overarching strategy in Richmond. Not surprisingly, they were disproportionately concerned with the importation of luxury goods, which were much more valuable by volume than commodities but which did little to actually support the Southern war effort. And the South desperately needed commodities, particularly foodstuffs: while the South had an agricultural economy, most of what it grew were cash crops like cotton and tobacco, and it imported great quantities of food from both the northern United States and overseas.

"From the beginning, the blockade reduced food imports into the South," writes the historian Andrew F. Smith in "Starving the South: How the North Won the Civil War." "Coffee, tea, spices, and wine quickly became difficult to acquire. More important losses from a nutritional standpoint were apples and dairy products, such as butter and cheese, which had been imported from New England; citrus fruits, dates, pineapples, and vegetables, which had been imported from Bermuda and the Caribbean Islands became scarce, as did salt which had been mainly imported from abroad before the war." With the halt of trade between the two halves of the country via the Mississippi, the South also lost its imports of grain from the Midwest.

Southerners also depended on external trade to provide most of their manufactured goods, including ones made from raw materials they produced. While the South grew more cotton than any other region in the world at the start of the Civil War, there were single towns in New England that produced more cloth in their mills than all those of the Confederacy combined.

But it was the loss of salt—most of it brought from Wales as ballast in ships—that perhaps most profoundly affected the South, because it was so critical in the preservation of food, particularly meat. Without adequate supplies of salt, Southern pork and beef could not be preserved and then sent from the areas where it was produced to the places where it was needed—particularly cities and wherever the rebel armies were located. The Confederate government encouraged domestic salt production but, despite some dramatic local successes, this never came anywhere near to meeting the South's civil or military needs.

"The obtaining of salt became extremely difficult when the war had cut off our supply," wrote the Alabama native Parthenia Antoinette Hague of her wartime experiences:

This was true especially in regions remote from the seacoast and border states, such as the interior of Alabama and Georgia. Here again we were obliged to have recourse to whatever expedient ingenuity suggested. All the brine left in troughs and barrels, where pork had been salted down, was carefully dipped up, boiled down, and converted into salt again. In some cases the salty soil under old smokehouses was dug up and placed in hoppers, which resembled backwoods ash-hoppers.

While the blockade precipitated increasingly severe and widespread shortages throughout the South, numerous other factors exacerbated their effects: the diversion of resources to the Confederate armies; the decrease in food production caused by so many ablebodied men being put under arms; wastage in areas exposed to combat; deliberate destruction of agricultural production by Union forces in occupied regions and coastal areas; reduced production caused by the flight or liberation of plantation slaves; the migration of refugees, many of whom had previously been involved in food production, from occupied zones into urban areas; and the degradation of the Southern railroad system.

Indeed, the blockade of Southern ports did not just shut down trade with third parties, it also curtailed coastal trade within the Confederacy itself and made such commerce dependent on other modes of transportation, primarily the railroads. Even as more strain was being placed upon the rail system, however, the non-industrialized South was less and less able to adequately maintain or repair them.

The 10 percent of Southerners who lived in urban areas were the first and most severely affected by shortages, and actual starvation threatened the populations of cities like New Orleans by midsummer 1861. Rural folk of all economic levels, black and white, were at least able to fall back on subsistence farming (though everyone was subject to being shaken down by commissaries collecting foodstuffs for the armies in the field).

The Confederate government did try to encourage plantation owners to curtail cotton production and shift over to food crops. While it had some limited success in this endeavor, the nature of the secessionist government, with its states' rights-centered constitution, was such that it did not force the issue, and most planters followed what they thought was still the path to profit and continued to grow cotton.

Aside from the effects of war and the blockade, Southerners also had to contend with maldistribution. In fact, throughout the conflict the South produced enough food for its civilians and soldiers, but it found it increasingly difficult to preserve surpluses and move them to areas of scarcity. Besides the preservation problem, interdiction of coastal traffic also meant that transportation of goods depended on the South's rickety railroad system, which was never adequate to the demands placed upon it. Confederate armies, at the far end of the supply lines, were nearly always short of food and materiel, especially as the war progressed.

Shortages led to inflation and, as the price of foodstuffs spiked, buying power steadily decreased, by about a sixth during the first year of the conflict. Increases in prices were especially marked in areas close to the front lines, where food distribution was directly affected by the fighting. A typical Southern family's food bill was $6.65 per month at the time of secession, $68 per month in 1863, and $400 per month in 1864. Indeed, by the spring of 1863, prices for food and dry goods were going up about 10 percent a month. Butter that cost 20 cents a pound when secession was declared commanded seven times as much a year later—and up to 100 times as much in some locales, if it was available at all, during the last year of the war. Untenable prices led to outbursts of civil unrest and incidents, ranging from the looting of supply trains to bread riots in Richmond and other Southern cities.

Before the first summer of the war was over, Southerners had already begun to suffer the effects of shortages imposed by the conflict. Few could conceive, however, just how severe the privations they would ultimately have to endure would become in the months and long years that followed.

The Wild Rose of Washington

By CATE LINEBERRY

Rose Greenhow

Washington, Aug. 23, 1861

Just before 11 a.m., Rose O'Neal Greenhow, a dark-haired, dark-eyed Washington widow in her 40s, walked toward her house on 16th Street. Greenhow circulated among the capital's elite social circles, and her home stood within sight of the White House. Despite the sweltering heat, she stopped to talk with a neighbor. A Union guard, she learned, had been placed in front of Greenhow's house earlier that morning.

Greenhow looked around and saw two men, one in uniform, watching her on the other side of the street. Just then an associate passed her by. "Those men will probably arrest me," she said. "Walk to Corcoran's corner and see. If I raise a handkerchief to my face, give out the information." She then removed a handwritten note from her pocket, put it in her mouth, and swallowed it before going to the home she shared with her eight-year-old daughter, Little Rose.

As Greenhow reached her front door, Allan Pinkerton, the famed Chicago detective, raced toward her with one of his men. Now in charge of counterintelligence in Washington for Gen. George B. McClellan and disguised as his nom de guerre, Maj. E.J. Allen, Pinkerton announced her arrest. While Greenhow demanded to see a warrant, she wiped her cheek with her handkerchief. Satisfied that her signal had been seen, she turned back to Pinkerton. "I have no power to resist you, but had I been inside of my house, I would have killed one of you before I submitted to this illegal process," she said.

Greenhow was already well-known as a fervent supporter of the Confederacy. But Pinkerton was arresting her for more than her inconvenient political leanings. She was also one of the South's most valuable spies.

Though the Civil War began on April 12, 1861, by then the South had spent months preparing a network of spies across the North, concentrated in Washington. Much of the groundwork in the capital was done by Capt. Thomas Jordan, at the time still an officer in the United States army. Knowing of Greenhow's sympathies and social position, he recruited her to lead the spy ring. As one of the premier hostesses in the city and a longtime friend of former President James Buchanan, Greenhow frequently entertained members of Congress and diplomats with elaborate dinner parties. She was also known for her beauty and charm, which she willingly used to get tight-lipped men to talk.

Greenhow was also familiar with tragedy, which likely added to her resolve to risk everything for the Confederacy. Born in southern Maryland to a wealthy family and nicknamed "Wild Rose," her father had been murdered by one of his slaves when Greenhow was still a girl. She and her siblings were separated and sent to live with relatives. In 1854, her husband was killed in an accident, and by August of 1861, five of the eight children she'd given birth to were dead. Her daughter Gertrude, who suffered for months from typhoid fever, had died that spring.

In the few months since the war began, Greenhow had already proved herself as an effective spymaster. In addition to passing along critical information collected by her agents, she used her sources to find out when the Union Army would march south to attack Manassas. On July 9, Greenhow sent a coded message to Gen. Gustave Toutant Beauregard, commander of Confederate forces in Northern Virginia, through her 16-year-old courier, Bettie Duvall. Duvall carried Greenhow's coded message in a black silk purse tucked in a chignon at the nape of her neck; she drove a wooden milk cart 20 miles through Union territory until she reached Beauregard's headquarters. The Confederates won the battle largely because Greenhow's message gave Beauregard time to request more troops. After the battle, Greenhow received a note from Richmond: "Our President and our General direct me to thank you. The Confederacy owes you a debt."

But now the game was up. On this hot August day, detectives escorted Greenhow into her house and ransacked her home. While they collected letters and notes that implicated her as a spy, Greenhow went to her bedroom under the guise of changing her clothes. As soon as she was alone, she destroyed papers she'd been carrying, including the cipher she used to communicate with Manassas.

The detectives arrested other women that day for "corresponding with the enemy" and within a week sent them to Greenhow's home, which would become known as "The House of Detention for Female Rebels." Newspapers called it "Fort Greenhow." Guards camped out for another week while they searched every corner of the house, tossing everything in their path, including the personal effects of Greenhow's recently deceased daughter.

For nearly five months, Greenhow was kept under house arrest with Little Rose. She was interrogated daily. Despite her confinement, some of her intelligence, gleaned from the guards or visitors, continued to reach Confederate headquarters. Pinkerton wrote, "She has not ceased to lay plans, to attempt the bribery of officers having her in charge, to make use of signs from the windows of her house to her friends on the street, to communicate with such friends and through them to the rebels." She even wrote a biting letter to Secretary of State William Seward, complaining about her poor treatment, and sent a copy of the letter to a Richmond newspaper. Seward and other Union officials were embarrassed and furious.

On Jan. 18, 1862, Pinkerton, having grown tired of Greenhow's behavior, insisted that all paper be removed from her home and the windows boarded up. In the late afternoon, Greenhow, Little Rose and another female prisoner were transferred to the military prison on Capitol Hill under the gaze of newspaper reporters. As the notorious spy left her home, she said to one of the guards, "I trust that in the future you may have a nobler employment than that of guarding defenseless women."

The women were the first females to arrive at the prison, which was packed with Confederate soldiers and crawling with vermin and disease. Greenhow's elitist and racist attitude, as well as her open disdain for the guards, only made her situation worse. She wasn't allowed out of her room for the first three months.

After five months of house arrest and more than four months in prison, Greenhow was finally brought before a commission to decide her fate. They finally agreed to release her, along with her young daughter, on the condition that Greenhow stayed in the South until the war was over.

The South greeted her as a heroine, and President Jefferson Davis asked her to travel to Europe on a diplomatic mission. While she championed the Confederacy overseas, she published her memoir, "My Imprisonment and the First Year of Abolition Rule at Washington." Her earnings were intended to be donated to the Confederacy.

On her way back to the South in October 1864, Greenhow's blockade runner, the Condor, encountered Northern forces and ran aground on Federal shoals. Despite the captain's warning, Greenhow insisted on trying to escape in a rowboat with several others. Wearing a heavy black silk dress, Greenhow carried dispatches and about $2,000 in gold from her book. Waves quickly battered the small boat and tossed its crew into the water. Greenhow drowned, carried under by the weight of the gold. Her body washed ashore the next morning; she was given a hero's funeral and buried in Oakdale Cemetery in Wilmington, N.C.

Go West, Young Confederacy

By RICHARD PARKER and NATALIE POSGATE

In the blistering August heat of 1861, an ambitious 45-year-old officer arrived in the dusty streets of San Antonio to organize one of the most daring Confederate offensives of the Civil War.

Freshly promoted to brigadier general by none other than President Jefferson Davis, Henry Hopkins Sibley was a distinguished soldier who had spent 22 years in the West. And Davis was suitably impressed with his plan: to cross 1,300 miles of forbidding desert, capturing New Mexico, present-day Arizona, the California gold fields, and the ports of San Francisco and San Diego.

If it succeeded, Davis and the Confederate leadership reasoned, the invasion could change the war overnight. Instead of a small number of states along the East and Gulf Coasts, hemmed in by the Union Navy's increasingly effective blockade, the Confederacy would at once be transformed into a Pacific power. The shackles of the blockade smashed, the South would trade with the world at will as gold poured into its coffers. A Confederate dream shimmered in that desert. Yet it would turn out to be a disastrous mirage.

Sibley was no homegrown Texas Ranger or state militia officer; when war called, increasingly in the West, Sibley answered. A Louisianan born to the influential physician and western explorer Samuel Hopkins Sibley, Henry was an 1838 graduate of West Point. He fought the Seminole in Florida. In Mexico, he fought bravely near Veracruz. After the Mexican War Sibley fought the Comanche in Texas and the Navajo in the New Mexico Territory. He pursued Mormons in the Utah Territory and quelled violence over slavery in Kansas.

When war broke out, Sibley was at Fort Union, in the New Mexico Territory. He knew where his loyalties lay, and he immediately resigned his Union commission. He then headed across the continent to see the Confederate president with his plan to strike west.

In hindsight, many would see the invasion of New Mexico as Sibley's grandiose vision. But in reality, Davis had seized upon a big Western offensive even before Sibley set foot in Richmond. A West Point graduate himself, Davis appears to have been influenced at the academy by the writings of Antoine Henri Jomini, a Swiss officer under Napoleon who coined the phrase "the offensive-defensive": a curious combination of a generally defensive posture that didn't wait on the enemy to seize the initiative. And Davis clearly had an appreciation for the riches on the frontier: in the Senate he had proposed that slave labor be imported for both mining and agriculture in the West.

As president of the Confederacy, Davis had at first said there was no Confederate interest in invading the West. But there were Confederate sympathizers in both Arizona and California, and they proved a handy excuse. Even the Union commander there reported that there were at least 20,000 sympathizers in California, and if the Confederacy "should ever get an organized force into this State, as a rallying point for all the secession element, it would inevitably inaugurate a civil war here immediately."

At his inauguration in Washington in March, President Lincoln seemed to anticipate the Confederate designs on the West, noting that the Constitution still applied to all states—and territories—that had not seceded. In April, Davis met with Secretary of War Leroy Pope Walker, where the two discussed not just the importance of defending Texas but how annexing New Mexico and Arizona would improve the situation.

Sibley presented his plan to the president in July. Raising a force at San Antonio, he would march 600 miles across the Hill Country, the Edwards Plateau and the Chihuahuan Desert to El Paso, settling into Fort Bliss. Already a small rebel force, the Second Texas Mounted Rifles under Lt. Col. John R. Baylor, had dashed into far southern New Mexico, linked up with Arizona confederates and defeated a small Union force.

Sibley proposed to vastly expand upon Baylor's initial—if modest—success. With a brigade of 2,500 men, he would move north, up the Rio Grande into New Mexico before striking west. The detour would be necessary because supply lines to El Paso would have already been stretched and nearly exhausted; Sibley's entire strategy depended upon seizing supplies from his Union enemies to keep his force headed westward to California.

Despite the huge risk of depending upon the enemy for supplies, Davis reasoned that it could work: it took only 1,500 soldiers to capture Santa Fe in 1846, after all. He approved the expedition and gave Sibley command of the Confederate Army of New Mexico. But not everyone would share this sunny perspective. The march up the Rio Grande had been fraught with danger for centuries. With burning desert on either side of the river and Apache lurking along its banks, the Spanish named this track northward the Jornada del Muerto—the Journey of Death.

Upon returning to Texas, Sibley found plenty of doubt there as well. Gov. Edward Clark was slow to provide troops. Military units not provided by the governor said they were waiting on orders. And the Texans worried about sending so many troops out West even as they feared an invasion from the sea, where they were hurriedly reinforcing shore batteries. Meanwhile, Sibley went about scratching up troops for his brigade where he could, drilling in the San Antonio sun.

John Shropshire, a 28-year-old volunteer officer, would be among them. Having left his family's cotton plantation in Columbus, Tex., he wrote home:

> My Dear Carrie,
>
> We are now stationed about 8 miles from San Antonio where we will probably remain 4 or 8 weeks. We have been mustered into the Confederate Army for the indefinite period of the war. When we will get back I can't tell. . . Remember me to all.
>
> Your, John

Tragically for his family, Shropshire would be one of many Texans not to return. Indeed, nearly a third of the 2,500-man brigade would die in New Mexico. The initial dash up the Rio Grande was followed by a ruinous defeat at Glorieta Pass, near Fort Union—where those precious supplies were lost—and a frantic retreat. The sheer boldness of the plan that Sibley and Davis hatched would be its undoing.

The proud general, Sibley, would make it back to Texas, but his reputation would be destroyed. Stripped of his command, he would be a broken man whose remaining years were filled with his only real battle, a losing one with the bottle. And it would all be the result of that bold but foolhardy invasion of the West.

The Star-Spangled Bummer

By ALBIN J. KOWALEWSKI

Music was everywhere in the North, it seemed during the summer of 1861. From presidential appearances to Union rallies, everyone was singing—usually emotional versions of "Yankee Doodle," or "Hail, Columbia" or the "Star-Spangled Banner." It's forgotten today, but in 1861 America didn't have an official national anthem; each one of those songs functioned more or less informally as the nation's rallying cry at some point in its history.

The problem was, few could agree which one, if any, was popular enough to stand as the country's official song—at a time when more and more people thought it needed one. In response, a group of Manhattan powerbrokers—lawyers, politicians, businessmen, scholars, and a former senator and New York governor—who called themselves the National Hymn Committee, decided to find a new, official anthem.

The committee wrote off the three existing contenders immediately: "Yankee Doodle" was "childish," they said. "Hail, Columbia" was "pretentious." The "Star-Spangled Banner" was just too hard to sing—indeed, according to the committee's spokesman, Richard Grant White, they found it "to be almost useless."

The committee turned to the literary public for help. From mid-May to early August, it held a contest challenging Yankee poets to compose "a national hymn or popular and patriotic song appealing to the national heart," as George Templeton Strong, a committee member, described it. The competition would be judged blindly, and the committee retained the rights to publish and market the entries, the proceeds of which would go to the local "Patriotic Fund." To the winner, however, the 13 committeemen promised $500 and the thanks of a grateful nation.

Though the hymn committee sought something with lasting appeal—something more than "a war song," it said—it was no coincidence that the competition took place early in the conflict. The "Star-Spangled Banner" was arguably the most-recognizable song in the Union, but in the context of the Civil War it suddenly felt out of place. It dated to the War of 1812 and had ridden the wave of popular nationalism that followed America's second war with the British. But after nearly two generations of contentious and equivocal compromise over slavery, many northerners were leaving that earlier world behind. Writing a new national anthem seemed a logical next step for a country in the process of reinventing itself. After all, White recalled that summer, following the Confederate attack on Fort Sumter "we all found ourselves side by side with one feeling, one purpose, forgetful of the past, absorbed in the present and the future."

It quickly became clear that many northerners shared in the hymn committee's opinions. Within six weeks of the contest's announcement, the committee had received 1,275 entries ("Four or five huge bales of patriotic hymnology," according to Strong) from as far afield as California and even Italy.

Over the next month and a half, the committee—assisted by an organist and choir—met to review the submissions. Its roster was a who's who of Manhattan's upper crust, but never once, it appears, did the full committee meet together. One member, John A. Dix, a former treasury secretary and now Union general, couldn't even attend. He was too busy maintaining law and order from his post at Fort McHenry in Maryland, where, just weeks after missing the hymn committee's first round of judging, he imprisoned Baltimore editor Frank Key Howard on charges of disloyalty. Howard, coincidentally, was the grandson of Francis Scott Key, the author of the "Star-Spangled Banner."

Unlike the committee members, little is known about the musicians and poets who scratched out those thousands of lines of verse. Because the judges promptly discarded most of the submissions, the authors' identities disappeared as well. But what we do know reveals a general cross section of northern society. The participants included the well educated and barely literate, the provincial and the worldly, ministers and musicians, and a middle-aged woman named Julia Ward Howe— who had yet to write her legendary "Battle Hymn of the Republic."

Likewise, the few of their poems that do exist convey a range of emotion: vengeance, militancy, confidence and optimism. They had such titles as "Union Forever," "The Ballot-Box," "Freedom's Jubilee," "Liberty's Beacon" and "1861." Many sought divine inspiration, though others offered comic relief. Some championed the war as "freedom's second birth," while others spoke of finding comfort in the "shades of our forefathers." One imaginative soul even set the Declaration of Independence to rhyme.

The problem was, the committee couldn't agree on a clear winner. But not because there were so many good options—rather, it was because there were hardly any. On Aug. 9, 1861, the hymn committee announced that it couldn't, in all fairness, choose a winner. "Although some of [the songs] have a degree of poetic excellence which will probably place them high in public favor as lyrical compositions," it said in The New York Times, "no one of them is well suited for a National Hymn." Strong was more blunt in private: most poems were "rubbish."

The controversy, however, didn't end there. The criticism from northern literary circles came hard and fast, and many agreed with Harper's Weekly that patriotism couldn't be "made to order." Not to be outdone, the committee itself refused to let the issue die. A few of the poems had been saved, and that fall Richard Grant White published them—good and bad—in the book "National Hymns: How They Are Written and How They Are Not Written, A Lyric and National Study for the Times." The volume was both a meditation on music and nationalism and a clarification of the committee's decision. Strangely enough, many newspapers gave the book rather positive reviews. Like most, the Christian Advocate and Journal appreciated the wartime gallows humor. "The worst [anthems]," it said, "will doubtless be the most entertaining."

Such cynicism didn't last long. Within months, the "Battle Hymn of the Republic" would hit the North, capturing the Union's voice in biblical terms unlike anything the hymn committee could have ever imagined.

The north would continue writing music throughout the war, but when it counted most many Yankees simply fell back on the songs they knew best. Roughly four years after his stint on the hymn committee, George Templeton Strong overheard something remarkable in the streets of New York. Richmond had just fallen to Union forces, and crowds began to fill Wall Street near the offices of the Commercial Advertiser:

> Never before did I hear cheering that came straight from the heart. . . . They sang "Old Hundred," the Doxology, "John Brown," and "The Star-Spangled Banner," repeating the last two lines of Key's song over and over, with a massive roar from the crowd and a unanimous wave of hats at the end of each repetition. I think I shall never lose the impression made by this rude, many-voiced chorale. It seemed a revelation of profound national feeling, underlying all our vulgarisms and corruptions, and vouchsafed to us in their very focus and centre, in Wall Street itself.

In 1931, as the Great Depression again tested the country's resolve, the "Star-Spangled Banner" was signed into law as America's official national anthem.

The First Emancipation Proclamation

By MICHAEL FELLMAN

O n Aug. 30, 1861, Maj. Gen. John C. Frémont, commander of the Union Western Department in St. Louis, issued a proclamation of martial law. "All persons who shall be taken with arms in their hands," he announced, "shall be tried by court-martial, and if found guilty will be shot." This was harsh, but perhaps to be expected in the strife-torn region. But Frémont went further. "The property, real and personal, of all persons in the State of Missouri, who shall take up arms against the United States, or who shall be directly proven to have taken an active part with their enemies in the field, is declared to be confiscated to their public use, and their slaves, if any they have, are hereby declared freemen."

In other words, acting completely on his own and without precedent, Frémont issued the first Emancipation Proclamation, a full year before Abraham Lincoln issued his own. Though the president would ultimately force him to rescind the order, Frémont, in declaring that the war for the Union was by necessity a war against slavery, amplified abolitionism as war policy, opening a road that would never be closed.

The president, to put it mildly, was not amused. However, as was his wont even when provoked, Lincoln stepped back from his emotions and, assuring Frémont that he was writing "in a spirit of caution and not of censure," sent by special courier on Sept. 2, an urgent but mildly phrased letter to Frémont. His first concern was the punitive steps promised by Frémont, which Lincoln feared would lead to reprisals: "Should you shoot a man according to the proclamation, the Confederates would very certainly shoot our best man in their hands in retaliation, and so, man for man, indefinitely. It is therefore my order that you allow no man to be shot without first having my consent."

Lincoln's concern regarding the slavery plank was more about grand political strategy. He still believed there were significant numbers of slave-holding Southern Unionists, who might yet be convinced to side with the North; at the same time, sympathizers with slavery in Union states needed reassurance to stay. Frémont's declaration would, he wrote, "alarm our Southern Union friends, and then turn them against us—perhaps ruin our rather fair prospect for Kentucky." He asked Frémont to voluntarily rewrite this part of the order to eliminate the abolition of slavery.

Whether out of obtuseness or egoism, Frémont replied to Lincoln on Sept. 8, saying that he had not intended to shoot "ordinary prisoners of war," but only guerrillas who were in the process of tearing Missouri apart. He requested that he be allowed to order them killed on the spot when captured in arms (already a practice among many Union units). And as for abolitionism, he asked Lincoln to "openly direct me to make the correction" to this part of his proclamation, as if willfully reading Lincoln's kindly previous admonition as ambivalence. Three days later, Lincoln replied that he "cheerfully" ordered Frémont to remove the statement from his proclamation.

By now Lincoln realized he had a problem that went beyond a single, zealous declaration, and he dispatched Postmaster General Frank Blair, of the politically powerful, and very conservative, Blair family, back home to Missouri, to sort things out. The Blairs, who had lobbied Lincoln heavily to make Frémont commander in Missouri, now turned violently against him, and set about destroying his reputation directly to Lincoln.

The problem lay in the manner by which Frémont, blind to the political landscape of Missouri, had drifted from the conservative camp, around the Blairs, into the arms of the radicals. The conservatives, however, held power in the state, and were staunchly against any step to weaken slavery. Gov. Hamilton Gamble, a conservative, had declared on Aug. 5, three weeks before Frémont's proclamation, that "No countenance will be afforded to any scheme or to any conduct calculated in any degree to interfere with the institution of slavery existing in the State. To the very utmost extent of my Executive power, that institution will be protected." In other words, state policy and Frémont's policy were directly at odds, in a state where the dual powers of the federal military and the state political system collided. Gamble shot off an extremely angry telegraph when he read what Frémont had proclaimed, adding his voice to that of the Blairs.

In response to this conservative bombardment, Lincoln also sent Gen. David Hunter to Missouri. Frémont, Lincoln told him, was "losing the confidence of men near him," and asked Hunter to lend Frémont "assistance which it is difficult to give him," due to the fact that he "isolates himself, & allows nobody to see him."

But Frémont, the 1856 Republican presidential candidate, was not completely deaf to politics. To get his own side of the story into the president's office, Frémont dispatched his wife, Jessie, to Washington. She was the daughter of the powerful politician, Thomas Hart Benton, and a forceful operator on her own. By all accounts the interview was a disaster, as Jessie lost her temper and told off the commander in chief. Then Frémont blundered: back in St. Louis, he arrested Frank Blair and charged him with insubordination. Life was imitating melodrama.

After many more moves, including Blair's release from prison, Lincoln finally removed Frémont from his post on Oct. 24. Although he ostensibly cashiered him for financial shenanigans, Lincoln had made it very clear that emancipation was impermissible. With Lincoln on their side, and his great need of their support, the Missouri conservatives had easily won this battle.

Many historians tend to over-simplify this story as a duel between a buffoonish maverick general and an ever-patient and sagacious president, and there is no doubt that Frémont was every bit as eccentric and strange as Lincoln was balanced and calm. Lincoln wasn't exaggerating when he said Frémont wouldn't let anyone see him. Frémont had excluded professional military officers from his inner circle, and had retreated into his office, where he surrounded himself with radical European revolutionaries whom he dressed up in splendid uniforms with feathers and epaulettes. Their main job seemed to be to keep everyone else at bay who disagreed with their radical politics while they bilked the army on supply contracts.

Moreover, Frémont was no lone wolf. Prior to issuing his proclamation, he had begun to listen to the growing chorus of abolitionists inside and outside Congress, including some very important figures like Representative Owen Lovejoy and Lincoln's close friend, Senator Charles Sumner, who were urging the Lincoln administration to broaden the war policy to include emancipation. And in fact, as Allan Nevins, the most astute historian of these events, has demonstrated, Frémont's proc-lamation received a widespread burst of approval in Congress, and not only among the radicals, but in many of the more moderate newspa-pers throughout the North. The proclamation was not just the demented product of a hare-brained egomaniac, but the outgrowth and amplifica-tion of a rising and spreading wave of public opinion.

Nevertheless, feeling beleaguered by a war that was not going well, Lincoln was deeply angered by Frémont's action, in considerable mea-sure because he must have believed that it was obvious that Frémont should have consulted him before making such a monumental deci-sion. But beyond that, and unusually for him, he let his hair down when the moderate Republican, Illinois Senator Orville H. Browning, one of his oldest and closest friends and supporters, wrote him on September 17 defending Frémont's declaration—a telling demonstration of just what a chord Frémont had struck. Your letter "astonishes me," Lincoln responded. Nothing about Frémont's act was due to "military law, or necessity," which might have made it somehow excusable. No, this was

a purely political act simply "dictatorship." It assumes
that the general may do anything he pleases—confiscate
the lands and free the slaves of loyal people, as well as of
disloyal ones. Can it be pretended that it is any longer the
government of the U.S.—any government of Constitution
and laws,—wherein a General, or a President, may make
permanent rules of property by proclamation?

What a terrible "principle" that would be. And as "policy," the proc-lamation had already led to a whole company of Union volunteers in Kentucky to throw down their arms and disband. "I think to lose Ken-tucky is nearly the same as to lose the whole game," with all the other slaveholding border-states going next, and with them the Union.

The greatest irony in this unusual burst of anger grounded in Lin-coln's great conservatism about military and executive action is that, a year later, he would issue just precisely the same declaration he was now decrying. When the Democrats in the North opposed Lincoln's proclamation they used exactly the same arguments against him. The difference, Lincoln would no doubt argue, was timing: by mid-1862, he believed, the necessities of war did indeed demand acts in defense of the Union that would have been considered unconstitutional before the war.

Still, Frémont's declaration was an important precedent. If the rebellion were concluded without abolition—if slavery remained unresolved—there would be another civil war over the same issue. However insufferably impolitic he may have been, Frémont articulated the previously unthinkable, employing means that were, as Lincoln emphasized, extra-constitutional under ordinary circumstances. Onto the scrap heap of historical ridicule he went, for all times. And yet his central misjudgment had been political prematurity: as emancipation transpired, Frémont served as a bellwether of what was to come at Lincoln's own hand.

Grant Goes to War
By CHRISTOPHER PHILLIPS

Since settlers arrived in the early 19th century, Southern Illinois has been referred to as "Little Egypt," a reference to the supposed similarity between the Nile Delta and the fertile soil found at the confluence of the Mississippi, Ohio and Tennessee rivers. Fittingly, this delta region was also home to that great Sphinx of the Civil War, Ulysses S. Grant. He had lived in all the surrounding states, often uncomfortably, before moving away in search of work. Residents of all these states would find things even more uncomfortable after his wartime return.

Perhaps no military commander knew the border region better. Grant was born only a few sloping yards from the Ohio River in Point Pleasant, Ohio, and raised in nearby Georgetown. His father, Jesse, was a mildly antislavery former Democrat-turned-Whig who served a term as mayor. The family moved frequently across the Ohio; as a child, young Grant attended schools in both Kentucky and Ripley, Ohio, the region's hotbed of abolitionism.

After graduating from West Point, Grant married the daughter of an affluent Missouri slaveholder and, after an undistinguished and often drunken army career, left to farm unsuccessfully on a rocky piece of

Missouri timber that his father-in-law gave him. (Appropriately, Grant named it "Hardscrabble.") Grant was even more ambivalent about slavery than his father—enough to free the only slave he ever owned (given to him by his wife's father), but he was not sufficiently opposed to it to deter him from hiring slave field hands or sell his wife's domestic servants. Or to drive him from the Democratic Party, or even from the slave states. Or to remain largely politically uninformed. Eventually, Grant's poor head for business and ineptitude at farming forced him, debt-ridden, to seek refuge in Galena, in extreme northern Illinois, where he clerked in his father's store only months before the war began.

There, the nation's ambition found him despite his best efforts. A veteran of the Mexican War (which he had opposed), Grant was the only man in town with military training, much less experience. He was soon beset by prominent Galenans, mostly Republicans who did not know the shut-mouthed Grant's politics, to lead its men into battle. He was unwilling to accept a volunteer commission, especially a subordinate one, and organized a company of volunteers and led them to the state capital, Springfield, where he helped to organize and train the thousands of men arriving daily.

Unsatisfied with the volunteers, Grant appealed to Nathaniel Lyon in St. Louis (where he witnessed the fallout from the Camp Jackson affair) as well as George B. McClellan in Cincinnati for a commission in the Regular Army. When none came, he accepted the colonelcy of the 21st Illinois Volunteers, and soon marched them westward to Missouri, already plagued by warfare. Reports from local home guards and vigilance committees of thousands of armed riders blanketing the Missouri countryside led Grant, who had seen guerrilla war in Mexico and knew about unreliable intelligence, to question their validity. But he saw firsthand that Southern sympathizers were using neutrality as a shield. He soon took the war to these "great fools," whom he considered disloyal, confronting them with arrests, fines and newspaper and trade suppressions.

Before his men had exchanged shots with either rebels or guerrillas, though, he received promotion to brigadier general and command of federal volunteers assembling at Cairo, Ill. The town was seen by most as a backwater command, made more so by residents' apparent disloyalty. "Our people," one Cairo editor declared, were "mainly with the South." Virtually none of Egypt's counties supported their state's Rail-splitter for president, and one reported to Gov. Richard Yates that "Some of them say . . . they are going to hang cut throts [sic] and shoot every Republican in Egypt."

But Grant, alone, saw this mudhole as perhaps the most strategic point on the entire continent. Cairo was near the point where four major strategic waterways—the Ohio, Mississippi, Tennessee and Cumberland rivers—joined to flow southward. It would be the site of the Union's chief riverine naval depot and construction site for the "fresh-water fleet" that would soon drive the war deep into the Confederacy. Victory, Grant believed, would ride the western rivers.

With an unerring sense of the course of both water and events, Grant took that wheel. "What I want," he would soon write his wife, Julia, "is to advance." His new superior, John C. Frémont, commanding the Department of the West, had given him his mission: clear Missouri's swampy southeastern Bootheel of marauding rebels and occupy the high Mississippi River bluffs at Columbus, Ky., the northern terminus of the only western railroad running southward to the Gulf of Mexico.

The problem for Grant was not logistical; it was political. In May, Kentucky's unionist legislature—which refused to call a secession convention despite demands from the state's governor, Beriah Magoffin—had declared itself "independent of both sides," a strict neutrality intended to "compel both sides to respect the inviolability of her soil." Whichever belligerent should invade first, Kentucky would side with the other. Just south of the Kentucky line, thousands of western Tennessee and Kentucky State Guard gathered in camps eager to invade, likewise held back by the state's neutrality.

Grant was not one to be hemmed. After he established and fortified camps across the Mississippi in Missouri, sympathizers living along the rivers told the Confederate commander, the Episcopalian bishop Leonidas K. Polk, of so-called "secret service" missions by federal river patrols and home guard scouts. Later, they reported armed river forays from Cairo aboard timber-clad gunboats and even the capture of civilians (one such expedition to Columbus was launched ostensibly to tear down a Confederate flag flying over it). All were clear violations of Kentucky's neutrality. Kentucky's State Guard commander, Simon B. Buckner, who in June had entered into a conciliatory agreement in Cincinnati with the federal commander there, George B. McClellan, claimed these forays had induced a "highly excited state of the citizens of Columbus and vicinity, and the indiscretion of many of them." Among these indiscretions was an invitation of the city's mayor to the commanders in Tennessee to occupy their city to prevent more of Grant's incursions from "imperilling[sic] the peace of the Commonwealth."

And so, "to quiet the unhealthy excitement which exists and to enforce the obligations which the state has undertaken to fulfill," on Sept. 3 Polk sent troops by river and by foot to the Columbus bluffs, which they quickly began fortifying to protect themselves and to seal off the Mississippi to river traffic. Eventually, Polk would have his men stretch a massive chain across its span, much as the revolutionary patriots had done across the lower Hudson, to create a self-styled "Gibraltar of the West." His troops soon after occupied the Kentucky towns of Bowling Green and Hopkinsville.

On Sept. 5, two days after Confederates occupied Columbus, Grant showed his own brand of impetuosity. He sent a telegram to the speaker of Kentucky's legislature, declaring that rebels were moving in great numbers into his state. It was more a warning of intent than a briefing, as a day later Grant dispatched troops to Paducah and Smithland, Ky., securing the mouths of the Tennessee and Cumberland rivers. He confidently declared to stony local citizens that "[t]he strong arm of the Government is here to protect its friends and to punish only its enemies." Columbus's secessionists scoffed. "[R]emember that it is our wives and daughters, our property, our slaves, and our homes, whose honor, safety, and indemnity is involved and not yours," they scolded their state's legislators.

But Grant's daring move paid off. Despite a last ditch effort of the state's secessionists to hold to strict neutrality, on Sept. 11 the legislature instructed the governor to order the Confederates, not the federals, to withdraw from the state; it also called out some 40,000 troops "for the purpose of repelling said invasion." Governor Magoffin vetoed the measure, but a week later, the solidly unionist legislature quickly overrode him. The governor dutifully complied, ending neutrality and declaring that Kentucky would side with the federal government. The Confederacy alone had violated the state's neutrality.

Kentucky then gave command of its federal volunteers to Robert Anderson, the heroic defender of Fort Sumter. Enlistments in the state began in earnest, for both sides. War had come, steaming south, with Grant at the helm. The Sphinx, by myth either a benevolent defender or monstrous devourer, had asked his first riddle.

The Iron Horse at War

By CHRISTIAN WOLMAR

A mong many other things, the Civil War marked the first significant use of the railroad as a military tool. Between the opening of the first European and American railroads in 1830 and the outbreak of the war in 1861, there had been a few short wars in which railways had played a supporting role in moving troops and supplying armies with ammunition. Never before, however, did it play such a central role in the strategic and tactical planning of both sides.

Troop and supply movement over hundreds of miles was now a question of hours or days, not weeks. Most of the major battles during Civil War were fought around key railway centers, including Chattanooga, Atlanta and Nashville. The location of many other battles was determined by their proximity to a railway line. And the railroads themselves became significant targets, as lines were torn up and destroyed by both sides to restrict their enemy's mobility, only to be rebuilt at great pace and with enormous skill once local territorial dominance had been achieved.

The two sides started with very different railway networks. By 1861, just three decades since the opening of the country's first railway, the Baltimore & Ohio, America had 30,000 miles of rail. Roughly two-thirds of it were in the North, leaving just 9,000 miles in what became the Confederacy. Moreover, the Northern lines were far better developed, with more advanced and reliable locomotives, rolling stock

The Potomac Creek Bridge, which Union engineers rebuilt in less than nine days.

and track. Most of the South's railroads were local, ramshackle affairs that did not cross state boundaries; co-ordinating the system was made more difficult by differences in gauge. This superiority of the North's railroads would prove crucial in helping the Yankee victory.

The North was also quicker to realize the importance of controlling the railroads, which at the time were all in private hands. Congress federalized all railroads in January 1862 and appointed an experienced railwayman, Daniel McCallum, as military director and superintendent of the railways with total power over them.

By contrast, in the South, the different railroad companies, having promised full co-operation and support for the war, soon started to squabble with the government over payments for the carriage of soldiers and prioritization of military convoys. The administration of Jefferson Davis never managed to impose itself on the railroad companies, partly because of the power of the states relative to the government in Richmond, informed by the ideology which had led them to break away in the first place. Although the Southern government created a Railroad Bureau, it was never able to exert the same power as McCallum over the frequently obstructionist railways, which were often more interested in short-term profit than the long-term prospect of military victory.

Nevertheless, the South scored a notable early military triumph:

at the First Battle of Bull Run, the turning point came when the Confederates, who seemed near the brink of defeat, managed to use the local Manassas Gap railroad to quickly bring in reinforcements from the northwest and launch a successful counter attack.

The South followed up its success at Bull Run with several other rail-based victories. But the battle, and in particular the use of rail, had shocked the North out of its complacency. Ironically, it was the North that seemed to take the lessons of Bull Run to heart and to develop more refined tactics. The first step was to appoint Herman Haupt, a famed veteran rail engineer, as McCallum's deputy. Haupt quickly became known as "the war's wizard of railroading" for his skill in building and destroying railways with great speed, and at making best use of their capability. His most famous exploit was to rebuild a 400-foot bridge over the Potomac, destroyed by the Confederates, in just nine days using locally sourced wood and a largely unskilled workforce. After inspecting the achievement, President Lincoln said, "I have seen the most remarkable structure that human eyes ever rested upon."

More important was Haupt's role as a tactician. He devised simple rules for using the railway in war, insisting, for example, that all wagons be emptied as quickly as possible and removed from the railhead so that they did not clog the unloading station and could be readily reused. It was a simple rule but one which the army, focussed on purely military objectives, was wont to forget. Indeed, Haupt's most fundamental rule was that railway personnel should be in charge of train movements, deciding on the timetable, rather than military officers, who would not understand the workings and limitations of the railway. Railways needed military discipline, but not the discipline of the military. In future wars, many generals paid a heavy price for ignoring these simple rules.

The war ended with General Sherman's great sweep south, and here too the railways were crucial. His army was supplied entirely by a single railway route, a combination of three lines stretching almost 500 miles from Louisville to Atlanta. Ever meticulous, in his memoirs Sherman paid tribute to this logistical miracle: "That single stem of railroad supplied an army of 100,000 men and 32,000 horses for the period of 196 days between May 1 and November 19 1864." To have delivered these supplies by road would have required 36,800 wagons, each with six mules—a logistical impossibility. Interestingly, once he had destroyed Atlanta and headed east, Sherman destroyed the railways behind him to ensure that the Confederates could not use it to pursue him.

Indeed, the length of the war, the number of battles—400, or more than one every four days—and the breadth of the conflict, over an area the size of Western Europe, were all the result of the ability of the railways to supply troops with both food and ammunition in an unprecedented way. The very bloodiness and intensity of the Civil War was a result of the invention of the railroad. Before the railways, battles were over in a day or so because of the inability to keep armies and their horses supplied by road. Now, battles could continue, in theory, indefinitely. A new way of war, borne by the iron horse, had arrived.

'No Language Like Song'
By AMANDA BRICKELL BELLOWS

Frederick Douglass spent much of his life speaking about the hardships of slavery—but even he, at times, realized that words were not enough. Instead, he turned to music: "The mere hearing of [slave] songs," he said, revealed the "physical cruelties of the slave system; for the heart has no language like song." Today, spirituals like "Go Down, Moses" and "God's Going to Trouble the Water" continue to convey American slaves' anguish, frustration and hope.

Less familiar to Americans, however, is the music of Russia's serfs, who were emancipated in 1861, on the eve of President Lincoln's inauguration. Although the slaves and serfs were separated by vast distances and significant historical experiences, each group endured years of bondage by turning to song. Likening the songs of Russian serfs to those of American slaves, early 20th-century actor and slave descendent Paul Robeson observed that both groups had "an instinctive flair for music . . . [a] faculty born in sorrow." But their musical traditions have striking differences, too—differences that help us understand the contrasts between the two systems.

Common types of American slaves' songs include work songs, sacred spirituals and social songs, a category comprised of narratives, ballads and dance songs. Pre-20th-century Russian folk songs consist of ritual songs, which relate to changing seasons or holidays, and family ceremonial songs, sung during weddings or funerals. Serfs also sang non-ritual songs, which included all other types of folk music, like historical epics, dance songs and work songs.

Both groups sang work songs as they labored in the fields; for both, such songs moderated the pace of labor. When African-American slaves hoed corn, for example, they sang songs like "Shock Along John" and "Round the Corn Sally." These tunes, found in the 1867 volume "Slave Songs of the United States," contain only two lines per verse and are repetitive and cadenced. In the hayfields, Russian serfs sang rhythmic pokos, or hay-making songs, to regulate the movement of their scythes.

The synchronization of action through song was crucial for physically challenging tasks. In Russia, groups of 50 to 125 serfs were harnessed to boats and forced to pull them upriver. A brutal job, barge-hauling was despised by all. Serfs endured this work by singing a song known as the "Song of the Volga Boatmen," or "Hey, Ukhnem." "Ukhnem" translates to the English equivalent of "heave-ho," and comes from the "ukh" sound that serfs made with each collective tug. As the serfs pulled in unison, this song coordinated their efforts.

American slaves employed song in a parallel way as they rowed together. In early-19th-century Savannah, the observer John Lambert recorded that four slaves rowed "to a boat-song of their own composing. The words were given out by one of them, and the rest joined the chorus. The tune of this ditty was rather monotonous, but had a pleasing effect, as they kept time with it at every stroke of their oars."

Such songs were an integral part of the serfs' and slaves' daily lives. Music served both a practical and a creative purpose as it helped slaves labor in unison and entertained them during, as one serf described it, the "heavy, monotonous work [that] much dulled [the] mind." Nineteenth-century observers noted the exceptional musical talent of both groups when they sang, danced or played musical instruments. The serfs and slaves each performed solo and group songs, employed forms of call and response, and danced as they sang.

Differences in sound were marked, however: American slaves created songs with complex overlapping rhythms that were enhanced by vocal performances of swooping, moaning and shouting, while Russian folk music was characterized by its dissonant heterophony and deep, resonant sound.

The content differed as well. Both groups drew strength from their Christian faith in times of anguish and joy. The lyrics and style of Protestant hymns were well-known to slaves, who sometimes attended church with their masters or participated in camp meetings. Blending African and Western musical traditions, however, American slaves created wholly original songs—spirituals—that are filled with religious language, symbols and ideas.

Rephrasing stories from the Old Testament in spirituals like "Go Down, Moses," slaves linked their bondage to that of the Israelites in Egypt. Inspired by New Testament stories as well, slaves sang spirituals like "Run to Jesus," "I am Bound for the Promised Land" and "Steal Away," which brought slaves hope of salvation in the mortal world and the divine.

Barely concealed messages lay embedded within the lines of these songs. In "Go Down, Moses," slaves sang: "No more shall they in bondage toil,/Let my people go;/Let them come out with Egypt's spoil,/Let my people go." Other spirituals like "Steal Away" functioned as direct invitations to flee. Phrases like "I hain't got long to stay here./Steal away, steal away, steal away to Jesus" served as a signal for potential runaway slaves. Christianity helped American slaves create a body of music that was both spiritually elevating and powerfully subversive, offering hope of heavenly peace or earthly escape.

The serfs' ritual songs, on the other hand, anticipated the occurrence of events or marked holidays and seasonal changes. For example, folk songs sung during Maslenitsa, or Shrovetide, the week-long period preceding Lent, contain themes of nature and fertility. In the song "We're Waiting for Maslenitsa," serfs sang: "We're waiting for Maslenitsa,/We're waiting, my dear, we're waiting./We'll treat ourselves with cheese and butter,/we'll treat, my dear, we'll treat./On the hill stands a green oak tree,/A green oak tree, my dear, a green oak tree." During their celebration, serfs feasted on special foods as they prayed for the swift arrival of spring, with its green oaks and abundant flowers.

One fascinating difference between slaves' spirituals and serfs' sacred folk songs is that while American slaves often sang about escape or emancipation, Russian serfs rarely did. According to the Russian scholar V. Ja. Propp, the number of songs that addressed the travails of serfdom was almost negligible when compared to the vast array of other types of folk songs.

What accounts for this surprising difference? Surely serfs did not prefer to remain enslaved? For one thing, serfs may have been hesitant to share subversive music with transcribers, or tsarist censorship might have prevented the publication of such music.

A more convincing answer is that a "free North" did not exist for the 23 million serfs who composed 40 percent of the Russian nation in 1860. Serfdom was concentrated in Russia's central and western provinces, but was legal throughout. Deterrents to serfs who considered flight included both the great distance from central Russia to its borderlands, where serfdom was less common, and the threat of capture once there. The Yale scholar John MacKay argues that an absence of sectionalism in Russia accounts for a general lack of an idea of a "land of liberty" in serf consciousness. Perhaps serfs viewed acts of insubordination or rebellion as more viable alternatives to escape; the existence of several Russian folk songs praising serf uprisings supports this theory.

By contrast, slaves comprised approximately 13 percent of the American population in 1860, where slavery was legal in only about half the country. Viewing the free Northern states and Canada as viable safe havens, slaves sang more frequently about escape than insurrection, revealing their abiding desire to "steal away" to a concrete destination where other blacks lived freely under the protection of law.

Each group's musical heritage was as unique as its conditions of bondage. Although Russian serfs and American slaves employed work songs in comparable ways, American slaves were singularly inspired to sing of their desire for earthly and heavenly escape. But for both groups, music ultimately served as a shared outlet of expression. Their songs were, in the words of Douglass, "like tears a relief to aching hearts."

Up South

By NICOLE ETCHESON

Abraham Lincoln may have won Indiana in the 1860 presidential election, but on a summer night in Greencastle, Ind., locals could see just how much the state was split between Unionists and Confederate sympathizers. On the evening of July 21, 1861, residents had gathered at the railroad depot, where the telegraph "dripped" news "from the wires indicating the rising or falling tide at the distant battle" at Bull Run. Eager anticipation turned to dismay when they learned that, at the end of the day, the tide had turned and the North had suffered a shocking defeat. But not everyone at the depot was discouraged: the face of Judge Delana Eckels, who publicly sided with the South even as he held a leading position in the community, was wreathed in smiles at the news of the Union army's panicked retreat.

Indiana, like its neighboring lower Midwestern states Ohio and Illinois, had been settled by Southern migrants, and many carried their old allegiances with them. Like many of his fellow townspeople, Judge Eckels had grown up in Kentucky. During the secession crisis, Indiana Representative Daniel W. Voorhees promised his constituents never to "vote one dollar, or one man, or one gun to the administration of ABRAHAM LINCOLN, to make war upon the South." Still, despite Voorhees's assertion, the firing on Fort Sumter sparked intense Union sentiment in the Midwest. When the war came, over half of adult Hoosier men signed up, many as three-year volunteers, placing Indiana second in the nation for the percentage of its military-age population in service.

Although the Civil War divided the nation, it especially divided Midwesterners whose strong ties to the South competed with a fierce attachment to the Union. No one embodied that paradox more strongly than Abraham Lincoln, who was born in Kentucky, raised in Indiana, married into a slaveowning family and rose to political power in Illinois.

In addition to family ties, the lower Midwest had important trade links to the South, which they knew would be hurt by sectional conflict. Farmers shipped pork, corn and other agricultural products down the

Ohio and Mississippi rivers to the market at New Orleans (Lincoln, as a youth in Indiana and Illinois, made two such trips to that port). War closed the Mississippi, hurting cities all along the Ohio River. Agricultural prices plummeted. In the fall of 1861, Peter Demaree, a farmer in Johnson County, Ind., complained to his brother that "times is very hard here every thing we have to sell is very low & every thing we buy is very high." True, as the war continued, railroads supplanted the rivers as the chief means of transportation, and the Northern army's demand for food and supplies brought Midwestern farmers high prices and prosperity: corn, which sold for 15 cents a bushel in the depressed days of 1861, rose to 95 cents by 1864. But in 1861 the good times were not apparent, and Midwesterners greeted the economic shocks with dismay.

Moreover, while Ohio, Indiana and Illinois were free states, all three maintained "black laws" that prohibited African-Americans from voting, serving on juries, marrying whites and testifying against whites in court. Informal segregation existed as well: Ellis Mitchell, a well-to-do free black man traveling through Ohio, had to eat in the kitchen while his white traveling companions were served in the dining room of a tavern. All three states also possessed or considered prohibitions against African-Americans moving into them; in Indiana such a bar was written into its 1851 constitution. David M. Dobson, an Owen County delegate to the state's constitutional convention, summed up the prevailing attitude, which worried that Indiana would become the "receptacle for . . . all the broke down and worthless slaves of the South."

States rights doctrine was also popular in the region. Sympathetic Midwesterners agreed with Southerners that the political quarrels of the 1850s constituted an attack on Southern rights. President James Buchanan appointed Judge Eckels, who was a powerful figure in the Indiana Democratic party, chief justice of Utah Territory; nevertheless, during the 1860 election Eckels campaigned in Indiana for the Southern rights candidate, John C. Breckinridge. Eckels wanted "complete enjoyment of every constitutional right," including to slaves, for "every portion of the Union, North and South."

Despite Eckels's endorsement, Breckinridge received less than 5 percent of Indiana's popular vote in 1860. Another pro-Southern candidate, John Bell, whose platform called for respecting the Fugitive

Slave Law, received less than 2 percent. Instead, the race in Indiana was between Abraham Lincoln and Stephen A. Douglas, both Illinoisans and both arguing that slavery could be prevented from expanding. Midwestern fear of black migration came as much from their dislike of haughty slaveowners, who often freed aging slaves and sent them north of the Ohio River, as it did from animosity toward African-Americans themselves.

In other words, many Midwesterners, especially those in the lower Midwest, opposed the Southern candidates not out of an ideological difference, but because they feared the growth of the "Slave Power" South that would force them to allow blacks to live in their region, whether as slaves or freedmen. To them, Douglas was a "Judas" who had authored legislation that opened Kansas Territory to slavery in exchange for Southern political support.

But in April 1861, the Confederate firing on Fort Sumter shifted the blame to the Confederacy. The "war spirit" infected entire communities. One Democrat in Greencastle, John A. Matson, "made a stirring and patriotic appeal in behalf of the Union." Another, Lewis Sands, opened a recruiting office. Sands raised two companies of soldiers and, despite his advancing age, hoped to enlist as well. His exertions, however, taxed his health and he died within a month. Matson's son, Courtland, quit college to volunteer and served throughout the war.

The entire community found ways to support the war. Most of the early volunteers were unmarried men like Courtland Matson, but nonetheless a committee formed to see that married soldiers' families would be cared for during their absence. Local women sewed uniforms for their sons, cooked farewell dinners for the troops and honored them with flags. George L. Chapin belonged to the first company to leave Putnam County for the muster grounds in Indianapolis. He described the farewell: "The Ladies of GreenCastle presented us with a beautiful Flag."

Shortly after the Confederacy formed, President-elect Lincoln wrote the new Republican governor of Indiana, Oliver P. Morton, that for "the salvation of this Union there needs but one single thing, the hearts of a people like yours." Yet Hoosier hearts were as deeply riven as the Union itself. In northern Indiana, the news of Fort Sumter caused Theodore Upson's grandmother to sob for those of her children who remained in the South: "Oh to think that I should have lived to see the day when Brother should rise against Brother." Her grandson would march through Georgia with Sherman's army.

Why Bismarck Loved Lincoln
By Kenneth Weisbrode

We usually think of the Civil War as a uniquely American event, a war unlike any other fought in the Western world during the 19th century. And of course that's true, strictly speaking: no other country saw itself split in two over slavery. But that's not the only way to think of the war. Put a different way, the Civil War was just one of several wars for national unification—including fighting in Italy and Germany—on both sides of the Atlantic during the mid-19th century.

While countries like Britain and France were concentrating on expansion through colonization, the United States, Germany and others were focused inward, developing—intentionally or not—the centralizing powers that have defined the modern state ever since. What seems like a particularly American event was really part of a much larger, and much more significant, historical trend.

As a war of national unification, the Civil War represented a sharp historical break, a moment of crisis that would define the country's course for decades to come. Beforehand, the notions of national unification and expansion had been indivisible: just 15 years prior, the United States defeated Mexico in a bloody war that brought vast territories under occupation and destroyed the delicate balance between slave and free states. Some people predicted the worst. "The United States will conquer Mexico," claimed Ralph Waldo Emerson in 1846, "but it will be as the man swallows the arsenic which brings him down in turn. Mexico will poison us." Ulysses S. Grant went so far as to declare the Civil War divine punishment for the Mexican conflict.

Indeed, the Mexican War fueled an ongoing debate about how large the country should get. Canada, or parts of Canada, had been sought by eager expansionists virtually since the two parts of British North America went their separate ways in 1776; spreading the plantation economy to Mexico and beyond—the so-called purple dream—had long animated the Southern imagination.

Even as the Civil War began, Mexico continued to fester and tempt interventionists. It announced in mid-July 1861 that it could not service its debts, having just ended its own civil war (called the War of the Reform), and so suspended payments to its European creditors. This was not unusual, but this time the country's creditors did more than reiterate demands for payment: the British, French and Spanish governments joined forces in October to compel Mexico to pay; by the end of the year the city of Vera Cruz was occupied.

The British and the Spanish soon reversed course, but Napoleon III of France, in league with Mexican reactionaries, persevered: he sought nothing less than a new Catholic empire in the Western Hemisphere under his auspices (thence the term "Latin" America). French troops occupied Mexico City and installed a Hapsburg archduke, Maximilian, as emperor. He lasted until 1867 when, having lost the war against his opponents and even the backing of Napoleon, he was executed by a Mexican firing squad.

Here, then, was a major challenge to Washington, an act of aggression in the Western Hemisphere by European countries and thus a direct violation of the Monroe Doctrine. Some in Abraham Lincoln's administration may have urged him to strike, to invade Mexico and push the Europeans out before they dug in. But Lincoln rejected any such advice.

In part it was a matter of expediency; the Union had more pressing matters to its south to deal with. But it was also a resetting of the course of the American state. As Lincoln saw it, "older" powers like Britain, France and Russia could go on to see imperial archipelagos flourish, but "younger" states should opt for geographic and political consolidation and centralization at home. Lincoln thus rebuffed the idea of conquering and colonizing Canadians and Mexicans in favor of building a new nation to the Pacific. It's no surprise that Lincoln would prefer this path: as a Midwesterner, his mental map extended more horizontally than vertically—east to west rather than north to south. But first he had to stop the American South from going its own way.

Lincoln wasn't alone in prioritizing centralization. Giuseppe Garibaldi and his fellow campaigners for Italy's unification—which had just been proclaimed in March—would have understood this, as would nationalists (sometimes called "unitarios") elsewhere in the Western Hemisphere, notably in Argentina, Colombia and Canada, whose confederation debate got going at about the same time. As a matter of fact, Lincoln authorized a commission for Garibaldi in the Union Army. Garibaldi turned it down—evidently because freeing the slaves was not yet sufficiently high on the list of the Union's war aims—yet Lincoln's offer underscores the fellowship between America's war of unification and those taking place in other parts of the world.

Perhaps no one was more in tune with Lincoln than Otto von Bismarck, the minister-president of Prussia. Beginning in 1862, Bismarck unified Germany, but he explicitly rejected the idea of a "Großdeutschland," or "Greater Germany," incorporating Austria, in favor of a "kleindeutsche Lösung," or "Little German Solution," that preferred centralization over maximum territorial expansion. This may have been one reason why, after the Civil War ended, Bismarck reportedly sounded out Washington on an alliance. It made sense: Europe's rising industrial and military power seeking common cause with an American counterpart that seemed destined for the same.

Unifying states needed more than just will; they needed propitious events and conditions. In Germany's case, it was the Crimean War—triggered, incidentally, by Napoleon III, following his 1851 coup—that made unification possible by putting an end to the Anglo-Russian condominium underpinning the European, and therefore global, balance of power. In the United States it was the country's "free" security (provided in large measure by the British Navy) that allowed for its territorial expansion and consolidation.

And so the old order gave way to a new, contested one on both sides of the Atlantic; unification would come in both places by force. If the Crimean War had set the stage for the wars of unification in Germany and Italy, and the Mexican War did so for the war of unification in the United States, then it's worth asking: if there had been no Crimean War, might there still have been an American Civil War? Probably so; civil wars by definition happen largely for internal reasons. But without the conflict in Europe, the American war would not have been the nationalist achievement of world-historical import, as Lincoln, Bismarck and later generations understood it.

In other words, the Civil War—as significant as it is for American history—is even more important when viewed through a comparative, transatlantic lens. The fight for internal unification rather than expansion meant that never again would the United States seek to conquer and annex its two largest neighbors. It would, along with Bismarck's Germany, be a new kind of state: centralized, rationalized and mobilized to dominate the coming century.

The Boys of War
By CATE LINEBERRY

With hopes of adventure and glory, tens of thousands of boys under the age of 18 answered the call of the Civil War, many of them rushing to join Union and Confederate troops in the earliest days of battle. Both sides had recruitment rules that barred underage men from enlisting, but that didn't stop those who wanted to be part of the action: some enlisted without their parents' permission and lied about their ages or bargained with recruiters for a trial period, while others joined along with their older brothers and fathers whose partisan passions overwhelmed their parental senses. Most of the youngest boys became drummers, messengers and orderlies, but thousands of others fought alongside the men.

As each side scrambled to get troops into the field in the early days of the war, many of these boys went to battle with just a few weeks of training. It didn't take long for them to understand what they'd gotten themselves into. Elisha Stockwell Jr., from Alma, Wis., was 15 when he enlisted. After the Battle of Shiloh in April 1862, he wrote, "I want to say, as we lay there and the shells were flying over us, my thoughts went back to my home, and I thought what a foolish boy I was to run away and get into such a mess as I was in. I would have been glad to have seen my father coming after me."

While some regiments protected their boy recruits by sending them to the rear when fighting broke out, others expected them to work in the front lines as stretcher bearers. Harry Kieffer, a musician for the 150th Pennsylvania, wrote about his experience at Gettysburg: "[I am called] away for a moment to look after some poor fellow whose arm is off at the shoulder, and it was just time I got away, too, for immediately a shell plunges into the sod where I had been sitting, tearing my stretcher to tatters." A 16-year-old musician, John A. Cockerill, who was also at Shiloh, later wrote,

> I passed the corpse of a beautiful boy in gray who lay
> with his blond curls scattered about his face and his hand
> folded peacefully across his breast. He was clad in a
> bright and neat uniform, well garnished with gold, which
> seemed to tell the story of a
> loving mother and sisters who
> had sent their household pet to
> the field of war. His neat little
> hat lying beside him bore the
> number of a Georgia regiment.
> He was about my age. At the
> sight of the poor boy's corpse,
> I burst into a regular boo hoo
> and started on.

Johnny Clem, perhaps the most famous drummer boy of the war, shot a Confederate officer who had ordered him to surrender.

Perhaps the most famous boy of the war was John Joseph Klem, better known as Johnny Clem. At only 9 years old and roughly four feet tall, Clem tried unsuccessfully to enlist with the 3rd Ohio in May 1861, soon after Lincoln first issued the call for volunteers. Clem left his father, brother and sister in Newark, Ohio, to join; his mother had been killed in a train accident earlier that year. Undeterred by the rejection of the 3rd Ohio, Clem tried his luck again with the 22nd Michigan, which allowed him to join as an unofficial drummer boy. Until he was added to the muster roll in 1863, the $13 he earned each month came from donations made by the officers of his regiment.

Clem became a celebrity for his actions at Chickamauga, Ga., in September 1863. The 22nd Michigan was assigned to defend Horseshoe Ridge, but Confederate soldiers soon surrounded it. A Confederate officer spotted Clem, who was armed with a musket modified for his size, and demanded that he surrender. In the face of danger, Clem shot the officer and ran, making his way back to Union lines. Though he escaped unharmed, 389 of the 455 men who made up the 22nd Michigan were captured, wounded or killed in the battle.

Sixteen days later, Confederates captured Clem while he was riding on a wagon train carrying provisions to nearby Chattanooga, Tenn. He was paroled after just three days and sent to Camp Chase, Ohio, where he was exchanged as a prisoner of war. On his way back to his regiment, Clem told his story to Gen. William S. Rosecrans, who had been relieved of his command of the Army of the Cumberland following the Union defeat at Chickamauga. Impressed with the boy's actions, Rosecrans informed the press. The Columbus Daily Express wrote, "The little fellow told his story simply and modestly, and the General determined to honor his bravery." How modestly Clem told his story is debated, but people in the North embraced it. The "Drummer Boy of Chickamauga," who had been promoted to sergeant, was now a Union hero. The daughter of Treasury Secretary Salmon P. Chase asked her father to honor Clem with a medal, which Clem wore in at least one of the many pictures taken by photographers hoping to profit from the young boy's newfound celebrity.

As his fame grew, Clem continued to serve in the Union Army. He mainly carried dispatches, suffering two minor wounds in Atlanta. Despite stories that claim Clem's drum was destroyed at Shiloh, giving him the nickname "Johnny Shiloh" and inspiring the song "The Drummer Boy of Shiloh," it's unlikely he was ever there.

On July 6, 1864, the War Department forbid any officers to enlist any soldier under 16 or face severe penalties. Almost a month later,

Lt. Col. Henry Dean of the 22nd Michigan requested Clem—who had changed his name during the war from John Joseph Klem to John Lincoln Clem in honor of the president—be released from service so that he "may have a better opportunity for educating himself."

While awaiting his discharge, Clem went to Carlinsville, Ill., where he started school. But the war remained very much on his mind. In a letter to Capt. Sanford C. Kellogg, an officer in his former unit, in September, he wrote, "I am going to school here and am very much pleased with the institution and my schoolmates. Please tell my Colonel to write to me as soon as he can How is Georgie Lutz getting along? Who has my little pony now? . . . If any of the officers are willing to write to me I would be very much pleased to hear from them."

Clem graduated from high school in 1870 and was nominated to West Point by President Ulysses S. Grant. He failed the entrance exam several times, but Grant nevertheless appointed him a second lieutenant in the Army. After serving 43 years in the military, Clem retired with the rank of major general—the last Civil War veteran to actively serve in the Army. He died in 1937 and was buried at Arlington National Cemetery.

Though he became one of the most famous drummer boys of the war, Clem was just one of thousands of young men who proved to be as brave as the men in their regiments. At least 48 boys under 18—11 of whom were under 16—received the Congressional Medal of Honor for their extraordinary valor in action. The youngest were mostly drummers: Willie Johnston, 11, was the only drummer in his brigade to hold onto his instrument during the Peninsula Campaign's heavy fighting; Orion Howe, 14, was a drummer who, despite being severely wounded, remained on the battlefield at Vicksburg, Miss., until he had reported that troops needed more cartridges; and William Horsfall, 14, was a drummer who saved the life of a wounded officer lying between the lines at Corinth, Miss. John Cook, 15, was a bugler who volunteered to act as a cannoneer under enemy fire at Antietam, Md., while Cpl. Thomas C. Murphy, 16, who was born in Ireland, voluntarily crossed the line of heavy fire at Vicksburg carrying a message to stop the firing of one Union regiment on another.

These and the other boys who served, whether as drummers,

orderlies or soldiers, risked their lives alongside men twice their age and, sometimes, size. Some became prisoners of war, while others were killed in the thick of battle or died from diseases that ravaged even the strongest men. Those who were lucky enough to survive were often left with a lifetime of haunted memories.

Sherman's Demons
By MICHAEL FELLMAN

By the end of the Civil War, William T. Sherman was one of the most important and celebrated Union commanders, and the most reviled in the Confederacy. During the last year of the conflict, his army conquered Atlanta, reversing a flagging Union war effort and securing Abraham Lincoln's re-election. After that his men scorched much of Georgia in his famous March to the Sea, then cut a huge swath up through the Carolinas. Not only did his army destroy men and material, but Sherman articulated a ruthless policy of destruction that deeply demoralized Southern morale. He gained perpetual infamy in the South as the grim reaper of the Union war effort, a task he undertook quite consciously, with both anger and joy.

Yet, as few Americans know, during the first year of the war, on Nov. 9, 1861, General Sherman, paralyzed by depression, was relieved of his command in Kentucky at his own request. Five weeks later, the wire services proclaimed to the nation: GENERAL WILLIAM T. SHERMAN INSANE. Just after his participation in the Civil War had begun, Sherman's service was nearly destroyed.

As all students of the war know, he came back and soared to prominence, but his mental collapse and his recovery, unusually well documented, present a riveting example of the understanding of depressive illness in the Victorian world, and the relationship of bipolar illness to creativity and inspired leadership during difficult times, which Sherman certainly demonstrated later in the war.

As was true of Ulysses S. Grant, Sherman's prewar life had careened from failure to failure. But where Grant self-medicated his frustrations with drink and retreated into stoic silence, Sherman experienced erratic emotional ups and downs that he shared with his friends and family in a manner that only intensified his self-laceration.

Grant and Sherman were both members of the broad cohort of West Point-trained officers who would populate the upper echelons of the war's opposing armies. But while others, including Grant, had fought heroic wars in Mexico, Sherman stewed in California, where most of his troops deserted his unit for the lures of the gold fields. Later, out of the Army, although backed by the powerful political forces of his family and wealthy supporters in St. Louis, his bank failed in San Francisco in the Panic of 1857. Subsequently, he bounced forlornly around Kansas and Ohio, achieving little worldly success.

When the war began, Sherman resigned his recently assumed presidency of the Louisiana military academy (which would become Louisiana State University), ran a streetcar line in St. Louis, very badly, and finally took command of a brigade at Bull Run that collapsed in the face of the Confederate advance. Nevertheless, in mid-August 1861, he was assigned to be second in command of the Army of the Cumberland, in Kentucky, a slaveholding, divided state, and the key to what would become of the Western theater—and perhaps of the Union itself.

Throughout the first six months of the war, Sherman's psyche was dominated by self-doubt and fear. In fact, when he was assigned to Kentucky, he informed Abraham Lincoln of his "extreme desire to serve in a subordinate capacity, and in no event to be left in a superior command." This reticence astounded Lincoln, who was far more used to braggart officers demanding important commands; but it was not modesty that led Sherman to his demonstration of uncertainty. Then, on Oct. 5, his superior, Robert Anderson (the commander at Fort Sumter when the war began) resigned because of health issues, almost certainly including major depression. Three days later, Sherman replaced him. Sherman lasted a tormented month before he was removed.

The day he took over, following a reconnaissance into the Kentucky hinterland, Sherman wrote anxiously to civilian supporters, and to Lincoln as well, that the whole countryside seethed with disunion, that the enemy was conspiring to create a "vast force" that would soon overwhelm Louisville. His own units were green, "too weak, far too weak" to resist the expected onslaught. He anticipated being "overwhelmed"—a defeat that would be "disastrous to the nation. Do not conclude that I exaggerate the facts. They are as stated, and the future looks as dark as possible. It would be better if a more sanguine mind were here, for I am forced to order according to my expectations." This was hardly the self-confidence one needs in leaders. And one can only imagine the degree to which Sherman dismayed others serving under him.

Thoroughly alarmed, Lincoln dispatched his secretary of war, Simon Cameron, to make a personal inspection. On Oct. 17, Sherman repeated these apprehensions to Cameron, and insisted that only a force of 200,000 men could hold Kentucky. Cameron replied that he was astonished by this analysis and that he had no idea where such an army might come from. And despite telling Sherman that he was among friends during this interview, Cameron had included Samuel Wilkerson of The New York Tribune in his party, who would later write the story declaring Sherman insane.

The other Union generals in Kentucky whom Cameron and Lincoln consulted assured them that the Confederate side was even more disorganized than they were, and that they did not share Sherman's negative certainties, which amounted, they were certain, to delusions.

Over the following weeks, Sherman's fears only intensified, while others observed a tortured man suffering what has long been defined in psychiatric terms as intense mania. For example, two sympathetic New York journalists who shared long nights at the Louisville telegraph office with the general grew deeply alarmed by his behavior. Sherman talked incessantly while never listening, all the while repeatedly making "quick, sharp odd gestures," pacing the floor, chain-smoking cigars, "twitching his red whiskers—his coat buttons—playing a tattoo on the table" with his fingers. All in all he was "a bundle of nerves all strung to their highest tension." Back at his hotel, other guests observed him pacing all night in the corridors, smoking and brooding, "and it was soon whispered about that he was suffering from mental depression." Such increased energy, talkativeness and hyperactivity (which can sometimes become impulsive and even psychotic), is the definition of mania, the twin—and opposite— of depression in the illness of bipolar disorder.

In letters to his wife, Ellen Ewing Sherman, Sherman himself confirmed and amplified what others observed. Everyone around him seemed poised to betray him, he wrote her. "I am up all night." He had lost his appetite. Viewing his situation from the perspective of this mental turmoil, he was convinced that he was caught in an impossible military contradiction where "to advance would be madness and to stand still folly." And he entirely lacked the means to lead others and to control himself: "I find myself riding a whirlwind unable to guide the storm." In the near future he anticipated total "failure and humiliation," an onrushing infamy that "nearly makes me crazy—indeed I may be so now."

Then, on Nov. 8, a captain on Sherman's staff telegraphed to ask her to come down to relieve him from the pressures of business. In a series of letters to the extended Ewing/Sherman clan over the next week, Ellen described what she found in Louisville: understanding that depression had what we would now call a genetic predisposition, she recalled that one of Sherman's uncles was a chronic "melancholic." And she also remembered quite vividly "having seen Cump [his boyhood nickname] in the seize of it in California," when the bank had failed, a mental event that was repeated at least twice prior to the war. To inheritance and personal history, Ellen Sherman added descriptions of his behavior: he seldom ate or slept, had lost human contact with others, and scarcely talked unless repeating his obsessions that "the whole country is gone irrevocably & ruin & desolation are at hand."

Sherman was relieved of his command on Nov. 8 and reassigned to a lesser post in St. Louis. When the downward spiral continued, Ellen Sherman came to collect him on Dec. 1, for three weeks' leave back home in Lancaster, Ohio. There she began to nurse him back to health with a rest cure, the frequently effective 19th-century therapy: favorite foods, reading him his most cherished books, especially Shakespeare, and calming him sufficiently so that he could sleep. The real cure, as in all bipolar illness, is nature: the average mood episode rarely lasts longer than six months before it goes into remission by itself.

Despite the public's awareness of his insanity, Sherman seemed somewhat strengthened by the time he returned to St. Louis on Dec. 19. His bipolar illness seems to have bottomed out, and he undertook a lengthy period of self-repair. Henry Halleck, Sherman's commander, who understood and sympathized with Sherman's inner turmoil, and also valued his intelligence and training, soon placed him in charge of the training camp in St. Louis under his direct supervision. Seven weeks later, trusting Sherman's recovery sufficiently, Halleck assigned him to Cairo, Ill., to serve as the logistical coordinator for Grant's army, the beginning of a long and intense friendship between two emotionally wounded warriors. Grant soon brought Sherman down to the front at Pittsburg Landing, Tenn., and put him in charge of a division.

There, on April 6, a vast surprise attack on Grant's army led to the horrific Battle of Shiloh, in which the casualties totaled 20,000 men. In the thick of things, Sherman led his men with considerable personal bravery and tactical skill. Following this battle, his spirits soared. He experienced an almost instant internal transformation: from the despairing, self-proclaimed loser in Kentucky to the confident and brilliantly creative commander who would do so much, in word as well as deed, to destroy the Confederacy.

Whistler's Brother
By RONALD S. CODDINGTON

Shortly after the Civil War broke out, Dr. William McNeill Whistler, scion of a storied Anglo-American military family and brother of the artist James McNeill Whistler, arrived in Richmond, Va., to lobby Confederate leaders for a medical officer's commission. Described as a genial, refined man with a soft and pleasant voice, the 25-year-old, Massachusetts-born Whistler was firmly determined to put his medical training to use.

Even after he gave up on the medical staff itself and applied for a clerk's position instead, he wrote in his application, "Being a physician by profession, I felt that the only true position for me was on the medical staff, as the want of any military education disqualified me for any other office." By war's end, though, he would find himself following more closely in his family's footsteps than he could have imagined.

Dr. Whistler's grandfather, John Whistler, had served in the British Army during the Revolution. He later immigrated to America, became a United States Army officer, and fought the British in the War of 1812. Dr. Whistler's father, George Washington Whistler, graduated from West Point and become a well-respected civil engineer during the early years of the railroad boom. He died unexpectedly in 1849 while overseeing the planning and construction of a Russian railroad, after which his widowed wife (and future world-famous portrait subject), Anna, and children, including 12-year-old William Whistler, returned to America. Even William's older brother, the acclaimed artist James Abbott McNeill Whistler, attended West Point (though he didn't graduate).

William Whistler, however, broke from the West Point tradition, earning a medical degree from the University of Pennsylvania in 1860. Later that year he married the Georgia-born Florida Bayard King—affectionately known as Ida. Dr. Whistler's mother, who hailed from North Carolina, embraced "precious Ida" with love and affection. She noted a few months after the Civil War began that the newlyweds "seem perfectly well and happy. Ida has made Willie a thorough secessionist thus verifying the saying 'A man forsakes all, for his wife.'"

The couple settled in Richmond, where Whistler failed to find a medical officer's commission and they ran into money problems. A year passed before his luck finally changed: in the fall of 1862, Confederate authorities commissioned Dr. Whistler as assistant surgeon and assigned him to duty in the Richmond area. But while his career prospects rose, Ida's health declined. Dr. Whistler's mother traveled to Richmond to care for her, but after an early and encouraging rally, Ida died in March 1863.

The loss devastated mother and son. Months later, a bereaved Mrs. Whistler wrote of Ida to a friend, "Each day I feel more sensibly what Willie & I have lost, she was such a rare combination of brightness & gentleness, so loving so confiding, just like one of my own little ones."

Whistler remained on duty in the vicinity of Richmond until April

1864, when he received a field assignment as an assistant surgeon in the veteran First South Carolina Rifles. The hard-fighting regiment was also known as Orr's Rifles after its original commander, Col. James Orr, a onetime speaker of the House of Representatives who resigned from the Army to serve in the Confederate Congress. Whistler served with Orr's Rifles on the front lines in Virginia as the Union Army of the Potomac advanced on Richmond in April 1864. "He was a total stranger to us," wrote Sgt. Maj. Robert Hemphill in a postwar memorial to Dr. Whistler. "The veterans of three years looked with discerning eyes upon the new assistant surgeon to see of what mettle he was made."

Dr. Whistler proved himself the following month during the Battle of Spotsylvania and the intense fighting in an area that came to be known as the Bloody Angle, some of the worst combat of the war. Driven, perhaps, to fill the void left by the death of his wife, Dr. Whistler proved fearless on the battlefield, even in the face of unrelenting enemy fire. "When the artillery opened," recalled Major Hemphill, Dr. Whistler ordered his servant to take his horse to the rear and out of danger, while he remained with the line of battle until it entered the Bloody Angle, and he was detained to look after such as had fallen in the charge. He thus established himself in the hearts of his comrades, and made a reputation for cool courage and fidelity to duty."

During the rest of the campaign, according to Major Hemphill, "Dr. Whistler was constantly on the line, sharing the hardships, dangers, and scant rations of the men. The humblest private received the same professional attention from him as did the highest officer." Major Hemphill included an anecdote that illustrated Dr. Whistler's compassion for the men in the ranks. During a raid outside Petersburg in December 1864, "The roads were covered with snow and ice, and the suffering of the men was great, for many were without shoes, and the broken ice lacerated their feet most painfully. Dr. Whistler gave up his horse to one of these wretched men, and marched on foot with the line. He walked for miles by the side of the writer." Whistler entertained his companions with stories of his boyhood adventures in Russia and other experiences. "In bivouac and camp he was a most agreeable comrade, his conversation being full of reminiscence, anecdote and philosophy," Major Hemphill added.

But the rigors of campaigning eventually compromised Dr. Whistler's health. He received a leave of absence in February 1865 and traveled to Richmond. He left soon after to join his mother, who had since departed for London to visit her artist son, James. Not letting an opportunity overseas go to waste, the Confederate government entrusted Dr. Whistler to deliver "certain dispatches of importance" to England. Dr. Whistler set out for South Carolina with the intention of crossing the Atlantic on a blockade-runner out of Charleston. He ran into elements of Maj. Gen. William T. Sherman's federal army, and changed course to Wilmington, N.C. There, the presence of Union forces foiled his plans again. He next traveled to the North under an assumed name and dressed in civilian clothes; he made his way through Philadelphia to New York, from where he sailed for England. He arrived in Liverpool and delivered the dispatches, then joined his family. One week later, Dr. Whistler learned that Gen. Robert E. Lee had surrendered the Army of Northern Virginia.

Dr. Whistler never returned to America. He wandered through Europe for about a year, and worked for a time in Paris, where he most likely posed for his carte de visite photograph wearing his Confederate uniform, perhaps for the last time. He eventually settled in London and rose to prominence as a physician and academic. In 1876 he married a Greek citizen, Helen Euphrosyne Ionides. She survived her husband after he died of influenza at age 63 in 1900.

Lincoln's Do-Nothing Generals

By MARK GREENBAUM

The Civil War's first year was one marked by inactivity and battlefield frustration. There was just one major battle, at Bull Run, and only a handful of minor engagements, most of them semi-guerrilla fighting in and around Missouri.

Yet as the leading Union generals in the field refused to directly engage Confederate troops, President Lincoln began to display an almost intuitive understanding of the aggressive military strategy that would win the war, a wisdom that would lead him to bring in new generals and push for more aggressive engagements in 1862. How did Lincoln, a lawyer by training with no military background to speak of—get the nature of the conflict so right, and his seasoned generals get it so wrong?

The Civil War was a West Point war. Even though the academy's alumni made up a tiny fraction of the Union's fighting force, West Point graduates dominated the general staff from Fort Sumter to Appomattox. Out of the approximately 560 Union generals to serve during the war, about 220 were West Point graduates (in the Confederacy, the ratio was a little lower but still significant, 140 out of 400). Given how rapidly and large the two armies grew, the dominance by West Point graduates of the top leadership positions is striking.

Nevertheless, virtually no one in the Union Army had any experience that could prepare him for the Civil War. In 1860, the Army numbered just over 16,000 men, a quarter of whom would soon resign. No wartime American army had ever exceeded 14,000, such that when Irvin McDowell took the field at Bull Run in July 1861, his 30,000 troops made up the largest force ever led by an American general. The Army thus lacked the experience to provide its cadets with proven doctrinal training.

Instead, in the decades leading up to the war, American military thought was overwhelmingly influenced by the French experience. Though eventually defeated by his European allies, Napoleon had left behind a world-class martial structure that other countries rushed to replicate. From the Army's uniforms, to its hard emphasis on drills, to its translated training manuals, French ideas pervaded and in many ways defined America's still-fledgling military, particularly in the nation's premier military education center.

Modeled on L'Ecole Polytechnique, West Point's curriculum emphasized mathematics and engineering almost exclusively. The school's only course on strategy, taught by Dennis Hart Mahan, was only a few lessons long and focused on the superiority of defensive postures and the building of fortifications and fieldworks. Mahan was a fierce student of the Napoleonic campaigns and helped found the

Napoleon Club, probably West Point's only real extracurricular group.

Mahan also taught the work of Antoine-Henri Jomini, a Swiss-born strategist who somehow managed to hold commissions from both the French and Russian armies during the Napoleonic wars. Widely regarded as the leading military theorist of the early 19th century, Jomini viewed war in precise, almost mathematical terms and believed that an enemy's territory was the primary objective of an army, not the opposing force. As a result, wars could be won through one large, well-planned battle.

The influence of Jomini's thinking in particular on Civil War battlefield strategy has long been controversial. While there were generals who studied and referenced his works, most had limited exposure to him. To directly impute his teachings to failed wartime maneuvers, therefore, is difficult. Still, the general ideas that pervaded his thinking—that modern wars could be limited affairs divorced from politics, defined by a few set-piece battles with little consequence to civilians—were an integral part of the foundations of American military teaching before the war.

But if the influence of Napoleonic campaigns was obvious, their relevance to the Civil War was not. Napoleon enjoyed several advantages the Union didn't, including shorter conflicts, narrower geography and population density, pockets of friendly population support, closer supply lines and an ability to defeat opposing armies completely (something that was achieved only once in the Civil War, at the Battle of Nashville in late 1864). The military's thinking circa 1861 was perhaps best delineated by Confederate Gen. Richard Ewell, who, reflecting on his West Point education, purportedly noted that it "taught officers of the 'old army' everything they needed to know about commanding a company of fifty dragoons on the western plains against the Cheyenne Indians, but nothing else."

Adding to their inexperience and inadequate education, Union officers also lacked a central command structure, trained troops and military maps, and suffered from the readjustment of generals returning from civilian life, harsh press coverage—particularly in the Eastern Theater—and a failure of strategic and tactical imagination.

Not surprisingly, when George B. McClellan took over command of eastern forces in July 1861, he was greeted as a savior. Here, finally, was a young man who seemed to understand the necessities of modern warfare, or at least spoke like he did. He quickly built up an army demoralized by the First Battle of Bull Run into a capable force of over 70,000. But with these men at ready, McClellan refused to move all through the year, despite mounting pressure from the press and Lincoln. A one-time member of the Napoleon Club, McClellan saw the conflict as one with limited objectives, minimal focus on the enemy army and battles never fought far from his supply base. He believed that the war could be won through quick battles and territorial expansion, leaving Southern civilians and property unmolested. Later, he would seek to concentrate all of his forces to capture Richmond by essentially going around the rebel army. His appointment of Henry Halleck and Don Carlos Buell as the commanders in the Western Theater led to similar approaches in Tennessee and Kentucky.

Nicknamed "Old Brains," Halleck was arguably the nation's leading military thinker. He had written extensively on strategy and had even translated Jomini's multi-volume biography of Napoleon. A by-the-book general who despised political interference, Halleck failed to move aggressively on Confederate positions throughout his western tenure. Buell followed a similar pattern, repeatedly finding excuses not to move, and focusing on taking Nashville over more strategic targets.

The generals' notions of what it would take to put down the rebellion ran counter to Lincoln's, whose pragmatic strategy would ultimately form the blueprint for Union victory. He had his work cut out for him: when he took office there wasn't just an absent system of command, but there had been no planning whatsoever by the previous administrations for war; no preparatory memos or regular briefings by the top brass awaited him.

But Lincoln—whose military experience was limited to a short and uneventful stint in the Black Hawk War—actively filled the void, soaking up military texts and regularly visiting with advisers, including General-in-Chief Winfield Scott and Quartermaster General Montgomery Meigs. Scott became a particularly important influence in Lincoln's military education. The leader of forces in the Mexican War and a veteran dating back to the War of 1812, he may have been the only man in history who knew both Thomas Jefferson and Abraham Lincoln. The old general believed that latent Southern Unionist sentiment, together with a coastal blockade and control of the Mississippi River, would eventually topple the rebel government. While Lincoln disagreed, believing that a large army would be central to subjugating the South and rejecting Scott's overarching "Anaconda" design as insufficient, Scott did much to help him understand the scope of the war.

From the beginning, Lincoln viewed every military decision through the single objective of defeating the rebellion and uniting the nation. Probably the clearest expression of Lincoln's views came in a letter to Buell and Halleck as he prodded the generals to move: "I state my general idea of this war to be, that we have the greater numbers that we must fail unless we can find some way of making our advantage an overmatch for his; and that this can only be done by menacing him with superior forces at different points at the same time."

While there is no evidence that Lincoln ever read his work, his views resembled the ideas of another 19th century theorist, Karl von Clausewitz. The Prussian officer emphasized the relationship between military strategy and politics, calling war "the use of engagement for the purpose of the war." He defined the new style of war as one based on broad objectives like taking over countries and overthrowing sitting governments through the annihilation of an enemy's center of gravity, generally its standing army.

Lincoln recognized the government's core policy (total defeat of the rebellion), the size of the conflict (unlimited, across two theaters), the South's keystone center of gravity (its army) and the Union's inherent advantage (manpower and industrial production) together in concert and divined a simple strategy: Directly engaging Southern armies repeatedly, and ignoring the alluring prize of rebel cities in favor of seizing strategic points like railroad hubs and lines of communication. His intuition soon proved right, as the capture of major Southern cities like New Orleans, Nashville and Memphis by mid-1862 did nothing to hasten the end of the war.

Lincoln's strategy was already taking shape by mid-1861. In late April he discussed a potential blockade, the importance of holding Fort Monroe on the tip of the Virginia Peninsula and even an attack on Charleston, S.C. Undaunted by the First Battle of Bull Run, in late July he pushed for dual offenses along the South Carolina coast once the Army was ready, and eventual joint movements on Memphis and East Tennessee. In early October, he called for large troop concentrations in Missouri, Louisville, western Virginia and Cincinnati, pushing Halleck and Buell to seize a crucial rail juncture between Tennessee and Virginia and later needling them to invade western Kentucky and Knoxville simultaneously.

The historian T. Harry Williams notes that Lincoln's generals rejected these ideas as "the product of a mind that didn't know the rules of war." But it was men like McClellan, Buell and Halleck, students of the old army, who were ill-equipped for unlimited war. Lincoln would have preferred his generals to dictate effective military strategy. They couldn't, and he performed well as an unofficial general-in-chief until he was able to find generals who could. In so doing, he supplanted the old army and built a modern force.

As McClellan, Buell and Halleck floundered in the field, the prospect of victory appeared remote in 1861. But just as McClellan began to shape the plans for his doomed Peninsula plan, Ulysses Grant won Forts Henry and Donelson. The great general who shared Lincoln's strategic outlook and understood unlimited war was emerging just as 1862 began.

CHAPTER 4

1862

Early 1862 found the Union armies slowly grinding into action. Plans were underway, in the east, for a massive amphibious assault on the Virginia Peninsula, through which Northern soldiers would move directly on the Southern capital at Richmond. In the west, General Grant's forces moved up the Tennessee and Cumberland rivers, quickly taking Nashville and, with it, control of Tennessee itself. Along the North and South Carolina coasts, Union forces solidified control of oceanfront territory—and in doing so opened up spaces where newly emancipated slaves could have a first taste of freedom, however tentative.

It was during this period when the war became, if not comfortable, then certainly routine. Wartime culture took root—songs were written, camp pastimes were developed, rumor mills and informal communications networks sprouted. Home became the homefront; wives and parents and children stopped waiting for news of the war's end, and learned to make do with errant dispatches from their loved ones. People who had never ventured beyond a few days' ride of their birthplace became familiar with unimaginably far-away places: Fort Donelson, the Shenandoah Valley, the James River. Men after battle spoke of "seeing the elephant"—a wonderfully 19th-century metaphor for confronting the exotic and unspeakably terrifying, a sadly regular occurrence for the typical soldier.

Then came Shiloh. On April 6, some 45,000 Confederate soldiers fell on 68,000 Union soldiers camped near Pittsburg Landing, in northern Mississippi. The Union men, caught largely unawares, scrambled to order, and fought to a narrow victory at a cost of 13,000 casualties, matched by 10,000 on the opposite side. But it was victory enough: simply by holding their ground, the Northerners broke the Southern forces apart and put an end to any significant threat to the Union's hold on Tennessee. A few weeks later, the Union Navy made that hold even stronger by fighting its way up the Mississippi River and capturing New Orleans, the largest city in the Confederacy.

The Union was not so lucky in the east. Gen. George McClellan's 121,000-man Army of the Potomac, massed at the tip of the Virginia Peninsula, began its long march north toward Richmond on April 4. But the going was rough; rains and wily Confederate generalship kept McClellan from coming within range of the Confederate capital until mid-May. By then, Gen. Thomas J. "Stonewall" Jackson, through a brilliant and backbreaking campaign up and down the Shenandoah, had reduced Union pressure on the capital from the west, freeing up Confederate defense forces. The end of May saw a short series of gruesome battles, including Seven Pines, that while technically Union victories, brought McClellan to a halt. A month later, Gen. Robert E. Lee defeated McClellan in the Seven Days Battles, effectively ending the Peninsula Campaign at a cost of 20,000 Confederate casualties to the Union's 15,000.

But if the South held firm at the front, changes were underway behind the lines that would ultimately doom the Confederacy. More and more slaves, never the docile servants their owners imagined them to be, saw opportunities to escape, either because Union forces were moving closer or because their masters were away fighting. At the same time, the Confederate government proved too weak to prosecute a major war and build a domestic state. Citizens, who had imbibed the secessionists' rhetoric of radical freedom, refused to consent to the sort of taxes and resource levies needed to make it possible to continue fighting. It was a testament of sorts to the Southern fighting spirit that many men would continue to live and die on the front lines long after Richmond stopped putting clothes on their backs or shoes on their feet.

Abraham Lincoln's Audacious Plan

By RICHARD STRINER

Abraham Lincoln is remembered by some as a thoughtful, often cautious leader. But in late 1861 he began to develop a plan that, even during that most unusual of times, was audacious in the extreme: the federal government would buy out Delaware's entire slave population.

In November 1861 he drafted legislation that he hoped would be introduced in the legislature of Delaware, the smallest of the slave states—and a slave state loyal to the Union. "Be it enacted by the State of Delaware," Lincoln's draft began, "that on condition the United States of America will, at the present session of Congress, engage by law to pay . . . in the six per cent bonds of the said United States, the sum of seven hundred and nineteen thousand and two hundred dollars, in five equal annual installments, there shall be neither slavery nor involuntary servitude, at any time after the first day of January in the year of our Lord one thousand, eight hundred and sixty-seven, within the said State of Delaware." An alternative version of Lincoln's text would have extended the phase-out of slavery in Delaware over 30 years.

The plan might sound outlandish, but it was wholly within Lincoln's often misunderstood antislavery position. The conventional view today holds that Lincoln's abolitionist sympathies evolved over time. But the real evolution wasn't in his opposition to slavery per se, but in his thinking on how to bring about its end. Unlike some of his firebrand antislavery colleagues, he understood that any plan for blanket abolition would tear the country apart; indeed, he was proven right when the mere fear of such a plan drove 11 Southern states to secede.

Rather, Lincoln, like many in his party, believed that the only workable solution short of violence was to restrict slavery gradually—hence his position, during the 1860 campaign, that slavery remain legal in the South but not be allowed into any new territories or states. The Delaware plan, though never enacted, demonstrates how his thinking was evolving once in office; by the end of 1862, it would flower as the Emancipation Proclamation.

Lincoln's plan was bigger than Delaware, of course. He hoped that, if the state successfully implemented his plan, it would prove attractive to the other border states and, maybe, even weaken the Confederacy. Lincoln predicted to his friend David Davis that "if Congress will pass a law authorizing the issue of bonds for the payment of the emancipated Negroes in the border states, Delaware, Maryland, Kentucky, and Missouri will accept the terms."

Why Delaware? For one, it was manageable: by 1861 its slave population had shrunk to fewer than 1,800. He also figured he could lean on Delaware Congressmen George P. Fisher and Benjamin Burton, who were friends of the administration—and the state's two largest slave owners.

And just to make sure that Republicans in Congress would be ready to take fast action in response to the Delaware request, Lincoln inserted some crafty lines in his annual message to Congress, which he delivered in early December 1861. After making reference to the "contraband" slaves who had crossed Union lines, Lincoln wrote that some process ought to be adopted to liberate them. Then he continued; it was "not impossible," he wrote, "that some of the States will pass similar enactments for their own benefit respectively."

But his hopes for the Delaware venture came to naught; his plan was rejected by the state house of representatives in February 1862 by a margin of one vote. Then the legislature worsened the situation by passing a declaration that if "the people of Delaware desire to abolish slavery within her borders, they will do so in their own way" and that "any interference from without, and all suggestions of saving expense to the people . . . are improper."

Though Lincoln's hopes for the Delaware plan were dashed, the experiment continued in the early months of 1862. In March, the president would send to Congress an unprecedented bill that put the offer of federal money for the liberation of slaves directly on the table. Republicans passed it over Democratic opposition, which declared the concept "taxes to buy Negroes."

Lincoln persisted. But when the offer of money made no impression on slave-owners, the president decided to radicalize his grand design. He started writing a draft of the Emancipation Proclamation.

Freedom Comes to Washington
By KATE MASUR

President Abraham Lincoln signed the District of Columbia Emancipation Act into law on April 16, 1862, a step heralded by abolitionists across the country. Never before had Congress passed a measure designed to destroy slavery in a place where it was already entrenched. As one newspaper put it: "The actual interest at stake was not extensive—a citadel never occupies a large proportion of the territory it represents—but the principle involved in the question was vital." The capital's liberation was, Frederick Douglass wrote, "a priceless and an unspeakable blessing" for those it freed and "the first great step towards that righteousness which exalts a nation."

Groundbreaking as it was, the act contained some provisions that look peculiar in light of later developments. The law provided for compensation to slave owners who remained loyal to the Union, and it suggested that emancipated slaves might benefit from leaving the United States entirely. It appropriated funds for these purposes: $1 million to distribute among loyal slave owners and $100,000 to support freedpeople who wanted to emigrate.

Such provisions were entirely absent from the Emancipation Proclamation, issued by Lincoln just eight and a half months later, and from the 13th Amendment, which finally made slavery illegal everywhere when it was ratified in December 1865. What changed? A look at how the District of Columbia Emancipation Act took shape in the Senate reveals the complexity of the wartime emancipation debate.

Senator Henry Wilson of Massachusetts first introduced legislation to abolish slavery in the capital in mid-December 1861, amid a national scandal about the incarceration of fugitive slaves in the Washington jail. Wilson and other Republican senators believed the Constitution gave Congress virtually unlimited power to legislate for the District of Columbia and that Congress was therefore fully within its rights to abolish slavery there, even if it could not touch slavery in the states. Indeed, for this reason, abolitionists had been attacking slavery in the capital for decades, arguing that it was an embarrassment and an insult to a nation supposedly devoted to human dignity and equality.

Even among those who favored ending slavery in the capital, however, there was considerable disagreement about how to do it. Lincoln had weighed in on the matter several times before becoming president. As a congressman in 1849, he had drafted legislation for emancipation in the District of Columbia that would be gradual, voluntary and compensated. Adults would remain enslaved, but beginning in 1850 all children born to enslaved mothers would be free and subject to apprenticeship to their owners. Slave owners would be compensated at market value for those liberated. And the gradual emancipation law would only go into effect if the voters of the District of Columbia approved it. Lincoln believed Congress had the power to enact abolition in the capital without voters' consent, he reiterated in his debates with Stephen Douglas, but he did not think it desirable to do so.

Congress never debated Lincoln's emancipation bill, but its parameters were well known in 1862 as the debate over Wilson's bill got under way. Among the three facets of Lincoln's proposal, the new emancipation bill picked up only one: compensation. The bill mandated a presidentially appointed three-man commission to hear slaveowners' claims for compensation, judge their loyalty to the Union, and assess the value of each slave. Some of Wilson's Republican colleagues complained about using federal funds to pay for slaves; Senator Samuel Pomeroy of Kansas even proposed compensating the slaves themselves for unpaid labor.

But Senator Charles Sumner of Massachusetts found a way forward, pitching the measure not as compensation but as ransom. "From time immemorial every Government has undertaken to ransom its subjects from captivity," he said. Just as the federal government had ransomed Americans held in slavery on the North African coast in the late 18th century, so too would it pay for the release of the slaves of the capital.

In lengthy speeches in late March and early April, senators marshaled their best arguments for and against the emancipation bill, making recourse to examples from world history and precedents from the founding fathers and the Supreme Court. Legislators from the loyal border states and nascent West Virginia adamantly opposed the measure. They had no love for slavery, most of them said, but they felt the measure was divisive, damaging to the tenuous loyalist movements in their states and especially threatening to the economic and social order of nearby Maryland.

Senator Garrett Davis of Kentucky insisted that it was unconstitutional for Congress to abolish slavery in the capital. Focused on the Fifth Amendment—which prohibited the government from taking "private property . . . for public use, without just compensation"—Davis argued that the government could purchase slaves from their owners, but it could not turn a piece of property into a free person. Even if it could, he added, the bill did not provide for "just compensation" because it limited the amount that owners could be compensated for each slave.

No one else in the Senate was willing to go to such lengths to defend property in human beings, and no one seemed to agree with Davis that Congress had no authority to abolish slavery in the capital. Democrats and moderate Republicans alike, however, cited Lincoln's earlier proposals—and his current bid to persuade the border slave states to find their own way toward emancipation—as they insisted that the emancipation bill should provide for gradual emancipation and for the consent of local voters. Still, a solid core of Republicans repeatedly voted down such suggestions. Pomeroy audaciously suggested that if local consent was necessary, Congress should seek it from all district residents over age 21, not just from the white men who currently composed the electorate. That idea got nowhere, but neither did border state senators' proposals to seek voters' approval.

The only substantive amendment to Wilson's bill concerned "colonization," or the proposal that the government should help African-Americans leave the United States once freed. Davis had initially introduced the issue, arguing that all persons liberated by the act be required to emigrate. But Senator James Doolittle of Wisconsin offered an alternative, that colonization be voluntary, and pressed his Republican colleagues to see the wisdom of the idea. Doolittle rested his argument on no less a figure than Thomas Jefferson. The author of the Declaration of Independence, he pointed out, had believed that blacks and whites were destined to live separately; that people of African descent would prosper in the tropics, leaving the northern climes for those of European origin.

Doolittle's proposal to appropriate $100,000 for voluntary colonization received little support at first, but as the debate wore on and Republican newspapers expressed concern that the bill was too radical, several senators came around. Finally, on April 3, the Senate approved Doolittle's colonization provision and then went on to pass the bill itself.

Colonization had not been part of Lincoln's 1849 proposal, but he had often voiced support for the idea. Lincoln believed all people were entitled to certain fundamental rights. At the same time, like many Americans of his era, he believed that the "races" were separate and distinct groups, and he doubted whether different races could live peacefully together as equals, in the same nation.

The colonization measure in the District of Columbia Emancipation Act was no anomaly. That summer Congress appropriated an additional $500,000 for the colonization of African-Americans freed during the war, and Lincoln urged a delegation of black men from Washington to help the government create a black colony on the Central American isthmus, where African-Americans would work in the coal industry and enjoy equal rights amid a racially mixed population. Lincoln appointed Pomeroy to oversee the project, but diplomatic obstacles proved insurmountable. Not a single government-sponsored ship ever set sail for that region.

The District of Columbia Emancipation Act (together with a supplemental act passed three months later) freed about 3,100 people held in bondage in the capital. Congress abolished slavery in the federal territories that summer, but in the main, it was the vicissitudes of war that would drive emancipation in the coming months. Congress and the president had far more latitude when they acted in the name of military necessity; besides, there were only so many places where the federal government enjoyed virtually unchallenged jurisdiction over slavery.

So it was that Congress passed legislation instructing army officers not to send fugitives back into slavery and, later, declared that all fugitives coming into Union lines were free. So it was, also, that Lincoln proclaimed emancipation in his capacity as commander in chief of the armed forces, leaving questions of gradualism, compensation and consent behind.

Laugh During Wartime
By JON GRINSPAN

Americans remember the Civil War for the carnage it caused, the people it liberated and the nation it rebuilt. Rarely do they remember it for the comedy it inspired.

Yet many considered the early 1860s to be "the age of practical joking." Throughout the conflict soldiers and civilians, Union and Confederate, laughed at "the comedies mixed up with our country's tragedy." From prisoners of war to members of Congress, Americans joked about serious subjects, meeting disastrous events with goofy gags. Northerners mocked recruiting officers as lascivious pimps. Southerners caricatured zealous gangs of excessively helpful nurses who swarmed tired officers. Newspapers on both sides printed grisly amputation puns with titles like "An 'Off-Hand' Joke." Americans met their brutal war with bold and honest comedy.

The United States already had an international reputation as a land of iconoclastic tricksters, and the fighting sharpened their wits even further. Girls larded letters to their enlisted sweethearts with the latest jokes told back home, and nurses slipped books by their favorite humorists under the pillows of recuperating soldiers. Though many joked, veterans led the way. The Army, some humorless civilians warned, is "deficient in reverence, and likes a laugh at anybody's expense."

Newspapers passed along much of the humor, often overseen by dedicated "funny editors," who filled their pages with war-themed

A Union cartoon mocking Gov. Henry Wise, his sons and other "First Families of Virginia" as "Fleet-Footed Virginians," presumably in retreat from Northern armies.

jokes. They "scissored" puns and anecdotes from other publications and passed them off as their own. The best bits went viral, popping up from North Carolina to South Dakota. Papers freely floated between the Union and Confederacy, further seeding the newest round of jokes behind the respective battle lines. Armies left trails of funny pages in their wake and civilians seemed fascinated by whatever was making their former countrymen laugh.

Most of the comedy during the first year of the conflict aimed at deflating puffed-up war talk. Comedians North and South met the initial alarm over secession with exaggerated panic. Northern newspapers printed false correspondences warning, in hysterical tones, that the little girls of Charleston, S.C., were organizing an invading army. Both sides mocked martial posturing, caricaturing volunteer companies made up entirely of self-appointed generals, more interested in epaulets than muskets.

Confederates soon debuted their own style of an aggressively macabre humor. When the Union called for 75,000 volunteers, rebel jokers published advertisements for "75,000 Coffins Wanted." Bill Arp, a daring and popular Georgia humorist, penned false letters to President Lincoln thoughtfully worrying that the Union's military strategy might be "too hard upon your burial squads and ambulance horses."

Abraham Lincoln became the war's most notorious jester, known for his backcountry yarns and goofy, self-deprecating style. Washington socialites complained that he simply would not stop telling jokes at their dinner parties. His cabinet—stiff, bearded, capable men, whom Navy Secretary Gideon Welles called "destitute of wit"—met his enthusiastic joking with blank stares and awkward sneezes; William P. Fessenden, the secretary of the treasury, objected that comedy was "hardly a proper subject." Lincoln ignored them, introducing his plan for emancipation by reading aloud a routine by his favorite humorist. He often joked with citizens who sought his aid: when a businessman requested a pass through Union lines to Richmond, Lincoln chuckled that he had already sent 250,000 men in that direction, but "not one has got there yet."

As casualties mounted, Lincoln's humor touched off a battle that would define Civil War comedy. Starting in late 1861 a faction of reverential Northerners pushed back against joking about the conflict, particularly by the president. Lincoln's political opponents waved banners screaming: "NO VULGAR JOKER FOR PRESIDENT!" Some Union soldiers, crushed by devastating defeat after devastating defeat, moaned that their comrades "are handed over to be butchered" while "Old Abe makes a joke." Even the president's supporters began to fret about Lincoln's "unfortunate habit of joking" at "the very crisis of our existence."

Lincoln's humor introduced a larger cultural struggle over how Northern society should address brutality. Victorian sentimentalists sought to suppress anything other than reverential mourning and denounced comedy as "fearfully out of season." By 1863 even the New York Herald, formerly a sarcastic paper in a sarcastic city, turned its back on humor, demanding, "Was Bull Run a joke? Was Fredericksburg a joke? Was Chancellorsville a joke? Does anyone laugh at the wholesale slaughter of brave men?" Faced with colossal defeats, disfigured veterans and eroding confidence, many argued it was simply too soon for joking.

But a new wave of humor, emanating from the barracks and brothels on both sides, squelched the sentimentalists. As the war grew bloodier, American men and women actually increased the audacity of their comedy. Those who kept joking tacitly argued that bold, comedic truth-telling was exactly what their nation needed.

In fact, Union and Confederate army camps generated the toughest comedy. At first their jokes were relatively tame. Some wondered how many court-martials a barrel of rum held. Others joked that draft exemptions were only open to "dead men who can establish proof of their demise by two reliable witnesses."

But the slaughter at Chancellorsville and Gettysburg introduced a new darkness. Soon, noted one wartime memoirist, "anything short of death is a capital joke." Many gags starred a battlefield surgeon— "Old Sawbones"—who could amputate a gangrenous leg without removing the cigar from his mouth. Surgery provided "an inexhaustible source of amusement," often involving amputation puns and jokes about former butchers finding their true vocation in the medics' tent. Not even the dead could escape the laughter: a genre of burial humor satirized sneaky mourners who stole graves dug by other companies.

As the fighting built to a bloody climax, Civil War humor reached its comedic peak. The unprecedented severity of Gen. William T. Sherman's march through Georgia and South Carolina challenged Americans' already dark humor. Bill Arp, the Confederacy's most talented comedian, responded with a hilarious series in which he bragged about chasing Sherman's "fleeing" army to the sea. Arp's fictitious wife was just as myopic, hoping that the "kind-hearted" Sherman would take good care of the things his men pillaged from her home. The joking was not limited to comedians: one Georgia girl, already a refugee, sent teasing notes to local boys falsely warning that Sherman's avenging army was just outside of town.

This all may sound callous to modern sensibilities, but there is an impressive honesty to it: the comedy of the Civil War preferred to directly engage suffering rather than hide behind stern reverence. While humor could not stop the onslaught of grand and terrible events, at least it helped Americans talk about them. Bill Arp acknowledged as much in a published letter at the end of the war, explaining, "I must explode myself generally so as to feel better." The very irreverent Union president agreed. Weighed down by the "fearful strain that is upon me night and day," Abraham Lincoln quipped, "if I did not laugh I should die."

News of the Wired
By SUSAN SCHULTEN

The advent of the Internet has prompted endless claims that we are living through an unprecedented revolution in communication, one that has annihilated the concept of distance. Yet the real revolution came with the arrival of the telegraph in the 19th century.

The innovations of Joseph Henry and Samuel F.B. Morse, among others, led to the first telegraphed message in 1844, and by the late 1850s President Buchanan was famously exchanging pleasantries with Queen Victoria. Over 50,000 miles of telegraph wire were strung across the country in the prior two decades, and by November 1861 a transcontinental network was complete.

Lincoln was aware that this new medium had great power as an instrument of both military and civilian communication. The telegraph had allowed him to follow the dramatic developments of the 1860 Republican Convention from his home in Springfield, Ill., and the same medium alerted him to his presidential victory in November. Yet when he took office in March, the telegraph extended only to the Navy Yard and the War Department, not the White House. For several months thereafter the administration had to use the city's central telegraph office to send its dispatches.

By contrast, the nerve center of the Union war effort in 1861 was found at the headquarters of Gen. George McClellan, who had actually issued a standing order that all messages were to be given solely to him. Such was the situation in October 1861, when telegrams reporting the disastrous Union defeat at Ball's Bluff were brought directly to McClellan as he met with Lincoln in the White House. McClellan withheld the news from Lincoln, who later learned of both the defeat at Ball's Bluff and that his close friend Edward Baker had been killed in action. Such a policy was unacceptable, and Lincoln soon transferred control of the telegraph from McClellan's headquarters to the War Department.

By the middle of 1862 Lincoln began to use the telegraph as a means to project his authority in both the eastern and western theaters. The telegraph office became his second home, where he spent more time than any other place outside the Executive Mansion, including many long nights waiting for unfiltered messages from the battle front.

Perhaps the most consequential adoption of the telegraph was in journalism. In the late 1840s, the establishment of the New York Associated Press made it possible for member newspapers to share the costs of the new technology in order to gather news. By the early 1850s, content from the A.P. comprised at least two columns of every major daily newspaper, and many readers considered this "telegraphic news" to be the most compelling and urgent part of the paper.

By 1860 the A.P. was distributing its news not just in New York but around the country, and this practice began to transform the very meaning of news. Local papers now had the capacity to report national events to their readers in a timely manner, so that "the news" gradually came to connote not just events, but events happening at almost that very moment. Prior to the telegraph, the distribution of news was regulated by the speed of the mail, but now news was potentially both instantaneous and simultaneous.

The immediacy of the news fed a public frenzy for the latest information. Circulation of New York papers rose by more than 40 percent during the war, and in other areas of the nation by as much as 63 percent. During a major battle, editors could expect to sell up to five times as many copies of their papers. While newspaper reporting remained highly competitive throughout the war, the A.P. came to dominate wire news, and this also served the interests of the Administration. The A.P. had regular access to the president and the War Department, and was given exclusive bulletins and announcements to disseminate to the papers. In exchange, the A.P. gave the administration a way to reach the public in a manner that could be carefully controlled and rapidly disseminated.

Telegraphic news of the war effort stimulated the spread of maps as well as newspapers. Among the most popular were those made by Louis Prang, who had emigrated from Germany in 1850 and built a thriving printing business in Boston. Prang's initial success came from small prints and cards (including the first Christmas cards), but with the arrival of the war he began to issue maps. And he could do it with lightning speed: within a day of learning of the attack on Fort Sumter, he had all Boston newsstands selling his newly engraved map of Charleston Harbor. Ultimately he sold 40,000 copies.

These were among the first war maps ever printed in America. The most successful was his War Telegram Marking Map, which Prang designed after hearing of the Union plan to invade the Virginia Peninsula. In February 1862 General McClellan confidently ferried thou-

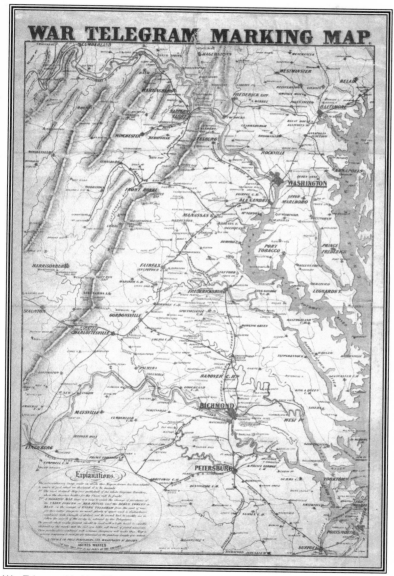

War Telegram Marking Map.

sands of troops to Fort Monroe in Virginia, planning an ambitious assault that would culminate with the capture of the Confederate capitol at Richmond. With similar confidence, Prang announced that his was the most distinct map of Virginia ever created, for he concentrated on the region "where the decisive battles of the Union will be fought."

Prang was responding to the public's desire not just for news, but the immediacy of "telegraphed" news. Unlike other battle maps which were issued after the fact, his was designed to follow the march in real time. He issued colored pencils—blue for Confederate forces, red for Union—to mark the advances, retreats and clashes that would be regularly reported by telegraph in any newspaper throughout the Union home front. Rather than waiting for maps to be issued after the battles, Prang enabled the viewer to track the invasion as it unfolded, with both victories but also terrible defeats and missed opportunities.

The map was a success, and went through six editions during 1862 alone. Prang's innovation reminds us not just of the centrality of the Peninsular campaign, but also that Americans in the 1860s were experiencing a revolution in communication that would come to define modern life.

Mr. Lincoln and Mr. Johnson
By PHILLIP W. MAGNESS and SEBASTIAN PAGE

One day in early 1864, a journalist found Abraham Lincoln busy counting greenbacks. "This, sir, is something out of my usual line," the president told the reporter, "but a president of the United States has a multiplicity of duties not specified in the Constitution or acts of Congress." The money belonged to a porter in the Treasury Department who was in the hospital and so ill from smallpox that he could not even draw his pay. The president had collected the outstanding wages himself and was dividing them into envelopes in accordance with the porter's wishes.

What makes Lincoln's concern for a low-ranking employee all the more remarkable is that the man was also an African-American.

Today we know little about that man, William H. Johnson. He has no surviving photograph, and we can only speculate as to his age, although there are strong hints that he was at least in his mid-20s. He was, however, very close to the president: the earliest records of him show that he began doing menial jobs for the Lincoln family in Springfield, Ill., around 1860 and soon accompanied them to Washington.

The working relationship between the two men attests to the complex and even enigmatic nature of Lincoln's racial attitudes. Indeed, the mystery that surrounds Johnson's death, and Lincoln's sense of responsibility for it, tells us much about the "Great Emancipator's" complex relationship with African-Americans and their quest for full citizenship.

Shortly after his arrival in the capital, the president referred to the adult Johnson as a "colored boy," attaching a belittling racial convention to the man he described as his "servant." At the same time, a more glaring display of racism quickly brought Lincoln to his valet's defense. Within a week of his arrival, Johnson fell victim to the rigid hierarchies of the White House staff, where lighter-skinned servants traditionally received preferential rank and responsibilities. Aware that prejudice had overshadowed Johnson's ability, the president secured him a messenger's post at the Treasury Department. "The difference of color between him and the other servants is the cause of our separation," explained Lincoln. "I have confidence as to his integrity and faithfulness."

And while he shared a racial view typical of many white northern moderates, Lincoln clearly thought highly of Johnson. Even after Johnson left for the Treasury, Lincoln allowed him to do side work as his barber and valet to eke out a living, wrote him checks to tide him over and apparently trusted him with carrying large sums of money. The president occasionally requested to borrow Johnson's services from the Treasury for a whole day or two, and Johnson accompanied Lincoln on his famous trip to Gettysburg on Nov. 18, 1863.

Even as Lincoln delivered his address, he was coming down with disease. Most accounts say that Lincoln had varioloid, the milder form of smallpox, but recent research suggests that he actually had a more serious strain and that his life was in very real danger. Whatever the case, the president recovered; his valet, who tended to Lincoln in those early stages, was not so lucky. Johnson contracted smallpox and died sometime between Jan. 11 and Jan. 28, 1864.

Washington was in the grip of a smallpox epidemic, so it was impossible to chart its transmission from person to person. "He did not catch it from me," explained Lincoln. "At least I think not." Whether through a nagging sense that he was responsible, or on the strength of their warm relationship—likely both—the president helped close his deceased servant's affairs. "William is gone," rued Lincoln to a Washington banker. "I bought a coffin for the poor fellow, and have had to help his family."

A Treasury clerk later confirmed that the "president had him buried at his expense." The anecdote reveals Lincoln's humanity at its best and appeared in a Republican campaign biography later that year, albeit stripped of any hint that Johnson may have contracted the disease from the president.

Such is the tale's magnetic appeal that it has subsequently picked up three embellishments. First, that Johnson's grave is still visible today at Arlington cemetery. Second, that Lincoln personally paid for his headstone. And third, that he personally ordered the stone inscribed "citizen," thereby symbolically repudiating the Supreme Court's notorious Dred Scott decision. All three, together, offer an attractive but misleading insight on Lincoln's views about African-American citizenship.

The story of Johnson's death is not much clearer than that of his life, since the chaos of war left death and burial records in disarray. Roy Basler, editor of Lincoln's "Collected Works," wondered if his grave was at Arlington on a "hunch," and duly found one William H. Johnson in Plot 3346, Section 27, whose corresponding burial record for an avowedly imprecise "1864" seemed to fit the bill. And the tombstone does indeed read "Citizen." Still, Johnson's name was a common one and the Custis-Lee estate's official conversion to a cemetery was still several months away when Johnson died (though there are hints of earlier, unrecorded burials thereabouts). Is it him, and if so, why would Lincoln have him buried there?

Another Lincoln biographer has accordingly placed Johnson in the Congressional Cemetery, while a local Washington historian, Tim Dennee, states that most black smallpox victims found their way to the Columbian Harmony Cemetery, in the capital's Northeast quadrant. Unfortunately, that site was cleared half a century ago for development.

What, then, are we to make of the supposed gravestone, or the accompanying tale of Lincoln's posthumous grant of citizenship to Johnson? Like others in the vicinity, the stone of the elusive "William H. Johnson" at Arlington is a 1990s replacement, though it repeats the original epitaph, "citizen." Yet this part of the cemetery is crowded with "citizens." Rather than conferring citizenship on the interred, the authorities merely wanted to make it clear that civilians, rather than soldiers, had been buried there during Arlington's earliest days, before it was restricted to the military. While it is not inconceivable that Lincoln tried to guarantee Johnson a marker of some description at an unknown location, he certainly had nothing to do with the stone we see today at Arlington, or its predecessor, which replaced a wooden headboard no sooner than 1877, or either's inscription of "citizen."

Ultimately, it's unclear what the term "citizen" even meant to the president. While Lincoln trod a fine line between his personal contempt for the Dred Scott decision, which denied citizenship to African-Americans, and public respect for the law, his attorney general, Edward Bates, lambasted the decision's distinction between national and state citizenship in a legal opinion of November 1862. Still, Bates could find no single definition of "citizen," and observed that it sometimes meant "civilian," in opposition to "soldier"; he also stressed that his opinion was only meant for free African-Americans, not slaves, and that individual citizenship meant nothing with regards to the right to vote.

Bates's opinion was likely in keeping with the president's views, though Lincoln offered no comment and did not personally address the issue of African-American citizenship between some brief remarks in 1858 and his death. Perhaps more significantly, Lincoln did tentatively recommend the vote for black veterans and "very intelligent" African-Americans by the end of his life.

Abraham Lincoln enjoyed a warm relationship with his valet, but also wrote of him and his replacement as "boy." We need hardly single out the president for such common usage to appreciate that it sits uneasily with placing so much weight on another solitary word, "citizen." That was not Lincoln's choice of inscription, and although the very suggestion of black citizenship could repel and inspire his contemporaries in equal measure, it is doubtful that an antislavery moderate would have deployed it as some kind of symbolic affirmation or withheld it as a calculated snub. It was a predominantly technical term, albeit one that ironically lacked definition. Its meaning to Lincoln died with him in 1865.

Damn the Torpedoes
By JOHN GRADY

On a hot summer day in 1861, Commander Matthew Fontaine Maury and his son Richard, now a junior officer in the Confederate Army, rowed from Rockett's Wharf in Richmond, Va., toward the middle of the James River and set afloat two kegs filled with rifle powder. The kegs bobbed down river toward a buoy, where they became entangled, as intended. But nothing happened.

Maury, however, was unwilling to admit defeat. He had his son row back toward the buoy. On his father's command, Richard pulled the rope connected to the mine's trigger. "Up went a column of water fifteen or twenty feet," Richard Maury wrote years later. "Many stunned or dead fish floated around."

The jubilant Maurys were drenched in the baptismal water of modern mine warfare in North America.

Matthew Maury, a respected engineer and the former superintendent of the National Observatory, was not the first American to successfully detonate percussion mines. The inventor David Bushnell had twice attacked anchored British warships during the Revolution, but with little success. Robert Fulton had for years tried to interest navies in Europe and the United States in his mines before and during the War of 1812. The Maurys were not even the first Americans to successfully explode electrically detonated mines, weapons not dependent on tides or currents, to sink a ship. Samuel Colt did that several times in 1844 in demonstrations in New York harbor and at the secretary of the Navy's request in Washington.

But these early efforts came to naught. Fulton, despite his fame, attracted only limited attention among naval officers more interested in blue-water warfare. Even progressive American naval officers, like Matthew C. Perry, preferred investing in steam power and blue water warships over mines.

This time, though, was different. The Confederate government lacked a navy of almost any kind, and it had thousands of miles of coast and inland waterways to defend. As a result, it was desperate enough to commit money to torpedoes, as mines were called then. As its military leaders realized early on, torpedoes were deadly and cheap; and for a government short of bullion, they could be a military godsend.

And so, although the Confederate Navy's top priority in 1861 remained rebuilding the scuttled frigate Merrimack as an ironclad, Secretary of the Navy Stephen Mallory requested $50,000 from the Confederate Congress for mines. Mallory also put Maury in charge of coastal defenses and detailed a few men to work out of an office at 9th and Bank Streets in Richmond to perfect the South's secret weapon.

Maury's task went far beyond mine technology, and within six months Mallory was being pilloried by Southern journalists and politicians for successive Confederate losses along the rivers of the Western theater, including Forts Henry and Donelson, Island No. 10 in the Mississippi and New Orleans. But Maury's attention was elsewhere: namely, the defense of Richmond. Largely out of sight of newspapermen and congressmen, Maury was turning the James River into a Union Navy death trap.

The first layer of the city's defense was already in place. Large guns from the naval shipyard in Portsmouth, Va., had been moved into positions at Drury's Bluff and Chaffin's farm, sites that commanded the river below Richmond. But Maury had bigger plans. In an 1862 report, he described three ranges of torpedoes he had placed downriver. There were 15 in all, encased in watertight casks, containing 160 pounds of explosives, electrically connected to a battery on shore and kept in place by buoys. They were connected in such a way that "each range are exploded at once," thus capable of destroying attacking gunboats approaching in pairs or single file.

Eleven other torpedoes with 70 pounds of explosives were being put in reserve. Also in reserve at Chaffin's farm were advanced galvanic batteries, at least one lent to Maury by Socrates Maupin, a professor of chemistry and pharmacy at the University of Virginia. Maury, as a member of the governor's advisory council, Virginia's de facto War Ministry after secession, had arranged with Maupin to use the university's laboratories to test and develop better batteries, different acid combinations, improved watertight casks and stronger insulated wires to make the torpedoes more deadly. Richmond's layered river defense, especially the mine ranges, became a model for other cities, including Wilmington, N.C., Mobile, Ala., and Charleston, S.C.

From the start, the Union Navy tried countering torpedoes with fenders and booms around large ships, as well as nets, grapnels and iron cutters to sever wires. Union ships dragged rivers all across the South, trying to break the electrical connections between batteries and torpedoes. Naval officers also asked their Army counterparts to sweep riverbanks for snipers and mine operators. Nevertheless, the deadly efficacy of torpedoes hampered Union advancement along rivers, as well as movement among blockade ships off the Southern coast. In explaining why his April 1863 attack of ironclads on Charleston had failed, Flag Officer Samuel F. DuPont blamed his ship commanders' "fear of these ghosts"—the hidden obstructions and invisible torpedoes that filled the harbor's channels.

While mines used to defend ports and rivers raised few ethical questions, their use on land and against nonmilitary targets troubled many Confederate leaders—especially army officers on the eastern front. In a debate that continues today, many argued that land mines were too indiscriminate to reliably kill only enemy combatants. And even then, they argued, such devices—tripped remotely, often from hiding—were a cowardly, unchivalrous method of war, unbecoming of Southern soldiers.

Nevertheless, exigency often trumped ethics, especially in the Western Theater. Gen. Leonidas Polk, a former bishop and a longtime Maury acquaintance, wrote from Columbus, Ky., "I feel constrained to urge upon you the necessity of at once furnishing me an officer familiar with the subject of submarine batteries and capable of a practicable application of this species of defense to the Mississippi River." But Polk had further plans for the devices: Lt. Isaac Brown, one of Maury's associates, not only mined the waters of southwestern Kentucky but also buried iron containers loaded with explosives to be detonated electrically along two routes leading into Columbus. Union soldiers discovered the torpedoes and dismantled them before they could explode.

Confederate officers soon began deploying land mines, also known as "subterra" mines, in the east as well. Brig. Gen. John Bankhead Magruder, commanding Confederate forces on the Virginia Peninsula, had witnessed how the Russians used mines during the Crimean War, knowledge he likely deepened in the late 1850s, when he was posted to Washington alongside his brother George, the chief of the Navy's ordnance bureau. He also established a strong friendship with Maury during that time.

Magruder, an amateur actor nicknamed "Prince John," is now best remembered for his successful deceptions during the siege of Yorktown in April 1862. He marched and countermarched his troops and cannons along a 13-mile defensive line, thus creating the impression of a much larger force than the 33,000 men under his command.

Less well known is the fact that Magruder was the first commander to employ mines on a large scale during the American Civil War. His soldiers hid mines in the sand around Yorktown, along its streets and roads and inside houses. After Yorktown was abandoned in May 1862, various Union units reported serious injuries and a few deaths from exploding mines.

Magruder wasn't alone in experimenting with mines. Gabriel Rains, an officer under Magruder, had even longer and more personal experience with mines than his commanding officer, having used them during the long-running Seminole Wars in Florida. A few months before the Confederate retreat from Yorktown, Rains was engaged in mining efforts in the James and the York Rivers to disrupt the Union Navy; why not, he wondered, place subterra mines leading up the peninsula from Fortress Monroe, the headquarters of the Union campaign? In the end he decided against it; too many civilians, he realized, were using the roads to flee advancing Union soldiers.

And yet a few weeks later, following a fierce skirmish at Williamsburg, Rains suppressed his earlier qualms. He had his soldiers bury four artillery shells on the main road leading to Richmond. As a lawyer watching a Union cavalry advance come to a standstill when the shells exploded on contact with the horses' hooves noted, "They never moved a peg after hearing the report." Years later, Rains boasted "these 4 shells checkmated the advance of 115,000 men under Gen. McClellan and turned them from their line of march."

In response, Maj. Gen. George B. McClellan, who also had been an American observer during the Crimean War, vowed to "make the prisoners remove [the mines] at their own peril," a threat repeated by Maj. Gen. William T. Sherman and Flag Officer David Dixon Porter.

Early Confederate successes with land mines set off new debates on the ethics of using "weapons that wait" to maim or kill soldiers, rather than against boats or ships. Secretary of War George Randolph finally stepped in to end the increasingly heated argument between Brig. Gen. James Longstreet and Rains over using mines. Randolph, Thomas Jefferson's grandson, drafted a series of ethical standards for mine use that may have eased some consciences in what was now becoming total war. And yet, in doing so, he helped make land mines an accepted part of the Southern arsenal.

As technology advanced and more officers employed torpedoes, new political and ethical questions surfaced. Mines, some argued, shouldn't be restricted to the battlefield; they could hamper all aspects of the Union war effort. But how far should the Confederacy go in taking mine warfare to all matters of Northern civilian life and commerce?

What prompted the most troubling debate was the "coal torpedo," an explosive device set in a block of cast iron "dipped in beeswax and pitch and covered with coal dust," so that it looked like a regular piece of coal. Confederate agents were to slip it into Union coal supplies; placed unknowingly into the burner of a steam engine, it would explode. The device was developed by the Belfast-born inventor Thomas Edgeworth Courtenay, who was quickly authorized to employ up to 25 men in a secret service to cast and distribute these devices.

Randolph's successor James A. Seddon now had to devise new rules of engagement. He ordered "passenger vessels of citizens of the United States on the high seas and private property in the water and [on] railroads or within the territory of the United States not to be subject of operations" using Courtenay's devices. "But the public property of the enemy may be destroyed wherever it may be found."

The use of mines never had a decisive impact on the war, though in one incident it came close. On Nov. 27, 1864, the Confederates found "the public property of the enemy"—a troop transport named Greyhound, steaming down the James River. Greyhound also served as Maj. Gen. Benjamin Butler's floating command post. Aboard with Butler were his staff, a convalescing major general and Flag Officer Porter, meeting in the ship's upper deck salon. It was, in the words of today's war, an especially "high value target."

Just as the ship passed the settlement of Bermuda Hundred, a few miles downriver from Richmond, there was a huge explosion in the engine room. Smoke began filling the ship, but the quick-thinking engineer "closed the throttle-valve, stopping the vessel, and opened the safety-valve," letting the steam escape. No one was killed in the blast. Nevertheless, the explosion gave the Union officers great pause. "In devices for blowing up vessels the Confederates were far ahead of us, putting Yankee ingenuity to shame," Porter wrote years later.

Indeed, by war's end the Confederates had added timers to the torpedoes to better sabotage barges, transports, warehouses and armories. By then serving in Europe, Maury provided the Confederacy with the latest exploders from the Continent; he was also exchanging letters with the head of the French Marine Ministry on developing self-propelled torpedoes for use at sea.

Historians estimate that mines claimed 35 Union ships and one Confederate vessel (in his postwar memoir, Rains claimed 58). There are no accurate figures on how many soldiers and civilians were maimed or killed by subterra explosives planted on land. While ethical debates remained, as the Civil War progressed and the Union brought its numerical and industrial superiority to bear in the total-war phase of the fighting, Confederate leaders felt they had no choice but to use mines to defend countless Southern cities (the Union also used mines on occasion, most famously at the Battle of the Crater outside Petersburg).

In the end, Rains firmly believed that he had advanced the science of war. He also best captured the moral dilemma of mine warfare. "Each new invention of war has been assailed and denounced as barbarous and anti-Christian," he wrote much later. "Yet each in its turn notwithstanding has taken its position by the universal consent of nations according to its efficiency in human slaughter."

'Our New Home Looks Inviting'
By MEGAN KATE NELSON

After a day spent exploring Hilton Head Island's beaches, fields and swampy forests, Wesley T. Harris ducked into his tent carrying several cotton bolls and a palm leaf. The cotton was for his family; he enclosed it in a letter he wrote to them that night. The palm leaf was for the tent, which he and his messmates had pitched earlier that day. Harris was hungrily looking forward to a dinner of fresh meat, "picked up" by a scouting party that afternoon. "This looks like living again," he wrote in his diary.

It was the second week of November 1861. Harris and his fellow soldiers in Company F, 3rd New Hampshire Volunteers, had taken part in the Port Royal expedition, establishing a foothold for the Union Army in South Carolina. Now they were setting up a permanent camp on Hilton Head and digging fortifications to shield them from Confederate attacks that could come by land or by sea. All hands were assigned to these duties, leveling out the campsite and transporting sand to the earthworks that reared up from the shore like breaching whales.

Fortified by his protein-packed dinner, Harris went out the next day and cut down several trees—most likely evergreens like loblolly or red bays, or perhaps a black gum, whose leaves would have been flaming a deep red in early November. These were not for burning in campfires, at least not yet. They were "shade trees," which he carefully placed in front of his tent. "Our new home looks the most inviting of any we have ever been in," he wrote proudly, "though it is quite sandy."

Throughout the war but especially during the winter months, both Union and Confederate quartermasters faced the challenge of housing tens of thousands of men in the fields and forests of the South. They issued A-frame tents, rectangles of canvas material raised up off the ground with poles often culled from nearby woodlands. Some soldiers received "Sibley" tents, which provided more interior space and headroom because of their conical shape. As the months passed and the temperatures fell, soldiers adapted.

By mid-December, Harris was trolling nearby wetlands for grass that "answers for straw & resembles it very much"—probably maidencane, which grows profusely in Hilton Head's lowlands. He likely spread this grass around to create a "floor" for his tent, or stuffed it into cotton sacks to make a mattress. This made Harris more comfortable but did little to ward off the cold. A few weeks later, while out on picket duty, he "got some boughs to make our shanty which was built of boughs a little warmer." By February 1862, Harris and his friends were cutting down trees to make beds, and taking lumber from winter camps abandoned by other Union regiments to lay floors and build "stockades," structures built of four cross-hatched logs, upon which they pitched their tents. Such structures appeared in all winter camps, both Union and Confederate; soldiers referred to them as their huts, cabins, shanties and log palaces.

Once their houses were built, soldiers turned to their interiors, building all manner of furniture for themselves. Many also demonstrated their talents in home décor. On Christmas Eve, all of the men of Company F "went out gathering brush and boughs to fix up our quarters." Harris was pleased with these efforts: "our Encampment looks fineally [sic]." When the Union photographer Alexander Gardner toured the Union army's winter camps in Virginia the next winter, he lauded "the ingenuity and taste" of Union soldiers. "The forests are ransacked for the brightest foliage, branches of the pine, cedar, and holly are laboriously collected," he noted approvingly, "and the work of beautifying the quarters continue[s] as long as material can be procured."

A federal camp on a South Carolina beach.

These were acts of self-preservation but also of domestication. Soldiers had left home, taken trains and boats—often for the first time—and landed in places that must have seemed like completely different worlds. For men from New England, the flat, lush and thickly humid lands of South Carolina were unsettling. Where were their granite hills, their evergreen forests? No wonder they walked sometimes as far as eight miles round trip to cut and drag trees back to their tents, anchoring them somewhat precariously in the sand. To have built a house surrounded by trees, to smell their sap and feel their leaves and needles under their fingers, gave soldiers a sense of place, of rootedness during a time of intense uncertainty and dislocation.

Many soldiers wrote proudly of these camp beautification and domestication projects, penning long letters to their family members full of detailed description of their huts, furniture and the camp streets. Others included sketches of their "streets," houses and floor plans. And when traveling photographers visited their camps, soldiers dragged their possessions to their front porches and dooryards, paying two dollars to fix images of their wartime homes on albumen paper.

One of the New Hampshire photographer Henry P. Moore's photographs of Harris's camp depicts three soldiers sitting around their tent, its flaps open to reveal a bed, writing desk (with a book, writing pen and jar of flowers arranged nicely on its top) and a floor made of planks. Moore has angled the shot to include the front walk, bordered on both sides with a neat fringe of maidencane. Another of Moore's images shows the headquarters of Lt. Col. John H. Jackson. The men stand somewhat stiffly and formally in front of their tents, surrounded by transplanted longleaf pines.

The effect of these images is somewhat surreal; the contrast of the tents and front walks, the longleafs' drooping needles and the smooth yards of sand suggest a kind of domesticity that would have been recognizable to viewers back in New Hampshire. But they also convey the utter strangeness of this military life and landscape.

Some soldiers never quite got used to the experience of building houses for themselves in the most unlikely of places. For others, the novelty wore off after they were ordered to build and then abandon two, then three, then four houses over the course of a winter. Wesley Harris remained with his regiment for the rest of his service, moving northward to take part in the siege of Charleston and building multiple houses along the way. He did not talk much about his shanties in his diary entries after that first winter. But Harris still found time to go out and explore the island landscapes in which he found himself; scattered throughout the three volumes he wrote during the war are flowers, pressed carefully between their pages.

A Capitol Dilemma
By GUY GUGLIOTTA

By the end of February 1862, construction of the enlarged Capitol building in Washington had been suspended for nine and a half months. The federal government had begun the project 12 years earlier, intending to add new House and Senate wings at either end of the original building, topped by a majestic cast-iron dome above the old central section. But now the country was deep in civil war, and the building was left towering but unfinished.

True, much had been completed. Both the Senate and House had new, elegantly appointed chambers. Floors were tiled in elaborately colored patterns. Many corridors and committee rooms were decorated with frescoes, wall paintings and ornately patterned motifs, featuring everything from native birds to the signs of the zodiac and trompe l'oeil cameos of famous Americans. Abraham Lincoln had been inaugurated on the East Front Capitol steps below the half-completed dome, an iron shell with a giant wooden derrick sticking out of the top of it, waiting to hoist chunks of cast iron nearly 300 feet in the air to be bolted into place.

But on May 15, 1861, Army Capt. Montgomery C. Meigs, the engineer in charge of the project, ordered construction suspended for the duration of the war. For the rest of the year, marble porticoes for the new Senate and House sat unfinished, and most of the new one-piece marble columns that were to girdle the new construction had not arrived. Terraces and steps still needed to be added in several locations.

There was too much else to do, too many other places to spend money and too many terrible things to think about. Building the Capitol was a luxury the country could ill afford. Two weeks after Meigs shut the Capitol down, Lincoln made him a brigadier general and appointed him chief of the Union Army's quartermaster corps, a job he would hold with great distinction for 21 years.

But by February 1862, it was clear Meigs had done the Capitol no favors. For several months, the Army had used it as a barracks. Soldiers scuffed the carpets, chopped up desks with their knives, lit campfires in the front yard, swung from ropes in the rotunda and used every byway and storeroom in the building as a privy. The commissary general had put ovens in the basement and was baking bread for the entire Army of the Potomac. Soot from the fires had invaded the stacks in the Library of Congress, with ruinous effect.

The Army had mercifully departed by the end of the year, but when the second session of the 37th Congress convened Dec. 2, 1861, the picture was truly grim. Loose pieces of cast-iron dome—$205,000 worth—lay on the grounds, stained and rusted. Inside, there was considerable water damage and mildew caused by seepage through cracks and crevices around the unfinished porticoes. Plaster was decaying in places and falling off the wall. Many stucco ornaments were already destroyed and others were heavily damaged. The Army had gobbled up most of the workforce. It was a mess.

A plan to resume construction had begun during the summer of 1861. The ringleader was Thomas U. Walter, the illustrious Philadelphia architect who had designed the new wings and the dome. He and Meigs had been close colleagues in the mid-1850s, but the pair had had a colossal and very public falling-out over Meigs's suspicion—justified, it turned out—that Walter was trying to undercut him and take his job, and Walter's fear—also justified—that Meigs was trying to minimize Walter's accomplishments and, where possible, take credit for them. The two men had barely spoken since 1858.

Walter's accomplices were his three most important contractors: John Rice, another Philadelphian whose quarry in Lee, Mass., was supplying the white marble for the facade of the Capitol; a local Washington entrepreneur, Alexander Provest, whose army of craftsmen was sawing, carving, polishing and setting the stone when it arrived; and Charles Fowler, a Bronx foundryman who was casting the dome.

"We are putting our heads together in reference to future operations," Walter wrote in a letter to his wife, Amanda, in July. "My present impression is that we will put things into a better shape than they have ever been before."

But the climate was not yet ripe. Congress was traumatized and unable to think about anything but the war, and Meigs, organizing the logistical juggernaut that would eventually destroy the Confederacy, could do no wrong. The conspirators' eventual solution, Walter told Rice in a note, was to get the project away from the War Department, which had had control of it for a decade, and transfer it to the Interior Department. Meigs would be bureaucratically eliminated.

It was then that Fowler made the decisive move. When Meigs suspended work on the Capitol, there were 1.3 million pounds of dome castings lying on the ground. Fowler could have stopped work, dismantled his workshops and put the iron in storage. But instead Fowler made a crucial decision to keep going, gambling that he would eventually be paid. Dome construction did not proceed rapidly after Meigs suspended operations, but it did proceed, and it was vital in establishing the earnest intentions of Walter and the contractors.

In mid-August 1861, Fowler made his case for resumption to Vermont Senator Solomon Foot, president pro tempore of the Senate, who endorsed his proposal. Then he went to see Meigs—Walter stayed out of sight—who told them he could not spare any money for the Capitol. So the plotters went over Meigs's head to Secretary of War Simon Cameron, who agreed to recommend that construction be resumed.

But then nothing happened—until Meigs made a crucial mistake in November. In his annual report on the Capitol extension, he spent most of his effort touting his past accomplishments: "The building has been in use for some years, and has realized all that I undertook to accomplish in regard to light, warmth, ventilation and fitness for debate and legislation," he wrote. "The health of the legislative bodies has never been better." The new chambers had conducted more business in a shorter time, he said, and the acoustics were flawless. The "spacious galleries" attracted crowds of people during the prewar hearings, and audiences "were able to hear the words of those who then debated the greatest questions discussed in our Congress since the revolution."

Congress had heard most of this so many times before, and members had long ago made up their minds about it and generally supported Meigs. But then Meigs noted that while troops had used the Capitol as a barracks, "the little injury done by them to the walls has been repaired." This was patently absurd. Meigs had at once insulted congressional intelligence and made it obvious that he had not visited the Capitol in months. Clearly he had way too much on his plate and needed to be gotten out of the way.

The trap was sprung. On March 5, 1862, Foot introduced a Senate resolution calling for Capitol construction to be transferred to Interior. The debate dusted off many old complaints about the project, several of which had long ago been overtaken by events. What business did the Army have building civilian structures? (They had the best, and cheapest, engineers.) Why does the Capitol need such fancy decoration? (It did not, but the decoration had been done.) Was this just another episode in the endless power struggle between Walter and Meigs? (Of course.) And why do the new chambers have no windows? Moving them to the middle of the building, noted New Hampshire abolitionist Senator John Hale, an outspoken opponent of the new Capitol for more than a decade, was about as useful as putting "a mousetrap in a pot." (The decision to put the chambers in the middle of the building had been made eight years earlier.)

Several things had changed, however. The building had taken a beating from troops and weather, and needed to be protected, and quickly. Foot, for one, had nothing against Meigs, but he and the War Department could not give the Capitol the attention it deserved.

Less obvious, but probably also true, Meigs may have had "a laudable ambition to distinguish himself by the completion of all of these works," as Massachusetts Republican Charles R. Train, the chairman of the House Committee on Public Buildings and Grounds, remarked, and "it would be a nice little entertainment for the decline of his life." However, Train asked, "Are we to suffer loss" until then because "Meigs would not allow Walter to complete the building?"

Finally, and most important, attitudes toward the Capitol had themselves changed. When the redesign began in 1850, Congress could barely be cajoled into financing it. Many lawmakers—perhaps the majority—were preoccupied with districts or states, regarded Washington as a dreary backwater and viewed the federal government as a barely necessary evil, to be tolerated, but never enhanced. And by tripling the size of the Capitol, the United States was putting on airs, like those decadent Europeans.

As the decade wore on, however, the new project had become a rallying point for increasingly fearful Northerners and Southerners who needed something to reaffirm the bonds that still held them together. The new Capitol was about hope for the future during a time of profound distress.

By March 1862, the future had arrived, and it was going to be a prolonged and bloody catastrophe. The Capitol was no longer simply a hope. It was, on the Union side, fulfillment, and by March 1862,

Congress saw this clearly. The United States was becoming a nation, embodied in the Capitol. Never again would individual states pretend to dictate the terms of their membership in the Union.

"Sir, we are strong enough yet, thank God, to put down this rebellion and to put up this our Capitol at the same time," Foot said on the Senate floor on March 25. "And when the rebellion shall have been suppressed—as suppressed it soon will be; when this war shall have been terminated and when this union of ours shall have been restored it will furnish a fitting and appropriate occasion to celebrate that welcome event." The joint resolution passed in both houses with fewer than 10 votes in opposition. Construction on the Capitol resumed in April.

Why Shiloh Matters
By WINSTON GROOM

The Battle of Shiloh began at sunrise on April 6, 1862—the Sabbath—as 45,000 Confederate soldiers swooped down on an unsuspecting Union army encamped at Pittsburg Landing, a nondescript hog-and-cotton steamboat dock on the Tennessee River. What followed were two of the bloodiest days of the Civil War, leaving 24,000 men on both sides dead, dying and wounded.

When it was over the nation—two nations as it were, for the moment—convulsed, horrified, at the results. A great battle had indeed been anticipated; at stake was control of the Mississippi River Valley, which would likely decide who won the war. But the Battle of Shiloh was not the outcome that anyone wanted.

Beyond the grisly statistics, Americans north and south of the Mason-Dixon line were suddenly confronted with the sobering fact that Shiloh hadn't been the decisive battle-to-end-all-battles; there was no crushing victory—only death and carnage on a scale previously unimaginable. The casualty figures at Shiloh were five times greater than its only major predecessor engagement, the Battle of Bull Run, and people were left with the shocking apprehension that more, and perhaps many more, such confrontations were in store before the thing was settled.

Shiloh National Military Park in Shiloh, Tenn.

Among the many ironies of the battle is that its name was taken from a small chink-and-mortar Methodist chapel on the battlefield that had been christened after the Hebrew expression for "Place of Peace." The building itself was hardly better than a respectable Tennessee corncrib, but it was a house of God and gave its name to the first of the great battles of the Civil War.

The fate of the armies was sealed in mid-March when Gen. Ulysses S. Grant's 49,000 men began disembarking at Pittsburg Landing. Elsie Duncan Hurt was nine years old at the time, a child of one of the area's farmers. Her black nurse returned from the Landing one day with word that "there were strange steamboats on the river and Yankees camped in the hills."

This news soon flashed to Corinth, Miss., a mere 20 miles to the south, where the renowned Confederate general Albert Sidney Johnston had gathered 45,000 rebel soldiers bound to the destruction of Yankee host invading Southern soil. At Johnston's side was the dashing and magnificently named Louisiana Creole general Pierre Gustave Toutant Beauregard, recently celebrated as the "hero" of Bull Run.

Noted as a master of strategy and tactics, Beauregard urged an immediate attack on Grant, who was awaiting the arrival of a second Union army marching overland from Nashville under Gen. Don Carlos Buell. When the two combined, they would constitute an irresistible force against any rebel army in the western theater.

Johnston also wanted to wait for another army, a 14,000-man force coming from Arkansas under Gen. Earl Van Dorn, but Beauregard persuaded him to strike at once, before Buell could arrive. Johnston told the Creole to draw up the attack order.

Confusion and disarray reigned from the outset. First came an appalling mix-up in the muddy streets of Corinth, where the 10,000-man corps of Gen. Leonidias Polk (a cousin of President James K. Polk and, until recently, the Episcopal bishop of Louisiana) was encamped with all of its wagons, animals and baggage.

For reasons unknown, Polk idiotically refused to march without a written order—which was still being composed—and it proved impossible for the other corps to move around him. At long last Polk shoved off, but the delay cost the Confederates precious time and prompted one of his officers to remark, "Polk had been in the cloth too long."

The remainder of the march quickly turned into such a ceaseless military fiasco that it reminded an artillery captain "of the temple scene from 'Orlando Furioso.'" A mighty rainstorm doused the countryside in floods and washed out roads. Men became lost during the night—whole regiments got lost, even guides got lost—and by dawn entire divisions were so hopelessly entangled that it became necessary to postpone the attack until April 6, perhaps a fatal error.

Meanwhile Grant's army languished at Pittsburg Landing, supremely ignorant of the menace slowly lurching toward it.

The Yankee soldiers had not been told to fortify their positions—in fact they were ordered not to—which left them camping in the open like Boy Scouts, while daily instruction was given in close-order drill, weapons training and latrine building.

This lack of preparation against attack has never been satisfactorily explained. After the battle, Gen. William Tecumseh Sherman suggested that fortifying adversely affected the courage of the men, implying that if they dug in it would look like they were scared of the rebels. Both he and Grant maintained that since there were so many green, or untrained, volunteers in the army, the men's time would be better spent learning military technique.

In any case, even as the attack was about to burst upon them, when Yankee officers in the most forward camps began reporting a strong enemy presence in their fronts, Sherman threatened to have them arrested for spreading false rumors.

On the morning of April 6, when these reports could no longer be ignored, Sherman crossly mounted and rode forward—just as the main Confederate battle line emerged from a hedge of trees. As he reached for his field glasses, a bullet struck his orderly in the head; the orderly toppled from his horse, dead. Sherman himself was hit in the hand and dashed off, shouting, "My God, we are attacked!"

All of this overshadowed an otherwise idyllic Sunday morning that had broken cool, bright and clear in the Yankee camps, where the men were finishing breakfast, polishing brass and leather or attending services. Orchards were in full flower, dogwoods were in bloom, the forest floor was carpeted with violets. A number of men recorded that a great many birds were singing in the trees, an ironic cacophony against the sudden spatter of gunfire.

The rebel army, together at last, presented a stirring and dismaying sight, as regiment after regiment, dressed in Confederate gray or butternut brown, emerged from the woods in three successive waves, each in a line two miles long. Banners waving, officers on horseback shouting orders, they marched in perfect order "as if they were on parade." Sunlight glinted off their gun barrels and bayonets and their bands played "Dixie," but above it all the bone-chilling Rebel Yell rose from tens of thousands of throats, nearly drowning out the music and the gunfire.

On they crashed forward through forest and field, preceded by a diaspora of frightened wildlife—bounding rabbits, leaping deer, whirring coveys of quail—while Union officers tried frantically to put their units into fighting order. Men, some of whom had only received their weapons the day before, were hastily shoved into a line of battle. Artillery batteries that had never fired a round were raced to the front, where they began blasting shot, shell, canister and grape into the surging enemy.

Among the first casualties was the rebel general Adley H. Gladden, a prominent New Orleans merchant and president of that city's exclusive Boston Club. Leading a charge, he was blown from his horse by a cannonball that tore off his arm at the shoulder, mortally wounding him.

His opposite in the Union line was 38-year-old Col. Everett Peabody, a 6-foot-1, 240-pound, Massachusetts-born and Harvard-educated engineer commanding a Missouri volunteer regiment that bore the brunt of Gladden's attack. He was struck by five bullets during the first two hours of fighting, buying time for the Yankee divisions in his rear, before a sixth slug shattered his skull, killing him.

All morning the Confederates drove the blue coats northward in a carnival of carnage that left the mutilated bodies of both sides strewn in heaps amid great heroism and equally great cowardice. An estimated 10,000 of Grant's troops fled the fighting and hid under the bluffs by the river, while a number of rebel regiments were banished to the rear for timidity in battle.

Grant had arrived on the battlefield about 9 a.m. after a two-hour steamboat trip from the mansion where he'd been staying, nine miles downriver. It was an unfortunate and unfair stain on his reputation that, even years afterward, the lady of the house was called upon to testify that Grant was sober when he left the premises.

Thirty-nine years old, flawed, an indifferent West Point student, disgraced as an army officer, gossiped about as an alcoholic, a failed farmer and a failed businessman, Ulysses Grant had come to his command almost as a fluke. Only nine months earlier the Illinois governor had appointed him to take charge of a dissolute regiment of volunteers that he described as "a mob of chicken-thieves, led by a drunkard."

Grant managed to whip these miscreants into shape so efficiently he was given two more troublesome regiments, which constituted a brigade. Under army regulations, such a command required a brigadier general, and thus the once-disgraced Grant suddenly found himself wearing the stars of a general officer in the United States Army.

Early on he had become friends with another flawed officer, Sherman, who had been publically accused of being both "timid" as well as "insane" and sent into military limbo before redeeming himself with the army during Grant's push south. It was suggested that at Shiloh Sherman might have been overcompensating for the accusation of timidity by belittling the notion of a rebel attack.

The rebel onslaught continued unabated, and the Union front lines grudgingly collapsed as the Confederates pressed forward. Elsie Duncan Hurt remembered: "The fighting began at our gate just past the house. As the battle raged it got further away leaving dead men and dead horses behind."

About midday the fighting coalesced around the Union center, at a scrubwood forest that became known as the Hornet's Nest for the interminable bullets zinging through the air. It was bisected by an old wagon trail called the Sunken Road, where so many soldiers of both sides perished. Men who went through there next day said that such trees as remained standing were riddled with so many thousands of bullet holes they were astonished anyone, or anything, had survived it.

By mid-afternoon General Johnston was exceedingly pleased with the progress of his assault. The original intention was to drive the Yankees northwestward, into the boggy, moccasin-infested swamps of Snake and Owl Creeks, where they could be rounded up as prisoners. Now they were simply being driven backward—due north.

But the fortunes of war frowned on General Johnston that day. Acclaimed personally by Jefferson Davis as the Confederacy's finest officer, Johnston was a perfect specimen of military prowess and acumen, and at 59, he was at the height of his career when the war broke out. He spurned an offer of high Union command to side with his native South and was put in charge of the Department of the West.

Even with the frequent bullet or cannonball whizzing overhead, and with death and destruction all around him, Johnston was in unabashedly good humor until word came from one of his corps commanders that a Tennessee brigade was refusing to fight. Shocked, he rode to the scene and shamed the Tennesseans by declaring that he would personally lead their charge. The attack was soon successful in taking a bloody Union strong point known as the Peach Orchard, amid a rain of bullet-clipped blossoms that fluttered down like snowflakes among the wounded, the dying and the dead.

Shattered refugees from both sides made their way nearby to the so-called Bloody Pond to bathe their wounds beneath an unspoken (and unauthorized) truce, as the savage fighting raged all around them.

Returning from his charge about 2 p.m., Johnston suddenly reeled in his saddle. When he was lowered from his horse it was discovered that a bullet had severed an artery behind his knee; within a few minutes he bled to death in his boot. In the rush of battle, he hadn't even known he was hit. A doctor would have immediately stanched the wound with a tourniquet, but as luck would have it, Johnston had sent his doctor away to tend some wounded Yankee soldiers.

Command abruptly devolved on Beauregard, whose headquarters had moved forward near the Shiloh church where Sherman had been encamped. Following Johnston's death a lull was said to have settled over the field for nearly an hour, which many Southerner's blamed on Beauregard's inaction. Nevertheless, as the afternoon wore on, the Confederates pressed nearer to Pittsburg Landing, the last Union stronghold.

The Hornet's Nest finally collapsed between 5 and 6 p.m. with the mortal wounding of Union Gen. W.H.L. Wallace, a division commander, whose young wife, come to surprise him, was waiting on a steamboat at the landing. Shortly afterward came the capture of Union Gen. Benjamin Prentiss, along with the surrender of his entire division. As the sun cast its last, long shadows, it was beginning to look like the end for the federal army.

Good news came with the arrival of Buell, whose army would cross the river near sundown. It was not a moment too soon, for Grant's army had begun to draw up for a last-ditch stand with its back to the miry wastes of Snake Creek. Gen. Braxton Bragg immediately ordered his corps to "Sweep everything forward. Drive the enemy into the river."

Grant's adjutant had placed a battery of enormous siege guns in the Union line at that particular point, and the very shock of its fire drove the Confederates back. As Grant was observing these proceedings, a rebel cannonball blew the head off of one of his aides standing not 10 feet away.

Soon Bragg was sending out reinforcements, organizing another, final charge to break the Union line. Then he was staggered by orders from a messenger: Beauregard, unaware that Buell had arrived, had called off the attack till morning.

Bragg was convinced that even though some of Buell's army was taking the field, one last great charge would split the line and the battle would be won. "My God!" Bragg cried, as he watched other rebel units pulling back. "Too late! My God! Too late!"

It was also too true. Beauregard, commanding from the Shiloh church nearly two miles from the present scene of battle, was unaware that Buell's army was arriving. He believed only the remaining Yankees of Grant were milling around Pittsburg Landing like goats being prepared for the sacrifice and could be mopped up in the morning.

But with morning instead came one of the great reversals of the Civil War. Dawn brought an uproar of Union artillery and word that the Yankees were attacking all across the Rebel front. For half a day Beauregard put up a good fight, if for no other reason than he couldn't think of anything better to do, but the odds were hopeless and his men were spent. At around 2 p.m. on April 7, Beauregard ordered a withdrawal back to the stronghold of Corinth.

That should have ended the matter, but instead the next day Sherman took a large force in pursuit until he ran into a man—Nathan Bedford Forrest—with whose name he would become well acquainted as the war progressed. At the Battle of Fallen Timbers on April 8, Forrest taught Sherman a lesson about the power of cavalry that he would not soon forget, and with that, the fighting at Shiloh came to an end.

There remained the repugnant task of burying the thousands of dead, as well as hundreds of dead horses. The butcher's bill at Shiloh was just shy of 24,000 killed, wounded and missing, about evenly divided between both sides.

Nothing like it had ever happened in the Western Hemisphere. By comparison, the combined casualties at the Battle of Bull Run were 4,800. In fact, the two days fighting at Shiloh had produced more casualties than all the previous wars of the United States, combined.

Word soon got out to the Union public that Grant's army had been surprised, that men were bayonetted to death in their tents while they slept, which was an exaggeration. The public was incensed to hear that an entire 8,000-man division never took the field on the terrible first day, which was true. (It belonged to Gen. Lew Wallace, who took the wrong road and would afterward write the novel "Ben Hur.")

There was also the shameful matter of the 10,000 of Grant's soldiers who ran away.

In the press and in the halls of Congress Grant was censured for dallying in a mansion miles from the battlefield, for failing to fortify, or reconnoiter, or to even have a battle plan in case of attack, as well as failing to pursue and destroy the beaten Confederate army. Much of this sticks. But there were also accusations of drunkenness, indifference and sloth, which do not.

In Washington, a chorus arose for Grant's removal, despite the fact that he had won the battle. Popular lore has it that when Grant was accused of drunkenness, Lincoln told the critics, "Then find out what kind of whiskey he drinks and send a barrel to my other generals." There is no real evidence he ever said this, but there is evidence that he said of Grant: "I can't spare that man. He fights."

In the South there was widespread dismay over the outcome and over the death of Sidney Johnston. Late on the first day of battle Beauregard had foolishly sent a telegram to Richmond saying, "The day is ours!" Disappointment was palpable, and Davis wept bitterly over Johnston's death—they had been at West Point together. He never forgave Beauregard for calling off the attack.

The significance of Shiloh cannot be overstated. If the Union had lost badly, there would have been practically nothing standing in the way of a Southern invasion of the North. Cities like St. Louis, Cincinnati, Chicago, even Cleveland, would have been exposed. Almost certainly Kentucky would have joined the Confederacy—and probably Missouri as well, a calamity for the Union. Southern states would have rallied and recruits poured in. Lincoln would have had to shift his armies to counter the threat, upsetting the military and political balance at the most critical time.

None of that happened, of course. But a very real and important result of the battle was that after Shiloh Grant reached the stark conclusion that the only way to restore the Union would be the total conquest—. or in his words, "subjugation"—of the South. Sherman had understood this long before Shiloh and began to indulge his soon-to-be well-known pyromaniacal urges along the Mississippi River near Memphis.

But the overarching significance of Shiloh was to impress on everyone that there was never going to be one neat, brilliant, military maneuver that would end the war—or even come close to winning it. It was as if Shiloh had unleashed some tremendous, murderous thing that was going to "drench the country in blood," as Sherman had prophesied on the eve of secession.

From the ordinary foot soldiers' point of view, they had "seen the elephant," as the expression of the day went. For many it was so terrible that they ran and hid behind the bluffs. It was terrible for others too, but they stood their ground and faced it, or died trying. None of them who went through Shiloh would be the same again.

Confederate private Sam Watkins of the First Tennessee summed it up in his countrified elegance: "I had been feeling mean all morning, as if I had stolen a sheep. I had heard and read of battlefields, seen pictures of battlefields, of horses and men, of cannons and wagons, all jumbled together, while the ground was strewn with dead and dying and wounded, but I must confess I never realized the 'pomp and circumstance' of the thing called 'glorious war' until I saw this."

The Great Locomotive Chase
By PHIL LEIGH

For Confederates, the quickest connection across the Appalachian Mountains, which roughly split the eastern and western theaters of the war, was a railroad line from Richmond, Va., to Chattanooga, Tenn. From Chattanooga other lines fanned west and south toward the Mississippi and the Gulf of Mexico. Consequently, the Mountain City's strategic significance was far greater than its population of just 2,500 people might lead one to believe.

Union forces would not gain undisputed control of the town until November 1863. But one general authorized a daring plan that could have led to Federal occupation more than a year and a half earlier: a scheme that, today, is popularly remembered as the Great Locomotive Chase.

After Ulysses S. Grant's capture of Fort Donelson, Tenn., in February 1862 and Samuel Curtis's victory at Pea Ridge, Ark., in early March, their theater commander in St. Louis, Henry Halleck, was awarded overall authority in the West. He promptly urged a previously uncooperative, and now subordinate, Don Carlos Buell in Nashville, Tenn., to join most of his army with Grant's in western Tennessee. Once combined, the two armies could better meet the challenge of a Confederate force concentrating at Corinth, Miss., under Gen. Albert Sidney Johnston and Gen. P.G.T. Beauregard. The result would become the Civil War's first epic battle, at Shiloh, on April 6 and 7.

But Buell could not responsibly ignore the rest of Tennessee. He left 18,000 soldiers around Nashville, and sent a division eastward to the Cumberland Gap, another point of passage through the Appalachians. At the same time, he authorized Gen. Ormsby Mitchel to take 8,000 troops southward into northern Alabama.

As Shiloh combatants were bedding down after the first day's fighting, 200 miles to the east, in Shelbyville, Tenn., General Mitchel was meeting with a spy named James Andrews who had a plan to capture Chattanooga.

Owing to the risk-everything Confederate concentration at Corinth, Chattanooga was lightly defended. If a Union force were to attack suddenly, the town would be nearly helpless—unless reinforcements could quickly come by rail from either Corinth or Atlanta. If Mitchel blocked the Chattanooga-to-Corinth railroad, he would thwart Confederate aid from the west. To prevent Confederate reinforcements from the south, Andrews proposed to covertly capture a train just north of Atlanta, ride it to Chattanooga, and destroy rail facilities along the way. Once at the Mountain City, he would switch to the line connecting with Mitchel, leaving an open door to Chattanooga behind. With luck, Mitchel might occupy Chattanooga and even strengthen his grip with reinforcements via rail from the troops Buell left in Nashville.

To surprise the enemy, Mitchel and Andrews agreed to synchronize their actions for April 11. Andrews selected about 20 volunteers. Traveling in small groups, they were to reassemble at Marietta, Ga., on April 10 and hijack a train for Chattanooga the following morning. That same morning Mitchel was to advance eastward along the Corinth-to-Chattanooga line and meet the raiders later in the day.

But April 7 was the first in a string of 10 rainy days, setting Andrews a full day behind schedule. The raiders finally boarded a train on April 12, about 6 a.m. Eight miles into the trip, at the Big Shanty breakfast stop, they took control of the train, which was pulled by a locomotive named the General. Continuing northward, the raiders repeatedly cut telegraph line and twice removed rails behind them, although the latter task was more time-consuming than expected.

Meanwhile, General Mitchel had blocked the Chattanooga-to-Corinth railroad by quickly seizing Huntsville, Ala., on April 11. The next morning he led a column toward Chattanooga. After capturing a key bridge, Mitchel halted 28 miles from the town to meet Andrews—if he was still coming.

Andrews was running behind; from Big Shanty the raiders were still 110 miles south of Chattanooga. However, if they could destroy the important Oostanaula River Bridge 60 miles up the line, it would be unlikely that anyone could follow them the same day—thereby enabling them to leisurely wreck multiple smaller bridges further ahead.

The Confederates weren't slow in pursuit. Led by a young conductor named William Fuller, several railroad employees set out after the General. They started on foot, but the men soon commandeered a push car, then a switching engine and finally another locomotive, the Smith, less powerful than the General.

It was a tough chase. They were thrown off the push car where the raiders had removed a rail and had to abandon the Smith where Andrews derailed track a second time. Two of them continued on foot to the next station, where they took over yet another locomotive, the Texas, this time a match in speed and strength to the General. Lacking a turntable in the rail yard, the Texas sidetracked its cars, shifted into reverse, and chased after the General, whistling frequently to warn southbound trains of its unscheduled run.

Andrews, meanwhile, had been delayed. Because Mitchel's forces now threatened Chattanooga, Confederates in the city had sent rolling stock southward to safety, and straight into the General's path. Andrews tried to bluff, claiming that the General was actually a priority munitions train destined for General Beauregard, but his plea didn't get him very far in the rush from the Union forces.

Two miles short of the Oostanaula Bridge, Andrews stopped to wreck track a third time, but by this time the Texas was coming into view. The raiders hurried off, dropping railroad ties out the back and de-coupling boxcars in an attempt to block the Texas. Eventually they had to refuel at a wood-and-water station, but didn't have enough time to complete the job.

Meanwhile, the Texas picked up a telegraph clerk and later dropped him at a station where the raiders had been too hurried to cut the line. The clerk sent word to the Confederate garrison in Chattanooga, which promptly dispatched a company to capture the raiders.

Eventually the General ran out of steam. The raiders scattered on foot, but none escaped. Being dressed as civilians, Andrews and seven others were tried and executed as unlawful combatants under military conventions applicable to both North and South.

The Confederate bureaucracy was undecided about the fate of the remaining men. They were imprisoned in Atlanta, but broke out in October 1862. Ten escaped prison grounds and only two were recaptured. Traveling in four separate pairs, the other eight eventually reached safety among various Union commands. (Their exploits would later form the basis for two movies, Buster Keaton's "The General" and "The Great Locomotive Chase," starring Fess Parker.)

Perhaps most remarkable were the two who paddled 400 miles down the Chattahoochee River, away from Atlanta and toward the Florida coast, for three weeks. Their clothes became shredded. Mosquitoes drove them to cover their bodies with moss. When they finally reached open waters, they paddled out to a blockading Federal warship, where their strange appearance dismayed the crew.

The remaining six were locked up until March 1863, when they were traded as part of a prisoner exchange. They were taken to Washington, where they met Secretary of War Edwin Stanton and President Abraham Lincoln. Stanton gave them a military decoration recently created by Congress (one that would be given to the eight Atlanta escapees later): the Congressional Medal of Honor.

The Civil War and Warfighting

By PETER COZZENS

The Civil War began as a grand delusion. Most everyone North and South expected a short conflict in which one battle would decide the outcome. Few thought much blood would be shed. Each army expected the other to run after the first shots were fired. President Abraham Lincoln initially called out a mere 75,000 three-month's volunteers to quell the rebellion. The new Confederacy mustered just 100,000 short-term volunteers. Aside from a few remaining veterans of the Mexican War, no one on either side had ever been in battle.

But the war developed its own logic. Pressure on Lincoln to end the conflict quickly overcame considerations of military preparedness, and in July 1861 he ordered an army of poorly trained volunteers to attack an equally green Confederate force at Manassas Junction, Va. The ensuing First Battle of Bull Run turned into a Federal rout, which tired and disorganized Confederates were unable to exploit—a pattern that would repeat itself in every major clash between then and the end of 1862.

After First Bull Run came nearly eight months of relative calm, as both sides geared up for a long war and trained huge armies totaling nearly a million men. Three theaters of operations emerged. The Eastern Theater embraced operations on the Atlantic side of the Allegheny Mountains; the Western Theater encompassed the territory between the Alleghenies and the Mississippi River; and the Trans-Mississippi Theater, largely forgotten in the early phases of the war, which included the states of Arkansas, Texas and Louisiana.

After licking its wounds, the Union devised a multi-prong strategy for 1862. Above all, it aimed to capture the Confederate capital at Richmond, Va. At the same time, forces in the West would seize as much of the Mississippi River as possible to cut the Confederacy in half. Other objectives included the bringing of neutral Kentucky into the Union fold and an advance into Tennessee and the Southern heartland. In response, the Confederacy dispersed its forces in the West, adopting a forward defense aimed at holding every inch of territory. In the East, the South concentrated forces to shield Richmond.

The year began promisingly for the Union. An obscure brigadier general named Ulysses S. Grant shattered the Confederate defensive cordon in February 1862, sweeping Tennessee nearly clear of Confederates with the capture of Fort Donelson, the first major Union victory of the war. In March, a Northern army secured Missouri for the Union with victory at the Battle of Pea Ridge, Ark. Then came the Battle of Shiloh in April 1862, the greatest bloodletting yet seen on the American continent. General Grant prevailed, but in his pyrrhic victory recognized a harsh truth: "Up to the battle of Shiloh, I believed the rebellion would collapse suddenly and soon if a decisive victory could be gained over any of its armies." But afterward, he said, "I gave up all idea of saving the Union except by complete conquest."

Nothing remotely approaching conquest came in 1862. In the Eastern Theater, Robert E. Lee blunted Maj. Gen. George B. McClellan's drive up the Virginia Peninsula toward Richmond in the Seven Days Battles, and then defeated a second Union army at the Second Battle of Bull Run. The initiative passed to the Confederates. Lee invaded Maryland, and in the Western Theater Gen. Braxton Bragg invaded Kentucky. The advance was part of an evolving Southern strategy of the offensive-defense, designed to ease pressure on the Confederate states, deflate Northern morale and perhaps gain European recognition. The autumn counteroffensives failed. McClellan defeated Lee at the Battle of Antietam, and Bragg abandoned Kentucky after the indecisive Battle of Perryville. Never again would the South come so close to victory.

In December, Lee defeated yet another Federal drive against Richmond, dealing Maj. Gen. Ambrose Burnside a crushing defeat at Fredericksburg. On New Year's Eve, the two principal armies in the Western Theater clashed at Murfreesboro, Tenn. in the Battle of Stones River; the New Year opened with the outcome of that pivotal battle, in doubt.

Europeans struggled to understand the conflict convulsing America. The Paris newspaper Le Figaro observed:

> These Americans are fighting on a military system
> inaugurated by the Kilkenny cats. The two armies meet
> and fight and slaughter each other with the utmost fury.
> Then they fall back and reorganize for another general
> massacre. Positively, the war will end when the last
> man is killed.

Common soldiers could understand that logic. Many had seen their regiments nearly obliterated during the war's second year. The First Texas Infantry entered the Battle of Antietam with 226 men and emerged with just 40. At Second Bull Run, the 21st Georgia lost 184 of 242 men. Regimental losses of 50 percent in a single battle were not uncommon. In part, the slaughter could be blamed on the failure of the generals to adapt to modern battlefield realities. Army commanders clung to outdated Napoleonic tactics. Infantry fought shoulder-to-shoulder in lines of battle or in densely packed columns. Opposing commanders tried to outflank one another, but more often than not battles degenerated into stand-up, close-range slugging matches. Artillery was primarily a defensive arm. Cavalry reconnoitered and raided, but played an insignificant role in the major battles of 1861–1862. It was an infantryman's war.

The tight combat formations depersonalized battle and rendered the common soldier as an individual largely irrelevant. "If a comrade falls, the column still moves on," a Union veteran explained to civilians. "No one, by the late rules of war, dare stop to bear off the wounded or sympathize with those in the throes of death." Because they fired as a unit and gun smoke blanketed the field after the first volleys, soldiers seldom saw the victims of their individual shots, or even knew if they had hit anyone—perhaps the only saving grace of Civil War combat.

The year 1862 had begun with stunning Union victories in the West and ended in bitter defeat in the East. Ten major battles had been fought, and tens of thousands had died, but the strategic chessboard remained largely unchanged. War weariness settled over the home fronts, and the flow of recruits grew thin. The federal government began to offer bounties to entice men to join, and the Confederacy introduced conscription. Yet the soldiers on both sides fought on, determined to see the war through and confident of final victory.

William Hammond and the End of the Medical Middle Ages

By PAT LEONARD

While other events of April 25, 1862, dominated the nation's headlines—most notably the Confederate surrender of New Orleans—perhaps the most significant single event in the life of the average Union soldier was a presidential appointment that day that was hardly noticed outside Washington. Over the objection of Edwin Stanton, his secretary of war, President Lincoln named William Alexander Hammond as surgeon general of the Army.

Hammond was the preferred candidate of Gen. George B. McClellan and the handpicked choice of the United States Sanitary Commission, a civilian organization created to improve Army living conditions. Though only 33 years old and holding just an assistant surgeon's rank, Hammond had attracted the commission's attention through his work as an inspector of camps and hospitals.

Hammond quickly proved he was up to the job. Possessing a brilliant organizational mind and boundless energy, he started making changes at every level of the Army Medical Department. He established more stringent requirements for physicians joining the service and set up examination boards to evaluate their qualifications. He initiated a hospital inspection system and designed new pavilion hospitals with strict specifications for layout, lighting, ventilation and patient space allotments.

He standardized a medication table for military use, established laboratories to manufacture needed pharmaceuticals, founded the

Army Medical Museum and collected information that formed the basis of "The Medical and Surgical History of the War of the Rebellion." Finding no suitable text on the subject of hygiene, Hammond took pen in hand and wrote the industry standard, one of 30 books and more than 400 articles he would write in his lifetime. Hammond revolutionized the practice of military medicine almost overnight, saving the lives of thousands of men in the process.

Much of what Hammond advocated he had learned from his 11 years as an Army assistant surgeon in remote outposts, including present-day Arizona, Kansas and Florida. Unable to sustain a growing family on military pay, he had resigned his commission in 1860 to become an instructor at the University of Maryland Medical School in Baltimore.

He was in this position when he first attended to wounded Union soldiers: the Sixth Massachusetts Regiment, passing through Baltimore on its way to Washington, was attacked by a proslavery mob in April 1861. Hammond's diligent treatment of the injured men led to his being offered the position of surgeon of a rebel regiment, an offer he rejected "with no great fastidiousness in the choice of his language."

Hammond rejoined the Union Army shortly thereafter and was made a hospital and camp inspector in Maryland and what would soon become West Virginia. He impressed his superiors, as well as the Sanitary Commission, with his detailed reports and strident requests for improved hygiene. Those who met him found him equally impressive in person, standing 6 feet 2 inches tall with a booming voice that, one admirer said, "could be heard upwind in a hurricane."

Appreciating Hammond's talents from a distance, however, was apparently easier than working with him directly. Throughout his tenure as surgeon general, peers and subordinates described him as arrogant, impetuous, boastful and insensitive. Stanton, who had favored another, more senior officer for the pre-eminent medical post, found Hammond's personality insufferable and his incessant demands excessive. Illustrating that point was Hammond's $10 million budget for the 1863 fiscal year, which was four times what his predecessor had requested for 1862—and which he still managed to overspend by 15 percent.

But the young surgeon general was effective. By one estimate— arrived at by taking the rate of mortality among sick and wounded soldiers in the war's first chaotic year and extrapolating it across the carnage that followed—Hammond's initiatives saved nearly 26,000 lives. Such calculations are guesswork, but there's no question that his measures resulted in substantial improvements in the care and outcomes afforded Union soldiers and captured Confederates.

Yet even with his state-of-the-art initiatives to improve sanitation and save lives, Hammond was fighting an uphill battle. The American Civil War was fought during what he would later describe as "the end of the medical Middle Ages." An understanding of germ theory was still a decade away, and thousands died not from their wounds but from infections or gangrene that developed later. During and following a major battle, doctors performed amputations by the hundreds, sawing off mangled limbs as quickly as men could be lifted onto makeshift operating tables, without so much as wiping their blades between procedures. The death rate following amputations ranged as high as 50 percent, especially when major limbs were involved or when soldiers had to wait more than a few hours to be treated.

And that wasn't the worst of it. The greatest menace to Civil War soldiers was not enemy fire, nor even the infections that almost always inflamed their wounds and/or stumps. The majority of field fatalities—an estimated three out of five among Union dead, and two out of three among Confederates—were caused by preventable diseases that swept through camps and hospitals, including dysentery, typhoid fever, pneumonia, tuberculosis and even "childhood" ailments like measles, chickenpox and whooping cough.

Writing home, soldiers often remarked that they didn't fear the big battles as much as being taken to a hospital, where they would be exposed to killers they couldn't see and didn't understand.

Hammond persevered through all of this, but at last his peremptory directives started to turn even some of his supporters against him, especially when he revised the approved medication table in 1863, removing two drugs that were very popular with surgeons in the field.

Sensing an opportunity, Stanton assembled a committee in July 1863 to investigate the Medical Department. Among the members of this committee were known rivals of Hammond, including a man he described as a "vulgar ignoramus" and another he had denounced as "unscrupulous, dishonest, cowardly and ignorant." It can safely be surmised that such men would not be favorably, or even impartially, disposed toward the surgeon general.

Five weeks after the committee began its investigation, Stanton dispatched Hammond on an inspection tour of facilities in the South and West, and two days later replaced him with a surrogate. Hammond's wife suspected something underhanded was taking place and asked Stanton if he intended to discharge her husband. The secretary denied her suspicions.

Returning from his inspection tour in late 1863, Hammond demanded his position back, or to be court-martialed. He tried to appeal to Lincoln, but—with the Sanitary Commission's influence waning and Hammond's former champion, McClellan, now a political foe—the president chose to ignore him. In all probability, Lincoln had tired of the bickering between Stanton and Hammond, and had decided to let his secretary of war handle the matter himself.

And handle it Stanton did, convening a court-martial staffed by nine generals hand-selected for the task, none of whom had a medical background but nearly all of whom either disliked Hammond or were beholden to Stanton. Hammond welcomed the trial, naïvely believing that his innocence would guarantee his exoneration.

Based on the investigating committee's report, 3 charges and 10 specifications were brought against Hammond. These included a hodgepodge of accusations ranging from overpayment of suppliers to procurement of inferior goods to that military catch-all, conduct unbecoming an officer and a gentleman. Some of the charges were absurd and some, though plausible, were hardly criminal, given the exigencies of an all-consuming war. (If everyone who ever overpaid for military supplies was court-martialed for doing so, the War Department would have ceased to exist long before Hammond came along.)

Stanton not only stacked the deck; he didn't even deal Hammond a playable hand. When Hammond requested a copy of the investigating committee's report, Stanton refused. When, during the trial, Hammond presented a purchase order showing that Stanton had approved a procurement named in the specifications, the court would not allow it to be placed into evidence. And Hammond was unable to present a letter that would have exculpated him of one of the more serious charges—because it had mysteriously disappeared when his office was burglarized.

After nearly seven months of trial and 25,000 pages of testimony, the board deliberated for just 90 minutes before returning a guilty verdict on all three charges and most of the specifications. They removed references to corruption and tainted goods from the verdict, but nevertheless ordered Hammond "dismissed from the service and to be forever disqualified from holding any office of profit or trust under the Government of the United States."

Again Hammond tried to appeal to Lincoln, as did his wife, but the president declined to see either of them. Lincoln approved the guilty verdict on Aug. 18, 1864, and Hammond was dishonorably discharged 10 days later

The New York Times piled on in an Aug. 23 editorial, calling Hammond's guilt "of a very vile sort," asserting he had "stooped to the level of the lowest shoddy knave" and predicting "he will be remembered only to be loathed." A day later, however, after receiving a letter from Hammond himself—in which he promised a review of the case and declared he had been "the victim of conspiracy, false swearing, and a malignant abuse of official power"—the Times backpedaled, admitting "we know nothing of the case beyond the fact of conviction," and maintaining "we shall be most heartily rejoiced to be convinced of his innocence."

Hammond moved to New York City and set out to have his conviction overturned and to rehabilitate his reputation. Though nearly penniless—"I did not know where my next meal was going to come from," he wrote of this period—Hammond used his connections to set up a practice in the still-infant field of neurology, and within a decade he was one of the highest-paid physicians in the country.

In 1878, Hammond returned to Washington to restore his good name. He received a Congressional hearing, and both houses passed a bill annulling the court-martial proceedings and sentence. It was signed by President Rutherford B. Hayes on Aug. 27, 1879, and Hammond's name was placed on the retired list of the Army as surgeon general with the rank of brigadier general.

Nine years later, Hammond sold his practice and moved from New York to Washington. He established a sanitarium and unfortunately engaged in some questionable business practices, which eroded the reputation he had fought so hard to regain. Ever flamboyant and ever the self-promoter, he had himself fitted with a surgeon general's uniform late in life, for no other purpose than to have a portrait of himself painted. He died in 1900 at the age of 71.

The Civil War's Rip Van Winkle

By ALBIN J. KOWALEWSKI

Great fiction, we all know, has the uncanny ability to imitate the unpredictability and emotion of real life. So it's a testament to the Civil War's otherworldliness that real life imitated great fiction in the remarkable story of Isaac Israel Hayes, one of America's most famous early Arctic explorers.

It's unclear if Hayes ever read Washington Irving's classic short story "Rip Van Winkle," or if he even knew the plot, in which the main character inadvertently sleeps through the American Revolution. But by the spring of 1862, Hayes would have easily identified with Irving's famously henpecked hero. Like Rip, Hayes had one day ventured off into the unknown, missed some of the most defining moments of his generation (in this case everything from Lincoln's election to the Battle of Balls Bluff) and returned to a country he barely understood.

Hayes didn't sleep through the opening of the Civil War, but he might as well have. The Pennsylvania native had instead spent 15 of the most important months in American history—from July 1860 to October 1861—looking for the North Pole between and above Greenland and Canada.

Because telegraphs and mail didn't run that far north, Hayes had no idea that the United States had been torn in two during his absence. He heard rumors of the conflict on his way home, but it wasn't until he finally anchored in Boston Harbor in late October 1861 that the war's terrible realness stopped him cold. Within moments of stepping ashore,

Hayes realized that "the country which I had known before could be the same no more." Quoting the Book of Exodus but also presaging the title of Robert A. Heinlein's sci-fi classic, he wrote, "I felt like a stranger in a strange land, and yet every object which I passed was familiar."

Hayes hadn't always longed for something so familiar. Born in 1832 and raised in a Quaker family in Chester County, Pa., he was a medical doctor by training, but rather unexcited about the predictable and ordinary rhythms of private practice. Instead, he was drawn to the barrens of the Arctic, an unforgiving and mysterious world where a young man could prove himself, and even achieve renown. If nothing else, the northernmost frontier would give Hayes the opportunity to lead what he would soon call "a novel sort of life."

Equal parts science and adventure—with undertones of national ambition—Arctic exploration during the mid-19th century captivated the world much like the space race would do a century later. The top of the planet was impossibly cold, dark and often fatal. But Victorian explorers kept going back: first, in a renewed search by the British and others for the Northwest Passage; then, in typically hopeless rescue missions for the crews that never returned; and finally, after much of the North American Arctic had been mapped, they began a dangerous, often obsessive race "to reach the north pole of the earth," as Hayes first proposed in early 1860, that would last into the 20th century.

Few American or European scientists had ever made it above 80 degrees north latitude, but Hayes believed, like other explorers, that an "open polar sea" blanketed the very top of the world: a navigable ocean, kept ice-free by a mixture of warm Gulf Stream waters, strong undersea currents and prevailing surface winds. He had been a member of an earlier Arctic team led by Elisha Kent Kane between 1853 and 1855 that claimed to have found evidence of the sea's existence, and now he desperately wanted confirmation. Anxious to go back, Hayes organized a follow-up expedition.

The small crew left Boston in early July 1860, vowing to cross the ice belt in the lower latitudes, reach the open sea and sail straight to the North Pole. Hayes's ship was "snug, jaunty looking," he said, but whether it would survive the dangerous and uncharted waters in its future remained to be seen. Hayes named his ship the United States.

After tacking up Greenland's west coast, dense pack ice forced them to make winter camp near Smith Sound above Baffin Bay. Hayes traded for sled dogs and provisions with the Arctic's native peoples; were it not for their guidance—they did, after all, live in the very place Hayes had come to discover—his expedition would have ended much differently. After a long and dark winter in which temperatures dropped to 68 degrees below Fahrenheit, Hayes and most of his crew survived into the spring.

Just days before the Confederacy opened fire on Fort Sumter, Hayes pushed northward in search of the open polar sea. Traveling by dogsled, he struggled across the Arctic's broken terrain and its fields of ice hummocks. In mid-May, at a latitude Hayes recorded as 81 degrees 35 minutes north, he observed veins of open water fanning out like a "delta" across what he believed was the polar basin. He took a few measurements, enjoyed the view, planted a flag and turned around. Severe damage to his ship prevented him from attempting to sail to the Pole, as he had originally intended.

Hayes later said that he "led a strange weird sort of life" in the Arctic. The irony, of course, is that it would only get stranger and weirder when he went back home. In 1860, Hayes had embarked as a celebrity; he returned over a year later as an afterthought, ridiculed in the news. "Surely," wrote the Detroit Free Press a short while after Hayes docked at Boston,

> enough of treasure and valuable life have been spent in
> search of facts to substantiate somebody's theory about
> the polar regions, which, whether it is this way or that
> way, is of no practical importance to anybody in the wide
> world. Suppose the continent of land does run up to the
> north pole, or suppose it don't. Suppose there is an open
> sea there or suppose there isn't. What does it amount to?
> Who will go there on a pleasure voyage or a trout fishing?

But if the country had no time for Hayes, the explorer found the war an all-consuming horror. He felt out of place in an America that now seemed more alien than the Arctic north, leaving him "sad and dejected," he said. Confident that he had found the open sea but disappointed at not having reached the Pole, Hayes's existential anxiety came rushing back. In the spring of 1862, despite his Quaker beliefs, he accepted a commission as a surgeon in the Union Army and was quickly appointed director of the massive Satterlee Hospital, outside Philadelphia.

After Hayes died in 1881, follow-up expeditions challenged his findings and overturned his claim about the existence of the open polar sea. He largely faded out of memory. But recent studies, including a 2009 biography by Douglas W. Wamsley, have begun resuscitating his legacy. Not only had Hayes pioneered the use of photography in the Arctic, Wamsley and others note, but he had also helped establish the route that later explorers—including his better-known rival, Charles Francis Hall—would follow in subsequent expeditions to locate the Pole.

Hayes once wondered if his time in the Arctic had been "set down in a dream." In a sense, he was right—and more like Rip Van Winkle than anyone had ever realized, if they realized it at all. Coming back to the States in 1861 had indeed been a rude awakening.

Black Babies and Blackboard Predictions

By JUDITH GIESBERG

Something very strange, but very telling, took place in the spring of 1862 during Congressional deliberations about a proposed measure to abolish slavery in the District of Columbia: senators debated black birth rates, colonization and the likelihood—the desirability, even—of blacks disappearing as a race. A debate that began as a consideration of the fate of 3,000 men and women in the District of Columbia became a wide-ranging discussion about the demographic future of the nation.

The fierce debate over the District of Columbia Emancipation Act preoccupied the Senate for the better part of a month. Since almost all the Southern senators had left with secession, there were few outright pro-slavery advocates. But that didn't mean there was a consensus. Of greatest concern was what to do with the District's freed slaves—integration being out of the question. Would blacks reproduce as quickly in freedom as they had in slavery? Or would they, as Wisconsin's James Doolittle suggested with census numbers he scratched on a blackboard in the Senate chamber, "dwindle and dwarf in the presence of the white man," like the Indians?

The final version of the law included a provision of $100,000 for the voluntary colonization of District slaves to Africa and compensation to white District slave owners. Both measures—colonization and slave-holder compensation—reflected the work of two senators from the slave states of Delaware and Maryland, Willard Saulsbury and Anthony Kennedy, respectively, who set the terms under which an estimated 3,000 black Washingtonians were to be freed. Dislodging the debate about emancipation from humanitarian considerations and attaching it instead to a hard-nosed assessment of the demographics and numbers, Saulsbury and Kennedy stole the measure out of the hands of Congressional abolitionists, like the bill's sponsor, Senator Henry Wilson of Massachusetts.

The demographic debate began when Kennedy sketched out what he believed would be the dire consequences for Maryland—and, by implication, other border states—of freeing the District's slaves. Proximity and demography would conspire to abruptly end slavery in Maryland and, Kennedy feared, to create a volatile and dangerous situation. With a total population in 1860 of 687,034, including 83,718 free blacks and 87,188 slaves, Kennedy explained, Maryland could not sustain an abrupt doubling of the free black population.

"These facts," Kennedy insisted, left white Marylanders with the "alarming consideration that we are likely to become, by this interference of Congress, the great free Negro colony of this country." Because of the "bitter antipathy between the laboring white people and free blacks," race war was certain. Kennedy predicted "scenes of blood and carnage," and concluded that one "race or another will ultimately perish."

Geographic size mattered as well, according to Kennedy, who took pains to point out how much space was available in each state for the races to either coexist peacefully or presumably stay out of one another's way. The senator estimated that whereas the New England states occupied 65,440 square miles, for example, white New Englanders shared the space with a free black population (in 1850) of only 23,021—just over a quarter the number of free blacks living in Maryland, with under a fifth of the land area.

With tongue firmly in cheek, Delaware's Saulsbury then proposed an amendment to resettle free slaves from the District in all of the free states, "pro rata according to population," a measure that would be "a sublime example of philanthropy." Referring to stories of federal soldiers who warmly greeted fugitives in the wartime South, Saulsbury wryly suggested that colonizing free blacks in New England and elsewhere would allow free staters to embrace them "in your own midst." Intended to make a statement, the amendment was roundly defeated.

There is no record of how James Doolittle voted on Willard Saulsbury's amendment, but a few days later the senator from Wisconsin offered his own solution. Senators, including among them Waitman T. Willey, the "loyal" senator from Virginia, had raised questions about the practicality of colonization. Could it really be done? And if so, where? It was a topic that Doolittle, as chairman of the Committee on Indian Affairs, had likely thought about before.

Inviting his fellow senators to "cipher" with him "at the blackboard," Doolittle shared census figures intended to allay fears of a post-emancipation racial Armageddon. First, to those who feared the black population would grow faster after emancipation, Doolittle showed that, since 1840, the nation's free black population had actually grown at a slower rate than the slave population while, in the same period, the white population had grown faster than both the slave and free-black population.

The reason? Quoting a previous study on the issue, Doolittle insisted that with education and the improved "capacity to provide for themselves and families," free black birth rates slow down. "There are no maids, and no widows among slaves," Doolittle continued, describing how enslaved women were pushed to the limits of their reproductive capacities. As a consequence, "like the Indian race," free blacks would likely "dwindle and dwarf in the presence of the white man."

If Doolittle's reassurances were not enough for his colleagues, the senator from Wisconsin had worked out the numbers of an ambitious colonization plan. Doolittle recommended that appropriate arrangements be made to relocate freed slaves to Central or South America to save the time and expense of repeated trips to Africa. Such a thing could be done, he thought, for about half the money Congress was spending "in taking care of the Indians"—about $3 million.

Based on a plan to relocate 150,000 "slaves" each year—and taking "natural increase" into consideration—Doolittle showed senators an American black population that shrunk to zero by 1907. At a more ambitious rate of 350,000 relocations a year, that same goal might be reached as early as 1877. These numbers were heavily couched in fantasy: based on estimates only of the slave population, Doolittle's calculations omitted any mention of the free black population; perhaps his previous mention of a "dwindling" free black population was enough. Nor did the figures seem to reflect Doolittle's firm insistence that all federally sponsored colonization be voluntary.

Doolittle also left out another set of numbers he had considered before he took to the blackboards in the Senate. When he acknowledged the help of a "gentleman from Philadelphia" who had provided him with the tables, he was likely referring to Robert Patterson, a Philadelphia banker who had supplied the pro-colonization statistics. In a letter addressed to Doolittle in the middle of the District emancipation debate, Patterson shared some other calculations of a "far more intimate character," though he admitted to having "some doubt about [their] practical bearing." The black population might be brought down even faster "by deporting females alone, as they arrive at child bearing age, which we may assume to be at 17." He estimated that by the "year 1905, there will be no females under 45, or in other words no child bearers."

(To be fair, Patterson recognized "the inhumanity" of his proposal, as "it involves the separation of families, and of the sexes at marriageable ages"; it would have also left "in the South an enormous disproportionate of male slaves under circumstances most of all calculated to dissatisfy and brutalize them.")

Doolittle did not chart the numbers of this plan on the Senate blackboard, but even so, Patterson's dystopian plan for eliminating the problem of race was not that far removed from Doolittle's own considerations of black birth rates and the probability of black racial suicide—or, for that matter, Anthony Kennedy's race war nightmare. Both proposals showed how easily humanitarianism could become Malthusianism in the context of the times; both should remind us of the limitations of assessing 19th century people based on current attitudes about race and gender.

Westward, Ho!
By Rick Beard

May 1862 found the Union fighting ferociously on two fronts, but it still had time for nonmilitary matters. Indeed, that month the Senate approved, and President Lincoln signed, a bill that would help define the course of American expansion after the war ended: the Homestead Act, which gave away vast tracts of western land for practically nothing, to anyone willing to settle and cultivate it.

The act's impact was immediately obvious: after the Senate passed the bill on May 6, Horace Greeley's New York Tribune called it "one of the most beneficent and vital reforms ever attempted," one "calculated to diminish sensibly the number of paupers and idlers and increase the proportion of working, independent, self-subsisting farmers in the land evermore."

The legislation's straightforward provisions belied its long, politically tangled gestation. Beginning on Jan. 1, 1863, the new law invited any male who had never taken up arms against the United States and was over 21 years of age or the head of a family—as well as freed slaves and widows—to engage in a three-step process to secure 160 acres of public land. The potential landowner first had to apply for a claim and pay a $12 fee. Next he had to live on the land for five years and demonstrate proof of improvements like farming, clearing timber or building a house. Union soldiers who had served two years had to occupy the land for only one year before filing their claims. Only then could the homesteader, with a $6 fee, file for a deed of title.

The Homestead Act was one of many attempts by the central government to control its vast acreage; its earliest efforts predated adoption of the Constitution. The Land Ordinance of 1785 had created six-mile-square townships divided into 36 sections, each measuring one square mile, or 640 acres. Purchasers could initially buy no less than a full section for $1 per acre, though in 1800 the minimum purchase was halved, to 320 acres, and the cost fixed at $1.25 per acre, a price that remained in force until 1854. The minimum cost of $400 for 320 acres proved prohibitive for all but the wealthiest Americans and encouraged speculation at the expense of settlement.

The first federal action intended to galvanize the settlement of public lands came at the urging of western politicians. In 1841, President Tyler signed the Preemption Act, permitting squatters living on federally owned land to purchase up to 160 acres at a price not less than $1.25 an acre. Claimants had to live on the land for 14 months. The legislation assured that the states then considered the "west"—including Ohio, Indiana, Illinois, Alabama, Mississippi, Missouri, Louisiana, Arkansas and Michigan—and any other state later received a 10 percent chunk of the proceeds, as well as 500,000 acres to sell. All proceeds were to support internal improvements.

The passage of the Preemption Act prefaced the emergence of a vocal reform movement embracing "homesteading"—the free distribution of public land—as a safety valve for an American political and economic order threatened by a growing poor population in Eastern cities. In 1844, George Henry Evans, a British immigrant devoted to workingmen's causes, formed the National Reform Association, rallying supporters with cries of "Land for the Landless" and "Vote Yourself a Farm."

Horace Greeley quickly adopted Evans' cause, using the Tribune's pages to make his case. "Every thousand hardy, efficient workers who float West on Free Lands," Greeley editorialized, "would leave places open for as many others; and these taking a step upward, would leave room for advancement of as many more and so on." At the same time, he issued a cautionary warning for those who chose not to move westward. "Secure all, so far as possible, a chance to earn a living," he wrote, "then if they will run away from the Soil and shiver and starve in cities, why there is no help for them but such as Charity will afford."

Evans, Greeley and other advocates of homesteading soon found themselves enmeshed in antislavery politics. Many Northern opponents of slavery, initially wary that free land might depopulate the North and hurt manufacturing, came to see homesteading as a useful tool in the escalating battle with the Southern slave power. Because slavery typically required large plantations to be economically feasible, free farmers settling small plots of the western territories would provide a bulwark against calls for the institution's expansion into those lands. Many Southerners no doubt felt as one Mississippian did, who argued, "Better for us that these territories should remain a waste, a howling wilderness, trod only by red hunters than be so settled."

Although the Free Soil Party as well as several Northern Whigs supported homesteading, the emergence of the Republican Party in the early 1850s gave the movement true political momentum. The party found the answer to urban poverty in the westward migration of the poor, and embraced Greeley's contention that "the public lands are the great regulator of the relations of Labor and Capital, the safety valve of our industrial and social engine." The Democratic Party, on the other hand, proved ambivalent on the issue. Missouri Senator Thomas Hart Benton endorsed the idea as early as the 1820s, and by the 1850s, such progressive Democratic leaders as Andrew Johnson of Tennessee, Stephen A. Douglas of Illinois and Sam Houston of Texas had become homesteading advocates. But most Democrats, especially in the South, opposed homesteading, often vehemently.

Throughout the 1850s, efforts to push homesteading legislation through Congress, led by Johnson and Pennsylvania Representative Galusha Grow, were unrelenting—and unrelentingly defeated. In 1852, 1854 and 1859 the House passed homestead acts, all of which the Senate subsequently vanquished. The Panic of 1857, which impoverished tens of thousands, provided further impetus to the movement. Orville Browning, a Lincoln confidant, worried that "in many of the free states, population is already pressing hard upon production and subsistence, and new homes must be provided, or the evils of an overcrowded country encountered."

Republicans were quick to counter any notion that homesteading would somehow redistribute wealth. George Julian, the Free Soil candidate for vice president in 1852 and a Republican congressman throughout the Civil War, assured the nation that his party advocated

The first homestead application, by Daniel Freeman.

"no leveling policy, designed to strip the rich of their possessions." And Richard Yates, who would serve as Illinois's wartime governor, was equally soothing: the measure "does not take your property and give it to me. It does not bring down the high, but it raises the low." Yet another party member assured doubters that the measure "will greatly increase the number of those who belong to . . . the middle class."

Yet Southern critics remained recalcitrant. In 1857 the Virginian George Fitzhugh wrote that the social tensions resulting from population increases as the West was settled would force the North to resort to slavery as a means of controlling an insubordinate and menacing laboring class. The following year a writer for The Southern Literary Messenger predicted that population growth would strain the available means of subsistence and incite urban violence, religious fanaticism, and political demagoguery.

In 1860 the proponents of homesteading finally succeeded in steering the bill through both houses, only to have President Buchanan veto it. The reaction was immediate and visceral: one editorial writer for The Dubuque Herald wrote, "This act . . . is one of the most infamous of his infamous administration. The Slave propagandists demanded that the Bill should be vetoed, and their pliant tool was swift to obey them. Let the pimps and hirelings of the old sinner defend this last act of his, if they dare."

The election of Abraham Lincoln, who favored "cutting up the wild lands into parcels so that every poor man may have a home," and the departure of Southern senators and representatives after the South's secession, forestalled a repeat of Buchanan's action. On Feb. 28, 1862, the House passed the Homestead Act by a vote of 107 to 16; the Senate approved the bill by a vote of 33 to 7 on May 6. On Jan. 1, 1863, Daniel Freeman of Nebraska and 417 others filed the first claims; by the end of the Civil War, homesteaders had made 26,500 claims. Over the life of the program, the government granted 1.6 million homesteads encompassing 270 million acres in 30 states, or 10 percent of all lands in the United States.

Still, the legacy of the Homestead Act, which remained in force until 1976 (a decade later in Alaska), is mixed. Its value as a safety valve was limited: unemployed workmen in Eastern cities seldom had the money to transport their families to the free public lands and to feed and shelter them until a crop could be made. Even if such a settler managed to establish himself on a western farm, he was not likely to succeed without skills that could be obtained only through long apprenticeship. Homesteaders were usually experienced farmers from nearby states. Except for European immigrants who were taken to the West by railway companies and other agencies with lands to sell, few settlers on the agricultural frontier came directly from eastern industrial centers. Moreover, only about 40 percent of the four million who started the homesteading process were able to complete it.

The Homestead Act did not replace other systems of distributing federal lands—railroads received up to 94 million acres between 1862 and 1871, and states granted them an additional 38 million acres. The federal government also set aside 140 million acres for schools, universities and other public buildings, and an equal amount of land for Indian reservations. Aside from the homesteaders themselves, the act probably had its greatest impact on Native Americans, who fought a series of bloody, futile wars against the constant encroachment of white settlers in the post-bellum years.

'Our Servants Do Pretty Much as They Please'
By ADAM ROTHMAN

Touring the United States for The Times of London, the war correspondent William Howard Russell reached New Orleans late in May 1861 to find a city ablaze. Confederate flags flew from the public buildings and private homes. Soldiers paraded through the streets in smart columns of dash and pomp. Gentlemen at the St. Charles Hotel pored over the latest papers for news of the dawning war. The police were rounding up suspected abolitionists, and every night mysterious fires flared up around the city—set, it was rumored, by the slaves.

After hobnobbing with politicians, planters and merchants, Russell observed that the Confederate elite "believe themselves, in fact, to be masters of the destiny of the world." But they soon discovered they were not even masters of their own homes.

New Orleans was a slave city: its fortunes depended on the slave-based sugar and cotton plantations of the lower Mississippi Valley, and the buying and selling of people was a big local business. More than 13,000 enslaved people (1 out of every 12 residents) lived in the city itself in 1860, working as stevedores, carpenters, valets, cooks and laundresses. Some were hired out and earned wages for their owners. Women made up a majority of adult slaves, performing "domestic" labor for masters and mistresses who could be just as abusive as any whip-wielding plantation overseer.

Yet daily routines took household slaves out to the city streets and shops, gave them the chance to socialize with friends and family and find refuge in hideaways outside their masters' gaze. Their skills as laborers, and their networks of kinship and community, would aid them when the Union Army arrived in May 1862, barely a year after the war began.

The Union "occupation" of New Orleans was also a liberation, if that is the appropriate word to describe the gnarled process of emancipation that took place there. Freedom did not arrive on board David Farragut's warships; the Union had not yet committed to a policy of emancipation. Nor did it arrive with the Emancipation Proclamation on Jan. 1, 1863, which exempted the city and other territory once part of the Confederacy but no longer "in rebellion." And yet slavery began to crumble in New Orleans from the moment Union troops arrived. The letters and diaries of Confederates in New Orleans in the weeks and months after the Federals arrived were already filling with despair and rage at the loss of authority over their slaves. What was going on?

We tend to look back at emancipation as a series of official acts. But in many places, including New Orleans, it was the result of local initiative as much as Union policy. In occupied New Orleans, slaves quickly recognized that the balance of power had shifted away from their owners, and they took advantage.

Many slaves, for example, ran away to the Union Army. Hundreds fled to Camp Parapet, a fortification just above the city, where the abolitionist commanding officer, Brig. Gen. John W. Phelps, welcomed them. Even those who were thought to be most loyal to their owners ran off. "There are many instances in which house-servants, those who have been raised by people, have deserted them," complained Clara Solomon, a teenager in the city.

Slaveowners felt robbed by the Federals and betrayed by their slaves. Owners claiming to be loyal to the Union petitioned for the return of their human property, sparking a controversy on "the negro question" between Phelps and Gen. Benjamin Butler, commander of the Department of the Gulf. The hard-nosed Butler was famous for his ingenious policy of confiscating slaves as "contrabands of war" in Virginia, but he did not want to wreck Louisiana's sugar plantations or alienate white Unionists. He thought that Phelps had crossed the line by fomenting slave unrest. "We shall have a negro insurrection here I fancy," Butler confided to his wife.

Butler and Phelps clashed, too, over Phelps's arming of black soldiers at Camp Parapet. Phelps resigned, but Butler eventually came around to the wisdom of the policy. By the end of 1862, black men—both free and slave—were joining the Union Army in southern Louisiana in droves. When asked whether slaves would fight their masters, one man told a Union officer, "Just put the gun into our hands, and you'll soon see that we not only know how to shoot, but who to shoot." The recruitment of black soldiers ate away at slavery, especially in Louisiana, which was credited with supplying over 24,000 black men to the Union Army, more than any other state.

Less well known are the contributions of enslaved women to the hastening of emancipation. Barred from battle, enslaved women fought daily skirmishes with masters and mistresses in their own kitchens and courtyards. They talked back. They refused to be beaten. They ran away, and returned with bayonets. "Our servants do pretty much as they please," protested Ann Wilkinson Penrose, whose son was off fighting in the Confederate Army. Penrose's torrential diary chronicles her family's loosening grip on their slaves after the arrival of the Union Army and offers a striking example of what the historian Thavolia Glymph calls "the war within" slaveholding households.

Simmering resentments boiled over on April 14, 1863. Penrose was angry at Becky, her cook, for baking bad bread and cakes. She went into the kitchen, slapped Becky, and "asked her how she dared to send in such bread & cakes." Becky took offense. "She started up, looked furiously at me, and exclaimed, 'don't you do that again, let it be the last time, or I'll just march out of this yard.'" Becky was told to hush or else a policeman would be called in. As Penrose recounts, Becky retorted that "she might send for whom she pleased she didn't care."

Penrose didn't send for a policeman; her family decided it wouldn't have done any good. The police were now on the slaves' side, they believed. Becky's defiance—and Penrose's inability to punish her for it—signaled the demise of slavery in New Orleans. The institution crumbled in New Orleans not from a single dramatic blow or stroke of a pen, but from the slow accumulation of resistance by slaves like Becky.

The law eventually caught up with the facts on the ground. Early in 1864, Union Gen. Nathaniel Banks (who had replaced Butler as commander of the Department of the Gulf) recognized that Louisiana's state constitutional provisions and laws concerning slavery were "inconsistent with the present condition of public affairs" and declared them "inoperable and void."

Finally, in September 1864, more than two years after the arrival of Union troops, Louisiana's all-white electorate ratified a new State Constitution that formally abolished slavery in the state. Heartened by the summer's debates over emancipation, one black soldier predicted that "under God, this will yet be a pleasant land for the colored man to dwell in."

CHAPTER 5

The War Expands

One can identify any number of turning points during the Civil War, but two events make the summer of 1862 stand out as critical moments. On the battlefield, the defeat of McClellan's Peninsula Campaign and the subsequent, inexorable northward movement of Robert E. Lee's forces (and the invasion of Kentucky in August) dashed any remaining hopes that the Union could bring the conflict to a rapid, and relatively painless, conclusion.

In Congress, the war's turn gave added fuel to the abolitionists' fire. For pragmatists, emancipation became a tool by which Union forces could draw away the Confederates' slave labor, undermining both front-line operations and morale on the homefront. Not that slaves needed encouragement: despite Union losses, slaves continued to pour north, filling up refugee camps across northern Mississippi and Tennessee.

But if the war was truly to be a fight to complete surrender, as that summer's battles implied, then many in the North began to feel it had to be about something more than mere reunification. The cost in blood had to buy much more. The end of slavery, long imagined, was suddenly a realistic possibility. Ironically, the Southern show of strength that summer, by steeling Union resolve for a long and total fight, made the end of the slave power more, not less, likely.

Much depended on July. On the 17th, the last day of Congress, Lincoln signed the Second Confiscation Act, which stated that all Confederates in territory under Union control had 60 days to surrender, or their slaves would be confiscated—that is, liberated. He also signed the Militia Act that same day, which allowed the enlistment of blacks as laborers "or any other military or naval service for which they may be found competent." Five days later, Lincoln first announced to his cabinet that he had written a proclamation of emancipation. But he decided to hold it until a Union victory, to make it clear that he was not acting from a position of weakness.

Meanwhile, the Confederacy was facing its own challenges. Enlistment rates were already dropping at the beginning of 1862, and even a draft that spring—the first ever, North or South—produced nearly as many evaders as conscripts.

But for now, the Confederacy seemed to all like a force unmatched, thanks to its charismatic battlefield leader, Robert E. Lee. Moving from strength to strength across Northern Virginia, by early September his army had crossed into Maryland, where he met General McClellan at the apocalyptic Battle of Antietam. Some 4,300 men died that day; another 2,000 were to die soon after of their wounds. Yet McClellan's victory, though it managed to break the wave of Lee's campaign, was sufficiently narrow, and his follow-up sufficiently lackluster, that Lincoln decided soon after to replace him completely. If the Union was to move decisively toward the next phase of a war that still held no prospect of ending, it would need new leadership, both in terms of men and in terms of ideals. By the end of the year, Lincoln would have both.

Grant on the Edge

By THOM BASSETT

I n early June 1862, a few days after Union forces captured the vital rail lines at Corinth, Miss., William Tecumseh Sherman sat chatting with Henry W. Halleck, his superior and commander of the victorious Yankee army. With elaborate casualness, Halleck mentioned that Ulysses S. Grant, another of his subordinates, was departing the next morning for 30 days' leave.

Sherman was immediately concerned that Grant might be seeking more than simply rest and recuperation. "Of course we all knew that [Grant] was chafing under the slights of his anomalous position," Sherman recounted in his memoirs, "and I determined to see him on my way back."

When Sherman arrived at Grant's camp, the scene there intensified his suspicions: officers were filling up chests and trunks scattered among the staff tents, and Sherman soon found Grant at a table piled with his papers and letters, silently sorting and bundling them. When Sherman asked why he was leaving, Grant replied, "You know that I am in the way here. I have stood it as long as I can, and can endure it no longer."

Grant wasn't simply going home on leave; he had decided to quit the Army. A few weeks earlier he had stood firm against a devastating rebel assault at Shiloh, and his stubborn resilience rescued the Union Army from what could have been total disaster. Now, sitting in front of a perplexed and worried Sherman, Grant was an unhappy, even sulking, man who wanted to surrender his position entirely.

Grant's decision to leave has been forgotten in light of his brilliant success later in the war. But it was a critical episode in his life—and, more important, a critical moment in the war, because it turned on differences between Halleck and Grant—one at the height of his power, one still unsure of his future—that highlighted two divergent paths forward in the drive toward Union victory.

Grant, like many, had benefited from Halleck's genius administration of the western military districts, while Halleck was headquartered in St. Louis. Things changed, though, a few days after Shiloh in mid-April, when Halleck arrived in Tennessee to take direct command of the 120,000 Union soldiers gathering in preparation for an assault against the beleaguered Confederates retreating south toward Corinth, just across the state line in Mississippi.

Sherman always held that Halleck was prejudiced against Grant due to recurrent rumors of his drinking, but the conflict between them involved much more than Halleck's simply imbibing innuendo. For one thing, his reorganization of the Union forces after arriving in Tennessee forced Grant into a position he was thoroughly unsuited for. Halleck pulled Grant from being head of his army and made him instead second in command of the entire Union force, reporting to Halleck, with no direct responsibilities for any troops. Grant's military abilities lay entirely in leading armies against the enemy, not in advising a superior or planning grand strategy, so it's no wonder he hated this position and later disparaged it as "a nominal command and yet no command."

Grant and Halleck also differed deeply about how armies in the field should conduct themselves. Halleck had never led a major campaign before, and the grimy disorder of army life appalled him. He was particularly displeased with the camp condition of Grant's own Army of the Tennessee under the latter's unfastidious leadership. The extent to which the generals' leadership styles differed became clear when, three days after he arrived, Halleck issued an order insisting on the proper folding of communications sent to him.

Most important, Grant and Halleck battled over how best to attack the rebels. For Grant, the matter was simple: war meant fighting the enemy relentlessly. Therefore, he insisted, Halleck should immediately attack the forces under the Confederate general P.G.T. Beauregard while they were still recovering from their bloodying at Shiloh.

Halleck, on the other hand, subscribed to a "places" theory of war, and thus aimed at depriving the Confederacy of important locations like the rail depots at Corinth and avoiding direct, set-piece battles wherever possible. Halleck had repeatedly said as much in his prewar book on military strategy, and he now adamantly intended to follow his own advice.

These strategic differences were compounded by the glacial pace at which Halleck led his forces toward Corinth. The city was only 20 miles away from the Union departure point, yet the march took almost a month, from April 30 to May 28. After moving minute distances during the day, Halleck required his soldiers to entrench for hours each evening, to defend against the attack by Beauregard he felt sure was imminent.

Grant disparagingly called it "a siege from start to finish," and he wasn't the only Union officer to find Halleck's approach frustrating. "My men will never dig another trench for Halleck except to bury him," one brigadier acidly remarked.

But though others disagreed with Halleck, Grant was embittered by the operation and, even more, his lack of a meaningful role in it. "For myself I was little more than an observer," Grant would complain in his memoirs. "Orders were sent direct to the right wing or reserves, ignoring me, and advances were made from one line of intrenchments [sic] to another without notifying me."

On May 11 Grant wrote to Halleck—even though they encamped nightly within 200 yards of one another—that he believed "it is generally understood through this army that my present position differs little from that of one in arrest." Grant wanted either to have his army back or to be removed entirely from service under Halleck.

Halleck was genuinely bewildered. "I am very much surprised," he replied, "that you should find any cause of complaint in the recent assignment of commands. You have precisely the position to which your rank entitles you." It reveals how fractured their relationship was that Halleck could think Grant would be mollified by an appeal to command protocol.

Sherman, on the other hand, was keenly aware of how Grant felt as they inched toward Corinth. Grant frequently visited him, and while he didn't speak openly Sherman nonetheless knew that "he felt deeply the indignity, if not the insult, heaped upon him." Grant had helped salvage Sherman's career after public accusations of insanity in late 1861, and Grant's refusal to abandon the field at Shiloh had only deepened Sherman's respect and loyalty. Now Sherman saw that Grant was suffering intensely (if perhaps a bit self-pityingly) as Halleck's subordinate.

Things came to a head once the Union Army arrived at Corinth. As the Yankees slowly invested the city, Grant argued for immediately encircling Beauregard's army, trapping it. But Halleck refused the suggestion so strongly that Grant blanched, thinking, as he wrote later, that "possibly I had suggested an unmilitary movement." The Confederates slipped away soon thereafter, leaving Corinth to Halleck. While he turned his attention to making it a Union stronghold, Grant seethed.

By the time Sherman came to see him, Grant was determined to leave the Army for good. Sherman recalls in his memoirs that he begged Grant not to strike his colors. He first reminded Grant that he himself had been "cast down by a mere newspaper assertion of 'crazy,'" but after recovering his confidence at Shiloh had been given "new life and now . . . was in high feather." He then entreated Grant to take heart from his own example. If he quit the Army, "events would go right along, and he would be left out; whereas, if he remained, some happy accident might restore him to favor and his true place."

His friend's encouragement rallied Grant, and he promised to think things over. On June 6, the day after Sherman's visit, Grant wrote him to say he would remain in the Army after all. Sherman's reply that same day shows how well he already understood Grant: "You could not be quiet at home for a week when armies were moving," he wrote, "and rest could not relieve your mind of the gnawing sense that injustice had been done you."

Sherman's advice soon proved prescient. On June 21, Halleck sent Grant to Memphis to oversee the military district there, which let Grant escape his direct control. Then, on July 11, after the Seven Days' debacle in Virginia, Halleck was called east to serve as general in chief of the Union armies. As a result, Grant replaced him as head of the Union forces scattered across northern Mississippi and western Tennessee.

While Grant still officially answered to Halleck, he was back where he belonged—in the field, at the head of an army that would soon once again aggressively battle the rebels. Sherman's exhorting words had not only repaid Grant for believing in him when he had faltered; they had also helped convince Grant not to quit on himself or surrender in the fight for the Union.

Where Was Stonewall?

By BEN CLEARY

n the early spring of 1862, the Confederate general Thomas J. "Stone-wall" Jackson won dazzling victories in Virginia's Shenandoah Valley that made him "the hero of the South." Combining incredible energy and audacity with a mastery of terrain and tactics, Jackson's Valley Campaign is internationally famous and still studied today.

Beginning later that year with the Second Battle of Bull Run, Jackson cemented his reputation as Gen. Robert E. Lee's hardest-hitting corps commander. After solid fighting at Antietam and a decisive victory at Fredericksburg, he was instrumental in the resounding Union defeat at Chancellorsville. Tragically for the Southern forces, he was wounded by friendly fire immediately following what was arguably his greatest success. He died a few days later, on May 10, 1863.

Between these two legendary pinnacles is the series of bloody engagements around Richmond in late June 1862 known collectively as the Seven Days. For most of the time, Jackson wasn't where he was supposed to be when he was supposed to be there; and, from all reports, he was ineffectual, listless and confused.

While historians cite a variety of causes—among them ambiguous orders and the difficulties of moving his troops in unfamiliar territory—sleep deprivation brought on by endless campaigning in the Shenandoah was the main reason. The unanswered, deeper question is why Jackson allowed himself to become so worn down that he let multiple opportunities for victory during the Seven Days slip through his fingers.

The Seven Days, in which Lee finally repulsed Gen. George B. McClellan's Army of the Potomac from the vicinity of Richmond and effectively ended the Union's Peninsula Campaign, opened only a few weeks after the close of Jackson's Valley Campaign. Lee communicated partial plans to Jackson, who started his troops toward Richmond from the valley shortly after midnight June 18. Leaving his soldiers en route, Jackson met with Lee at his headquarters east of Richmond on June 23, along with the generals A.P. Hill, D.H. Hill (no relation) and James Longstreet, to work out the details of Lee's plan for the campaign. To get there, Jackson traveled 52 miles in a mere 14 hours.

McClellan had been maneuvering toward Richmond through much of the spring. Now he was in the final stages of his Peninsula Campaign, so close to the capital that his soldiers could set their watches by the chiming of the city's clocks. Siege operations by the enormous, finely equipped Union Army, Lee and his generals concluded, would certainly be successful and would probably start soon. McClellan must be aggressively forced back. Jackson's assignment: open the fighting June 26 with an attack on McClellan's right flank. This would begin an assault by all four generals against the part of the Union Army north of the Chickahominy River. The conference concluded, Jackson rode 40 miles through the rainy night to rejoin his troops and prepare for battle.

But as the morning of June 26 waned into afternoon, Jackson and his men were nowhere to be seen. Lee didn't even know where he was. Shortly after 3 p.m., an exasperated and impetuous A.P. Hill opened the battle, "rather than hazard the whole plan by longer deferring it." Hill drove the Federals before him until he reached their strong position on the high ground east of the hamlet of Mechanicsville and Beaver Dam Creek, where—with no flanking support from the absent Jackson—he was bloodily repulsed.

Where was Jackson? We now know he had reached Hundley's Corner, about three miles from Beaver Dam Creek, a couple of hours after A.P. Hill started fighting. Though there was ample daylight and he could clearly hear sounds of the battle, Jackson bivouacked for the night. He did not send Lee word of where he was. He stayed up all night—conflicting reports say he was writing dispatches, or simply could not sleep because of dueling artillery.

By this point, if not before, it became obvious that Jackson was seriously sleep-deprived. Residual stress from the Valley Campaign, followed by exertions of the march to Richmond, took their toll. The historian Douglas Freeman estimates that Jackson got only 10 hours sleep during the four busy, tension-filled days leading up to June 26.

Yet even as a non-combatant, Jackson's presence was formidable. His presence in the area was the reason McClellan decided to "change his base" of supply from the Pamunkey River south to the

James River. The Confederates—and almost everyone else besides McClellan himself—looked on this movement as a retreat.

Jackson met with Lee on the morning of June 27 at Walnut Grove Church, near the front. His assignment: another attack on the Union right flank. During the march to the staging area he gave confusing instructions, first to a guide, which resulted in a time-consuming countermarch; and then to his subordinates, which led to yet more costly delays. That day's fighting, known as the Battle of Gaines Mill, opened about 2 p.m. Jackson did not get his troops into position until close to sunset.

He met Lee on the battlefield. "Ah, General," Lee said with gentle irony. "I am very glad to see you. I had hoped to be with you before." Jackson did not reply. The battle raged fiercely and inconclusively before them. "That fire is very heavy," said Lee. "Do you think your men can stand it?"

"They can stand almost anything," asserted Jackson. "They can stand that!"

Now Jackson was animated, as though he had drawn strength from the encounter. He saluted, galloped back to his men, issued crisp orders. An observer witnessed his "fiery spirit his face and person were literally transfigured." Jackson sent word to his division commanders: "Tell them this affair must hang in suspense no longer! Sweep the field with the bayonet!" In spite of Jackson's lateness, his soldiers were part of the final assault that broke the Union line and forced a bloody retreat.

His behavior during the rest of the Seven Days was comparable. Short glimpses of the fiery warrior vied with an overall impression of a man in a somnambulistic trance.

His torpor was most evident at White Oak Swamp on June 30. Jackson pursued the retreating Federals to the bridge over White Oak Swamp Creek, which they had destroyed. He brought up his artillery for a highly effective bombardment, but that was as far as it went. Efforts to rebuild the bridge failed, but his cavalryman Col. Thomas Munford found a crossing a quarter mile downstream, while Gen. Wade Hampton found a crossing 400 yards in the other direction, built a rude but effective bridge and reported back. According to Hampton, Jackson "sat in silence for some time, then rose and walked off in silence."

His artillery dueled with that of the Union. The heat was oppressive. Jackson napped. That evening, at the mess table, he fell asleep with a biscuit between his teeth.

His troops were minimally engaged in the disastrous Confederate defeat on July 1 at Malvern Hill. Fortunately for Jackson, McClellan nevertheless retreated, as he had after defeats as well as victories throughout the Seven Days. Had the Union general done otherwise, history might have treated Jackson less kindly than it has.

Stonewall Jackson is justly famous for ferocious and innovative fighting, as well as for his piety and eccentricities. An unshakable belief in the effectiveness of his will is also part of his legacy. "You may be whatever you resolve to be," a favorite quotation, is inscribed above the Jackson Arch at the Virginia Military Institute, where he was once a professor. Like his men, he believed he could "stand almost anything."

He couldn't. Jackson may have relied on his will to push himself beyond the limits of human endurance, but those limits are very real, and he encountered them in the hot, swampy lowlands east of Richmond in the summer of 1862.

Schools for Soldiers

By MICHAEL DAVID COHEN

By the first anniversary of the outbreak of the Civil War, Northerners had discovered how ill-prepared they were for a crisis. The peacetime Army had been tiny. Volunteers rallied to defend the Union, but what they brought in enthusiasm they lacked in experience. Many were too young to have fought in the Mexican War and, since most military academies were located in the South, few Northern youths had formal training in combat. To win the war, the Army had to create citizen-soldiers from scratch.

On July 2, 1862, Abraham Lincoln signed a bill designed to change that: the Morrill Land-Grant College Act, which offered federal financing to colleges that taught military tactics. When the next war began, its supporters believed, alumni of those colleges would be ready for battle. The law also required funded colleges to teach agriculture and engineering, thus preparing young men to serve their nation in both war and peace.

Since the United States' founding, education had remained a local and state concern. Now, in the midst of the Civil War, the federal government began to play a major educational role. Indeed, while its requirements were responses to the country's security and economic needs, the act proved to be one of the most transformative pieces of legislation in American history, seeding the ground for scores of high-quality public colleges and universities around the country.

The Morrill Act had been a long time coming. Justin Morrill, a Republican congressman from Vermont, had proposed it in 1857. He thought a network of colleges teaching scientific methods of farming would increase the country's agricultural output and encourage settlement of the West. So he introduced a bill to give federal land to each of the states, which would sell the land and use the proceeds to support colleges teaching agriculture, engineering and the liberal arts. States could award the money to either state or private colleges. Although the federal government had previously made a few land grants to aid in the founding of state colleges, this program would go far beyond any educational project it had attempted before.

Despite opposition from some Southerners (who opposed federal intrusion into state matters) and Westerners (who opposed giving Western federal land to Eastern states to sell), the bill passed Congress in 1858. But President James Buchanan, believing it unconstitutional, issued a veto. Lacking a two-thirds majority in Congress, Morrill had to wait for a new president. Lincoln, who before his election had expressed support for agricultural education, was just the man.

In December 1861 Morrill reintroduced his land-grant bill. This time, given the wartime context, he added the military-education requirement. In a speech the next June advocating the bill, he put special emphasis on that provision. Bemoaning the unreadiness of Northern men to fight the rebels a year earlier, he blamed politicians in Washington for having "long assumed that military discipline" was as "spontaneous" as patriotism. That assumption, he said, had cost many lives. Had Congress earlier passed a law like the one he now proposed, "The young men might have had more of fitness for their sphere of duties, whether on the farm, in the workshop, or in the battle-field." It was too late to start training for the Civil War, but Congress should pass the bill now so the country would be ready the next time disaster struck.

This time, Morrill succeeded; Congress approved the bill with large majorities and Lincoln signed it into law. But that was only the beginning. After the war, Congress followed the Morrill Act with laws expanding federal support of military training. In 1866 it authorized the dispatch of Army officers to colleges to teach military lessons, and in 1870 it authorized the loan of small arms and field artillery to colleges for use in those lessons. In less than a decade, the federal government had gone from having virtually no relationship with colleges to playing a direct role in their curriculum: it provided general financing, military professors and military supplies and underwrote instruction in agriculture, engineering, the liberal arts and especially military tactics.

Colleges, in the meantime, had introduced military lessons without any government assistance. Sometimes they did so at students' request. Barely a week after the attack on Fort Sumter in April 1861, Harvard students signed a petition asking the faculty to institute a military drill at the Massachusetts school. The faculty obliged and 352 young men signed up for the College Drill Club. Among them was Robert Todd Lincoln, son of the president.

Drilling was not confined to the North. South Carolina College students formed the College Cadets a month before Fort Sumter. When they heard of the impending battle, they rushed to Charleston to join the Confederates. Later in the war, Wesleyan Female College in Macon, Ga., even formed its young women into military companies that marched around town in paper hats with artificial guns. In wartime, military activities had become a part of college life.

After the war, colleges made use of the new laws. By 1879 the Morrill Act was supporting 43 land-grant colleges and the Army was supplying the legal maximum of 30 officer-professors. The University of Missouri, for example, took advantage of both federal programs: it welcomed Gen. Richard W. Johnson to the faculty to drill its young men in 1868 and opened its Agricultural and Mechanical College using Morrill Act money in 1870. In the 1880s, following Wesleyan's wartime precedent, it added an armed drill company for the women who recently had been admitted to the university.

The Morrill Act also enabled the creation of new colleges. New York's Cornell University opened in 1868 and Arkansas Industrial University opened in 1872 using income from land sales under the law. Both of these schools also brought in Army officers as military professors.

The act had something of a knock-on effect as well. Neither Harvard nor South Carolina obtained federal support; nevertheless, as during the war, they diversified their curriculums to keep up with the times. Both introduced engineering courses, Harvard built an agricultural school and both taught at least limited military lessons, subjects that had become standard components of higher education.

The federal government's role in education only grew. In 1867, with some Northern politicians attributing secession to poor education in the South, Congress created the Department of Education to keep watch on the country's schools; it quickly became America's central repository for educational statistics. Congress gradually expanded the officer-professor program and, in 1916, transformed it into the modern Reserve Officers' Training Corps.

In time for the United States' entry into World War I in 1917, Justin Morrill had gotten his wish: civilian colleges were training men to defend the county's interests. The close link between higher education and the federal government, forged during and right after the Civil War, had become a key feature of both American defense policy and college campus life.

The Author of the Civil War
By CYNTHIA WACHTELL

At the height of the holiday shopping season of 1860, a bookseller in Richmond, Va., placed a telling advertisement in The Daily Dispatch promoting a selection of "Elegant

Books for Christmas and New Year's Presents." Notably, the list of two dozen "choice books, suitable for Holiday Gifts" included five works by the late Scottish novelist and poet Sir Walter Scott in "various beautiful bindings."

Sir Walter Scott not only dominated gift book lists on the eve of the Civil War but also dominated Southern literary taste throughout the conflict. His highly idealized depiction of the age of chivalry allowed Southern readers and writers to find positive meaning in war's horrors, hardships and innumerable deaths. And his works inspired countless wartime imitators, who drew upon his romantic conception of combat.

In 1814 Scott had begun his ascension to the heights of literary stardom with the publication of the historical romance "Waverley," which was soon followed by other novels in the so-called Waverley series. The works were an immediate and immense success in Great Britain and America. Over the course of many volumes, Scott glamorized the Middle Ages, at once shaping and popularizing what we now consider the classic tale of chivalry. As one enamored 19th-century reader explained, each of Scott's romances focused upon the "manners and habits of the most interesting and chivalrous periods of Scottish [and] British history."

Among Scott's most famous works was "Ivanhoe," published in 1820. The romance, set in the 12th century, presents a tale of intrigue, love and valor. The plot traces the fortunes of young Wilfred of Ivanhoe as he strives, despite his father's opposition, to gain the hand of the beautiful Lady Rowena. In the course of Ivanhoe's adventures, Richard the Lionheart and Robin Hood appear, and Ivanhoe performs many a remarkable feat. He travels to Palestine, gains fame in the Crusades, returns home in disguise, bravely distinguishes himself in a two-day jousting tournament, and last but surely not least, single-handedly rescues a raven-haired Jewess named Rebecca, who has been abducted and is in grave peril.

In the first half of the 19th century, America caught a highly infectious case of what Mark Twain would later diagnose as "the Sir Walter disease." Northerners and Southerners alike were smitten. The more far-fetched the plot and remote the setting of Scott's works, the more pleased his American readers seemed to be. In less than a decade, from 1814–1823, more than half a million volumes of Scott's novels and poems were sold in the United States, and even after Scott's death in 1832, his books remained extremely popular.

Henry Adams, the great-grandson of President John Adams and grandson of President John Quincy Adams, would recall that the "happiest hours" of his boyhood in the late 1840s and early 1850s "were passed in summer lying on a musty heap of Congressional Documents" in his grandfather's farmhouse reading "Ivanhoe" and other of Scott's historical romances. John Hay, who served as President Lincoln's assistant secretary during the Civil War, would explain decades later, "The books a boy reads are those most ardently admired and longest remembered. . . . Through all [the] important formative days of the Republic, Scott was the favourite author of Americans. . . . [The influence of his books] was enormous upon the taste and sentiments of a people peculiarly sensitive to such influences."

If anything, Scott's romances were even more popular on the other side of the Mason-Dixon Line. Some southern families even went so far as to name their estates and children after places and characters in Scott's stories. As Mark Twain would later write, "Sir Walter Scott had so large a hand in making Southern character, as it existed before the war, that he is in great measure responsible for the war."

In 1850, a year commonly recalled for the fierce sectional debate that culminated in the Compromise of 1850 (which included the passage of the Fugitive Slave Act), one admirer of Scott's works wrote in The Southern Literary Messenger, "Scott's purpose was not to give an analytic account of man in general, but to present a bold and glowing picture of the men of a particular age, and the age selected by him was that when knighthood was the profession of every gentleman, and war the principal occupation of almost every monarch."

Even the outbreak of fighting—and the nation's rude initiation into the pain and suffering of an extended fratricidal war—did not diminish the popularity of Scott's works. As one soldier wrote home from his military camp, "I have read all of Sir Walter Scott's novels within the last month." Indeed, Scott provided both readers and writers with the very tools that allowed them to overlook the hardships and brutality of the ongoing war.

The lofty language, lofty sentiments and lofty deeds popularized by Scott imbued nearly all Southern wartime poetry with the fragrant smell of romanticism. And poetry enjoyed a degree of near-universal popularity during the Civil War years that is hard for modern readers to imagine. Newspapers and magazines throughout the Confederacy published an abundance of war poems written by both amateur and accomplished poets. Indeed, Southerners bombarded newspapers with such a quantity of unsolicited poetry on war-related topics that one publication apparently threatened to charge aspiring poets the same rate to print their verses as it charged to print obituaries.

Even as writers experienced the raw reality of the Civil War, the days and ways of chivalry held imaginative sway in the verses they drafted. "The Virginians of the Valley" is a fine example. The work was written in late 1861 by Francis Orray Ticknor, a physician who would later run the war hospitals in the area of Columbus, Ga.

However, it was not the weaponry or the wreckage of the unfolding war that Ticknor chose for poetic material. Instead, Ticknor celebrated the men and women of his wife's home state, Virginia. He begins his poem by describing Virginians as:

> The knightliest of the knightly race,
> Who, since the days of old,
> Have kept the lamp of chivalry
> Alight in hearts of gold

After recounting the great accomplishments of Virginians of the past, Ticknor pays tribute to the sons of Virginia of the present. These "Golden Horse-shoe knights" do not slumber as danger looms. Instead, they band together and prove themselves worthy of their "noble sires."

A poem titled "Ashby" by the popular Southern poet John Reuben Thompson offers another example of Scott's powerful influence on wartime writers. General Turner Ashby, a Virginia gentleman and Confederate cavalry officer, was killed while fighting a rear-guard action under General Stonewall Jackson's command in early June 1862.

Thompson, who served as editor of The Southern Literary Messenger from 1847 to 1860 and of The Richmond Record and The Southern Illustrated News during the war, was one of many Southern writers who memorialized the man who had been called the "Knight of the Confederacy." His poem begins:

> To the brave all homage render,
> Weep, ye skies of June!
> With a radiance pure and tender,
> Shine, oh saddened moon!
> "Dead upon the field of glory,"
> Hero fit for song and story,
> Lies our bold dragoon.

General Ashby was shot in the chest in a skirmish that took place more than a year into an unremitting, full-scale war in a still rustic America. But Thompson's poem, full of romantic flourish, all but omits these fundamental facts.

Instead, Thompson focuses upon Ashby's knightly fortitude and compares Ashby to warriors of bygone days and faraway lands. In the second stanza he writes:

> Well they learned, whose hands have slain him,
> Braver, knightlier foe
> Never fought with Moor nor [Pagan],
> Rode at Templestowe,
> With a mien how high and joyous,
> 'Gainst the hordes that would destroy us
> Went he forth we know.

Later in the poem, Thompson refers to Ashby's "saber," "crest" and "manly breast." Indeed, in Thompson's adoring portrait, Ashby seems better outfitted for a medieval joust than for mid-19th-century armed combat.

Perhaps most interestingly, Thompson makes reference to Templestowe, the mythical place from which Ivanhoe rescues Rebecca. He clearly trusted that his readers would recognize the reference and would likewise remember that an important jousting tournament in

Ivanhoe occurs in the town of Ashby.

General Turner Ashby was the son of Colonel Turner Ashby, who fought in the War of 1812, and the grandson of Captain Jack Ashby, who fought in the Revolutionary War, yet Thompson makes no mention of Ashby's actual martial lineage. Thompson's emphasis on Ashby's knightly qualities and Ashby's nickname, "the Knight of the Confederacy," point to the literary preferences and references of the Civil War generation.

Sir Walter Scott, more than any other writer, shaped Americans' conception of manliness, bravery and combat in the period leading up to the Civil War. And his influence did not end once the fighting began.

If the lived reality of four years of suffering and slaughter did not neatly conform to Scott's knightly norms, the war as presented in romantic Southern poetry very often did.

In 1866 a contributor to DeBow's Review, published in New Orleans, wrote:

> Without question, [Scott] opened new paths
> of thought and feeling. He was a benefactor
> to his race, for he lit up the common life
> of man with the beautiful lights of a vivid
> imagination; and with the radiancy of a fine humor he flashed
> an honest glow into the
> hearts of thousands.

The Confederacy had died, but the cult of Scott remained robust. Not until the rise of realism in the late 19th century—with the publication of such works as Stephen Crane's "Red Badge of Courage"— would Scott and his imitators fall out of favor.

The Civil War and the Foreign Context

By AMANDA FOREMAN

When the American Civil War erupted in 1861, it was jostling for headline space alongside a half dozen other rebellions and conflicts around the world. Some, like Colombia's civil war, were small-scale affairs between rival parties. But others, like the Taiping Rebellion in China, were causing death and destruction on an epic scale. To the average European, America's travails seemed self-inflicted and unnecessary. And yet its effect on the continent's own politics and military affairs would be profound, both during and long after the war.

The European press was generally united in treating the Civil War with a mixture of exasperation and confusion. The South was no Italy struggling for reunification, or Poland chafing under Russian autocratic dominion, or Ireland seeking liberation from British misrule. Editors lambasted the Confederacy for demanding international recognition, on the threat of withholding cotton—the gasoline for Europe's industrial engine—if compliance was not immediate. The failure of the great powers, primarily France and Britain, to behave as expected was a great blow to Richmond.

The Confederates had assumed that recognition would be swift, and in the case of France they were not far wrong. Even before the guns fired on Fort Sumter, the British minister in Washington, Lord Lyons, reported that the French were pushing for the powers to come together and recognize the Confederacy. London balked, preferring to wait and see how events progressed without European interference. Napoleon III dared not strike out alone and reluctantly followed suit. The reason Britain could adopt such an apparently self-defeating stance was that rather than fearing a cotton embargo, the country had every reason to welcome a temporary slow-down in imports. The bumper cotton crops of the preceding two years had produced a massive over-supply, potentially bringing ruin to the British textile industry. The South had inadvertently provided the perfect solution to Britain's cotton glut.

President Lincoln's call to arms, followed by the Federal blockade of Southern ports, helped to clarify Europe's position on secession and the subsequent war. Although some histories have labeled Britain's subsequent declaration of neutrality (a legal move that recognizes two belligerents in a bona fide war) as an act of hostility toward the North, the historian Allan Nevins effectively debunked this assertion. Since Britain had been a signatory to the 1856 Declaration of Paris regarding maritime law, the Union blockade offered it only two choices: respect it and declare neutrality, or deny its legitimacy and turn the Southern coastline into a violent free-for-all. Other countries quickly followed with their own neutrality declarations, with the French agreeing to join the British in a united front regarding Union policy.

On balance the neutrality proclamation contained rules and provisions that were more helpful to the North than the South. But the awarding of belligerent status to both sides did confer on the Confederacy some useful rights that it used with impunity, including the right to send out privateers in place of a navy, and the ability to raise money on the international market. Despite the angry assertions from Washington that belligerent status was overly generous to the Confederacy, and protests from Richmond that it did not go far enough, Europe stayed neutral for the rest of the war. This was no mean feat, bearing in mind that for the next four years the North and the South variously ignored, subverted or attempted to overturn French and British neutrality.

High profile threats to British neutrality, like the Trent Affair of late 1861, the clandestine construction of Southern sea raiders and Confederate guerilla operations out of Canada have tended to overshadow the fact that the reach of the Civil War went far beyond individual incidents. The Southern manipulation of news and public opinion was more sophisticated than anything the world had yet seen. At one point, the South's chief foreign propagandist, Henry Hotze, had both the Reuters and Havas news services using his reports as their sole source of Civil War information, as well as the most of the leading English-, French- and German-language newspapers. The North was never able to match the South's overseas lobbying and propaganda efforts.

There was no single over-riding reason why Britain (and therefore Europe) decided against interfering in the Civil War. The part played by the American minister Charles Francis Adams has been grossly overstated. His most important contribution to Anglo-American relations was not that he stopped Britain from supporting the South, but that he prevented Secretary of State William H. Seward's foreign policy blunders from turning the British cabinet irremediably against the North. Economic, political, cultural and moral factors also had a role in shaping the motivations of those for and against intervention. But more often they tended to cancel one another out. For example, the Southern cotton famine that began in 1862 did less damage than expected to the British economy because it was offset by the bonanza that other industries enjoyed from increased orders from the North.

On the other hand, the impact of the Civil War on Europe's balance of power continued long after the war concluded. Napoleon III's rule was fatally wounded not only by his misjudged invasion of Mexico, but also by the political lift his republican opponents gained after the North's victory. Britain's position as the world's superpower was also undermined by the war. Prime Minister Lord Palmerston was reduced to making empty threats. He was unable to interfere militarily in events that were redrawing the map of Europe, for fear of losing either Canada or the Caribbean to an American sneak attack; and, vice versa, he dared not be dragged into a transatlantic war that could leave Britain exposed to the machinations of either the emperor or the tsar.

It has often been said that the Civil War did not alter European methods of warfare as much as it should have, and that it had no more than a tangential impact on homegrown movements for political reform. Neither is the case. As the French who endured the Prussian interpretation of Philip Sheridan's "total war" in 1870 could attest, and the British who demanded a government of the people and by the people in 1867, 1884 and 1918 would aver, the Northern victory at Appomattox was a beacon seen by millions.

The Coming of the Emancipation Proclamation

By PAUL FINKELMAN

On July 12, 1862, Abraham Lincoln met privately in the White House, for the second time, with most of the senators and congressmen from the loyal slave states—Delaware, Maryland, Kentucky and Missouri. It wasn't the most relaxed of meetings: most of these delegates were Democrats; some grudgingly supported the war effort, while others were more enthusiastic about the Union cause, as long as the conflict was solely for the purpose of restoring the Union.

Many of them were slave owners, and virtually all supported slavery—like the Confederates, they believed that the proper status of blacks was as slaves, or, where circumstances warranted, as free people with limited rights. Most agreed with Chief Justice Roger B. Taney's conclusion in the 1857 case Dred Scott v. Sandford that blacks could never be citizens of the United States. Except for the handful of Republicans in the gathering, the delegation undoubtedly hoped to see Lincoln defeated in the 1864 election.

But more uncomfortable than the makeup of the meeting was its message: Lincoln asked these border-state politicians to return to their home states and lobby for abolition. Congress was willing to offer compensated emancipation if any of the loyal slave states would begin to end bondage, so the president needed one or more of them to take the initiative.

Lincoln's strategy was to argue that the loyal slave states would help the war effort by showing the rebels "that, in no event, will the states you represent ever join their proposed Confederacy." While Lincoln did not expect the border states to secede and join the Confederacy, he argued that voluntary emancipation in those states would be a blow to Confederate hopes and morale. If the upper South ended slavery, even the most optimistic Confederates would know that the four loyal slave states would not be leaving the Union.

This proposal dovetailed with Lincoln's personal hatred of slavery and his "oft-expressed personal wish that all men everywhere could be free." It also would increase his stature with the antislavery wing for the Republican Party, which was clamoring for some direct attack on slavery.

Lincoln's position was also a practical one. One way or the other, he said, slavery was done for—he famously told them that "incidents of war" could "not be avoided" and that "mere friction and abrasion" would destroy slavery. He bluntly predicted that the institution "will be gone and you will have nothing valuable in lieu of it." He also pointed out that Gen. David Hunter had just issued a proclamation in Union-held coastal South Carolina to end slavery there. Lincoln had countermanded that proclamation (he saw it as a usurpation of the president's role), but he also noted that Hunter's proclamation had been very popular, and that he personally considered Hunter an "honest man" and "my friend." The message was clear: slavery would soon end, and the border state representatives should take what they could get for themselves and their constituents.

But the gathered representatives and senators did not take the hint, probably still believing, as pro-slavery forces had argued before the war, that any move against slavery would be unconstitutional. Indeed, two days later more than two-thirds of them—20 in all—signed a letter saying precisely that (eight border state representatives then published letters of their own, supporting the president).

On July 14, the same day that the border state representatives denounced emancipation, Lincoln made one final stab at gradualism with a bill to compensate states that ended slavery. The bill left blank the amount that Congress would appropriate for each slave, but it provided that the money would come in the form of federal bonds given to the states. The bill was part of Lincoln's strategy to end slavery at the state level where possible, as a way of setting up the possibility of ending it on the national level. If he could get Kentucky or Maryland to end slavery, he felt, it would be easier to end it in the South. Such an approach was also consistent with prewar notions of constitutionalism—that the states had sole authority over issues of property. The bill went through two readings, but Congress adjourned before acting on it.

Lincoln surely knew that this bill, like his meeting with the border state representatives, would go nowhere. Nevertheless, this very public attempt was valuable. As in his response to Hunter, Lincoln was demonstrating to the nation that he was not acting precipitously or incautiously. On the contrary, he was doing everything he could, at least publicly, to end slavery with the least amount of turmoil and social dislocation.

The proposed bill must also be seen in the context of Lincoln's actions on July 13, the day before he introduced the bill and the day after his meeting with the border state representatives. That day he privately told Secretary of State William H. Seward and Secretary of the Navy Gideon Welles that he was going to issue a proclamation declaring emancipation for all slaves in the Confederacy.

This was not a sudden response to the border state representatives' rejection of compensated emancipation: even had they accepted Lincoln's proposal, it would not have affected slavery in the Confederacy, where most slaves lived. Indeed, Lincoln told Welles that for weeks the issue had "occupied his mind and thoughts day and night."

Lincoln told Welles the issue was one of military necessity. "We must free the slaves," he said, "or be ourselves subdued." Slaves, Lincoln argued "were undeniably an element of strength to those who had their service, and we must decide whether that element should be with us or against us." Lincoln also rejected the idea that the Constitution still protected slavery in the Confederacy. The rebels," he said, "could not at the same time throw off the Constitution and invoke its aid. Having made war on the Government, they were subject to the incidents and calamities of war."

Lincoln had found a constitutional theory that would be acceptable to most Northerners. Regardless of how they felt about slavery or the constitutional power of the federal government, few were willing to come to the defense of the rebels. And in any case, the legal questions were largely moot: until the war ended with a Union victory, the South couldn't very easily challenge the proclamation in court. After decades of political and constitutional stalemate over slavery, Lincoln had figured out a path toward freedom for millions of men and women in bondage.

Congress Confiscates Confederates' Slaves

By SEAN WILENTZ

O n July 17, 1862, the last day of the congressional session, President Lincoln signed into law "An Act to suppress Insurrection, to punish Treason and Rebellion, to seize and confiscate the Property of Rebels, and for other Purposes," commonly known as the Second Confiscation Act. That same day, Lincoln also signed a Militia Act, which authorized the enlistment of "persons of African descent" to serve in the Union military as laborers "or any other military or naval service for which they may be found competent." Together, the measures were important markers in the fitful transformation of the war against the slaveholders' rebellion into a war of emancipation—a war in which ex-slaves and free blacks would play important roles. Both acts also signified the important role congressional Republicans played in advancing that transformation.

With so much historical attention fixed on Lincoln and his generals, it is easy to overlook the contributions of the peculiar but forceful 37th Congress. Elected alongside Lincoln in 1860, the Congress's size was diminished by Southern secession even before it had assembled. A handful of Unionists from Virginia, Tennessee and Louisiana would serve in the House beyond its first brief special session, called by Lincoln to open on July 4, 1861; otherwise, both chambers were composed entirely of Northern and Border States representatives. Of these, about one-quarter of both the House and Senate were Democrats, a considerably smaller portion were independent Unionists, while roughly three in five were Republicans.

Under Republican leadership, the Congress quickly passed a series of bold measures, some directly related to the war and some not. First, during the opening special session in the summer of 1861, came the Revenue Act, which included the first provision for a federal income tax in the United States. Thereafter, during the ensuing regular session, came the Legal Tender Act (authorizing the issuing of paper money, or "greenbacks"), the act abolishing slavery in the District of Columbia, the Homestead Act, a second Revenue Act, the Pacific Railway Act and the Morrill Land Grant Colleges Act, among other measures.

As in the case of abolition of slavery in the capital, the Republican legislators were making good on their campaign vows to curtail or abolish slavery wherever the Congress had, in their view, the clear constitutional authority to do so. (This effort aimed to advance what had been the Republicans' avowed purpose even before secession: placing slavery on the road to extinction.) Much of the rest of the legislation concerned funding the war effort. But by opening the way for building a transcontinental railroad, providing inexpensive homesteads to prospective western settlers, and expanding opportunities for higher education, the Republican Congress was also acting on the impulse, most closely identified with the old Whig Party, to deploy the federal government's power vigorously in pursuit of the public welfare.

During its opening months, the Congress displayed bipartisan unity in supporting war measures. But the question of what to do with slaves who had escaped to Union lines, which appeared when three slaves turned up at the Union-held Fortress Monroe in Virginia in May 1861, caused division. The administration approved General Benjamin Butler's policy of treating the escapees as "contrabands of war," just as Congress was wrestling with the same problem while debating a bill to confiscate all property—including, presumably, slave labor—used to aid the rebellion.

Some Border State representatives objected to any form of confiscation. The Constitution's prohibition of Congress's legislating against slavery in the states, they claimed—a prohibition almost universally recognized and honored—was no less intact during wartime than in peacetime. Northern Republicans replied by, in effect, drawing a distinction between abolition and emancipation: although Congress was powerless to abolish slavery in the states, they asserted, it could certainly confiscate and, some believed, emancipate the slaves of traitors. With remarkable accord, erasing factional lines that divided the so-called Radicals from more moderate Republicans, the Republican majority pushed forward with confiscation.

Over the strenuous objections of Border unionists and Demo-crats—the 37th Congress's first serious partisan breach—both houses passed a bill that confiscated all slaves utilized in the Confederate war effort and declared that their masters would "forfeit" their claims to ownership. Despite the controversy it stirred, the act was extremely limited in substance, confiscating only that minority of refugee slaves who had actually worked for the Confederate military while leaving it unclear whether those slaves were emancipated.

Nevertheless, the constitutional experts who designed the bill made subtle but portentous changes to the federal government's rela-tions to slavery. By treating the confiscated slaves not as chattel prop-erty but as persons "held to labor," the bill implicitly endorsed the argument, long advanced by Republican political leaders, that there could be no legitimate property in human beings. (As a result, con-fiscation of slaves, unlike other property, would require no further legal proceedings.) The law also applied to owners in loyal Border States as well as seceded states that permitted the Confederates to employ their slaves' labor. President Lincoln, saying that he feared the bill would anger the Border States and doubted its constitution-ality, approached signing the measure, according to The New York Times, "with great reluctance," yet he signed it anyway, ostensibly bowing to the political reality that, as virtually every Republican in both the House and Senate had voted for the bill, he had no choice.

The ensuing bloody year pushed the White House as well as the Congress to take more forceful steps toward emancipation. A minority of abolitionists and Radical Republicans had held to the idea from the war's commencement that secession and war empowered the federal government to abolish slavery. But by early 1862, in the face of military setbacks, moderates and even conservatives in Congress were coming around to the idea that military necessity required freeing the slaves in order to rob the rebellion of the bondsmen's labor. Something of a revo-lution in thought ensued. "You can form no conception of the change of opinion here as to the Negro question," the conservative Senator John Sherman wrote to his brother, General William Tecumseh Sherman, in August. "I am prepared for one to meet the broad issue of universal emancipation." The Second Confiscation Act, far more drastic than the first, was the great signal of Congress's shift months before Lincoln's Emancipation Proclamation.

Unlike the First Confiscation Act, passed swiftly under the immediate pressure of the contraband question, winning approval for the second act required nearly the entire regular first session of the 37th Congress. On Dec. 5, 1861, three days after the session opened, Senator Lyman Trumbull of Illinois introduced a bill that would free the slaves of all who had participated in or abetted what Trumbull called "this wicked Rebellion." Also in December, the House took up a similar bill. The proposals then languished for months in congressional committees. A separate, similar Senate resolution came up for debate the following February, after which various senators offered amendments and alternative proposals. Only in the late spring of 1862 did the Congress begin considering the bill in earnest.

A tall and nervously animated lawyer who squinted behind gold-framed spectacles, Trumbull had joined the Republican Party at its inception in the mid-1850s after serving for eight years as a Democrat in the Illinois State Legislature and for five years as an associate justice on the state supreme court. Selected in 1855 by the state legislature to serve in the United States Senate—in preference to Abraham Lincoln—Trumbull gravitated to the ranks of the Radicals in 1861, badly underestimating the newly elected President Lincoln as an expedient opportunist, and perceiving himself and his allies as a necessary force to goad the supposedly ineffectual president into action. In rising to explain his new confiscation bill, Trumbull left little doubt that he intended to help make emancipation not simply an effect but an aim of the Union cause. The bill, he announced, would not only compel the rebels and their abettors to forfeit "the persons they hold in slavery," it would declare the slaves thus forfeited free.

Trumbull explained the underlying logic: "The right to free the slaves of rebels would be equally clear with that to confiscate their property generally; for it is as property that they profess to hold them: but, as one of the most efficient means for attaining the end for which the armies of the Union have been called forth, the right to restore to them the God-given liberty of which they have been unjustly deprived is doubly clear." Emancipation, in short, was a matter of military necessity that would also end the oppressive fiction that slaves actually were the property their masters claimed they were.

When they finally turned to the confiscation question, congressional Republicans argued over numerous details, most important whether the bill ought to compel or permit the president to put its terms into effect. The complicated bill that finally passed authorized severe penalties for all rebels, especially high-ranking Confederate officials. It also authorized, although it did not require, the president to warn the Confederacy's supporters to cease their rebellion or face confiscation. The army would be forbidden to return fugitive slaves to disloyal owners, and Lincoln would be permitted to enlist blacks in any capacity he thought necessary to suppress the rebellion. Above all, the bill's ninth section declared "forever free of their servitude" all rebel-owned slaves who had escaped to Union lines or who lived in all territories currently or subsequently held by Union troops. As with the First Confiscation Act, the confiscation of slaves would be self-executing and require no further legal proceedings. In sum, the bill turned the Union army into an army of liberation not just for refugee slaves, but for the vast preponderance of those slaves who lived in conquered portions of the South. And it helped clear the way for the emancipation of slaves in the unconquered areas by presidential proclamation.

While the debate over the Second Confiscation Bill reached its climax, Congress also considered a new bill concerning the raising of black troops. Radical Republicans had vainly advocated such a measure from the very beginning of the regular congressional session, but by July, more moderate Republicans, alarmed by heavy Union military losses, began moving to support an amendment to the Militia Act of 1795. The amendment would authorize the president to open service to blacks for manual labor jobs or (much as the new confiscation bill would stipulate) any other task they could handle—which presumably might include combat duties. Rebel-owned slaves who enlisted would, along with their immediate families, be declared free. Although it opened up the possibility of blacks serving in combat, the proposal presumed that they would serve mainly as laborers, their value being in freeing up white soldiers for combat duty.

As they did in response to any proposal that even touched on emancipation, Border State representatives howled in opposition. It was thus all the more remarkable when the conservative and highly influential Republican Senator William Pitt Fessenden of Maine delivered a long speech supporting the amendment, challenging those representatives who grow "so sensitive the moment that you speak of employing negroes, the slaves of rebels, in the service of the country." As he finished mulling over the Second Confiscation Act, passed less than a week earlier, Lincoln signed the Militia Act, secure in the knowledge that it would go into effect only following a presidential order.

The new confiscation act caused Lincoln more difficulty, as he had hoped the Congress would not pass any legislation touching on confiscation that might complicate his own efforts to hold together the disparate pro-Union alliance. Craftily, he drafted a veto message that criticized the bill for, among other things, failing to provide the means for distinguishing fugitive slaves owned by Confederates from those owned by loyal Unionists. But he also consulted with several members of Congress and obtained a resolution specifying that no forfeiture of rebel real estate would last beyond the life of the owner, in line with the Constitution's provisions regarding attainder of treason. Congress stayed in session one extra day to get the resolution approved—and that same day, along with the Militia Act, Lincoln signed the confiscation bill, even as he released his draft veto message.

Lincoln's seemingly ambivalent actions irritated and even incensed some Radical Republicans, in and out of Congress. So did, thereafter, what his critics unfairly took to be his slowness to enforce the Second Confiscation Act—in deference to what Horace Greeley called the "fossil politicians" of the Border States—as well as public statements that seemed to hedge on emancipation. As usual, though, the Radicals were underestimating Lincoln, who was heeding his own counsel— and quietly following his own course on emancipation.

Exactly how and when Lincoln devised his new approach remains unclear, though he had plainly been pondering it, as was his wont, for some time before July 17. On July 21, only four days after he signed the Second Confiscation Act and the Militia Act, Lincoln informed his cabinet he had resolved to implement provisions of the acts. And the following day, he delivered to the cabinet a new draft order—what would later be known as the draft of the Emancipation Proclamation. It began by warning Confederates, under the stipulations of the new confiscation act, to cease their rebellion in 60 days or face the confiscation of their property, including slaves. The order then reaffirmed Lincoln's longtime support for gradual emancipation with compensation to the slaveholders. The last sentence contained Lincoln's bombshell: under his authority as commander in chief, he would declare that on Jan. 1, 1863, "all persons held as slaves" in states still controlled by the rebels "shall then, thenceforward, and forever, be free."

The congressional Republicans had labored hard, and on July 17, 1862, their pursuit of emancipation, as well as black military enlistment, brought the enactment of legislation that, as one Illinois congressman would later remark "has not been fully appreciated." What they did not know was that President Lincoln, whom a number of them distrusted, was silently hard at work on his own, preparing the way for a proclamation beyond anything Congress had yet envisaged.

The Painter and the President
By LOUIS P. MASUR

Francis Bicknell Carpenter dreamed of greatness. Born in Homer, N.Y., in 1830, the portrait painter studied at the Cortland Academy and then moved to Manhattan to make his name. But he knew portraits would take him only so far. The most distinguished art critics ranked them, along with domestic scenes and still life, as a lesser genre. It was history painting that reigned pre-eminent—works like John Trumbull's "Death of General Warren at the Battle of Bunker Hill" (1786) and Emmanuel Leutze's "Washington Crossing the Delaware" (1851), which drew throngs when first exhibited and was hailed as "the best painting yet executed for an American subject."

After Abraham Lincoln issued the Emancipation Proclamation on Jan. 1, 1863, Carpenter knew he had found the subject for his masterpiece. He sought an audience with the president and asked Owen Lovejoy, an Illinois congressman and abolitionist, to arrange a meeting. "I wish to paint this picture *now*, while all the actors in the scene are living," he told Lovejoy. "I wish to make it the standard authority for the portrait of . . . Mr. Lincoln as it is the great act of his life by which he will be remembered and honored through all generations."

Carpenter met the president on Feb. 6, 1864. As the artist remembered it, Lincoln said, "we will turn you loose here and try to give you a good chance to work out your ideas."

Shortly after their February interview, Carpenter moved into the White House, where he remained for six months. The artist had Lincoln and cabinet members pose for him again and again, he arranged for them to be photographed, he borrowed books and maps to portray them accurately on the canvas. Much to the dismay of Mrs. Lincoln, he took over the state dining room. Visitors would look at the artist engaged in his work and President Lincoln would explain, "Oh, you need not mind him; he is but a painter."

An artist's most important decision is what to paint, and Carpenter chose to commemorate the first reading of the Emancipation Proclamation to the cabinet on July 22, 1862. It had taken Lincoln time to arrive at that moment, but he had become convinced of the necessity, according to one cabinet member at the meeting, of "proclaiming the emancipation of all slaves within States remaining in insurrection on the first of January, 1863." Lincoln later told Carpenter, "I felt that we had reached the end of our rope on the plan of operations we had been pursuing; that we had about played our last card, and must change our tactics, or lose the game."

Carpenter explained his artistic intentions:

I conceived of that band of men, upon whom the eyes of the world centered as never before upon ministers of state, gathered in council, depressed, perhaps disheartened at the vain efforts of many months to restore the supremacy of the government. I saw, in thought, the head of the nation,

"President Lincoln Reading the Emancipation Proclamation to His Cabinet," by Francis Bicknell Carpenter.

bowed down with the weight of care and responsibility, solemnly announcing, as he unfolds the prepared draft of the Proclamation, that the time for the inauguration of this policy had arrived; I endeavored to imagine the conflicting emotions of satisfaction, doubt, and distrust with which such an announcement would be received by men of the varied characteristics of the assembled councilors.

Whatever his vision, Carpenter had chosen an odd moment to commemorate. Even Lincoln didn't recollect the exact date of the first reading, telling the painter it "was the last of July, or the first part of the month of August." Salmon P. Chase later said that "not the slightest trace" of the meeting on July 22 "remains on my memory." The artist might have picked any of a number of other occasions that were more memorable and could have proven more visually compelling and dramatic: Sept. 22, for example, when a resolute Lincoln read to the cabinet a story by Artemus Ward and spoke of God's providence before issuing the preliminary Emancipation Proclamation. Or the signing of the Emancipation Proclamation itself on Jan. 1, when Lincoln struggled to still his hand which trembled from the exertion of greeting visitors all day.

But having chosen July 22, Carpenter stuck with it. On July 22, 1864, two years to the day after Lincoln's announcement to the cabinet, he was ready to unveil for the president and his councilors the huge canvas, 9 feet by 14.5 feet, which was titled "First Reading of the Emancipation Proclamation of President Lincoln."

Carpenter had indeed created a tableau of the cabinet meeting. Lincoln sits just left of center, proclamation and quill in hand. To the far left are Secretary of War Edwin Stanton and Secretary of the Treasury Salmon P. Chase. Secretary of the Navy Gideon Welles is seated, with his back to the wall, and standing beside him are Secretary of the Interior Caleb Smith and Postmaster General Montgomery Blair. To the far right of the canvas, arms crossed, sits Attorney General Edward Bates. Secretary of State William Seward, is in profile, speaking. There are two portraits in the room—the departed Secretary of War Simon Cameron on the left and Andrew Jackson, above the mantel. Read left to right, the painting depicts cabinet members in descending order of their enthusiasm for the Emancipation Proclamation.

Carpenter has also included a selection of books, newspapers and maps. The New York Tribune rests on the floor beside Stanton; on the table is a parchment copy of the Constitution and, before Bates, a map of the seat of war in Virginia; another map, showing the distribution of slave population, is propped up on the right-hand side, and on the floor nearby are William Whiting's "War Powers of the President" and Joseph Story's "Commentaries on the Constitution," two works that influenced Lincoln's decision; beneath the table are volumes of the Congressional Globe.

Despite the artist's heroic efforts, the painting was not a success. Lincoln diplomatically said, "It is as good as it can be made." Noah Brooks, correspondent for The Sacramento Daily Union, was less tactful. The problem, Brooks thought, was that the scene did not lend itself to history painting: "a group of men, wearing the somber-hued garments of American gentlemen, assembled in a plainly furnished apartment, though earnestly discussing a matter which is now historic, does not furnish a tempting subject for the tricks and bewildering cheats of art." William O. Stoddard, one of Lincoln's secretaries, thought the painting uninspiring and joked that the title should have been "Table, surrounded with gentlemen waiting to have their picture taken."

The review in The New York Times was more kind, stating that "the picture will be viewed with satisfaction by succeeding generations for its special merits of portraiture." But the reference to portraiture must have irritated an artist who aspired to being feted as a history painter. The Times review concluded, "when slavery has become a surprise and a horror to everyone in the land; when the Proclamation of President Lincoln has passed into history as a splendid trophy of a sanguinary war; when the gratitude of a people that no longer knows a bondman reverts to the heroes that made them glorious, then will such a canvas be gazed upon with respectful admiration."

Carpenter took the canvas on tour to several cities (special hinges in the frame allowed him to fold the work, thus making it easy to transport), and then brought it to his studio and continued to tinker with the portraits. In 1877, a philanthropist purchased the painting and donated it to Congress, where a dedication ceremony was held the following year on Lincoln's birthday. On that day, of the eight men depicted, only Montgomery Blair survived. The painting now hangs far from the spotlight, near the west staircase in the Senate. A print, engraved by Alexander Hay Ritchie, achieved greater success. It "will be prized in every liberty-loving household," declared Noah Brooks. Lincoln was the first to subscribe for a copy; when it appeared in 1866, it went to his widow.

Although Carpenter may not have satisfied his ambitions as a painter, he succeeded as a writer. In 1866, he published "Six Months at the White House With Abraham Lincoln." The book was a sensation, and it remains an essential volume in any Lincoln library. A review in The Times praised the work for facts and anecdotes as "pointedly illustrative of Mr. Lincoln's character and inner life as any that have yet found that way into print." Another publication declared "this is a book that will live when many of the heavy biographies of its central figure shall have been forgotten." Carpenter had created an unforgettable historical portrait after all—only he had done so not with brush but with pen.

The McClellan Problem

By RICHARD SLOTKIN

On Aug. 3, 1862, Gen. George B. McClellan received orders to begin withdrawing the Army of the Potomac from its position in front of Richmond, Va. The new Union general in chief, Henry Halleck, had given McClellan a choice: to renew his offensive against Richmond or ship his army back to Washington. McClellan resented and resisted Halleck's authority, and stubbornly refused to advance, thinking Halleck would eventually recognize the folly of a withdrawal.

And folly it was, McClellan's obstinacy and lack of battlefield success notwithstanding. Once McClellan's troops were in transit, half the Union forces in the Virginia theater were out of action. With the threat to Richmond removed, Gen. Robert E. Lee was free to stage a bold counter-offensive into northern Virginia, which would lead to the near destruction of the Union Army under General John Pope at the Second Battle of Bull Run, the invasion of Maryland, the bloody Battle of Antietam and the Confederacy's best chance to win the war outright.

The root of this tactical blunder was the radical and absolutely necessary transformation of Federal strategy initiated by President Abraham Lincoln in July 1862. At the start of the war, he had hoped that aggressive military action, coupled with a "conciliatory" policy on slavery, would induce the South to negotiate a return to the Union in short order. But a year of costly fighting had proved that the Confederacy's military strength and political will could not be overcome without a far longer and more destructive war. By the summer of 1862, the situation was clear: Union troop strength had to be greatly increased—Lincoln was asking for 300,000 new volunteers—and offensives had to be pressed with greater energy.

But Lincoln had also concluded that the elimination of slavery must become a Federal war aim. He had always believed slavery was morally wrong and incompatible with democracy. It was the motive for secession and the basis of the South's economic and military strength. So long as slavery existed it would remain a source of conflict between the states. Lincoln concluded that the longer, costlier war for the Union that now seemed necessary could be justified only if it removed the root cause of conflict.

To carry out such a strategy he needed a general whose determination and commitment matched his own. What he had instead was General McClellan, who was both a balky and reluctant field commander and the symbolic champion of the opposition Democratic Party. On July 8, 1862, he met with McClellan at the general's headquarters, to see whether he was able and willing to fight the long war.

McClellan was a highly respected West Point professional, who had been put in command of the Army immediately after the disaster at Bull Run in July 1861. For the first months of his tenure he received universal acclaim, and was given a free hand in organizing the Federal armies. But the accolades went to his head: he believed the outpouring of public support he enjoyed during his first six months in command was a kind of symbolic election, which gave him moral authority comparable to the president's. Although he saw himself as a disinterested military professional, he was in fact a partisan Democrat "of the Stephen A. Douglas school," who maintained close contact with the leaders of the Democratic Party and pressed Lincoln to adopt the "conservative" policies favored by his party.

He thought antislavery Republicans were just as responsible as secessionists for the outbreak of war, and that if he was to restore the Union he had to defeat both the Southern armies on his front and the Radical Republicans who would stab him in the back. He even flirted with idea of a Congressionally sanctioned "dictatorship," which would give him control of war policy, leaving Lincoln as a figurehead. From the start of his tenure he had waged a series of political and bureaucratic battles, trying to make himself the dominant voice in the president's councils. "I have no choice," he told his wife. "The people call upon me to save the country—I must save it & cannot respect anything that stands in the way."

His illusions flourished in the hothouse of his headquarters, where he was surrounded by loyalists who mirrored and even exaggerated his moods. He saw himself as the agent of Divine Providence, chosen by God to save the Republic—and visit judgment on his enemies. Even his defeat by Lee in the Seven Days battles was a sign that God was on his side. "I think I begin to see His wise purpose in all this," he wrote his wife on July 10. "If I had succeeded in taking Richmond now the fanatics of the North might have been too powerful & reunion impossible."

Most dangerously, McClellan was utterly contemptuous of Abraham Lincoln's character, intelligence, social origins and morals. He dismissed the president as "the original Gorilla," a well-meaning but weak-minded "baboon" surrounded by fools and traitors. He believed that his July 8 meeting was his opportunity to impress his will and his ideas on the president.

They met on the deck of Lincoln's steamer, where a canvas awning shaded them from the day's insufferable heat. Lincoln asked McClellan when he planned to resume the offensive. Instead of answering, McClellan begged leave to submit a letter detailing his views, which he handed the president. Instead of taking it and leaving, Lincoln read it right there. But if its contents astonished him he gave no sign.

The letter said nothing about the Army's defeat, nor did it propose a plan for renewing the offensive. It was instead a political manifesto, laying out McClellan's grand design for the future civil and military policy of the country. McClellan demanded a "conservative" approach to three basic policies: the legal consequences of secession, the status of slavery and the division of power between civil and military authorities. He denied the basic premise of Lincoln's policy, that secession was an act of rebellion. Instead, he declared that the government had no right to "subjugate" the seceded states. So when their districts were occupied by Union forces, the "political rights" of Southerners must be automatically restored. As McClellan well knew, such a policy would slowly restore the Democratic Party's national majority.

McClellan also warned that "a declaration of radical views, upon slavery, will rapidly disintegrate our present Armies." Coming from the commander of the nation's most powerful army, which was imbued with his cult of personal loyalty, that warning had threatening implications. Finally, McClellan wanted Lincoln to delegate control of all war-related policy to "a Commander in Chief of the Army; one who possesses your confidence, understands your views and who is competent to execute your orders." McClellan was clearly nominating himself for the post.

In effect, McClellan was demanding that Lincoln abandon the responsibilities of his office and the platform of his party, and turn power over to the general who had just lost the war's greatest battle at the time.

Lincoln pocketed the letter and kept his poker face, but the meeting had crystallized his strategic ideas. In the two weeks that followed he made a series of decisions which radically transformed Federal strategy. On July 11 he ordered Gen. Henry Halleck, commander of Federal armies in the West, to assume command, under the president, of all Federal armies—thus making him McClellan's superior.

Then, on July 12, in a private conversation with Secretary of State William Seward and Navy Secretary Gideon Welles, Lincoln declared his intention to issue an emancipation proclamation, freeing all slaves in the rebellious states; and on July 22 he presented a draft proclamation to an astonished cabinet. He acted with full awareness that such a proclamation would end all hope of conciliation and commit the Union to an all-out war.

First, however, he had to deal with McClellan. Indeed, Halleck's first task would be to force General McClellan to resume the offensive—but McClellan was immovable, confident that his popular prestige and political support gave him sovereign immunity. On July 11, the very day of Halleck's appointment, he boasted to his wife, "I have commenced receiving letters from the North urging me to march on Washington & assume the Govt!!"

Fearful of removing him outright, Halleck and Lincoln chose the half-measure of shipping McClellan's Army north without him. They thus set the stage of Lee's invasion of Maryland, and McClellan's return to command for the Antietam campaign.

Women at War

By C. KAY LARSON

On Aug. 29, 1862, during the Second Battle of Bull Run, Union soldiers could see a young woman helping the wounded seek shelter under a rock ledge, while taking fire herself. At Petersburg in June 1864, Sgt. Frederick O. Talbot, of the First Maine Heavy Artillery, found himself standing beside this same woman as she beckoned soldiers to the frontline breastwork to be treated. He was told that the men of the Fifth Michigan Infantry would have anyone's "life in a minute" for saying "any harm of her."

Annie Etheridge had gone off to war with her husband, James, in 1861. He deserted after the First Battle of Bull Run, but Annie remained, serving as a battlefield medic with the Second and Third Michigan, a unit eventually incorporated into the Fifth Infantry Regiment.

Etheridge is the most famous of the Civil War "daughters of regiments," who, along with "mothers," tended soldiers in camp, sometimes in battle, and on the march. She went on foot and horseback, treating the wounded and taking them off the field. Although she participated in 28 battles, she was wounded only once. And she did more than tend to the wounded. On two occasions she rallied the troops: at Chancellorsville, riding along the line, urging the soldiers to hold it, and at Spotsylvania, leading retreating troops back into battle, under hot fire. Etheridge received the coveted Kearny Cross, awarded to enlisted personnel of the First Division, Third Army Corps who "most distinguished" themselves in combat.

Etheridge, along with Marie Tepe of the 114th Pennsylvania, are perhaps the most romantic heroines of the war, because they served under fire, undisguised, in feminine attire. An additional 400 women, according to the Sanitary Commission agent Mary Livermore, were known to have disguised themselves as men.

They include Jennie Hodgers, who enlisted in the 95th Illinois Infantry, serving for three years and participating in 40 battles. Her motive: "I wanted excitement." Hodgers developed a reputation for being a daring soldier, evincing "nerveless performance in combat situations and tirelessness on the march." She returned to Illinois and lived out the next 50 years as a man, her gender revealed only when she became an elderly victim of an automobile accident.

Like Hodgers, many disguised women maintained their cover by adopting male lifestyles and mannerisms. Others were discovered in sad, obvious, odd and funny ways. Most women were identified as such when they came sick or wounded into hospitals. Having sweet

A woman, Union officer and children, possibly a family, in camp.

faces, peachy complexions and small hands and feet were clear give-aways. Yet a Rochester recruit got up one morning and, completely forgetting herself, put her pants on over her head, thinking they were her dress. A cavalryman and teamster working for Gen. Philip Sheridan were revealed when they fell drunk into a river and attempts were made to revive them. Conversely, Pvt. Franklin Thompson, a k a Sarah Emma Edmonds, of the Second Michigan Infantry, kept the secret for one woman who died on the field at Antietam: Edmonds buried her in an unmarked grave.

Female soldiers passing as men could be determined to stay the course, enlisting in new regiments after each discovery. Fourteen-year-old Lizzie Compton, a Canadian, served in eight regiments. Frances Hook holds the record for serving in 10 different regiments. Versatile Fanny Wilson of Williamsburg, N.Y., enlisted in the 24th New Jersey, took sick at Vicksburg and was discharged, did a stint as a ballet dancer, and then joined the Third Illinois Cavalry.

The Civil War women also carried on a century-old family tradition. Continental Army women traveled with their husbands' units, working as nurses, cooks, laundresses and water carriers for artillery units. The Civil War carried on this family tradition. Civil War soldiers were mostly farmers, and farm families worked together in the home and the fields, so separation in war would have been the odd circumstance. Keith Blalock of the 26th North Carolina told his recruiter that he wouldn't enlist unless his wife was enrolled with him. They fought in three battles together.

Often they enlisted from the same motives as men: a patriotic sense of duty, to uphold family traditions, to gain better or any pay, for abolition. Private Lyons Wakeman, a k a Sarah Rosetta, of the 153rd New York Infantry, wrote home: "I am as independent as a hog on the ice."

Most women, however, seemed to have joined to be with their husbands, boyfriends or brothers. Reportedly, the husband of Mary Owens, a Pennsylvanian, "was killed by her side in their first battle." In one Philadelphia case, after the husband enlisted, the wife was unable to support herself and their new baby; so she left the infant with neighbors and joined her husband's regiment. The baby died shortly thereafter. Melverina Peppercorn of Tennessee saw no reason why she should not enlist. She was older than her brother and could shoot as well as he. Twenty-year-old Eliza Wilson, a "daughter" of the Fifth Wisconsin Regiment, in which several family members had enrolled, trudged along "in storm and sunshine" with her compatriots.

In the Victorian era, women's lives could be tenuous: a number of female soldiers were orphans, widows and escaping abused children and wives and prostitutes. A 19-year-old drummer girl in the 112th Indiana Regiment joined to be with her three orphaned siblings in 1861. By the time The Chicago Tribune reported her medical treatment in September 1864, all her brothers had been killed in battle.

Women performed multiple duties. Cuban-born Loreta Janeta Velazquez, a k a Lt. Harry T. Buford of the Confederate Army, was surely the busiest devotee: soldier, smuggler, secret and double agent, detective, courier and bounty-jumper agent. Mary Ellis, wife of the colonel of the Union First Missouri Cavalry, assisted with surgeries, nursed on the battlefield and served as a courier and detective.

Women also served in naval roles. Elizabeth Taylor, a British volunteer, served disguised as a sailor, likely on a Confederate raider. In January 1863, presumably, Augusta Devereaux, the captain's wife, retook their merchant ship, J. P. Ellicott, from a Confederate prize crew, with the help of mostly Caribbean seamen. She commanded the vessel to St. Thomas, where it was turned over to the United States consul. In mid-February 1862, Mary Louvest, a Norfolk free black, hand delivered traced plans of the Confederate ironclad Merrimac to Secretary of the Navy Gideon Welles, advising that the Merrimac would soon go on the attack.

Of course, women's primary role was medical. Some 20,000 female doctors, nurses, matrons and other hospital workers enrolled. Otherwise, women served as clerks, cooks, scouts, telegraphers, recruiters and arsenal workers. A few women rose to officer rank, the reported highest being a Union major. They held federal- and state-appointed positions as Sanitary Commission and military state agents. There was one chaplain, and Christian Commission workers and freedmen teachers. Southern women formed militia groups like the Rhea County, Tenn., Cavalry and the Nancy Hart Girls of La Grange, Ga., and joined and aided guerrillas as well.

Whatever duties they performed, the Civil War women who valiantly served their causes distinguished themselves from men in one major way: They were all volunteers, as has been every woman who ever enrolled in military service in our nation's history.

The Breadbasket of the Union

By CHRISTOPHER PHILLIPS

The summer of 1862 saw the Civil War's two fronts as a mirror image. In the West, Federal troops had harnessed long stretches of the Cumberland, Tennessee and Mississippi Rivers to drive deep into the Confederacy. Fort Henry, Fort Donelson, Nashville and Memphis had all fallen, leaving Union forces largely in control of Kentucky, middle and western Tennessee, northern Mississippi and northern Alabama.

But in Virginia, Confederates were having a summer of unprecedented successes. Stonewall Jackson humiliated five different federal commanders in the Shenandoah Valley and at the Battle of Cedar Mountain. Robert E. Lee had stymied George B. McClellan's Peninsula Campaign aimed at Richmond, and in August joined Jackson to humiliate John Pope at Second Manassas.

Confederate leaders saw this as the moment to capitalize on these successes with a bold military incursion into Kentucky in August. The Union's breadbasket, the western border states lying astride the Ohio River, was about to become the next front.

Beginning in the mid-18th century, the Ohio River was one of the great highways of North America. Tens of thousands of people used it to float westward down from the Appalachian Mountains into the interior of the continent. The region filled up quickly: by 1790, 73,677 people lived in Kentucky, then a Virginia county, and 35,691 more in Tennessee. By 1810, 15 percent of the American population lived west of the Appalachians, by then including the newest state, Ohio. Within a decade, six more Western states would be added to the national Union. Three decades later, in 1840, more than a third of all Americans lived in this so-called First West.

The early settlements in the western region quickly thrived because of the river trade. The Ohio and its tributaries, which stretched north to nearly the Great Lakes, south to the Nashville Basin, and east to the Cumberland Plateau, sustained the growing population of the valley with crops and goods. Farmers loaded flatboats filled with products of their summer labors, with wheat milled into flour, corn distilled into whiskey and hogs slaughtered into bacon and soap. These and innumerable other goods floated down the Big Sandy, Scioto, Licking, Kentucky, Wabash, Cumberland and Tennessee, then down the Ohio to the Mississippi and on to even hungrier markets in Memphis, Natchez, New Orleans and beyond.

The appearance of the steamboat in the first decade of the 1800s revolutionized river traffic, making it possible to return upriver without walking, riding, pushing or pulling against the river currents. Before the arrival of the steamboat, items had to be carried over the Appalachians to western Pennsylvania and floated downriver. By

1820, 73 steamboats were working the Ohio and Mississippi rivers, bringing as much as 33,000 tons of goods back up to Louisville, Cincinnati and Pittsburgh. A canal-building craze soon followed, cheaply and efficiently connecting the inland areas, especially north of the Ohio, with the rivers. In 1852, at the peak of the steamboat trade, 8,000 landings were recorded at Cincinnati.

Owing in large part to the steamboat, in a single generation after the Revolution, bustling cities grew from these once isolated river towns: Pittsburgh, St. Louis, Louisville, Lexington, Cincinnati, Evansville. These were business towns—with regularity of design standard in all of these river cities, travelers talked of their attractive business climates rather than their physical beauty. Merchants dominated local society and politics, accumulating wealth by the southern river trade that both drove and exemplified their cities' growing class stratification.

But civic leaders also planted and cultivated the seeds of culture that sprouted first in these cities: newspapers, churches, opera houses and theaters, bookstores, museums, lyceums and debating societies, libraries and schools and colleges. Although St. Louis led all cities in the West in sophistication, by the early 19th century Lexington, Ky., was known as the "Athens of the West" because of its educational facilities, most notably Transylvania University. Other cities were not far behind. By the 1830s Cincinnati, the West's Queen City with nearly 50,000 people, had replaced Lexington as the region's cultural and commercial epicenter.

Fast on the heels of the steamboat boom came rail. By the eve of the Civil War, Ohio boasted some 3,000 miles of track, 76 times what it had in 1840 and the most of any state in the entire nation. Illinois was second in the region and nation with 2,799 miles, and Indiana followed (fifth in the country) with 2,163; only New York and Pennsylvania boasted more. Missouri and Kentucky, too, had engaged heavily in railroad construction, but their 817 and 534 miles of track, respectively, left them lagging far behind even most of the cotton states, much less their immediate neighbors. Even in Missouri, virtually all of the main railroad lines ran along or north of the Missouri River.

Industrial expansion in the West followed these states' respective railroad booms, contributing to population explosions in all of them. The 1850s saw the floodtide. In 1860, Ohio's 2.3 million residents represented a more than 50 percent increase since 1840, making it the third largest state in the country. Illinois' population doubled each decade, reaching 1.8 million, while Indiana's population had nearly doubled to 1.4 million. Kentucky's population had, like Ohio's, increased by half to some 919,000 residents and had spread noticeably westward.

Some of the new settlers came from Eastern cities, but many of them came from a new wave of immigration from Europe, which favored the railroaded portions of these states, creating new population centers away from the traditional riverine sections. As late as the 1840s, many of the unorganized areas or fledgling counties of the northern portions of the Northwestern states had been sparsely settled. But soon boggy forests were drained by industrious laborers and settlers, with railroads following, allowing these counties to account for much of their states' growth in the final antebellum decade. All of the counties of northern Indiana and Illinois saw their populations double or more; even in Ohio, they increased by half in the decade. Propelled by the lake trade, Cleveland became a city and Chicago became the region's colossus within decades of its founding.

The northward shift of these states' populations contributed much to the western region's population's exceeding those of all other national regions, including the fast-growing cotton frontier. The towns and villages of the southern portions of these states, their traditional locus of population, declined proportionally. By 1860, between a quarter and a sixth of the population of the Ohio River states lay in the valley itself.

At the same time, though, the Ohio Valley cities thrived. Where in 1840 just less than four percent of the region's overall population was urban (and only three cities boasted as many as 8,000 residents), by 1860 some 14 percent lived in villages, towns and cities, and the region boasted 14 cities with 10,000 or more residents.

This new urban population was unlike any the region had seen before. Between 1820 and 1849, nearly 2.5 million foreigners came to the United States, largely from northern Europe, representing a seven-fold increase in the incidence of immigration. By 1850, 47.2 percent of Cincinnatians were immigrants, and more than 70 percent came from either Ireland or Germany, in part responses to the terrible potato famine of the later 1840s in Ireland and the failed democratic revolutions of 1848 for the Germans. Nearly a contiguous square mile of the cityscape was a virtual German "stadt," with bustling streets bearing names like Berlin, Schiller and Goethe, and with street signs and business placards posted in German script. The vibrant 10th Ward was known simply as "Über der Rhein," or for Anglos, "Over-the-Rhine," a descriptive term that originated from the area's proximity to the Miami Canal, which separated it from the rest of the city.

Many, like those in Cincinnati, were Catholics, which for many native-born Protestants caused more consternation than the newcomers' ethnicities. By 1850, Cincinnati was only the third most densely immigrant city in the nation. But those with more were also Western cities: Chicago and St. Louis. (Surprisingly, all three led New York City, in which foreigners constituted 45.7 percent of the population.) But immigrants flocked to all the Western cities. They made up some 17 percent of Louisville's population. They likewise settled heavily in Covington, Ky., and Evansville, Ind., creating a unique culture. The diversity that became much of America was as much the western border region's as the nation's.

Many of these Germans were strongly antislavery. Yet as the second year of the war began, positions on slavery did not easily divide north and south of the Ohio. Many of the region's Irish Catholics supported slavery's protection, while in large sections of the free states fighting-age "Butternut" men, called "Copperheads" by their Republican opponents, laid out of the fight altogether or threatened to leave it, should they be conscripted or slavery be abolished by the "friction of war," as Abraham Lincoln put it. Others sympathized outright with the Confederacy, and fights commonly broke out between them and their pro-war Republican neighbors.

For many of the border region's dissenting white residents, the course and events of the Civil War pointed out clearly that a new alliance had emerged, one in which Republicans in the Northern and Northwestern states appeared to be uniting in a conspiracy against liberty, which for many included the right of slaveholding. Angry and disillusioned, many of these Westerner dissenters sympathized with the region that now embodied their sense of betrayal and victimization—the beleaguered South. In the rural areas of Missouri, and western Kentucky and Tennessee, guerrillas were waging a desperate fight against occupying troops and local unionists that grew out of their recognition that the cities in their states were virtual fortresses: recruiting and staging centers for the Federal armies impossibly defended by hordes of blue-clad troops who guarded the supply and munitions depots and manufacturing centers for the federal government's war machine

As the newly appointed general in chief, Henry Halleck, later realized, Jefferson Davis and his advisers had "boldly determined to reoccupy Arkansas, Missouri, Tennessee, and Kentucky and, if possible, invade the states of Ohio, Indiana and Illinois while our attention was distracted by the invasion of Maryland." Coordinated invasions of the border states on both sides of the Appalachians, as well as west of the Mississippi, would threaten the West's major river cities and even the nation's capital, perhaps turning the tide militarily.

But the decision was more than strategic; it was political. The federal government's midterm elections loomed. Success on the new war front would embolden dissenters and moderates in the border states, especially in the Ohio Valley, to vote against Lincoln's party, turn public support in the free states against the war, and possibly gain for the Confederacy its most elusive prize: foreign recognition. The cumulative effect would be to force the Lincoln administration to sue for peace. The Confederacy's Tet Offensive was set to begin.

The Minister of Death
By CAROLE EMBERTON

From April 29 to May 30, 1862, some 300,000 men—including my great-great-grandfather, Pvt. Edward Willis—converged at the tiny railroad depot of Corinth, in northern Mississippi, where they laid siege to the Confederate forces under Gen. P.G.T. Beauregard. The Union soldiers scarred the landscape with miles of earthen fortifications. But the trenches could not protect Edward and his fellow soldiers from what Thomas Macaulay called "the most terrible of all the ministers of death," a predator that craved those close, confined spaces, where men's blood, breath and spit mingled freely. Although they fought on opposite sides of the trenches, the Union and Confederate forces shared a common enemy: smallpox.

Edward was hospitalized for the two months following the Union's capture of Corinth. While his service record gives no reason for his hospitalization, his wife Edith's pension application after his death in 1878 claimed that he had contracted smallpox while in the Army, "which afflicted his eyes and head, from which condition said soldier never recovered." It is likely that he spent June and July in a "pest house," quarantined along with other soldiers displaying signs of what Army doctors called "eruptive fevers"—smallpox, scarlet fever, measles and erysipelas (a bacterial skin infection caused by streptococcus).

Of these infectious diseases, smallpox was not the most common, but it was the most feared. During the course of the war, the Union Army reported only about 12,000 cases of smallpox among white troops, compared to nearly 68,000 cases of measles. However, total deaths from both diseases were about the same—4,700 and 4,200, respectively—with the death rate from smallpox hovering around 39 percent.

It is little wonder that medical personnel in both armies wrung their hands over the prospect of an impending smallpox epidemic, scouring Northern cities and the Southern countryside in search of small children to inoculate so that their scabs could be harvested to produce "pure vaccine" free from other diseases, like syphilis, that might be transmitted from adults. Fear of the "speckled monster" also led soldiers to take desperate measures, including self-inoculation with the pus from other men's sores that they believed to be smallpox but could, in fact, be syphilis or some other gangrenous lesion. The resulting infections incapacitated thousands of soldiers for weeks and sometimes months. The inspector general for the Army of Northern Virginia estimated that when the battle of Chancellorsville was fought in May 1863, as many as 5,000 men were unfit for duty due to these "spurious vaccinations."

It is widely accepted that disease claimed more lives than bullets during the Civil War. The first wave of infection hit new recruits soon after they arrived in camp. Men from rural areas were especially vulnerable, lacking immunity to the childhood diseases to which their urban counterparts most likely had been exposed. Before Edward's regiment, the 17th Kentucky, left camp at Calhoun where they enrolled, an outbreak of measles "raged through the camp like some attacking army." According to the unit's historian, more than 20 men died in those first few months, before they even heard a rebel gun.

Historians of medicine commonly refer to the mid-19th century as the "medical Middle Ages" in the United States because of the lack of understanding about sanitation and contagion, and thanks to a medical profession that lagged behind its European counterparts in procedural knowledge, institutional structure and numbers of certified physicians. When the war began, the Union Army medical division consisted of fewer than 100 surgeons and assistant surgeons. There was no organized ambulance service to remove wounded soldiers from the battlefield, and those who did make it to a squalid camp hospital fared little better than those left to die where they fell. With the help of the United States Sanitary Commission and a reorganization of the Army medical corps, which included the creation of an ambulance corps to rival any European army and a modern general hospital system across the nation, the Civil War revolutionized medical care in the United States. But for those men who fell victim to smallpox and other infectious diseases, modernity mattered little.

Smallpox was an ancient disease. For millenniums, it had followed the routes of trade, empire and war. The earliest descriptions of smallpox's telltale pustules date from the fourth century A.D. in China. However, scientists believe they have identified smallpox scars on the bodies of Egyptian mummies from the 12th century B.C. "An inveterate camp follower," according to the historian Michael Willrich, the virus, whose Latin name variola means "spotted," spread across the globe along with the armies of the Roman, Mongol and Ottoman Empires, claiming the lives of kings, queens and emperors as well as common folk. No one was safe. It followed Europeans to the "New World," wiping out as much as 90 percent of the indigenous populations of North and South America and the Caribbean. By the time the English physician Edward Jenner introduced the first vaccine for smallpox in 1798, at least 400,000 Europeans were dying each year from the disease.

What made smallpox so deadly? W.W. Brown, a surgeon with the 7th New Hampshire stationed in St. Augustine, Fla., wrote that the disease, "when uncomplicated, requires no medication except an occasional anodyne to allay nervous irritation and procure rest." Unfortunately, in an era before modern sanitation or antibiotics, not to mention in the middle of a war, few cases were "uncomplicated." Many of the men stricken with smallpox were already suffering from other ailments—fatigue, malnutrition, typhoid or dysentery. With their immune systems compromised, smallpox struck a deadly blow. In the worst cases of "fulminating and malignant" smallpox, the patient began to bleed out through the mucus membranes and the skin sloughed off in great patches. The virus attacked the internal organs, resulting in "general toxemia" and eventual death. Postmortem examinations revealed considerable tissue deterioration and severe internal hemorrhaging.

The case of 25-year-old Enos W. Bratcher of the Third Kentucky Cavalry was typical. Bratcher contracted smallpox while in the hospital near Madison, Ind., being treated for tonsillitis. Although the doctors noted that "his general health appeared good," he also suffered from chronic diarrhea. As with other smallpox patients, doctors treated Bratcher's sores with a tincture of iodine applied with a small brush to his face, where the pustules congregated and ran together. For pain, he was given the ubiquitous "Dover's powders," a crystallized combination of ipecac and morphine dissolved in liquid. He was encouraged to drink fluids, although the prescribed mix of "ale, milk-punch, egg-nog, chicken and beef tea" probably did not appeal to a man suffering from violent nausea. In other cases, when the oozing pustules invaded the mouth and throat, making it difficult for the sufferer to breathe or swallow, doctors gave a small dose of potassium chlorate as a gargle, a solution that could prove fatal if swallowed. In any case, nothing worked for Bratcher. Delirious with fever and with his tongue and teeth turned black, a common occurrence in patients suffering from dehydration and prolonged infection, he died after two weeks of hellish suffering.

For those like Edward, who survived smallpox, the road to recovery could be long. In addition to the pockmarks left on the skin, the disease could cause permanent hair loss, recurring eczema and deformities in limbs resulting from muscle and tissue damage. In men, it could result in sterility. The virus infected the eyes, causing eruptions on the eyelids and scarring of the cornea (the eye problems cited in Edith Willis's pension application were consistent with the long-term effects of smallpox).

There were psychological effects as well. Walt Whitman may have admired "faces pitted with small-pox over all latherers," but not everyone saw the scars as symbols of rugged masculinity. Instead, the disease's association with filth, vagrancy and foreignness could stigmatize survivors long after their bodies had recovered, condemning them to social ostracism and loss of employment.

The racial politics of disease in the era of emancipation also complicated the cultural understanding of smallpox. After multiple epidemics among freed people, smallpox assumed a negative association with blackness, further adding to the popular belief that sufferers were both filthy and inferior. But if black soldiers and freed people suffered from smallpox disproportionately, it wasn't because they were inherently susceptible to it because of their race. As the historian Jim Downs points out in his recent book on the health care of former slaves, smallpox spread among the freed population because of unsanitary living conditions, including the refusal of local officials to properly bury the dead and burn their belongings, which carried the contagion. Already malnourished and in poor health, many of the slaves flocking to Union lines and joining the ranks of the Federal Army stood little chance against the disease.

Other than his eye problems, I do not know what other scars Edward bore from his battle with smallpox. He had faced down an enemy much older, and in the grand scheme of things far deadlier, than the Confederacy. But there were no medals earned from his victory. By August 1862, he was back on duty, driving the commissary wagon.

A Separate Peace
By KATE MASUR

Those interested in the history of abolition and racial equality would find few incidents in Lincoln's presidency as dispiriting as the president's Aug. 14, 1862, meeting with a delegation of five black men from Washington. It was dispiriting then as well: to the dismay of those hoping the Civil War would lead to full citizenship for African-Americans, Lincoln informed the delegation that "you and we are different races" and proposed that the five men be progenitors of a black colony the government would establish in Chiriquí, a region of what is now Panama.

Historians have debated Lincoln's remarks and their context for decades. It was once conventional to claim that Lincoln's proposal was an attempt to appease conservatives while he pursued the policy he truly believed in: a presidential proclamation of emancipation. But the more recent consensus is that Lincoln was speaking very much in character. The "Great Emancipator" was one of the many white Americans of the era who believed that if slavery were abolished, a "race war" would inevitably ensue. Since the United States was destined to be a white nation, emancipation must be accompanied by the emigration of freedpeople out of the United States.

For all the attention to Lincoln's ideas and motivations, however, there has been very little focus on the delegates' side of the story. For decades no one even knew who they were, much less what they stood for. Drawing on the work of the historian Benjamin Quarles, many believed that four of the five delegates were uneducated former slaves, hand-picked by Lincoln and his colonization commissioner, James Mitchell, to be pliable and subservient.

In fact, all five of the men who listened to Lincoln's case for colonization were members of Washington's free black elite, chosen by a formal meeting of representatives from Washington's independent black churches. The delegation's history—and more broadly, black Washingtonians' responses to the variety of emigration proposals on offer in 1862—reveal a vigorous and complex debate among African-Americans regarding their future in the United States.

In the spring and summer of 1862, Washington was the national hub for debate about black emigration, both within the United States government and among African-Americans themselves. Congress had appropriated $600,000 to support voluntary colonization of people freed by the D.C. Emancipation Act and continuing military operations. Lobbyists hoping to settle African-Americans in Liberia, Haiti and Central America converged on Washington to recruit emigrants and persuade the government that the appropriation should go to their pet projects.

African-Americans in Washington met the lobbyists and their Congressional allies with mixed responses. Among the newly freed slaves in Washington, some lived in miserable camps and were open to the idea of making their lives elsewhere. Henry McNeal Turner, a prominent minister in the African Methodist Episcopal Church, advocated a fair hearing for proponents of emigration and signed a petition asking Lincoln to choose Chiriquí as the location of a colony. Two other local A.M.E. ministers also expressed support for emigration in some form, and in June a ship left Alexandria, Va., for Haiti with about 150 emigrants on board.

Frederick Douglass was appalled by the support emigration agents seemed to be receiving among black Washingtonians, writing in his newspaper that even a small number of voluntary emigrants helped vindicate white colonizationists "who have made the ridding of the country of negroes, the object of long years of unwearied but vain exertion."

Although Douglass was loath to acknowledge it, the prospect of leaving the United States had always appealed to a subset of black Americans, especially at moments when their future in the United States seemed particularly bleak—for example, after the passage of the 1850 Fugitive Slave Act. In the summer of 1862, it was difficult to tell which way the wind was blowing. The president had decided to issue an emancipation proclamation, but only his closest circle knew about it. The war was eroding slavery, but who was to say what the ultimate outcome would be?

Late July witnessed an outpouring of animosity toward colonization agents in Washington. It began when John D. Johnson, one of three Liberian "commissioners" then touring the United States, was said to have voiced support for forced—not voluntary—colonization in Liberia and declared that newly freed slaves required the supervision of "the superior race." Johnson was black, but his comments smacked of the racism and coercion many Africans-Americans associated with the American Colonization Society, a white-led group whose members had founded Liberia decades earlier as a colony for American ex-slaves.

The members of the Social Civil and Statistical Association, a black civic association, decided that Johnson was no longer welcome in town. Hours after the group asked Johnson to leave, two of its members instigated a fight with him and were arrested. Rumors flew that the Haitian colonization agents would be banished next, and a group of young men confronted an African-American agent of Central American colonization at his hotel and sent him packing. The S.C.S.A. had not intended a blanket condemnation of black emigration, one of its supporters later commented. It was fighting only "the machinations and schemes of the old Colonization Society and their leaders and abettors."

It was in this climate of debate and suspicion that representatives of several of Washington's black churches convened in Union Bethel A.M.E. Church to hear from the president's assistant, James Mitchell.

When Mitchell informed them that the president wished to speak to a black delegation about government-sponsored colonization, the response was chilly. According to a reporter who was there, attendees discussed "to a great length" the president's intentions and the implications of sending representatives. They ultimately decided to send a delegation, but not before they passed two resolutions expressing grave doubts about the entire enterprise. The first stated that it was "inexpedient, inauspicious, and impolitic" to support emigration; the second expressed skepticism that delegates chosen at that meeting could represent "the interests of over four-and-a-half millions of our race."

Who were the men who reluctantly convened with Lincoln that day? Edward Thomas, who became the delegation's chairman, was a messenger in the House of Representatives and renowned for his collections of fine art, coins and books. John F. Cook Jr., who also became a delegate, was the son of the city's most prominent black minister; he had attended college in the North and was a respected teacher. Both Cook and Thomas, as well as another delegate—Cornelius Clark—

were active in the S.C.S.A., whose main purpose was racial uplift, or "to improve our condition by use of all proper means calculated to exalt our people." The other two delegates, Benjamin McCoy and John T. Costin, were, respectively, a leader in religion and education and a scion of one of Washington's most illustrious black families.

Lincoln might not have known of the resolutions that immediately preceded his meeting with the delegation, but he clearly understood that these were men of considerable stature. In his address, the president acknowledged that the delegates were "intelligent colored men" and that they probably had "long been free." He urged them to emigrate not for their own well-being, but to help "those who are not so fortunate as yourselves." In fact, Lincoln may have heard something of these men from the lead servant in the White House, William Slade, who as president of the S.C.S.A. would have known at least three of them well.

When Lincoln ended his speech, the delegates promised to give a response soon. Newspapers immediately published Lincoln's remarks, giving rise to a storm of criticism from black and white abolitionists.

In Washington, however, African-Americans' reaction was neither simple nor unified. Two days after the meeting, Edward Thomas, the chairman of the delegation, informed Lincoln that he had changed his mind and that he was interested in pursuing emigration to Chiriquí. As plans for a government-sponsored voyage got under way, one of Frederick Douglass's sons sought to join the expedition. Hundreds of African-Americans from the Washington area volunteered to go, hoping to rebuild their lives far outside the ambit of slaveowners and the United States government. Many sold their belongings and moved out of their homes in preparation for the trip.

Unfortunately, they were caught up in dynamics much larger than themselves. The government voyage was delayed and finally canceled because of resistance from Central American governments. The stranded migrants wrote Lincoln that they faced destitution in the coming winter and lamented that he would "create hopes within us, and stimulate us to struggle for national independence and respectable quality" only to abandon them. They sought a meeting; Lincoln, through a secretary, asked them to be patient.

Black leaders like Frederick Douglass, who insisted that African-Americans put their faith in the United States—and who demanded that the government see black men as soldiers and African-Americans as citizens—are the ones whose rhetoric fits most easily into our national narratives of inclusion and multiculturalism. But it is well to remember, also, how many white Americans rejected the idea of a multiracial nation and how many black Americans, recognizing the implications of that rejection, took steps to build their lives elsewhere.

Lincoln and the Sioux
By RON SOODALTER

During his term as president, Abraham Lincoln was responsible for the largest mass execution—and the greatest act of clemency—in our nation's history.

Indeed, as every schoolchild is aware, the history of our government's relations with the American Indians is disgraceful. Congress never made a treaty that it wasn't more than willing to break at the slightest provocation. Throughout the 18th and 19th centuries, tribe after tribe was left with no recourse other than rebellion or starvation, and the Dakota Sioux were no exception.

In 1851—10 years before the Civil War—the United States signed two treaties with the Sioux that resulted in the Indians' ceding huge portions of the Minnesota Territory. In exchange, they were promised compensation in the form of cash and trade goods, and directed to live on a reservation along the upper Minnesota River. The thoroughly corrupt Bureau of Indian Affairs was responsible for overseeing the terms of the treaties. Not surprisingly, many of the trade goods were substandard and overvalued by several hundred percent, and the promised payments were often not forthcoming—stolen by Washington functionaries, or simply channeled directly to the crooked traders and Indian agents.

This situation continued for years. Finally, in 1858—the year Minnesota entered the Union—a party of Sioux led by Chief Little Crow visited Washington to see about proper enforcement of the treaties. It did not go the way they'd hoped; instead of acknowledging the Sioux grievances, the government took back half their reservation, and opened it up to white settlement. The land was cleared, and the hunting and fishing that had in large measure sustained the Sioux virtually ended.

The situation worsened with each passing year, with the Sioux suffering increasing hunger and hardship. There was nothing to be gained by appealing to the traders; reportedly, their representative—a clod of a fellow fittingly named Andrew Jackson Myrick—responded to the Indians' appeal for food with the comment, "So far as I am concerned, if they are hungry, let them eat grass or their own dung."

In August 1862, the powder keg exploded. It began almost randomly, when a party of four braves on an egg-stealing foray impulsively killed five white settlers. From there, it escalated rapidly. Under the leadership of a somewhat reluctant Little Crow, several bands held a war council, and set about attacking the new settlements. They seized the Lower Sioux Agency, killing whites and burning the buildings. At the outbreak of hostilities, Myrick was one of the first casualties, and when his body was discovered, his mouth was stuffed with grass.

A combined force of militia and volunteer infantry set out to subdue the Indians. The two sides met at Redwood Ferry, where the Indians gave the soldiers a thorough drubbing, killing 24 men. Flush with victory, roving bands of Sioux destroyed entire townships throughout the month and into September, plundering and killing as they went. A number of desperate appeals for help had gone to Lincoln, but he was immersed in such day-to-day matters as the stunning debacle at Second Bull Run, Gen. Robert E. Lee's invasion of Maryland, Gen. George B. McClellan's heartbreaking failure to follow up after Antietam, and the release of the Preliminary Emancipation Proclamation.

Finally, over a month after the outbreak of the Sioux uprising, Lincoln responded, assigning Gen. John Pope, fresh from his defeat at Bull Run, the task of ending the uprising. A pompous, self-righteous man, Pope declared his "purpose to utterly exterminate the Sioux. They are to be treated as maniacs and wild beasts."

The Army finally subdued the Sioux in the battle of Wood Lake on Sept. 23. The butcher's bill at the end of the fighting totaled some

77 soldiers killed, between 75 and 100 Sioux, and—no one took an accurate count—between 300 and 800 white settlers.

The Sioux who surrendered were promised safety. But once the hostilities were over, hundreds of Sioux—some of whom had had nothing to do with the uprising—were arrested and summarily tried by a five-man military commission. The trials were perfunctory affairs, some lasting less than five minutes. More than 40 cases were adjudicated in one day alone. Due process played no part; most of the defendants hadn't a clue what was happening. Of the 393 tried for "murder and other outrages," 323 were convicted, and 303 sentenced to hang—including those who had surrendered with a promise of safety.

The final approval for the executions rested with the president. General Pope, seeking a quick and dramatic finish to the affair, pressured Lincoln to sign the orders for all 303 executions. Nor was he alone; outraged newspaper editors and congressmen advocated a speedy hanging as well. Alexander Ramsey, the governor of Minnesota—who had made a fortune cheating the Sioux—threatened that if the president didn't hang all the condemned, the citizens of his state would.

The Sioux had a rare friend, however, in Minnesota's Episcopal bishop, Henry Whipple. The clergyman traveled to Washington and met with Lincoln, who was so impressed with Whipple's account that he ordered that every case be re-examined on its own merits. After thorough analysis, only 38 Sioux could be proved to have participated in the uprising. Lincoln immediately approved their execution order, and commuted the sentences of the others. In a finish that is pure Lincoln, the president hand wrote the list of long, difficult, phonetically spelled Sioux names himself, and advised the telegrapher on the vital necessity of sending them correctly, lest the wrong men be hanged.

On Dec. 26, 38 Dakota Sioux were led to the scaffold; they sang their death songs as they walked, and when they had mounted the scaffold and the hoods were drawn down over their faces, they continued to sing and sway, and clasp one another's manacled hands. At a drum signal, the trap was sprung, and the watching crowd of thousands cheered.

The year after the uprising, Congress expunged all Sioux treaties from the record, took back their reservation and ordered that the entire tribe be expelled from Minnesota. As an incentive, a bounty of $25 was offered for the scalp of any Sioux found living in the state after the edict. There still was scattered resistance, but the Dakota War was over. The Sioux would continue to fight for years to come, until 1890, when the Army marked paid to their account by massacring at least 150 men, women and children from the tribe at Wounded Knee.

Given the mood of the country regarding what were seen as unprovoked savage depredations, what drove Lincoln to spare the lives of so many Sioux? The wonder isn't that Lincoln allowed more than three dozen men to hang; it's that he took the time away from a war that was going badly—and that threatened the very existence of our nation—to examine one at a time the cases of more than 300 Sioux, and to spare the lives of all but 38 of them.

While Lincoln felt that there must be a reckoning, and that the wholesale killing of settlers could neither be condoned nor ignored, he would not allow the law to be used to elicit indiscriminate revenge, despite the tremendous pressure on him to do just that. When it was suggested to him that he would have garnered political support by allowing the original orders to stand, he responded, "I could not hang men for votes."

The Duel
By JAMIE MALANOWSKI

The story thus far: In the tradition-bound old navy of the 1850s, little interest was devoted to building ironclad ships. Learning from their experiences in the Crimean War, the European naval powers drove to update their fleets, while America's naval leaders, many with a half century of service or more, preferred to keep building wooden ships that had masts and rigging, even when they also had steam engines.

But the war changed that. Southern leaders, knowing they would have to break the Union blockade but lacking ships to match, tossed away comfortable old ideas and fixed upon the potential of ironclads to compensate for their fleet's inequality, and to wreck the Yankees' walls of wood. Failing to buy an ironclad from the Europeans, the confederates focused on building one at home. They latched onto the idea of attaching iron plating to the sides of the Merrimack, a sunken frigate salvaged from the Gosport Navy Yard in Norfolk.

Meanwhile, in the North, a new broom had swept clean. The Navy that had no interest in ironclads now wanted them, and fast. Gosport was a sieve, and word that the Merrimack was being converted reached Washington about the same instant the scheme was hatched. After much debate and discussion, a Navy board convened to evaluate proposals for a Union ironclad reluctantly approved a controversial design by the brilliant but iconoclastic John Ericsson of Brooklyn. Everyone who saw his model knew it was different and intriguing; but not even the most discerning eyes realized that this was most revolutionary vessel of the century.

And so two societies, two approaches, and a race between them. An underindustrialized South stretched and scavenged and taught itself a new process, while the North had to overcome doubt and tradition, and embrace the brilliance of its industrial ingenuity.

The South built a behemoth, 260 feet long, 50 feet wide, with a draft of more than 20 feet, 3 inches of iron over 22 inches of pine attached to a scaffolding built onto the hull of the salvaged Merrimack. It bore 10 guns and, as an afterthought, a 1,500-pound cast iron ram that protruded from its bow. The North built a raptor, 100 feet smaller than its counterpart, lighter, faster, more nimble in the water, covered in five inches of armor and topped with an amazing 9-foot revolving turret out of which stared two powerful 11-inch Dahlgren guns.

The South wanted its ship, renamed the CSS Virginia, to get down the Elizabeth River into the Chesapeake as soon as possible, to sink the Yankee squadron and to disrupt Gen. George McClellan's planned offensive up the Virginia peninsula. The mission of the northern ship was simple: stop the Virginia. And after Ericsson was quoted as saying, "This ironclad will prove a severe monitor to the confederate leaders," the Union ship finally had a name.

In February, both ships were in the water, siting their guns, building their crews. The Monitor received its commander, Lt. John Worden, at 44 a 27-year veteran of the Navy, and by one account its toughest and saltiest officer. In April 1861 he had been sent on a mission to deliver orders to the command at Fort Pickens in Pensacola, Fla., and on the way back was captured and held as a prisoner of war for 9 months. In his orders, Navy Secretary Gideon Welles says, "I believe you have the right sort of qualities for the job." Perhaps that meant he was a man with something to prove, willing even to take command of an untested and entirely preposterous-looking ship.

Both ships experienced setbacks. The Monitor suffered steering problems, spending a day drifting from one side of the East River to the other before finally washing ashore by the New York Gas Works. Ericsson had to remove its rudder and replace it. In Norfolk, the Virginia, which most observers thought would be too heavy, turned out to be light, with a high center of gravity. That made her difficult to turn, and worse, because the iron plates extended only a foot below the surface, it left her unprotected underside dangerously vulnerable to shots at her water line. Immediately 200 tons of pig iron was added to her bilge to settle her, but she was still hard to steer, still rode high in the water and now had a deeper draft.

On Feb. 24, the Virginia received her master, Captain Franklin Buchanan, a 61-year-old Marylander who was a 46-year veteran of the old Navy. Buchanan was a fighting man, not an architect or engineer. Asked how he planned to treat the Virginia's lingering problems, the old salt replied, "I mean to try her against the enemy, sir! There will be time to complete the shutters and armor after we have proved her in action!" He fixed the Virginia's maiden voyage for the night of March 6.

It didn't happen. The ship needed to be navigated down the twisty, tricky Elizabeth River to where the federal Navy waited at Hampton Roads, and all the local pilots refused to try to negotiate the river in the dark. Very well, the impatient Buchanan allowed, first thing in the morning. Sorry, the chief pilot told him, but this ship draws 23 feet, you won't be going anywhere until high tide, which will be about 2 p.m. on Friday the 6th. But the afternoon arrived with rain, heavy winds and roiling water. The ungainly Virginia took a half an hour to make a half circle, and Buchanan called it a day.

On March 6, however, at 4 p.m., the Monitor left Brooklyn, headed for the Chesapeake Bay. She made fine time in the Atlantic, answering the doubts about her seaworthiness that had been brought up by skeptics on the Navy board. But as night began to fall on the 7th, the same storm that had caused a delay in the launch of the Virginia began causing trouble for the Monitor, now off the coast of Maryland. There, gale force winds pounded the ship as high waves washed her deck, and unexpectedly, leaked into her hold. Ericsson had specified that the turret be lowered in the event of a storm, contending that it would seal itself against its brass ring.

The Navy felt otherwise, and specified that the turret be raised to its highest position, and that the bottom be wrapped in oakum to prevent leakage. But the oakum washed away in no time, and water poured below decks, soaking the fan belts of the blower pipes and preventing them from working. Soon the entire area was filled with gas, steam and smoke, and choking, gasping men were fleeing the area. The chief engineer led a gang of men below, who struggled with the blowers until they lapsed into unconsciousness.

Then, with the Monitor on the verge of foundering, the storm blew itself out. A doughty tug traveling with the Monitor towed it to shallow water, where repairs could be made and the toxic air below decks could clear. After a perilous night, the crew worked all the next morning; the ship got underway by midday, and by late afternoon reached Cape Henry, about 20 miles from Fortress Monroe. They could hear cannon fire from up the bay.

Saturday the 8th dawned bright and clear, and Buchanan could at last get his ship on the water. Concerned about the notoriously unreliable engines—the Merrimack, commissioned in 1856 and widely hailed as the pride of the fleet, was handsome but widely known to be a lemon, with balky boilers—Buchanan treated the first part of the trip down the Elizabeth River as a trial run, but after 10 miles of reliable performance, every man on board knew that the next stop would be Hampton Roads, and the guns of the federal blockade squadron.

All of the Virginia's faults were evident—the deep draft, slow speed, stubborn handling, but she was making good time, her engines performing better than ever. Emerging from the mouth of the river, Buchanan could see five large federal warships: Minnesota and Roanoke, both sister ships of the Merrimack; Congress and St. Lawrence, two 50-gun frigates; and the 30-gun sloop Cumberland. The leviathan prepared to feast.

Saturday was laundry day in the Union Navy, and the rigging on the vessels was covered with drying clothes. That didn't pose much of a delay, however, and soon the federal ships were ready for action. Buchanan steamed straight for the two nearest, Congress and Cumberland, both of which opened fire, as did Union army batteries stationed on shore. The well-aimed shells just bounced off the iron plating, like hailstones on a tin shed.

Then the Virginia laid a broadside into the Congress, ramming the Cumberland, which caved in like an apple basket. She began sinking so fast that she almost took the Virginia down with her, and might have, had the weld on the ram been stronger. Instead it snapped off, freeing the Virginia, which turned and laid more fire into the Congress, which had run aground. Helpless to move, her captain dead, her decks awash in blood, she ran up the white flag.

As was the custom, the Virginia halted firing, and sent two officers to the ship to take prisoners. The army batteries on shore, however, continued to fire, and their shells killed the emissaries from the Virginia. "I know the damn ship surrendered," General Mansfield later explained, "but we hadn't." Furious that the truce had been violated, Buchanan shouted, "Sink that damn ship!" and had red-hot cannonballs fired into the Congress, setting it ablaze. He did this even though he knew that his brother McKean was paymaster on the vessel. Then, grabbing a rifle, the feisty Buchanan began shooting at Yankee soldiers on the shore. This lasted but a moment, until he was then shot in the leg. His second in command, Lt. Catesby ap Roger Jones, took the bridge.

While this was happening, the frigates Minnesota, Roanoke and St. Lawrence came to the join the battle, but in the tricky currents and shallow of Hampton Roads, each ran aground. After finishing with the Congress, Lt. Jones turned the Virginia and began to fire on the Minnesota. His shells smashed her decks and splintered her sides, but he could get no closer than 200 yards, and now the light was going. His men were exhausted and hungry, and some were wounded; he was low on coal; his ship has sustained 98 hits, leaving three guns damaged and the funnel resembling Swiss cheese.

Jones elected to return to Gosport and refit. Those wooden ships would be there in the morning, he reasoned. He left victorious: two ships destroyed, three frigates aground, 400 Yankee sailors dead against two of his own. The United States Navy would not suffer another defeat on this scale for 79 years.

When word of this calamity reached Washington, President Lincoln summoned his cabinet for a rare Sunday morning meeting. The awful report of ships sunk, aground and hopeless brought out the worst in some of the officials. A frantic secretary of war, Edwin Stanton, paced about, envisioning calamities to come. The Merrimack could destroy every ship in the Navy! Take Fortress Monroe! Hold every city on the coast under ransom! "It's likely she'll come up the Potomac, disperse the Congress, and destroy the Capitol! Or she may go to Philadelphia! Or New York! Or Boston! It's not unlikely that we shall have a shell or a cannonball from one of her guns in the White House before we leave this room!"

The Navy secretary, Gideon Welles, usually as excitable as a rooster, sat calmly as Stanton raved. A deep draft vessel like the Merrimack, he finally replied, with her heavy armor, wouldn't make it up the Potomac past Kettle Bottom Shoals, and that's 50 miles away. It's unlikely we'll see cannon balls this morning. "Besides," he added archly, "if she did attack Washington, she couldn't be attacking Philadelphia, New York and Boston, too." He then shared with his colleagues a reassuring piece of information. "We have an ironclad, too," he said. "It left New York for the Chesapeake on Thursday. It should be there any time."

This news relieved the cabinet's anxieties immensely. "How many guns does it have?" Stanton asked eagerly.

"Two," Welles replied confidently, "but of large caliber."

Indeed, they were of large caliber, and at the same time Welles was talking, they were being fired. The Virginia had come down river early on Sunday morning confident that it would resume thrashing the Yankee Navy right where it had left off the previous evening. By 7:30 she was opposite the Minnesota. As she was preparing for action, out of the shadows of the union frigate came this short, squat, alien machine, famously derided by one southern sailor as "a cheese on a raft"; it placed itself between the enfeebled Minnesota and Virginia. Aboard the Confederate ironclad, some men thought it was just a raft taking away one of the Minnesota's boilers or its magazines, although one better-informed sailor wondered if this could be the Ericsson machine. Meanwhile, the ruling impression from the other side was best expressed by one of the Monitor's mates: "You can see surprise in a ship just as you can see it in a man, and there was surprise all over the Merrimack."

The appraisals ended abruptly when the crippled, pugnacious Minnesota fired a broadside, and the Virginia responded. On the Monitor, Lt. Worden, hearing the gunfire above his iron-hooded head, saw two of his men manhandling a 166-pound cannon ball into the muzzle of one of his 11-foot guns. "Send them that with our compliments, my lads," Worden said, and ordered the ship to open fire, a surprise pop in the jaw from an undersized opponent. The Virginia replied with a broadside that shook the smaller vessel, which then closed on its fearsome opponent. The fight was on.

It lasted about four hours. The ships kept steaming in circles, the Virginia in its large, ungainly arcs, the Monitor in sharper, tighter turns. As a result, the ships closed on each other, and then pulled apart; sometimes they shot at each other at a distance of 100 yards, and sometimes at 15 feet. One time Jones aimed to ram the Monitor, but the best he could manage was a glancing blow that shook the teeth of everyone on both ships but that did no harm. Worden tried to fire into the Virginia's lightly clad stern, but couldn't quite manage so precise a shot. Jones aimed to pull up to the Monitor and board her with crew members armed with cutlasses, a maneuver Drake or Nelson would have known aboard ships they could never have dreamed of; at the last moment, the Monitor veered away.

Once, the Virginia ran aground, but managed to free herself before the Monitor could react; once, Worden thought he had the Virginia lined up for a damaging shot, but his cannon jammed. Despite hit after hit, neither side pierced through the other's armor, though the Monitor kept banging the Virginia like a blacksmith, and had split and chipped the plate. Had she been able to aim better—the revolving turret allowed the ship to maintain a high rate of fire, but it couldn't be stopped precisely in its spin—it might well have stripped away some of the iron plating and exposed a vulnerable underside. In time, the gunners grew frustrated; when one on board the Virginia stopped, his commander asked him why. "Our powder is precious," he replied, "and I find I can do as much damage by snapping my thumb at her every two minutes."

After more than three hours of this, neither side had gained an advantage, although there were so many holes in the Virginia's smokestack that she could hardly get any draft for her boilers, which meant that the speed of the already sluggish southern ironclad was cut in half. Jones maneuvered his ship opposite the Monitor, and from a distance of 10 yards, delivered a 9-inch shell against the Monitor's pilot house. It exploded directly against a narrow slit though which Worden was at that moment peering. Blinded, eyes full of powder, ears ringing, his beard smoldering, Worden collapsed on the floor. "Sheer off!" he shouted. And his helmsman turned away.

The Monitor headed for the shoals to take stock. Worden was taken to his cabin, though not before ordering his subordinates to turn back and save the Minnesota. But the Virginia, having waited what it took to be a suitable period, assessed its wheezy boilers and leaky seams and decided that the best course of action would be to declare victory and head home.

That night, the officers and crews of both ships were celebrated for their efforts. Both sides claimed victory, though any fair-minded person would have called the fight a draw. But that night, the captains of wooden vessels everywhere did not sleep a wink, and prayed for the Congress and the Cumberland.

The Bullet That Changed History

By PAT LEONARD

It was late afternoon on Aug. 30, 1862, the concluding day of the Second Battle of Bull Run, and the largest simultaneous massed assault of the Civil War was about to be unleashed. The Confederate general James Longstreet's corps was in position on the left flank of the Union general John Pope's unsuspecting Army of Virginia, and when the signal was given 25,000 Rebels surged forward, catching the surprised Federals in an immense "hammer on anvil" movement.

Leading the charge was John Bell Hood's Texas Brigade, a force of roughly 2,500 men that included Pvt. William Fletcher, Company F, 5th Texas Infantry. When Fletcher and his fellow Texans had advanced to within 150 yards, a line of Union soldiers stood and fired, then turned to run, precipitating a retreat that would nearly result in Pope's annihilation.

The Federals' parting volley was mostly ineffective, but one bullet struck Private Fletcher in the stomach, knocking him to the ground and momentarily rendering him unconscious. When he came to, he saw the "long and ugly wound" and guessed that his bowels had been pierced. Fletcher sat up and actually faced into the raging battle, hoping he "might be so fortunate as to get a dead shot" that would "put an end to his existence."

Private Fletcher had good reason to wish for a mercy shot. Earlier battles had taught veterans like him that serious gunshot wounds to the head, chest and abdomen were most often fatal. But while the first two were very likely to kill quickly, abdominal wounds condemned their victims to agonizingly slow deaths. Fletcher cursed his fate but resigned himself to it.

In the history of armed conflicts, there has never been a good time to be wounded in battle, but the soldiers of the American Civil War were especially unlucky that their battles took place during the early 1860s. Those four years were a brief period when recent developments in arms and ammunition made battlefields far more lethal than they had been a decade before, while discoveries in medicine—which could have partially counterbalanced the awful effects of the new ordnance—were still a handful of years in the future.

Almost as soon as the war ended, historians began to study the factors that contributed to so much bloodshed—more than 200,000 killed and nearly 500,000 wounded—and concluded that the introduction of the rifle musket was the primary cause of the staggering casualty rates. And not without reason: the rifle musket combined the best features of the smoothbore musket and the Kentucky flint-

lock rifle. It could be loaded quickly and easily—an experienced soldier could load and fire up to four rounds a minute—while its long,
grooved barrel gave it an effective range up to four times that of a
smoothbore, with similar improvements in accuracy.

Many chroniclers noted that, unlike the tactics of the American
Revolution, when defenders would hold their fire until they could
"see the whites" of their attackers' eyes, Civil War defenders armed
with rifle muskets could aim at and frequently hit targets at 400 yards
or more. It was the rifle musket, researchers determined, that had
made the bayonet obsolete and drastically transformed the roles of
cavalry and field artillery.

Statistics appear to bear out this theory. Of all the wounds treated
by Union Army doctors throughout the war, nearly 95 percent were
caused by small-arms fire, less than 1 percent were attributable to
bayonets and swords, and all but a handful of the remainder resulted
from artillery shells and shrapnel.

Several modern historians, however, have disputed the notion that
the rifle musket alone deserves the credit—or rather the blame—for
the Civil War's incredible carnage. They note that many battles were
fought at close quarters, effectively negating the superior range and
accuracy of rifle muskets over smoothbores, and that in any case most
Civil War soldiers lacked the training and practice to take advantage
of the new weapon's awesome killing capacity. Of the millions of
rounds fired at the enemy during the war, far more sailed over the
heads of their intended targets than actually struck home.

What these discussions tend to overlook, though, is that it was not
just the accuracy or frequency of fire that killed and maimed so many
men, but the characteristics of the ammunition that encountered flesh
and bone. While a smoothbore musket could expel a solid ball with a
greater muzzle velocity than a rifle musket, it was the projectile that
the latter weapon fired—the slightly smaller Minié ball—that made
all the difference.

The Minié ball (properly pronounced "min-YAY" after its devel-
oper, the French Army officer Claude-Étienne Minié, but pronounced
"minnie ball" by the Americans) wasn't a ball but a conical-shaped
bullet. Popularized during the Crimean War, it was perfected in early

1850s America. An armorer at the arsenal in Harpers Ferry named James Burton simplified the design that had made Minié famous and developed a hollow-based, .58-caliber lead projectile that could be cheaply mass produced.

The first generation of rifled projectiles were hard to load, since they had to fit snugly within the rifling grooves inside the barrel. Minié balls were slightly smaller in circumference than the inside of the barrel, so they could be dropped in quickly. When fired, the base of the bullet expanded and gripped the rifle grooves, which imparted a spiral on the projectile and thereby gave it its greater range and accuracy. In 1855, Secretary of War Jefferson Davis adopted the rifle musket and Burton's improved Minié ball, or bullet, for the United States Army.

The intent of the designers of the rifle musket/Minié ball combination was to increase the firepower of the individual soldier, and in this quest they succeeded. But in developing a defender's dream they also created a nightmare, not just for the men felled by the bullet, but for the medical corps stewards and surgeons who had to deal with its effects. The very attributes that increased the bullet's range and accuracy also increased its destructive potential when it struck its target. Unlike a solid ball, which could pass through the human body nearly intact, leaving an exit wound not much larger than the entrance wound, the soft, hollow-based Minié ball flattened and deformed upon impact, while creating a shock wave that emanated outward.

The Minié ball didn't just break bones, it shattered them. It didn't just pierce tissue and internal organs, it shredded them. And if the ragged, tumbling bullet had enough force to cleave completely through the body, which it often did, it tore out an exit wound several times the size of the entrance wound. Civil War surgeons were quickly overwhelmed by the gaping wounds, mangled bodies and mutilated limbs they were asked to repair as the scope of the war broadened and casualties mounted. Though often accused of being too partial to their bone saws, amputating arms and legs as quickly as the men could be placed on their operating tables and subdued with chloroform or ether, the surgeons really had no choice. Even if they'd had the skills and resources to attempt reconstructive surgery, in the heat of battle they didn't have the time.

Over all, Civil War surgeons did a respectable and generally successful job of trying to save lives, given the unrelenting slaughter with which they had to cope. They were notably less successful, however, in convincing the public of this fact, as cries of "Butchery!" continued to dog the medical corps throughout and after the war. As an editorial writer noted in the Cincinnati Lancet and Observer, following the Union victory at Gettysburg: "Our readers will not fail to have noticed that everybody connected to the army has been thanked, excepting the surgeons."

As for Pvt. William Fletcher, he survived the abdominal wound he suffered at the Second Battle of Bull Run, thanks in part to a "Kentucky button"—a plug of dried oak he had whittled to hold up his pants. The minié ball that knocked him down fractured the button, dissipating enough of the bullet's force to prevent it from penetrating too deeply. Fletcher recovered and went on to fight at the battles of Fredericksburg, Gettysburg and Chickamauga, where he was again wounded, this time in the foot.

Fletcher credited the care he received from the Sisters of Charity with saving his foot from amputation and enabling him to return to duty. Thirty-four years later, as a successful businessman in Beaumont, Tex., he acted on the gratitude he felt by donating the land and lumber to build the order's hospital in that city, the Hotel Dieu. His memoir of the Civil War—"Rebel Private: Front and Rear"—was said by author Margaret Mitchell to be "her single most valuable research tool when writing 'Gone With the Wind.'"

Killing Time
By JEAN HUETS

The temptations that will beset you will be very great," a Mississippi man, already a veteran in the Civil War, warned his newly enlisted younger brother. The evil he warned of wasn't treason or desertion or theft. It was cards. "Of all the evil practices that abound in Camp, gambling is the most pernicious and fraught with the most direful consequences."

Civil War soldiers, like all soldiers, spent the vast majority of their time in camp, waiting for action and looking for anything they could find to fill the long empty hours. For many, card playing more than met the need, and provided a chance to make a little money besides. "It was a poor hut that could not boast of a pack of well-thumbed cards," reminisced George Forrester Williams. Union men could even claim card playing as a patriotic duty, since the Revenue Act of 1862 slapped an excise tax on decks and just about everything else under the Yankee sun.

The monotony of sutlers' wares squelched games like taroc, which German and Hungarian immigrants would have played with a 78-card deck. Fortunately for card makers, the 52-card deck, like speaking English and playing baseball, quickly became part of the common camp culture among both Rebs and Yanks, native-born and immigrant. That deck, in turn, determined the range of card games they played.

Whist claimed gentlemen, and ladies when available. Seven-up, or old sledge, seemed to have been favored by rustics and roughs. Twenty-one, keno and faro also stood ready to strip soldiers of everything from coin to clothing to "a chicken which had been pressed into service," as one Union soldier, Napier Bartlett, recalled. In describing furtive games played for "postal currency," paper issued by the Post Office and used in lieu of hard-to-get coins, the New York volunteer Albert Rowe Barlow mentioned euchre as a "standard game"— though for Barlow and other gamblers North and South, poker was the hands-down favorite.

Gaming, combined with alcohol, boredom and any suspicion of cheating, ignited duels and brawls as enthralling as the game itself, at least to bystanders. But serious gamers played not to fight but to win, and then as now they demanded that the cards be easily recognized, undistracting and clearly denominated.

The standard deck, laid down by French cartiers in the 16th century, was as familiar to the Civil War soldier as it is today. The black suits of spades and clubs and the red suits of hearts and diamonds each comprise 10 pips, or numbered cards, and three "face" or court cards. The graphic design that persists to this day had also by then been set: the arrangement of the suit signs, and the oddly stylized court figures, with their stringlike hair, simple color schemes and geometric patterning. So universally known were playing cards that an examiner tested a New York recruit's vision by walking to the other end of the room and holding up the 9 of clubs and the 10 of hearts.

Not that card makers never dared something new. The Union deck, produced by the American Card Company, featured "national emblems" of eagles, shields, stars and flags in place of normal suit signs. The goddess of liberty, colonel and major replaced the woefully un-American queen, king and jack. Despite the maker's "fullest confidence that the time is not far distant when they will be the leading Card in the American market," the deck, like most novelties in the card world, died a quiet death. For the most part, card players accepted only changes that made the deck easier to manipulate and harder to cheat with.

One such innovation was indices, the suit sign and value marked in the upper left corner of each card. Before indices were adopted, if Johnny Reb held the four or five of spades, for example, he would have to see nearly the entire card to know its value, since the fifth spade is in the middle. Indices allow a tight fan of cards, easier to hold and hide.

Another design change came with the double-figure court card, which mirrors the top half of king, queen or jack. By contrast with the full-length, single-figure personage, a double-figure is never upside down (though only the most naïve infant—or maybe the craftiest bluffer—would tip his hand by rescuing that queen of hearts from standing on her head). Yet however a novice holds his cards, his own face is what gives it all away. The Ohio volunteer John Calvin Hartzell described being fleeced by "Uncle Dan, who has the face of a graven image, while mine always told tales."

Card faces weren't the only thing that changed in the mid-19th century. Early decks nearly always had blank backs, making the cards easier to

Civil War-era playing cards featuring Union and Confederate generals.

mark and easier to see through. (Today, a deck of decent quality bears a layer of dark "cartridge" paper within the cardboard.) In the Civil War era, back designs became not only standard, but artistic. Patterns of asterisks and dots, wavy lines and dashes, and "pebbles" gave way to intricate images, often with patriotic and military themes. Flags, a shield and an anchor backed the Union deck.

The most radical change, the joker, pranced into the deck around 1860. Trickster that he is, he stands out as the only major innovation not inspired by convenience or caution. The joker most likely hopped over to American decks via the German immigrants who fought on both sides of the war. Some attribute his name to the German word for euchre, "juker," a game so engrossing that, as the Rebel soldier David Holt recounted, when hymns wafting through camp forced the men to realize it was Sunday, "We would lay down our cards, even in a game of euchre."

Like baseball, cards occasionally brought the two lines together. During the siege of Petersburg, Va., in the autumn of 1864, the Gray and the Blue would "creep into . . . a neutral cornfield," one soldier recalled, "for a friendly chat, for a barter, or for a game of cards!" Their money being worthless to each other, a few gamers staked Abe Lincoln and Jeff Davis. "The Lincolnite lost. 'There,' says the winner, 'Old Abe belongs to me.' 'Well, I'll send him over by the Petersburg express,'" said the Union soldier, using a nickname for the shells bombarding the city.

Camp gambling became one of the great moral crusades of the war, North and South. Gen. Robert E. Lee was "pained to learn that the vice of gambling exists"—he must have been the last to know—and issued an order forbidding it, to little effect. As the Union soldier David Lane put it, "so far as my observation goes, nine out of ten play cards for money."

Players did, under pressure from family, chaplains and commanding officers, occasionally cast off their "evil practices." One Confederate soldier, Samuel Hankins, recalled, "When the cannonading became more frequent, you could hear, 'Boys, we are going to get into it.' Then there would begin the searching of pockets for gambling goods, playing cards especially. The thought of being killed with such in their pockets induced the soldiers to throw them away." Once the battle was over, though, the so-called Devil's Picture Book once again trumped the Good Book, with players so avid that even "the breast of a wounded comrade" did for a table, wrote Thomas Wise Durham, a Zouave.

For gambling or for simple fun, playing cards are a staple in memoirs of Civil War camp life. All up and down the ranks, men played cards under fire, men played cards between battles, sworn enemies played cards together in cornfields, prisons, and hospitals. Far from home, often lacking even the simple diversion of a dime novel, as one soldier put it, "card playing seemed to be as popular a way of killing time as any."

America's Bloodiest Day
By RICK BEARD

In a letter to his wife, the Union general Alpheus Williams recorded his feelings on the eve of the fighting at Antietam Creek, Md. "There was a half-dreamy sensation about it all," he wrote, "but with a certain impression that the morrow was to be great with the future fate of our country. So much responsibility, so much intense, future anxiety." The morrow was indeed great—a pivotal moment in the struggle between North and South.

The battle of Antietam, or Sharpsburg, the bloodiest day in American history, rebuffed the Confederate Army of Northern Virginia's first invasion of Northern territory, convinced European nations to withhold recognition from the Confederacy, assured Republican control of the House of Representatives in the upcoming midterm elections, gave Abraham Lincoln political cover to announce the preliminary Emancipation Proclamation and finally persuaded the president that the Union could no longer afford Gen. George B. McClellan.

Such momentous outcomes would have seemed unlikely a few months earlier. Throughout 1862, momentum on the battlefield had swung back and forth between the Union and Confederate armies. Northern troops had won a number of important victories, most notably at Shiloh in April, but in May Gen. Thomas J. "Stonewall" Jackson befuddled Union forces in Virginia's Shenandoah Valley. And by July 2 McClellan's much ballyhooed advance on Richmond had become a retreat, as Robert E. Lee audaciously drove federal forces back to the James River. On June 26, the Army of the Potomac was five miles from Richmond; it would not threaten the Confederate capital again until 1865.

The failure of the Peninsula Campaign stunned the North. The diarist George Templeton Strong captured the mood: "We . . . are in a depressed, dismal . . . state of anxiety." And things quickly got worse. Lee and the Army of Northern Virginia pivoted to confront the newly formed Army of Virginia, commanded by Maj. Gen. John Pope. After a series of modest successes in the Western theater, Pope arrived in Washington, announcing, "I have come to you from the West, where we have always seen the backs of our enemies."

Pope got his comeuppance at the Second Battle of Bull Run on Aug. 29 and 30. After bitter and repeated assaults against Stonewall Jackson's forces, Pope was driven from the field when Gen. James Longstreet's five divisions smashed into the Union Army's left flank. Pope blamed defeat on McClellan's failure to send reinforcements; McClellan gave credence to the charge, suggesting to Lincoln on Aug. 29 that they "leave Pope to get out of his scrape & at once use all our means to make the Capitol perfectly safe."

McClellan's refusal to reinforce Pope infuriated members of the cabinet, especially Secretary of War Edwin Stanton and Treasury Secretary Salmon Chase. Stanton took the extraordinary step of drafting a "remonstrance" (later softened by Attorney General Bates) to the president expressing the fear that "the destruction of our armies, the protraction of the war, the waste of our national resources, and the overthrow of the government . . . must be the inevitable consequence of George B. McClellan being continued in command."

At a fractious cabinet meeting on Sept. 2, Lincoln overrode Stanton's and Chase's objections to McClellan, who unbeknownst to them had that morning accepted Lincoln's request to take command of the combined Union armies (after Gen. Ambrose Burnside had declined). Lincoln, described as "extremely distressed" by McClellan's actions, nonetheless argued that the troops were "utterly demoralized" and only McClellan could "reorganize the army and bring it out of chaos."

On Sept. 4, Lee led the Army of Northern Virginia across the Potomac River into western Maryland. Lee believed that the South must strike a blow that would reduce the Northern enthusiasm for the conflict or face a war of attrition it could not win. In a letter to Jefferson Davis, Lee acknowledged that "the army is not properly equipped" but that "I do not consider success impossible." The Confederacy had long contended that it was only defending itself against an aggressive "foreign invasion," but now, in Davis's words, "we are driven to protect our own country by transferring the seat of war to that of an enemy who pursues us with a relentless and apparently aimless hostility."

Lee fully expected his army to be greeted as liberators in Maryland, a slave state, issuing a proclamation identifying Marylanders as "citizens of a commonwealth allied to the States of the South by the strongest social, political, and commercial ties" and promising "to aid you in throwing off this foreign yoke." But the farmers and townspeople of western Maryland, where slavery was scarce, offered the invading army scant support.

Meanwhile the Northern press panicked at the presence of Lee and his army on Union soil. The New York Times wrote that people believed the government was "actually falling to pieces," while The New York Herald predicted that defeat would produce "ten or twenty petty republics of the South American school."

Some among the Union military privately voiced similar distress. Brig. Gen. George Meade wrote: "The morale of the army is much impaired by recent events. I must confess I am not very sanguine of our power." But many Union foot soldiers, called upon for the first time to defend their homes, felt otherwise. "I am willing to fight as long as there is a man left in the 2nd regt before I will see the north invaded," wrote one Michigan private.

Lee, who had taken McClellan's measure months earlier in Virginia, was certain the Union leader would be slow to reach western Maryland and felt secure in dividing his army. On Sept. 9, he issued his famous "Lost Orders," directing Stonewall Jackson to re-cross the Potomac and circle around to attack the Union garrison at Harpers Ferry from the west, while Gen. Lafayette McLaws and Gen. John Walker were to assist by capturing Maryland and Loudon Heights overlooking Harpers Ferry. Lee, along with Longstreet's corps, would remain near Hagerstown. The inexplicable discovery, four days later, of Lee's battle plan, wrapped around three cigars lying by a roadside, was an intelligence bonanza. "Now I know what to do," McClellan crowed to one officer. To Lincoln, McClellan wrote: "I have all the plans of the rebels, and will catch them in their own trap. Will send you trophies."

Ever cautious, McClellan squandered much of his advantage by waiting more than 17 hours before getting underway. Alerted by a Southern sympathizer that McClellan had a copy of his orders, Lee moved to block the Union advance. On Sept. 14, some 38,000 Union troops drove west through three passes in South Mountain and by day's end had routed the 12,000 Confederate defenders. Lee became convinced that he needed to abandon his plans, but word from Jackson that Harpers Ferry would surely fall the next day restored his determination and he ordered his army to march to Sharpsburg.

Had McClellan attacked at this moment, he would almost surely have overwhelmed Lee's force. But convinced as ever that he was outnumbered, McClellan hesitated east of Antietam Creek. Harpers Ferry fell to the Confederates the next day, and by midday on Sept. 16 all but three of Lee's nine divisions had arrived in Sharpsburg. A cataclysmic battle was at hand.

Lee arrayed his forces in a crescent, anchored on the right by Antietam Creek and on the left by the Potomac River. While the rebel army enjoyed interior lines of communication, it had its back to a river that was not easily crossed. Late in the day, Maj. Gen. "Fighting" Joe Hooker led a Union foray across Antietam Creek, thereby alerting Lee to where McClellan would strike first. Although McClellan had a sound battle plan, he failed to communicate it to his corps commanders or to coordinate their assaults. Each corps operated independently, and no more than 20,000 of his 75,000 troops were ever engaged at any one time during the battle: 20,000 troops saw no action at all.

The fighting began in earnest early the next morning. Amidst a fierce artillery duel, Hooker led sustained Union assaults on Jackson's troops, who were well positioned in the West Woods near the

Dunker Church (Dunkers were a German Baptist denomination). For a time, the Union troops made progress, but attack and counterattack soon transformed a now-iconic landscape—the Cornfield, the East and West Woods, the Dunker Church—into a slaughter pen. "In the time I am writing," Hooker later reported, "every stalk of corn in the northern and greater part of the field was cut as closely as could have been done with a knife, and the slain lay in rows precisely as they had stood in their ranks a few moments before."

By mid-morning, the Confederates had managed to blunt the attack, and the battle's focus shifted to the center of the Southern lines. Wave after wave of federal troops sought to dislodge rebel troops from a sunken farm road, often exchanging fire at 30 paces. For over four hours, the deadly aim of Confederate cannons and troops blanketed the land with dead or wounded Union soldiers, but in the early afternoon the Yankee's superior numbers finally overran the Confederates positioned in what has been known ever since as the Bloody Lane. The carnage, captured in Mathew Brady and Alexander Gardner's famous photographs, was horrific. "In the road the dead covered the ground," remembered a Union lieutenant colonel. "It seemed . . . that it was the Valley of Death. I think that in the space of less than ten acres, lay the bodies of a thousand dead men and as many more wounded."

At the southern end of the battlefield, three Confederate batteries and an infantry brigade commanded by Brig. Gen. Robert Toombs looked down from a steep hill onto Rohrbach Bridge. Despite repeated urging from McClellan, General Burnside made only a few desultory attempts to cross the bridge until early afternoon, when troops from New York and Pennsylvania regiments finally braved the withering fire and established themselves on the other side of Antietam Creek. By late afternoon Burnside's 13,000-man force had advanced almost to Sharpsburg, threatening to cut off Lee's line of retreat across the Potomac. At the last minute, Gen. A. P. Hill's division arrived from Harpers Ferry and drove the federal troops back to the heights near what we now know as the Burnside Bridge.

By 5 p.m., the Battle of Antietam was over. Over 22,000 Americans lay dead or wounded or were among the missing: the highest single-day casualty total of the Civil War. As one particularly literate

Union private later wrote, "the whole landscape for an instant turned slightly red." (Sept. 17 also proved to be the war's deadliest day for civilians, when 78 workers in the Allegheny Arsenal were killed in an explosion.) An official with the Sanitary Commission wrote: "No words can convey the utter destruction and ruin. For four miles in length, and nearly a half mile in width, the ground is strewn with . . . hats, caps, clothing, canteens, knapsacks, shells, and shot. . . . Visit a battlefield and see what a victory costs."

Lee, who was sure McClellan would not attack the next day, elected not to withdraw during the night of Sept. 17, but the following night the Army of Northern Virginia crossed the Potomac. It took more than a month—until Oct. 26—for McClellan to follow, taking six days to do what Lee had done in one, prompting Gen. Henry Halleck to exclaim: "There is an immobility here that exceeds all that any man can conceive of."

Antietam was a Union victory only because McClellan had retained command of the field. But it gave President Lincoln political cover to release the preliminary Emancipation Proclamation on Sept. 22, telling his cabinet that God "had decided this question in favor of the slaves." A month later, Lord Palmerston, the British prime minister, wrote that the British would remain neutral "lookers-on till the war shall have taken a more decided turn." And on Nov. 7, Lincoln fired McClellan: "I began to fear . . . that he did not want to hurt the enemy. I saw how he could intercept the enemy on the way to Richmond. . . . If he let them get away, I would remove him. He did so & I relieved him."

Lincoln's Great Gamble
By RICHARD STRINER

Countless school children have been taught that Abraham Lincoln was the Great Emancipator. Others have been taught—and many have concluded—that the Emancipation Proclamation, which Abraham Lincoln announced on Sept. 22, 1862, has been overemphasized, that it was inefficacious, a sham, that Lincoln's motivations were somehow unworthy, that slavery was ended by other ways and means, and that slavery was on the way out in any case.

The truth is that Lincoln's proclamation was an exercise in risk, a huge gamble by a leader who sought to be—and who became—America's great liberator.

Since before his election in 1860, Lincoln and his fellow Republicans had vowed to keep slavery from spreading. The leaders of the slave states refused to go along. When Lincoln was elected and his party took control of Congress, the leaders of most of the slave states turned to secession rather than allow the existing bloc of slave states to be outnumbered.

The Union, divided from the Confederacy, was also divided itself. Many Democrats who fought to stop secession blamed Republicans for pushing the slave states over the brink; some were open supporters of slavery. And if the Democrats were to capture control of Congress in the mid-term elections of November 1862, there was no telling what the consequences might be for the Republicans' anti-slavery policies.

The Emancipation Proclamation wasn't always part of the plan. Republicans, Lincoln included, tried push their antislavery program by measured degrees, since they feared a white supremacist backlash. That was what made Lincoln's decision to issue an emancipation edict, and to do it before the mid-term congressional elections of 1862, so extraordinarily risky.

In the first half of 1862, he had tried to institute a program of gradual and compensated emancipation in Delaware, Kentucky and Maryland, the slave states that had not fallen under the control of secessionists. But the border-state leaders refused to listen. So Lincoln decided in July that he would turn his attention to rebellious slave states, and there, in the name of preserving the Union, he would institute immediate and uncompensated emancipation.

In the months that followed, he worked to soften public opinion in the North—to get the public ready for the fact that he intended to free some slaves. In August, he wrote a letter to Horace Greeley, editor of The New York Tribune. This letter would soon become famous. Lincoln claimed that his "paramount object in this struggle is to save the Union, and is not either to save or to destroy slavery. If I could save the Union without freeing any slave I would do it, and if I could save it by freeing all the slaves I would do it; and if I could save it by freeing some and leaving others alone I would also do that."

This was a clever deception in light of the fact that no breach in the Union would have happened in the first place had Lincoln and his fellow Republicans not refused to admit more slave states to the Union. Lincoln's letter to Greeley was misleading; he wrote it in an effort to appeal to patriotic Unionists and get them used to the idea that he might start freeing slaves. What he hoped was that people would view the proclamation as a patriotic necessity.

Some observers got the point; Sydney Howard Gay, a leading abolitionist, wrote to Lincoln:

> Your letter to Mr. Greeley has infused new hope among
> us at the North who are anxiously awaiting that move-
> ment on your part that they believe will end the rebellion
> by removing its cause. I think the general impression is
> that as you are determined to save the Union tho' slavery
> perish, you mean presently to announce that the destruc-
> tion of Slavery is the price of our salvation.

Lincoln himself confided to Representative Isaac N. Arnold that, as Arnold recounted, "the meaning of his letter to Mr. Greeley was this: he was ready to declare emancipation when he was convinced that it could be made effective, and that the people were with him."

Others, however, concluded from the letter that Lincoln was hopelessly obtuse in regard to the moral issues of the war. Wendell Phillips, another abolitionist leader, called the letter a "disgraceful document" and asserted that Lincoln "can only be frightened or bullied into the right policy. . . . He's a Spaniel by nature—nothing broad, generous, or highhearted about him."

In early September the deceptions thickened as Lincoln pretended he had not yet decided on the matter; he even played devil's advocate and told a group of visiting abolitionists that he was plagued with doubts about emancipation: "how can we feed and care for such a multitude," he asked a group of Chicago antislavery petitioners who visited him on Sept. 13. Once again, he was being deceptive; not only was he positive that he would take this step—the proclamation had been written already—but he was ready to act in advance of the November elections. He was waiting for a battlefield victory that would permit him to issue the proclamation from a position of strength. At one point he made this very clear to his listeners: "There is a question of expediency as to time, should such a proclamation be issued. Matters look dark just now. I fear that a proclamation on the heels of a defeat would be interpreted as a cry of despair. It would come better, if at all, immediately after a victory."

After Lee's invasion of Maryland was stopped in the battle of Antietam on Sept. 17, Lincoln made up his mind to go ahead. He later told a Massachusetts congressman that "when Lee came over the river, I made a resolution that if McClellan drove him back I would send the Proclamation after him." On Sept. 22, he read the proclamation to his cabinet.

The Preliminary Emancipation Proclamation is called "preliminary" because it was framed as a warning to rebels, a threat to take action by a certain date if they refused to lay down their arms. Lincoln warned that if the rebellion continued past Jan. 1, 1863,

> All persons held as slaves within any state, or designated
> part of a state, the people whereof shall then be in rebel-
> lion against the United States shall be then, thencefor-
> ward, and forever free; and the executive government of
> the United States, including the military and naval author-
> ity thereof, will recognize and maintain the freedom of
> such persons, and will do no act or acts to repress such
> persons, or any of them, in any efforts they may make for
> their actual freedom.

The warning was clear: the rebels were risking the permanent loss of their slaves if they refused to lay down their arms by New Year's Day. Lincoln's armies would not only "recognize" the freedom of slaves, they would work to "maintain" that freedom.

When the proclamation was released to the press later that day, reactions spanned a very broad range. The black abolitionist Frederick Douglass complained that it "touched neither justice nor mercy. Had there been one expression of sound moral feeling against Slavery, one word of regret and shame that this accursed system had remained so long the disgrace and scandal of the Republic, one word of satisfaction in the hope of burying slavery and the rebellion in one common grave, a thrill of joy would have run round the world." The abolitionist Lydia Maria Child wrote that "it was done reluctantly and stintedly. . . . It was merely a war measure, to which we were forced by our own perils and necessities." "How cold the president's proclamation is," remarked abolitionist Sallie Holley.

But other antislavery leaders were ecstatic. Theodore Tilton wrote that he was "half crazy with enthusiasm." Samuel J. May Jr. wrote that "joy, gratitude, thanksgiving, renewed hope and courage fill my soul." The Radical Republican Senator Charles Sumner wrote that "the skies are brighter and the air is purer now that Slavery is handed over to judgment." Horace Greeley editorialized thus: "Let the President know that everywhere throughout the land he is hailed as Wisest and Best. . . . He re-creates a nation." The editor of The Pittsburgh Gazette called the proclamation "the most important document in world history." Even Frederick Douglass, despite his doubts, spoke words of praise for public consumption: "We shout for joy that we live to record this righteous decree."

On Sept. 24, some administration revelers met at the home of Salmon P. Chase, the Treasury secretary, an ardent pre-war Free Soiler and a rival of Lincoln's for the 1860 nomination. "They all seemed to feel a sort of new and exhilarated life; they breathed freer," one of Lincoln's secretaries, John Hay, recorded. "They gleefully and merrily called each other and themselves abolitionists."

Some regarded the proclamation as an act of great political shrewdness. The editor of The Boston Commonwealth wrote that while "we complained bitterly that the President was slow," it was obvious that "his slowness has been the means of committing the whole flock of you to a rule of loyalty, which you cannot abandon. . . . Those who do not stand by the Proclamation will be branded as those who would rather see the United States Government overthrown than the end of Human Bondage on this continent."

But others worried that Lincoln's proclamation might prove a political mistake. Postmaster General Montgomery Blair warned that it would "endanger our power in Congress, and put the next House of Representatives in the hands of those opposed to the war, or to our mode of carrying it on."

White supremacist Democrats vilified the proclamation. The Louisville Democrat editorialized that "the President has as much right to abolish the institution of marriage, or the laws of a State regulating the relation of parent and child, as to nullify the right of a State to regulate the relations of the white and black races." The New York Express excoriated the proclamation; no president had ever before "conceived a policy so well fitted, utterly to degrade and destroy white labor, and to reduce the white man to the level of the negro."

Lincoln's gamble was dangerous indeed. But he did what he believed he had to do. It was not, in the end, a political calculation. According to the diary of Navy Secretary Gideon Welles, Lincoln told his cabinet on Sept. 22 he had made a promise to God. "He had made a vow, a covenant," Welles recounted, "that if God gave us the victory in the approaching battle, he would . . . move forward in the cause of emancipation."

And so the stakes of the war would be raised to a level commensurate with all of the carnage and all of the sacrifice. The meaning of the war would be changed—forever changed—by Lincoln's proclamation.

CHAPTER 6

Toward Emancipation

The Union victory at Antietam, slim as it was, provided Lincoln the opening he needed to make his Emancipation Proclamation public. On September 22, he announced that if the Confederacy did not surrender by the end of the year, he would issue a decree that "all persons held as slaves within any State or designated part of a State, the people whereof shall then be in rebellion against the United States shall be then, thenceforward, and forever free."

The proclamation went as far as Lincoln's powers as a wartime president could reach: not all slaves everywhere, and not a single slave in territory under Union control. But every slave on every inch of land that would be conquered from the date of issuance forward would be set free. Each Union advance, then, was not just a step toward reunification, but a step toward the end of slavery. And every Union unit was no longer simply a conquering force, but a liberating one—and almost immediately, thousands upon thousands of slaves set off north, often at great peril, to reach them. The document gave the war a new direction, a new purpose. It would be, from then on, a war for freedom.

Lincoln did, of course, hedge his reasoning; emancipation, he told Democratic and moderate skeptics, was a means to the war's original end: every slave drawn away from the Confederacy, or freed by advancing troops, was a slave that could no longer support the Confederate war effort. But there can be no doubt where Lincoln's real emphasis lay—he had always been a critic of slavery, but not necessarily an advocate of black freedom as a good in itself. The war, with its sacrifices past and long road still to come, had changed that.

Lincoln's new tack on slavery was ill received in many places, particularly the southern Great Lake states, including his own, Illinois. That November the Republicans suffered extensive losses in the midterm elections, as Americans skeptical of both the legality of Lincoln's proclamation and its import for the war turned toward the Democratic Party.

The president had other concerns, though: in early November he relieved General McClellan of his duties. Since Antietam, "Little Mac" had done almost nothing to take advantage of Lee's retreat, even as he made public statements criticizing Lincoln's Emancipation Proclamation. In his place Lincoln put Gen. Ambrose Burnside, a dubious choice, even at the time, given Burnside's mixed battlefield performance. But Burnside had one thing Lincoln wanted: a zeal, and a plan, for moving swiftly toward Richmond. He set out quickly south, with a massive army. But the bewhiskered general's momentum would come to a halt at Fredericksburg, where in mid-December dug-in Confederate troops slaughtered thousands of Union men before the survivors retreated across the Rappahannock River.

Better news came from the west. The Confederate invasion of Kentucky, during which the rebels took the state capital of Frankfort and even installed a puppet governor, had broken down, thanks to a surprisingly hostile local population and a string of Union victories, culminating at the Battle of Perryville. In October the South retreated from the state, though Confederate raids would continue through almost the end of the war. The 35,0000 rebel soldiers, under Gen. Braxton Bragg, settled in Middle Tennessee near Nashville, where, in the last days of December, a 41,000-strong Union army under Gen. William Rosecrans defeated them at the Battle of Stones River. The victory meant the end, for the moment, of Confederate military strength in the Upper South, relieving pressure on Ulysses S. Grant's forces in Mississippi, which would turn, in spring 1862, on the last bastion of Southern strength along the Mississippi: Vicksburg.

As the Battle of Stones River raged in Tennessee, hundreds of miles away President Lincoln gathered with friends and family in Washington to welcome the new year. That afternoon, he excused himself to his study, where he sat down for one last reading of the Emancipation Proclamation. Then he picked up his pen, dipped it in his ink bottle, and signed it.

Rights During Wartime
By SUSAN SCHULTEN

Did President Lincoln violate civil liberties during the war? In July, Lincoln revealed to his cabinet his intent to emancipate slaves; in September he announced the policy to the entire nation. The proclamation applied only to states in rebellion, and excluded areas occupied by Union forces. Such limitations disheartened those who hoped for the destruction of slavery altogether. But Lincoln insisted that emancipation could only be considered constitutional as a military measure, and therefore could be deployed only to areas actively in rebellion. In other words, he thought very carefully about his constitutional power before making his proclamation.

By contrast, Lincoln worried little about curbing civil liberties to protect the war effort. As president he sharply limited freedom by suspending the writ of habeas corpus. The "great writ" forbade authorities to hold citizens indefinitely without being charged. This protection against tyranny was one of few that appeared in the original constitution, prior to the Bill of Rights.

At first Lincoln seemed reluctant to wield this power. After the crisis at Fort Sumter, generals Benjamin Butler and Winfield Scott announced their intent to arrest Maryland legislators who advocated secession, but Lincoln overruled them. By June, Marylanders intensified their opposition to the new administration by attacking volunteers and destroying communication lines and bridges that connected Baltimore to the capital. Lincoln responded swiftly, imposing martial law on the route from Washington to Philadelphia and suspending the writ of habeas corpus throughout Maryland.

The public supported these measures to secure order in Maryland, but Chief Justice Roger Taney vehemently denied that Lincoln had the constitutional power do to so. For Taney, for the power to suspend the writ was the domain of Congress, not the president, for it appeared in Article I of the Constitution.

In response, Lincoln openly defied Taney. He argued that such a narrow ruling of presidential power was hopelessly inadequate to the crisis at hand. As he wrote, if the Union was dissolving, "are all the laws, but one, to go unexecuted, and the government itself go to pieces, lest that one be violated?" Lincoln refused to believe that the framers would not have endorsed his efforts to restore the Union. After all, the Constitution did not specify which branch had the power to suspend the writ, only that it could be suspended "when in cases of rebellion or invasion the public safety may require it." This was, above all, a case of rebellion.

The following summer it was not Lincoln, but Secretary of War Edwin Stanton, who vastly intensified a crackdown on disloyalty. On Aug. 8, 1862, Stanton issued a nationwide order that anyone "engaged, by act, speech, or writing, in discouraging volunteer enlistments, or in any way giving aid and comfort to the enemy, or in any other disloyal practice against the United States," would be subject to arrest and trial "before a military commission." The vague order made it nearly impossible to distinguish between dissent and disloyalty, and widespread arrests followed.

In the 30 days after Stanton issued the order, more than 350 individuals were imprisoned on these charges, far more than had been arrested prior to that point. The majority of these were avoiding the draft, which was the administration's primary justification. Yet by deputizing local authorities to enforce the order, Stanton created serious problems. Lincoln was all too frequently frustrated to discover that some of those arrested were speaking against the war rather than actively obstructing enlistments. The editor of the Dubuque Herald, for instance, was arrested for publishing material hostile to the draft. After being held without charges for three months, he was released, but as a result his opposition to the war—and especially to Lincoln-had immensely intensified.

Two days after Lincoln issued the Emancipation Proclamation in September 1862, he renewed the nationwide suspension of the writ. Once again, the administration justified the action as a measure to protect the draft passed by Congress in July. Arrests of civilians north of the border states increased dramatically that August and September. This unwittingly fueled the criticism of the administration at a perilous political moment, on the eve of the midterm elections.

In this period, Lincoln came under increasing fire from artists and cartoonists, but not all were unsympathetic to his plight. In his satirical painting "Lincoln Crushing the Dragon of Rebellion," David Gilmour Blythe portrayed Lincoln as a hamstrung commander, simultaneously struggling against the "dragon of rebellion" and northern subversion. New York Democrats, including New York City Mayor Fernando Wood, are ridiculed for "using" the Constitution to invalidate not just the draft but the war effort generally.

Criticism of Lincoln intensified after Congress approved the draft in March 1863. The unsigned image "Abraham the Last" from August 1864 rendered Lincoln as a subhuman beast with kingly aspirations to power. He dangles the "joke of emancipation" in front of a small African-American soldier hoping to earn his freedom, and blithely tramples over the rights of citizens and the press. Secretary of State William H. Seward reportedly boasted that he could arrest citizens from New York to Ohio with the ring of a bell, powers not even the queen of England could claim.

The political opposition to these wartime measures did worry Lincoln, particularly as he approached reelection in 1864. But he was certain that these actions were constitutional. As he wrote in a public letter to New York Democrats, the use of military courts was absolutely necessary, and arrests of those protesting the draft was done to protect the military. In Lincoln's mind these actions were temporary, and taken to advance a much larger cause. This must have been cold comfort to the thousands arrested and held without charges during the war.

The problem with Lincoln's justification is that it was premised on the assumption that major threats to the Union cause existed throughout the north. There are certainly instances of individuals speaking out against Lincoln and the draft, and the persistence of a virulent anti-war press suggests that the administration did not widely prosecute speech. But there is little evidence of widespread insurrection in the Union.

After the war, the Supreme Court concurred, ruling in Ex parte Milligan (1866) that while the suspension of the writ was lawful, the use of military trials was unconstitutional where civilian courts were in operation. No longer alive to respond, Lincoln would likely have taken the ruling with a grain of salt. Yet he did worry that military emancipation might be reversed after the end of the war, and this led him to press Congress to enshrine emancipation in the 13th Amendment.

Lincoln's reputation as the violator of civil liberties is far overshadowed—and rightly so—by his reputation for defending the Union and striking against slavery. But we should remember that these are in fact interdependent, and in Lincoln's own mind one necessitated the other.

The Drought That Changed the War
By KENNETH W. NOE

I n August 1862, two Confederate armies turned north from Tennessee, hoping to revive their nation's faltering hopes west of the Appalachians. And yet, despite a stunning victory at Richmond, Ky., the capture of Frankfort, the state capital, the installation of a Confederate governor, and a tactical victory at Perryville on Oct. 8, by fall the two forces were limping back south. What happened?

Even as the two Confederate armies, one under Maj. Gen. Edmund Kirby Smith, the other under Gen. Braxton Bragg, as well as a pursuing force under Gen. Don Carlos Buell, all raced north across central Kentucky on parallel paths in what many soldiers likened to a great foot race, the men were suffering—brought low not just by the summer heat, but by vast dust clouds, increasingly short rations and a growing dearth of potable water. Both armies had marched headlong into a drought.

Food shortages, inflation and other hardships the Confederate plain folk suffered, as well as at least part of the disillusionment that grew out of those issues—the entire litany of the so-called "internalist" interpretation of Confederate defeat as a "rich man's war and poor man's fight"—actually can be traced back at least in part to the drought of 1862, its negative effect on Southern food production, and the choices the Jefferson Davis administration made when confronting the situation. The newborn Confederacy simply had been born at perhaps the worst possible moment in the 19th century to launch an agricultural republic. Meanwhile, Northern crops, especially Midwestern wheat, boomed.

Months earlier, Civil War soldiers would have found it hard to even imagine such a situation. The winter and spring of 1862 were unusually wet. High water and mud shaped campaigns in places as far apart as Fort Henry in western Tennessee and the bottomless swamps that Maj. Gen. George B. McClellan encountered on the Virginia Peninsula.

The rains created problems of their own. Wet conditions led to widespread wheat rust, a fungus, which destroyed perhaps a sixth of the South's wheat crop. Flooding along the Mississippi and other rivers wrecked other spring crops in the field.

Then, in the early summer, the heavens closed, and drought conditions set in. Agriculture suffered. With the notable exception of Georgia, the corn crop of 1862 largely failed, while the Montgomery Advertiser pronounced the Confederacy's wheat crop all but ruined.

The armies confronted the great drought as well. The army of Union General Don Carlos Buell, sent from Corinth, Miss., in July to take Chattanooga, had endured much as rivers fell to levels too low to permit the shipping of supplies, leaving the men dependent on railroads that soon proved easy prey for marauding Rebel cavalry.

The "great foot race" north in late August and September proved more agonizing still. James Iredell Hall of the 9th Tennessee wrote that "the only water accessible was pond water and that was warm and muddy. The water we were compelled to drink, was so muddy that we could not wash our faces in it." A Confederate soldier in the 33rd Alabama remembered that "we obtained water under deep limesinks, some of these being partly full of water, and Federals had utilized some of the partly filled sinks as a place to butcher cattle and dumped offal into them, making the water unfit to drink."

The food situation was just as bad. Back in Tennessee and northern Alabama, both sides already had encountered trouble filling their bellies. Part of Buell's decision to retreat from Chattanooga was his supply situation; elderly locals testified that 1862 was the driest summer in their memory. Pillaging and disorder increased as hungry soldiers took what their commissaries could not supply.

For his part, Bragg's plan depended upon living off the land as the Confederates marched north, a decision that quickly smashed into a dry reality: drought and the occupying Federal army had left little for them to eat. Bragg changed course with every new rumor of ample foodstuffs ahead. On Sept. 14, acting without orders, Brig. Gen. James Chalmers of Bragg's army and Col. John Scott, commanding a detachment of Kirby Smith's cavalry, initiated an ill-advised attack on the entrenched Federal garrison at Munfordville, Ky. Hoping to secure an easy victory, Chalmers had also heard that Munfordville contained large stores of wheat. Worried that the repulse would undermine Confederate sentiments in the Bluegrass State, Bragg veered his entire force to Munfordville and compelled the garrison to surrender.

But the delay allowed Buell to draw near. Briefly Bragg considered making a stand against Buell there, but instead returned to the march. Real hunger now appeared: Buell's men complained that they were reduced to half-rations, then quarter-rations, and when the hardtack they brought with them finally ran out, received only wormy flour without the necessary utensils to make bread.

On Sept. 22 Confederate forces halted at Bardstown, in the middle of the state, disappointing many Johnny Rebs who had assumed they were hurrying to take Louisville. Buell's exhausted men began arriving in that city on Sept. 25, furious that their commander had allowed Bragg to come so far north without a fight. Indicative of the soldiers' collapsing morale, wild rumors circulated that the two generals actually were brothers-in-law who slept together nightly while making plans for another day's nonviolent marching. Some Hoosier troops were in fact so angry that they deserted by walking home across the drought-ravaged Ohio River.

On Oct. 1, augmented by new recruits, Buell marched his army out of Louisville, determined to drive Bragg's smaller army from the state. Again, the water crisis stymied the two armies. By Oct. 7, at least one corps in the Federal army was so dehydrated and so sick from pondborne bacteria that it lurched into camp at the point of collapse and mutiny. Before dawn the next morning, other elements of Buell's army moved forward in the darkness, determined to drive Confederates away from the precious springs of water they zealously safeguarded.

So opened the Battle of Perryville, Kentucky's largest battle, fought in the dusty hills just west of a town where the Chaplin River had all but run dry. Gaining a tactical victory, Bragg decided to retreat to Tennessee when he finally realized that he faced a numerically superior force, and he abandoned Kentucky entirely upon learning that his planned supply base was all but empty.

The drought that turned the war in the West would continue for another two years.

The War Democrats' Big Night
By NICOLE ETCHESON

When the Army of Northern Virginia invaded Maryland in September 1862, it did so in part to influence the upcoming Northern elections—an effort to "conquer a peace." The presence of a Southern army on Union soil, Confederate General Robert E. Lee wrote President Jefferson Davis, "would enable the people of the United States to determine at their coming elections whether they will support those who favor a prolongation of the war, or those who wish to bring it to a termination." Even if the Confederacy lost its war for independence on the battlefield, the reasoning went, it could still hope to undermine the Northern public's will to fight.

Confederates were right to see Northern political will as a Union vulnerability. When the South seceded from the Union, Illinois Senator Stephen A. Douglas declared that "there can be no neutrals in this war, only patriots—or traitors." As the leading Northern Democrat, Douglas's support was important to the new administration of his old rival, Abraham Lincoln. But Douglas died in the summer of 1861. While many of his followers became "War Democrats," and some even officially joined the Republican Party, a faction of the Democrats quickly emerged as an antiwar opposition.

These Peace Democrats rejected administration policies like suspending the writ of habeas corpus as violations of American liberties, and they blamed the Republicans, not the South, for bringing on the war. Named "Copperheads" by their detractors—a reference to a venomous snake, native to Midwestern states like Indiana, where Peace Democrats were strong—they also vehemently rejected the idea that winning the war necessitated freeing the slaves.

Indeed, Indiana was a bellwether for the Republicans' political dilemma at the midterms. In 1860, the party had captured 7 of Indiana's 11 congressional districts, while Democrats retained control of only 4 districts in southern Indiana. Indiana's new Republican governor, Oliver P. Morton, was a former Democrat who, like Douglas, had promised he would "denounce treason and uphold the cause of the Union."

Still, the state's Republican leaders were careful not to throw themselves wholly behind the war and antislavery. Although the party controlled the state legislature, it had not yet embraced emancipation. After the firing on Fort Sumter, legislators resolved that while Indiana would help suppress the rebellion, the state would not participate "in any aggression upon the institution of slavery or any other constitutional right belonging to any of the states." At the same time, an Indiana Democratic convention in January 1862 blamed Northern extremists and Southern secessionists equally for causing the war. And they blamed Republicans for refusing to compromise with the South during the secession winter, while supporting the legislature's refusal to use the war to end slavery.

But that didn't help the Republicans two years later. By the fall of 1862, the party had to defend a record that included controversial military policies, setbacks on the battlefield and emancipation. In the months leading up to the elections (then held in October), military authorities had arrested a number of Indiana Democrats, including some candidates for office, for allegedly aiding the enemy, either by speaking against the war or discouraging enlistments. A few days before Indiana's state elections, the state had to resort to a draft of 3,000 men to meet the War Department's quota. Earlier, in July, Kentucky guerrillas had raided Newburg, Ind., causing the state militia to mobilize, which frightened Hoosiers with the possibility of an invasion. And later that summer, the Confederate generals Kirby Smith and Braxton Bragg invaded neighboring Kentucky, a campaign that—a week before the Indiana elections—culminated in the Battle of Perryville.

Indeed, 1862 was a difficult year for the Union as a whole. It had abandoned the Peninsula campaign after a series of bloody battles and suffered defeat at Second Bull Run. Although it claimed Antietam as a victory, the North had suffered staggering, historically unprecedented losses. After the election, The Indianapolis Journal, which was the state's leading Republican newspaper, admitted: "The terrible inefficiency with which the war has been conducted, had done more than all the President's proclamations to dissatisfy and alienate the people from the Administration. They see their blood spilled, their money wasted, and they see no results at all commensurate with the fearful outlay."

Many Hoosiers also felt betrayed by the Lincoln administration's change of war aims with the preliminary emancipation proclamation. Postmaster General Montgomery Blair warned Lincoln that such a proclamation would give Democrats "a club . . . to beat the Administration." Indiana Democrats objected that the proclamation was "a confession of weakness—an acknowledgement that twenty millions of white people . . . can not conquer six millions of whites" without black help.

According to an observer of the Democratic convention in Putnam County, Ind., "The resolutions and the speeches showed a terrible fear of negro equality." In particular, Putnam Democrats worried that the abolitionist tendencies of the war would threaten Indiana's constitutional provision that "no negro or mulatto shall come into or settle in the State." Before the war, Indiana Congressman William H. English had warned that if the "Black" Republicans triumphed, the "free States" would be "overrun with free negroes, to eat out the substance of the white man, compete with his labor, and trespass upon his political rights." Putnam Democrats called for a "vigorous prosecution" of the war to restore the national government's authority, but "when this is accomplished the war ought to cease."

Not surprisingly, that fall the state Republicans tried to distance themselves from the national party—a tactic they would use again in 1864—by labeling themselves the Union Party. In doing so, Governor Morton claimed, Republicans had renounced partisanship and chosen "to lay down the partisan on the altar of country." This title also implicitly grouped the Democrats with the opponents of the Union. James S. Athon, the successful Democratic candidate for secretary of state in 1862, called the resort to the Union label "hoodwinking," an effort to conceal Republicans' true identity that indicated the party's political weakness.

The Democrats did well in the fall 1862 elections. The historian Kenneth M. Stampp wrote that voters in Indiana went to the polls on Oct. 14 in an "atmosphere of gloom." They reversed the results of the 1860 elections, giving 7 of Indiana's 11 congressional districts and control of both houses of the legislature to the Democrats. The margin of victory, 9,000 votes to 10,000 votes, may have been made possible by the absence of volunteer soldiers, a claim pressed by Indiana Republicans.

Indiana wasn't the only place where Democrats made gains: they also won the governorships of New York and New Jersey; Republicans also lost control of the legislatures of Illinois and New Jersey. After the state elections, The Cincinnati Enquirer called on Morton and David Tod, the governor of Ohio, to resign, saying their administrations had been repudiated. (The gains should be put in context, though: the historian James M. McPherson has noted that Republicans not only gained seats in the Senate but also lost fewer seats in the House of Representatives than was normal for an off-year election.)

A few weeks after the election, the Democratic state central committee issued an address "to the Freemen of Indiana." Denying Republican accusations of treasonable collusion with the Confederacy, they insisted that "Armed rebellion must be suppressed by force." But the Indiana Democrats also added that "the insane and infuriated faction of Abolitionists must retire before the ballots of a free people." They considered the election a victory won for "Constitutional liberty." Governor Morton could not have disagreed more. That same day, he wrote to Lincoln warning that Northern Democrats expected the election results to mean acknowledgement of Confederate independence. As a result of the election, the governor told the president, "The fate of the North is trembling in the balance."

The Free Men of Color Go to War

By TERRY L. JONES

A s in all things, 19th-century New Orleans was a world apart from much of the rest of the South. When the Civil War began, it had a large population of so-called free men of color, citizens descended from French and Spanish men, on the one side, and slave women on the other.

Colonial-era slave codes granted them complete equality; the "hommes de couleur libre" could own land, businesses and even slaves; they could be educated and serve in the military. They created a niche for themselves in the Crescent City's multicultural society and became important to Louisiana's defense, maintaining their own militia units that served in various Indian wars and against the British during the Revolutionary War.

After the United States acquired Louisiana in 1803, the status of the free men of color changed significantly. Louisiana's Constitution of 1812 specifically restricted the right to vote to white men who owned property. The free men of color could still own property and serve in the militia, but they were left out of politics, and their status began to decline. Nonetheless, they once again volunteered to defend their homes during the War of 1812 and bravely fought for Andrew Jackson at the Battle of New Orleans.

A week after civil war erupted in April 1861, some of New Orleans' free men of color offered to form military companies to protect the state against the Union. In an announcement published in the Daily Picayune, the men declared that they were prepared to defend their homes "against any enemy who may come and disturb its tranquillity." The Daily Crescent newspaper declared: "Our free colored men . . . are certainly as much attached to the land of their birth as their white brethren here in Louisiana. . . . [They] will fight the Black Republican with as much determination and gallantry as any body of white men in the service of the Confederate States."

Soldiers from the First Louisiana Native Guard guarding the New Orleans, Opelousas and Great Western Railroad.

Soon afterward, hundreds of free men of color gathered in the street to show their support for the Confederacy. A regiment known as the Native Guards was soon formed and mustered into the state militia, but the Confederate government refused to accept them into the national army. All of the regiment's line officers were of African descent, although Gov. Thomas O. Moore appointed a white officer to command it.

Popular history clams that many of the Native Guards were wealthy slave owners who were members of New Orleans' upper class, but that is not true. While a few might have been well-to-do and owned slaves, and some certainly were related to prominent citizens, the 1860 census shows that a vast majority were clerks, artisans and skilled laborers—lower middle class at the time.

The black militia disbanded when Union forces occupied New Orleans in the spring of 1862. After the Battle of Baton Rouge in August, Gen. Benjamin F. Butler, the Union's military governor of Louisiana, requested reinforcements to defend New Orleans, but none were forthcoming. In desperation, Butler informed Secretary of War Edwin M. Stanton that he planned to raise a regiment of free blacks. On Sept. 27, 1862, Butler mustered the First Regiment of Louisiana Native Guards into Union service, making it the first sanctioned regiment of African-American troops in the United States Army.

It has generally been assumed that the African-Americans who joined Butler's Native Guards were the same ones who had served earlier in the state militia regiment by the same name. Butler, in fact, claimed that was the case. As a result, historians have questioned the sincerity of the black militiamen who volunteered for Confederate service in 1861. Their supposed change in loyalty seems to indicate that their offer to fight for the South was made only to protect their economic and social status within the community; to not volunteer would make white neighbors suspicious and possibly lead to retaliation. Some Native Guards said as much to Butler and others.

Military service records, however, call this assumption into question. Despite Butler's claim to the contrary, a vast majority of his Native Guards were not free men of color but slaves who had made their way into Union lines. James G. Hollandsworth Jr., a professor at the University of Southern Mississippi who wrote the definitive study of the Native Guards, found that only 108 of the 1,035 members of the Louisiana militia regiment, or about 10 percent, went on to serve in the Union's Native Guards. This would seem to indicate that a large number of the black militiamen were indeed sincere in their desire to fight for the South and defend their homes against invasion.

(That's very different, of course, from saying that a large number of African-Americans voluntarily served in the rebel army, a claim made by some. The men of the first Native Guard had unique circumstances and motives that should be understood in their specific context, and not extrapolated to the entire black free and enslaved population. One extensive study of Louisiana's 65,000 Confederate soldiers identified only 15 who were known to be of African descent.)

While most of Butler's Louisiana Native Guards were runaway slaves, some were free men with connections to prominent white families. During an inspection, the Native Guards' white colonel told another officer: "Sir, the best blood of Louisiana is in that regiment! Do you see that tall, slim fellow, third file from the right of the second company? One of the ex-governors of the state is his father. That orderly sergeant in the next company is the son of a man who has been six years in the United States Senate. Just beyond him is the grandson of Judge_____ . . . ; and all through the ranks you will find the same state of facts. . . . Their fathers are disloyal; [but] these black Ishmaels will more than compensate for their treason by fighting it in the field."

Later, the Second and Third Regiments of Native Guards, likewise made up overwhelmingly of former slaves, were mustered into service. In July 1863, the three regiments were brigaded together in what became known as the Corps D'Afrique. All three regiments had white colonels, but the line officers in the First and Second Regiments were black, while the Third Regiment had both black and white officers.

These Louisianians were the only black officers in the Union Army, but their racist superiors eventually purged most of them. To weed out incompetence, all officers in the Army had to pass an oral examination given by a board of experienced officers; those who failed either resigned or were stripped of their commissions. Army examiners routinely failed black officers or harassed them to make them resign their commissions. By war's end only two African-American officers remained on duty in the entire army, and both were with the Louisiana Native Guards.

Like all African-American soldiers who served in the Civil War, the Native Guards suffered from blatant discrimination. Not only were they paid less than white soldiers, they were also issued inferior arms and rations, and white soldiers often insulted and harassed them.

Despite their poor treatment, the men served well, and they became the first black soldiers to see combat in a major battle when the First and Third Regiments attacked the Confederate defenses at Port Hudson, La., on May 27, 1863. Most of the men fought bravely in their baptism of fire, and the Native Guards suffered 169 casualties in the attack. Afterward, the bodies of the dead were left to rot between the lines.

Why that happened is a matter of dispute. In her book "This Republic of Suffering," the Harvard historian Drew Gilpin Faust claims that Confederate sharpshooters prevented Union soldiers from retrieving the Native Guards' dead during a truce that was arranged for that purpose the next day. On the other hand, the historian Lawrence Lee Hewitt, from Southeastern Louisiana University, and the late Arthur W. Bergeron Jr., the former manager and curator of Port Hudson State Commemorative Area, wrote in their book "Louisianians in the Civil War" that the Union soldiers "inexplicably" failed to collect their dead on that part of the field. The stench of decaying bodies became so great that the Confederates finally requested permission from Union Gen. Nathaniel P. Banks to bury the dead Native Guards themselves. According to Hewitt and Bergeron, "Banks refused, claiming that he had no dead in that area."

Northern newspapers and magazines wrote extensively about the black soldiers' bravery at Port Hudson, although they greatly exaggerated their success. A Harper's Weekly illustration showed the Native Guards mounting the rebel breastworks and engaging in hand-to-hand combat. But in fact, none of the black soldiers got anywhere near the Confederate position, and their entire attack may have lasted only 15 minutes. In contrast to the Native Guards' heavy casualties, the Confederates who turned back their assault did not lose a single soldier.

Rather, the most significant contribution the Native Guards made at Port Hudson was demonstrating to their white comrades and superiors that African-Americans would fight as well as white soldiers. In the days following the doomed attack, many officers and men made note of the Native Guards' bravery and heavy losses. General Banks told his wife, "They fought splendidly!" Col. Benjamin H. Grierson wrote, "There can be no question about the good fighting quality of negroes, hereafter, that question was settled beyond a doubt yesterday." Largely because of the Native Guards' service at Port Hudson, Union officers began recruiting African-Americans for combat roles.

The three Native Guards regiments went on to further glory in the war. After serving in the 1864 Red River Campaign, they were re-designated the 73rd, 74th and 75th United States Colored Infantry. When the Union Army attacked and captured Fort Blakely, Ala., in April 1865, it was the Native Guards who led the charge. Afterward, one Union general wrote, "To the Seventy-third U.S. Colored Infantry belongs the honor of first planting their colors on the enemy parapet." Capt. Louis A. Snaer, a free man of color, led his men in the successful assault on Fort Blakely. Commending his courage, Snaer's commanding officer wrote, "Captain Snaer fell with a severe wound at my feet as I reached the line. He refused to sheathe his sword or to be carried off the field. . . . No braver officer has honored any flag."

The Louisiana Native Guards were mustered out of service soon after the last Confederate surrender, and many of its veterans became active in Reconstruction politics. One, P.B.S. Pinchback, became America's first black governor when, in 1872, he filled out the remaining term of the impeached Louisiana governor Henry Clay Warmoth.

The Civil War and Emancipation

By DAVID W. BLIGHT

I n December 1860, Frederick Douglass, America's most prominent African-American abolitionist, welcomed the news of
South Carolina's secession from the Union. Heaping scorn
upon the Palmetto state's rash act while relishing the opportunity
is offered to confront the evil of slavery, Douglass all but thanked
the secessionists for "preferring to be a large piece of nothing, to
being any longer a small piece of something."

To Douglass, secessionists provided what he initially hoped
would be the long-awaited opening for the antislavery cause: disunion, political crisis and some form of sanctioned military action
against the South and therefore against slavery. By the beginning of
1863 he would get his wish, but only through two years both disappointing and astonishing.

Few events in American history match the drama and significance of emancipation in the midst of the Civil War. How, when
and where slaves became free was the result of a complex interplay
of at least four factors: the policies enforced at any given time by
the Union and Confederate governments through military forces;
the geographic course of the war; the size of the slave population in
any given region; and the volition of the slaves themselves in seizing their chances and paths to freedom.

The emancipation policies of the federal government evolved
both with and against the tides of public opinion. In April 1861, the
Ohio abolitionist Congressman, Joshua Giddings, wrote to his ideological comrade in the Senate, Massachusetts' Charles Sumner,
with a declaration of certainty: "The first gun fired at Fort Sumter
rang out the death-knell of slavery." But equally vehement opposition came from conservative Democrats, as well as many Republican moderates. Representative Aaron Harding of Kentucky spoke
for many in claiming that the federal government had no power to
take anyone's "property." "The war should have nothing to do with

the institution of slavery," he insisted. "Let slavery alone; it will take care of itself."

In the first year of war, President Abraham Lincoln moved cautiously, worrying that any suggestion of emancipation might force the four loyal border slave states to join the Confederacy. He hoped for a short, limited war, and to avoid, he said, "a remorseless revolutionary struggle." If emancipation ever came from this war, Lincoln's preferred plan was for a gradual (involving decades), compensated process, with slaveholders paid for their slaves, black freedom enacted by the states themselves and large numbers of African Americans voluntarily "colonized" to foreign lands in the Americas or Africa. Although Lincoln tried assiduously to convince border state representatives, especially in Kentucky and Delaware, to go along with such a course, his proposals were soundly rejected.

Federal emancipation policies evolved in relation to escalating military imperatives. Through 1861 and into 1862, the Union Army operated with an official policy of exclusion (what it called "denial of asylum"), turning away fugitive slaves who reached the front lines. The official purpose for the war was to restore the Union, not to uproot slavery. But events steadily overtook this unworkable plan, as slaves began to flee in large numbers to Union forces in Virginia, Tennessee, and along the coasts. In May 1861 at Fortress Monroe, Va., Gen. Benjamin F. Butler declared the slaves who entered his lines "contraband of war." The idea of escaped slaves as confiscated enemy property caught on among the troops and in the popular imagination.

Congress soon followed Butler's lead. In early August 1861, striking a balance between legality and "military necessity," a phrase heard now all over the Northern press, Congress passed and Lincoln signed the First Confiscation Act, allowing for the seizure of all Confederate property—specifically including slaves "employed in or upon any fort, navy yard, dock, armory, ship, entrenchment, or in any military or naval service."

That same month, Gen. John C. Frémont proclaimed martial law in Missouri, and declared free the slaves of all rebel masters in the loyal, unseceded state. Frémont's preemptive action was widely celebrated by abolitionists, but Lincoln quickly countermanded the general's order, fearing its impact on other border states and eager to restrain the social impact of the war. But that winter at the front, the ambiguous policy of returning fugitive slaves to "loyal" owners, if their allegiance could be determined, proved unworkable and very divisive in the ranks of Union officers.

By the spring and summer of 1862, with the war surging across many fronts, east and west, both Congress and President Lincoln began to address emancipation more aggressively. In April Congress abolished slavery in the District of Columbia, providing compensation to the owners of some 3,100 bondsmen. The law marked the first time the federal government had enacted immediate emancipation. By June Congress abolished slavery in the Western territories, sweeping the war's overriding cause into one marvelously ironic heap of refuse. As Union armies advanced in this ever-widening conflagration, black people were the human asset both sides desperately needed, and they forced a new moral economy on each side's leadership.

In July 1862 Congress passed the Second Confiscation Act, which explicitly freed slaves of all persons "in rebellion," declared blacks "forever free of their servitude," and excluded no part of the slaveholding South. The law encouraged colonization to some "tropical" land, but it also suggested enlistment of freedmen as soldiers. Lincoln, meanwhile, with his armies enduring bloody defeats in Virginia from June to August, began to draft an executive order about slavery.

In the tense weeks of August 1862, Lincoln invited a delegation of African-American leaders from the Washington area to the White House to hear his views on colonization. The encounter was decidedly Lincoln's worst hour in race relations. Whites and blacks, the president lectured his guests, were "different races" that ultimately "should be separated." Lincoln acknowledged slavery as "the greatest wrong," but also maintained that without the "presence" of blacks, the war would not exist. Then he aggressively recruited these leaders to volunteer to lead colonization efforts to remove black people from the country. The meeting was roundly condemned by prominent black spokesmen, including Douglass.

But the ambiguous Lincoln kept everyone guessing, as he prepared to launch a bombshell that would reorient the purpose of the war.

On Sept. 22, 1862, five days after the horrible battle of Antietam, Lincoln, sensing an opportunity proffered by military success, issued his preliminary Emancipation Proclamation. In this document, he announced his intention to free all slaves in the states still "in rebellion" on Jan. 1, 1863. He promised compensation for the loss of slave property and aid in colonization schemes if a state wished to create them. Most important, the president pledged the full "military and naval authority" in helping blacks in "any efforts they may make for their actual freedom." Critics said this was merely "military" emancipation with limited legal scope. But it was an extraordinary beginning to a larger story.

The 100 days between Lincoln's preliminary and final emancipation proclamations were an uncertain and hopeful time for both advocates and opponents of black freedom. In Lincoln's Annual Message to Congress in early December 1862, he once again offered an elaborate defense of compensation, colonization and gradual abolition. But he also made amply clear that if the nation was to live, slavery would have to die.

On New Year's Day, 1863, Lincoln signed a great document, which he would later describe as the "central act of my administration, and the greatest event of the nineteenth century." Throughout the war zones Union forces received thousands of copies of the proclamation, some in miniature, to distribute among the black population. In some places the document was read aloud among throngs of freedpeople.

Despite its apparent limitations—critics then and since have argued that it is a dry legal letter that applied only to those regions over which federal forces exercised no immediate power—the resounding phrase "then, thenceforward and forever free" entered the lexicon of American civil religion. Lincoln wrote the proclamation in the language of a legal brief because he anticipated that slaveholders would challenge it in court for restitution of their property once the war was over.

Lincoln freed slaves as a war measure under his powers as commander in chief, and some have argued that such a reality robs the document of moral grandeur. But the proclamation's impact on the war and on slaves in the South was no less real for all its legal dullness and Constitutional caution. Every forward movement of the Union armies and navies would now be a liberating step. The proclamation served as an open invitation to slaves to flee at every opportunity to Union forces; even more important, it authorized the enlistment of black soldiers and sailors.

At a contraband camp in Washington, a crowd of 600 black men, women and children gathered to sing and testify through most of the evening of Dec. 31, 1862. In chorus after chorus of "Go Down Moses," they announced the magnitude of their exodus. One newly supplied verse concluded with "Go Down, Abraham, away down Dixie's land, tell Jeff Davis to let my people go!" In between songs and chants, members of the group stood up and told personal stories of their experience as slaves. At two minutes before midnight, the entire assemblage knelt on the ground in silent prayer.

But those contraband camps were not model refugee stations merely for the freedmen's celebrations. They were destinations of hope, but also disease-ridden death traps. Harriet Jacobs, the former fugitive slave and author of the now celebrated narrative, "Incidents in the Life of a Slave Girl," labored heroically as a relief worker during 1862 in the Washington camps. In September, she observed "men, women, and children all huddled together...in the most pitiable condition...sick with measles, diphtheria, scarlet and typhoid fever." It was not uncommon to see 10 deaths a day at the camp, Jacobs reported. Despite the misery, Jacobs felt overwhelmed by the courage and determination of the freedpeople as they arrived in droves. "What but the love of freedom," she concluded, "could bring these old people thither?"

The choices and agonies that emancipation wrought are exhibited in a letter written by John Boston, a Maryland fugitive slave, to his wife, Elizabeth, in January 1862:

"It is with grate joy I take this time to let you know Whare I am now in Safety in the 14th regiment of Brooklyn this day I can Adres you thank god as a free man...as the lord led the Children of Isrel to the land of Canon So he led me to a land Whare Freedom Will

rain in spite of earth and hell...I am free from the Slavers Lash."
Boston concluded tenderly: "Dear wife I must Close rest yourself
Contented I am free...Write my dear Soon...Kiss Daniel For me."

Surviving sources do not tell us whether the Bostons were
ever reunited in freedom. But such a letter demonstrates the depth
with which former slaves embraced freedom and the human pain
through which it was achieved.

'The Best Servant by Far'
By KEVIN LEVIN

In the spring of 1861 John Christopher Winsmith of Spartanburg,
S.C., went to war with all the enthusiasm, determination and
clarity of a member of the slaveholding class. Winsmith understood what was at stake, and he urged "the whole South to make
common cause against the hordes of abolitionists who are swarming
Southwards."

The framing of the war in such stark terms not only reflected
the region's economic and political dependency on slave labor, but a
sense of urgency manifested in the violent memory of Nat Turner's
1831 insurrection and, more recently, the failed raid at Harpers Ferry
led by John Brown. White Southerners convinced themselves that
only outsiders could upset what they believed to be an organic, pater-
nalistic master-slave relationship.

The Winsmith family, like other slaveholding families, expected
their slaves to remain loyal and productive in exchange for a benevolent hand. Christopher, as he was known to his family, not only set
out to defend this way of life, but he brought a piece of it with him—
in the form of a personal body servant named Spencer.

During the next 16 months Christopher and Spencer remained
side by side, moving from South Carolina to Virginia and back again.
Although Spencer's legal status never changed, the challenges associated with being away from home, as well as the exigencies of war,
stretched the boundaries of the master-slave relationship to its limit.

Their story fits into a broader narrative of the dissolution of slavery on a personal level and, ultimately, the defeat of the Confederacy.

John Christopher Winsmith was born in 1834 to John Winsmith, a member of the state General Assembly, and his wife, Catherine. At age 15, Winsmith attended the Citadel Military Academy in Charleston, but he did not graduate owing to poor conduct: in November 1851 he was brought in front of the college's board of visitors for defrauding "a Negro woman by passing to her a copper coin covered with quicksilver for amount greater than its value." One can only guess at the nature of this transaction, but it may have been sufficiently embarrassing to prevent him from reapplying when given the opportunity.

Dismissal from the Citadel, however, did not prevent Winsmith from pursuing a law degree at Charleston College, which he completed in 1859. Two years later, he left for war.

Both Winsmith and Spencer departed the family home of Camp Hill with heavy responsibilities, the former having been commissioned a lieutenant in Company G of the Fifth South Carolina Volunteer Infantry. While Winsmith learned the art of command, Spencer acclimated himself to his role as camp servant. Early in the war thousands of slaves followed their masters to war; their presence not only pointed to the social rank of their owners, but also satisfied the need to mobilize as much of the Confederacy's population as possible in the face of a much larger enemy. Indeed, tens of thousands of slaves would be impressed by the Confederate government by the end of the war to work on military projects, often against the protests of their owners, who viewed the policy as a violation of their property rights.

In addition to ensuring that Winsmith's quarters were kept clean, Spencer washed his master's clothes, prepared his food, brushed his uniforms, polished his swords and buckles, ran errands, foraged and tended his horse. Among all these responsibilities, Winsmith noted, "Spencer has proved himself an excellent cook."

While it is impossible to ignore Spencer's instrumental value to Winsmith, the two likely found comfort in the shared experience of living away from loved ones. For Spencer, communication with his wife, Peg, and children took place through Winsmith's letters, which regularly included a passing "howdye" or thanks for a recent package toward the end before signing off.

The emotional pain of separation for Spencer was most likely balanced to some degree by the experience of increased privileges. His responsibilities left him with free time to earn extra money, which he did by washing for other men in the company—an arrangement that Winsmith consented to and acknowledged: "He is making more money than any of us."

Winsmith could have said no, of course, but one thing comes clearly through his letters: Winsmith trusted Spencer, and, in a way, vice versa. Spencer tended to Winsmith during a brief bout with measles, and was even on the receiving end of care when dealing with his own health problems. Spencer performed his duties admirably, and even continued them when Winsmith was assigned to serve on a court-martial trial in May 1861. Winsmith declared Spencer to be "the best servant by far in Camp."

A reflection of Winsmith's trust can be found in his decision to take Spencer along on picket duty while stationed in Northern Virginia in September 1861. Along with the rest of the patrol, Spencer "could see the Yankees moving about," but he made no attempt to flee. A few days after returning from picket duty, Winsmith told his family that "I do not have any fears of his being deceived by the Yankees."

Winsmith's confidence in Spencer persisted through the first winter of the war and during their journey back to South Carolina in May 1862. By then Winsmith had been transferred to Company H of the First South Carolina Volunteer Infantry and elected as its captain. The unit was first assigned to a Confederate force on James Island, just outside Charleston. Following the battle of Secessionville in June 1862, and as part of the organization of his new regiment, Winsmith spent more time away from camp, first to procure bounties for new enlistees and later to organize conscripts from the area around Columbia. This meant leaving "Spencer in charge of my affairs at camp."

It was in Columbia where Winsmith learned that Spencer was "missing." Writing to his father, Winsmith promised to provide additional details once he was back in camp, but he urged his father to send another servant as if assuming the unlikelihood of Spencer's return. He learned little upon returning to camp in July:

> He went out on Sunday morning the 20th in company with another boy from the Regt, having obtained a permit from Lt. Nesbitt to go for potatoes near River's house, which is not more than ¾ mile from the Stono River, in which there were some Boats. They did not return, and their absence being reported to Maj. Duncan, he sent out several companies to scour the surrounding wood, but nothing could be seen of them, nor of any trace where the Yankees had been. It seems to be a doubtful point whether they went off to the Yankees of their own accord, or were captured. Most of the men in the Co. think Spencer was captured, as he took nothing away with him and went off in his shirt sleeves, and from his conduct nothing had occurred to make them suspect that he meditated on escape. The watch, which he wished to take, was a galvanized one. I hear, that he had bought it in town, and wanted to dispose of it as I had told him he would go home soon. He brought all my things over right when our Regt moved, and I have missed nothing. If he was captured he will very probably make his escape at the first opportunity.

As that last sentence indicates, Winsmith struggled coming to terms with Spencer's sudden and unexpected disappearance, even going so far as to suggest that his partner had "persuaded him off after they left camp." He would consider any number of explanations but for a desire on his part to be free. Finally Winsmith comforted himself by falling back on the common stereotype that, "negroes are very uncertain and tricky creatures so it is difficult to tell what is the real truth in this case."

The loss of Spencer tugged at Winsmith's emotions, at least at first. "You may know I miss him very much," he admitted to his father, "but I will not let the matter worry me in the least as I know it will do no good." Winsmith's sincere feelings of loss, however, did not overshadow the instrumental role that Spencer had played in his life, and in short order he pressured his father to send along another slave. By the beginning of August, Winsmith had "nothing more to write" about his former servant.

One of the many tragedies of slavery is its legacy of illiteracy and the lack of a substantial record that gives voice to slaves such as Spencer. In this case, as in so many others, we are forced to rely on brief references from the man who claimed legal title to him to discern what he thought of his own condition. Unfortunately, we know precious little about how Spencer experienced the war. The most we can say is that Winsmith, for all his claims to "know" Spencer, understood very little about him.

Under the Knife
By TERRY L. JONES

On Aug. 28, 1862, Maj. Gen. Richard S. Ewell's Confederate division was fighting desperately in the fields and pine thickets near Groveton, Va., during the Second Bull Run campaign. Heavy fire was coming from unidentified soldiers in a thicket 100 yards in front. To get a better look, Ewell knelt on his left knee to peer under the limbs. Suddenly a 500-grain (about 1.1 ounces) lead Minié ball skimmed the ground and struck him on the left kneecap. Some nearby Alabama soldiers lay down their muskets and hurried over to carry him from the field, but the fiery Ewell barked: "Put me down, and give them hell! I'm no better than any other wounded soldier, to stay on the field."

The general lay on a pile of rocks while two badly wounded soldiers nearby cried out for help until stretcher bearers finally arrived on the scene. Despite their own painful wounds, the two men insisted Ewell be carried off first, but he instructed the litter bearers to take them away. Hours after being wounded, Ewell was finally placed on a stretcher and taken to the rear. Dr. Hunter McGuire, Gen. Thomas J. "Stonewall" Jackson's medical director, amputated Ewell's leg the next day.

Campbell Brown, Ewell's aide and future stepson, witnessed the operation. McGuire and his assistants sedated Ewell with chloroform and used a scalpel to cut around his leg just above the knee. In his drug-induced fog, Ewell feverishly issued orders to troops, but he did not appear to feel any pain until McGuire applied the bone saw. According to Brown, the general then "stretched both arms upward & said: 'Oh! My God!'"

McGuire opened up the amputated limb to show the officers in the room that the operation had been necessary. The bullet had "pierced the joint & followed the leg down for some inches," Brown later wrote. "When the leg was opened, we found the knee-cap split half in two—the head of the tibia knocked into several pieces—& that the ball had followed the marrow of the bone for six inches breaking the bone itself into small splinters & finally had split into two pieces on a sharp edge of bone." Brown and a slave wrapped the bloody limb in an oilcloth, and the slave "decently buried" it in the garden. Brown kept the two pieces of bullet as souvenirs for his mother, who was engaged to Ewell, although he never told the general he had done so.

Rank was no protection from such brutal operations, and General Ewell was just one of many high-ranking officers to face the surgeon's knife. In fact, statistically speaking, a Confederate general was more likely to require medical treatment than a private. Almost one out of four died in the war, compared with 1 out of 10 Union generals. Of the 250 Confederate generals who were wounded, 24 underwent amputations. General Ewell was one of the lucky ones who survived and returned to duty many months later with an artificial leg.

Approximately two out of every three Civil War wounds treated by surgeons were to the extremities because few soldiers hit in the head, chest or stomach lived long enough to make it back to a field hospital. From a technical point of view, damaged limb bones presented the greatest challenge to surgeons. The war's most common projectile, the large, oblong Minié ball, often tumbled when it hit the body and caused much more damage to bone than smoothbore musket balls. One Confederate surgeon observed, "The shattering, splintering, and splitting of a long bone by the impact of a minié or Enfield ball were, in many instances, both remarkable and frightful." When bone was damaged, surgeons had to decide quickly on one of three possible treatments. If it was a simple fracture, a wooden or plaster splint was applied, but if the bone was shattered the surgeon performed either a resection or an amputation.

Resection involved cutting open the limb, sawing out the damaged bone, and then closing the incision. It was a time-consuming procedure and required considerable surgical skill, but some surgeons became quite proficient at it. After the Battle of Savage's Station in 1862, one Union surgeon completed 26 resections of the shoulder and elbow in a single day. He was said to be able to eat and drink coffee at the operating table while pieces of bone, muscle and ligaments piled up around him.

Besides being a difficult procedure, resection also carried a high risk of profuse bleeding, infection and postoperative necrosis of the flesh. Successful resections, however, allowed the patient to keep his limb, although it was limp, useful merely to "fill a sleeve." Because of the time required, resections were not always practical when there were large numbers of patients to treat, but they were used more frequently after surgeons learned that amputations had a much higher mortality rate.

The amputation process was fairly simple. After a circular cut was made completely around the limb, the bone was sawed through, and the blood vessels and arteries sewn shut. To prevent future pain, nerves were then pulled out as far as possible with forceps, cut and released to retract away from the end of the stump. Finally, clippers and a rasp were used to smooth the end of the exposed bone. Sometimes the raw and bloody stump was left untreated to heal gradually, and sometimes excess skin was pulled down and sewn over the wound. Speed was essential in all amputations to lessen blood loss and prevent shock. An amputation at the knee was expected to take just three minutes.

Civil War surgeons almost always had chloroform to anesthetize patients before an amputation. The chloroform was dripped onto a piece of cloth held over the patient's face until he was unconscious. Although not an exact science, the procedure worked well, and few patients died from overdose. Opium pills, opium dust and injections were also available to control postoperative pain.

The mistaken belief that amputations were routinely performed without anesthetics can be partially attributed to the fact that chloroform did not put patients into a deep unconscious state. Bystanders who saw moaning, writhing patients being held down on the table assumed no anesthetic was being used. As in the case of General Ewell, patients often reacted to the scalpel and bone saw as if in pain, but they did not remember it afterward. After his left arm was amputated (Dr. McGuire also performed that operation), Stonewall Jackson mentioned that he had heard the most beautiful music while under the chloroform. Upon reflection, he said, "I believe it was the sawing of the bone."

Because surgeons preferred to operate outdoors where lighting and ventilation were better, thousands of soldiers witnessed amputations firsthand. Passers-by and even wounded men waiting their turn watched as surgeons sawed off arms and legs and tossed them onto ever growing piles. The poet Walt Whitman witnessed such a scene when he visited Fredericksburg in search of his wounded brother. "One of the first things that met my eyes in camp," he wrote, "was a heap of feet, arms, legs, etc., under a tree in front of a hospital." Indeed, after the December 1862 Battle of Fredericksburg, Union surgeons performed almost 500 amputations.

Early in the war surgeons earned the nickname "Saw-bones" because they seemed eager to amputate. This eagerness stemmed not from overzealousness but from the knowledge that infections developed quickly in mangled flesh, and amputation was the most effective way to prevent it. Those limbs removed within 48 hours of injury were called primary amputations, and those removed after 48 hours were called secondary amputations. The mortality rate for primary amputations was about 25 percent; that for secondary amputations was twice as high, thanks to the fact that most secondary amputations were performed after gangrene or blood poisoning developed in the wound. Surgeons learned that amputating the limb after it became infected actually caused the infection to spread, and patients frequently died. Thus, the patient was much more likely to survive if a primary amputation was performed before infection set in.

Primary amputations were also preferred because it was easier and less painful to transport an amputee than a soldier whose broken bones and inflamed tissue made the slightest jostle sheer torture. One surgeon admitted that an excessive number of amputations may have been performed during the war, but he added, "I have no hesitation in saying that far more lives were lost from refusal to amputate than by amputation."

Where the amputation was made on the limb was as vital to survival as when it was done. Generally, the higher up the amputation was made, the higher the mortality rate. This was especially true for thigh wounds. More than half of all soldiers who suffered a femur wound died, and amputations at or near the hip joint had a 66 percent mortality rate in the Confederate Army.

Nonetheless, it is estimated that approximately three out of four soldiers survived amputations. Amazingly, some, like Confederate Brig. Gen. Francis T. Nicholls, endured more than one. His lower left arm was amputated after he was shot at the First Battle of Winchester and his left foot was taken off when he was wounded at Chancellorsville. After the war, Nicholls was a popular Louisiana governor who was said to ask people to vote for "all that's left of General Nicholls" and to support him for governor because he was "too one sided to be a judge."

Often, surviving an amputation seemed to be completely random. While some, like Ewell and Nicholls, seemed unhindered by the surgery, others died from what appeared to be rather minor wounds. Two members of Company B, 19th Michigan Infantry, were shot in the index finger in the same battle during the Atlanta campaign. One man treated himself by cutting off the mangled finger with his pocket knife. He wrapped the stub in a handkerchief and waited until the battle was over to have the wound dressed at the field hospital. The other soldier went immediately to the surgeon for a proper amputation. Gangrene set in within days, and the surgeon was later forced to amputate his arm at the shoulder. The soldier died soon afterward. The man who treated himself made a full recovery and lived to a ripe old age.

Taking care of amputees put a significant strain on both wartime governments. The Union provided its disabled soldiers with prosthetic limbs made from cork wood, metal or rubber and gave amputees $8 a month as a pension. The Confederacy was unable to be so generous and by 1864 was providing just 10 percent of the needed prostheses. Incredibly, Mississippi's single greatest state expenditure a year after the war ended was the purchase of artificial limbs for its veterans, which consumed 20 percent of the state's budget. Some amputee veterans were forced to look after themselves and paired up to form "shoe exchanges" where they chipped in to buy a pair of shoes and each man took the one he needed.

Amputation was the most common Civil War surgical procedure. Union surgeons performed approximately 30,000 compared to just over 16,000 by American surgeons in World War II. One postwar British traveler noted that amputees were "everywhere in town and farm communities through the South." The men who had survived the surgeon's knife were a visible reminder of the Civil War for decades.

The South's Man in London
By ANDRE M. FLECHE

I n late 1861, a 27-year-old naturalized Alabamian from Switzerland named Henry Hotze was sent on a secret mission to London. Officially, he would be a Confederate commercial agent, negotiating trade deals between Britain and the South. But his real task, given to him by the Confederate secretary of state, Robert Mercer Taliaferro Hunter, was much more sensitive: to persuade the British people to support the Confederate cause.

Hotze's mission represented a departure in Confederate foreign policy. When the war began in April 1861, Confederate officials had hoped that the economic power of cotton alone would force the British government to intervene on the Confederacy's behalf. For much of the 19th century, Britain had carried on a booming trade with the American South; Southern plantations supplied cotton fiber to the bustling textile mills of Birmingham and Manchester, and, in return, Southern planters furnished their homes with British goods and filled their libraries with British books. Few Confederate patriots could have imagined that Britain could long tolerate any disruption to this lucrative commerce.

To speed British action, early in the war the Confederate president, Jefferson Davis, ordered growers and shippers to withhold cotton from the world market. He imagined that his embargo would wreak financial havoc, causing factories to close and throwing thousands of laborers out of work—and that, to save the world financial system from collapse, the British government would have no choice but to help arrange a cease-fire, or, better yet, join the war against the Union. Davis's stratagem became known as "King Cotton Diplomacy."

It was a miserable failure. London was less reliant on Southern cotton than Davis had assumed. A Union naval blockade began to gradually choke off Southern ports, making the very premise of King Cotton diplomacy moot. The Royal Navy had not taken to the seas to ensure the flow of cotton, nor had officials in London committed troops to the cause of Southern independence. The British government had not yet even agreed to officially recognize the Confederacy as an independent nation. It was Henry Hotze's job to figure out what had gone wrong.

Hotze arrived in London in early 1862. What he found worried him. The lack of Southern cotton had not troubled the English people nearly as much as the Confederate leadership had assumed it would. A mild winter had allowed British workingmen and -women to make ends meet, even while working fewer hours. Some speculators, cotton wholesalers and merchants had actually profited by the cotton shortage as prices rose and importers shifted to growers in India and Egypt to meet demand. In general, Hotze found most Englishmen "cold and indifferent" toward what he called the Confederacy's "great war for a nation's life."

Though the picture looked bleak at the moment, Hotze didn't give up all hope. British public opinion might seem apathetic, but he also found it "in a fusible state." He concluded that Southern officials had put too much faith in economic self-interest and had not spent enough time appealing to the hearts and minds of the British people. Determined to seize the opportunity, he proposed to carry out a propaganda campaign on behalf of the Confederacy.

To many white Southerners, Henry Hotze appeared to be the perfect person to represent their cause abroad. In the years before the war, the young European-born American had earned a growing reputation as an academic celebrity in the South. After immigrating to the United States, he took up a career in journalism and quickly embraced Southern causes. During the 1850s, he explained that, as a native of the Swiss republic, he cherished the principles of local self-government. "States rights and federal powers," he declared, had been frequently "discussed over his cradle."

White Southerners found his views on slavery especially acceptable. As a student in Switzerland, Hotze had developed a keen interest in history, anthropology and the study of race, and he came to the United States convinced that racial characteristics played a key role in determining a person's character, capabilities and intellect. He first became widely known in the South when he translated into English the work of the French count Arthur de Gobineau, who had argued that mankind was divided into three different and inherently unequal races, the white, the black and the yellow. Hotze left his reading of Gobineau a believer in the superiority of the white race and a defender of slavery.

In England, Hotze came determined to employ his views in defense of the Confederacy. He believed that if Englishmen only understood the principles undergirding the struggle of the South, then they would enthusiastically embrace the Southern cause. In early 1862, he published several editorials in British newspapers arguing for recognition of the Confederacy, but in the weeks after they appeared he began to work on a much more ambitious undertaking. In May, he began publishing his own weekly newspaper, which he named the Index.

Under Hotze's direction, the Index became the leading expositor of the Confederate cause in Europe, and one of the most important anywhere. Though the front page always printed information on cotton markets to call attention to English economic interests, the real substance of the paper came in its editorial columns. Hotze recruited writers from Europe and America who shared his intellectual commitments. He chose one of his English writers for his "devotion to the cause of national independence," and he worked hard to recruit famous Southern intellectuals, including the University of Virginia professor Albert Taylor Bledsoe and John Rueben Thompson, former editor of the Southern Literary Messenger.

Together, Hotze and his writers outlined the intellectual substance of the Confederate cause. First and foremost, they seized on the right of national self-determination. They proclaimed that 19th-century people lived in an "age of liberal thought," in which no serious thinker could deny the right of any people to establish their own government if they wished. The American Revolution of the 1770s and the French Revolution of 1789 had made that quite clear to the world, and the Confederate revolution should benefit from the precedents they had set. The South, one editorial maintained, fought for rights "which have never been disputed to any people in modern times."

The editorials in Hotze's paper worked hard to depict Confederates as heroic patriots fighting for home rule, and they pleaded with Englishmen to recognize the fact. Southerners, one article reasoned, desired only "that self-government which Englishmen practice themselves and usually commend in others." Hotze and his contributors wholeheartedly believed that Southerners had already established a nation, and it only awaited British action to secure its well-deserved independence. "We have just witnessed in the New World," one article declared, "the sublime spectacle of the birth and fiery baptism of a nation."

While these articles appealed to the liberal sentiments of the British people, ultimately Hotze and his collaborators refused to apologize that this new nation was founded on a defense of slavery. In fact, they argued that slavery would give the Confederate nation peculiar unity and strength. Slavery, the argument went, would endow the South with the "intrinsic power to create wealth," while at the same time managing the social inequality between whites that wealth engendered. The British social system had not fared so well. In Britain, a wealthy ruling class had shut out white workingmen from political power, which led to class resentment and hatred. Southerners, however, had extended political rights to all white men by basing social divisions on what Hotze believed to be the natural fault lines of race. Hotze called the position "liberal conservatism," and he believed it would redeem the world.

Despite Hotze's high-profile efforts, "liberal conservatism" did not work any better than had "King Cotton Diplomacy" in persuading the British to join the war. Though Hotze published his paper into April 1865 and beyond, Britain never officially recognized the Confederacy as an independent nation.

Hotze's efforts did, however, effectively elucidate the principles of Confederate nationalism by linking the achievement of self-determination with the practices of racial subordination and slavery—principles that, in various forms, continued to shape nation-building efforts well into the 20th century, as segregation, imperialism and the tragic history of the First and Second World Wars amply demonstrated.

Boxers, Briefs and Battles
By JEAN HUETS

Civil War soldiers carried many valuables: letters from home, photographs, and locks of hair from wives, sweethearts and babies. But they held a less romantic article much nearer to their hearts, and sometimes much dearer: their undergarments.

History favors epic battles, stirring speeches, presidents and generals and the economic and political forces that transform the lives of millions. Yet mere underwear has a story to tell, a story that covers the breadth of the Civil War, from home front to battlefield.

A full suit of mid-19th-century men's underwear consisted of a shirt, "drawers" and socks. Like today, men's underwear at the time, unlike women's, did not provide structure to the body. Rather, cover, warmth and hygiene were the order of the day—though the hygiene part did not always work out. The term for undershirt was usually just "shirt"; shirts as we know them today were often called blouses or top-shirts. Undershirts were square-cut pullovers, voluminous and long. Buttons and sometimes laces at the neck fastened them.

Drawers, meanwhile, were sometimes knee-length, usually ankle-length. Two or three buttons closed a center fly. Lacing or a buckle at the back waistband adjusted the fit. Tape ties or drawstrings at the ankle (or knee) kept drawer legs from riding up. Possibly the drawstrings also functioned as sock garters. For many men of the period, shirt tails stood in for drawers. Ribbed and knit fabric primarily went to socks, which were nearly always woolen. When not hand-knit, the tubular body was knit at mills, with heels and toes added by hand.

Mills provided the fabric, which women pieceworkers assembled at home by hand and sewing machines. "In certain districts" of rural New Hampshire, Maine and Vermont, reported one New England manufacturer, "the whole female population is employed, in spare moments, at this work."

It's nearly impossible to imagine rural women enjoying "spare moments" while running farms in the absence of men, in addition to housekeeping and child care. Women who relied solely on piece-work struggled as well. One "smart operator" finished four pairs of drawers daily, breaking "long enough to make herself a cup of tea and eat a piece of bread," reported The New York Times. For her 12-hour day, she earned 16 and a quarter cents. Women in mills might make even less. By comparison, a Union private earned about 43 cents a day, plus rations and clothing. Pieceworkers in New York and other cities organized, but contractors, or as The New York Sun described them, "fiends in the shape of men," continued to reap huge profits while "driving ten thousand working women into the very jaws of hell."

For subsistence, patriotism, love or profit, women North and South worked hard to supplement Army-issue underwear, sometimes ripping their own clothes apart for fabric. And many soldiers, especially those in the South, preferred their underwear homemade; wives, sisters and enslaved women stitched a variety of fabrics, especially canton flannel (cotton flannel fleeced on one side) and cotton-and-wool blend flannel, into drawers and shirts.

Recruits whose mothers never issued underpants could be fooled into wearing their new drawers on parade. They presented themselves in august company. Gen. Ulysses S. Grant himself once appeared in "parade uniform": one night, when gunboats threatened the depot at City Point, Va., reported an eyewitness in The Century magazine, "the general came hurriedly into the office. He had drawn on his top-boots over his drawers, and put on his uniform frock-coat, the skirt of which reached about to the tops of the boots and made up for the absence of trousers."

Underwear was always in short supply. Prisoners of war suffered most. Lincoln's quartermaster general, Montgomery Meigs, stipulated that "from the 30th of April to the 1st of October neither drawers nor socks will be issued to prisoners of war, except to the sick." A Union prisoner testified that hundreds of his fellow captives went "without even a pair of drawers to cover their nakedness."

Such shortages made underwear coveted spoils of war. When Gen. Thomas J. "Stonewall" Jackson's men raided a Union supply depot, "sumptuous underclothing was fitted over limbs sunburnt, sore and vermin-splotched." A Confederate cadet spotted his own monogram on underwear worn by a Federal whose pants were cut open to tend a wound. The soldier confessed to looting a Lynchburg, Va., house where the cadet had stowed his trunk.

Getting fresh underwear by issue, mail or pillage was easier than laundering and carrying extra. One Confederate soldier, Carlton McCarthy, preferred to wear all his clothes "until the enemy's knapsacks or the folks at home supplied a change. Certainly it did not pay to carry around clean clothes while waiting for the time to use them."

Francis Ackerman, a volunteer from New York, gleaned fresh clothes from the fields at the Third Battle of Winchester, in September 1864. His account of finding a riderless horse mingles the grotesque tragedy of battle with the dry humor so characteristic of War memoirs. "I discovered a horse with one of his legs shot off, on his back a good outfit," he wrote. "Feeling rather lively from life inside my clothes," he "concluded to examine the wounded horse, and was rewarded by finding a clean full suit of underwear. I stripped on the battle field, and with thankful heart put it on, the first change I had in six weeks." More fastidious men changed into clean underwear faithfully—once a week.

Regardless of how often one changed his drawers, the louse ruled. "It preyed alike on the just and the unjust. It inserted its bill as confidingly into the body of the major-general as of the lowest private," wrote one memoirist. Laundering in boiling water didn't rout the "gray backs"; instead, taking a page from their battlefield playbooks, soldiers relied on "skirmishing," or painstaking search-and-destroy efforts to pick them off one by one.

In any case, boiling underwear could get a man into hot water. When

Gen. Thomas Lanier Clingman of North Carolina wrote his mother to send drawers, she answered back, "I am certain that your flannel is injured by washing. It should not be put in very hot water or boiled at all," and it should be washed in "moderately warm water with soap and rinsed in warm soap suds, which will keep it soft and free from shrinking. At least, you can direct your washer to do so." General Clingman was 50 years old when his mom told him how to wash his underwear.

Even clean and vermin-free, underwear was rarely comfortable. Harsh laundering subtracted durability and comfort. Availability and cost, not fit or season, dictated cut and fabric. In summer a soldier sweltered in flannel or discarded his drawers and got chafed raw by rough, sweaty wool pants.

The manufacture and use of underwear reflects several aspects of the Civil War, and it holds a mirror to our own times. Labor was both empowered and exploited by the cascade of contract money that poured in for its production, which in turn helped usher in the corruption and wealth of the Gilded Age. Slavery and regionalism weren't the only things that fractured our country. A chasm existed between the "dainty men" in their boiled shirts and the common herd in homespun plaid and flannel, between impoverished millworkers and pieceworkers—often immigrants—and women whose elegance was purchased by their husbands' manufacturing enterprises.

Most of all, the humble suit of underwear highlights the Civil War soldier himself: his endurance and fortitude, his ability to make do with whatever conditions and supplies came along and his sense of humor, which pervades even the most dire accounts of battle and camp life.

General Grant's Infamous Order

By JONATHAN D. SARNA

I, a peaceable, law abiding citizen, pursuing my legitimate business at Paducah, Kentucky, where I have been a resident for nearly four years, have been driven from my home, my business, and all that is dear to me, at the short notice of twenty-four hours; not for any crime committed, but simply because I was born of Jewish parents," said a young merchant named Cesar Kaskel to reporters in late December 1862. The accompanying headline disclosed why Kaskel was so abruptly ordered out. It read: "Expulsion of Jews from General Grant's Department."

The order, known as General Orders No. 11, expelled Jews from the territory under Gen. Ulysses S. Grant's command—which stretched from Northern Mississippi to Cairo, Ill. and from the Mississippi River to the Tennessee River. It was issued on Dec. 17, 1862, and came directly from Grant's headquarters in Holly Springs, Miss. It read:

> The Jews, as a class violating every regulation of trade established by the Treasury Department and also department orders, are hereby expelled from the department within twenty-four hours from the receipt of this order.
>
> Post commanders will see that all of this class of people be furnished passes and required to leave, and any one returning after such notification will be arrested and held in confinement until an opportunity occurs of sending them out as prisoners, unless furnished with permit from headquarters.
>
> No passes will be given these people to visit headquarters for the purpose of making personal application for trade permits.
>
> By order of Maj. Gen. U.S. Grant
>
> JNO. A. RAWLINS, Assistant Adjutant-General

For months, Grant had been worried about cotton speculators and smugglers in the area under his command. His department seethed with blockade runners who traded "upon the miseries of the country." Canny traders could turn $100 into $2,000 by smuggling Southern cotton to Northern ports and quinine, bacon and finished goods in the other direction. If he could just put a stop to the smuggling, Grant thought, he could put real economic pressure on the South and the terrible war would end sooner.

Such trade was, of course, illegal, and some of the smugglers that

Grant's men caught were Jews. America's Jewish population had bal-
looned from about 15,000 in 1840 to some 150,000 in 1860, mostly
immigrants from Central Europe. Large numbers of those immigrants
became peddlers and merchants, marked by their European accents
and foreign ways. Some of them, during the war, peddled contraband.

Lots of non-Jews, including many soldiers, likewise pursued fast
money by trading in illicit goods. Assistant Secretary of War Charles
A. Dana (who himself secretly speculated in cotton) reported in early
1863 that "every colonel, captain of quartermaster is in secret partnership with some operator in cotton; every soldier dreams of adding
a bale of cotton to his monthly pay." In Memphis, the leading city in
Grant's territory, "the amount of plunder & bribery" was "beyond all
calculation," according to Dana. "Honesty is the exception and pecu-
lation"—that is, embezzlement—"the rule."

Nevertheless, in the eyes of Grant and of many other Americans,
all smugglers and speculators and traders were Jews, whether they
were actually Jewish or not—just as Southerners dubbed all Northerners "Yankees," whether or not they hailed from New England. Grant
wanted as few of them as possible in the area under his command.

In July 1862, Grant ordered the commander of the District of
the Mississippi to "examine all baggage of all speculators coming
South," and to turn back those who were carrying gold. "Jews," he
admonished, "should receive special attention." In August, a soldier
newspaper quoted Grant as calling Jews "a nuisance" that he had
plans to "abate." On Nov. 9, as he prepared to move South in preparation for the decisive battle at Vicksburg, Grant tightened his regulations against Jews: "Refuse all permits to come south of Jackson for
the present," he ordered. "The Isrealites especially should be kept
out." The very next day he strengthened that order: "no Jews are to
be permitted to travel on the Rail Road southward from any point . . .
they are such an intolerable nuisance that the Department must be
purged" of them. Writing in early December to Gen. William T. Sherman, whose quartermaster had created problems by selling cotton "to
a Jew by the name of Haas," Grant explained that "in consequence of
the total disregard and evasion of orders by the Jews my policy is to
exclude them so far as practicable from the Dept."

But until Dec. 17, Grant had not gone so far as to expel Jews from his department. Indeed, when Col. John Van Deusen Du Bois on Dec. 8 angrily ordered "all Cotton-Speculators, Jews and other Vagrants having no honest means of support, except trading upon the miseries of their Country" to leave Holly Springs, and gave them "twenty-four hours or they will be sent to duty in the trenches," Grant insisted that the Draconian order be rescinded. "Instructions from Washington," he reminded Du Bois, "are to encourage getting Cotton out of the country." Notwithstanding his private opinions and actions, Grant understood that he still had publicly to uphold official government policy, which permitted those loyal to the Union to trade in cotton.

All that changed on Dec. 17. Grant, according to multiple sources, received a visit that day from his 68-year-old father, Jesse R. Grant, accompanied by members the prominent Mack family of Cincinnati, significant Jewish clothing manufacturers. Harman, Henry and Simon Mack, as part of an ingenious scheme, had formed a secret partnership with the elder Grant. In return for 25 percent of their profits, he agreed to accompany them to his son's Mississippi headquarters, act as their agent to "procure a permit for them to purchase cotton" and help them secure the means to transport that cotton to New York.

According to the journalist Sylvanus Cadwallader, a witness, General Grant waxed indignant at his father's crass attempt to profit from his son's military status, and raged at the Jewish traders who "entrapped his old father into such an unworthy undertaking." He refused to provide the permit, sent the Macks homeward "on the first train for the north" and, in high dudgeon, immediately issued the order expelling "Jews as a class" from his territory.

Fortunately for the thousands of Jews who lived in the territory under his command, Grant was soon distracted. Less than 72 hours after his order was issued, his forces at Holly Springs were raided by 3,500 Confederate troops. Simultaneous raids to the north inflicted significant damage to Grant's lines and tore up 50 miles of railroad and telegraph lines. Communications to and from Grant's headquarters were disrupted for weeks. As a result, news of Grant's order spread slowly, sparing many Jews who might otherwise have been banished.

To be sure, some Jewish traders in the vicinity of Grant's army were treated roughly. A "Mr. Silberman" from Chicago, temporarily in Holly Springs, was reportedly imprisoned for 12 hours for the "crime" of seeking to telegraph General Grant to find out if the expulsion order he received was genuine. An unnamed young Jewish trader and his fiancée, traveling through Grant's department on their way east, described in The Jewish Record how they were detained, forbidden to change out of wet clothes, robbed of their horses and buggy and verbally abused, and also had one of their trunks burned and their pockets picked in the wake of the order. Their expulsion, if not their mistreatment, was explained by Brig. Gen. James Tuttle, commander of the Union garrison in Cairo, Ill., with the utmost simplicity: "you are Jews, and neither a benefit to the Union or Confederacy."

But it was only when Grant's order reached Paducah, Ken., 11 days after it was issued, that a whole community of Jews found itself expelled. On Dec. 28, Paducah's provost marshal, L.J. Waddell, sent Cesar Kaskel and every other Jew in the city an official notice ordering them to leave within 24 hours. Women and children were expelled, too, and in the confusion—so it was recalled years later—one baby was almost forgotten, and two dying women had to be left behind in the care of neighbors. (The historian John E.L. Robertson of Paducah recounts, somewhat dubiously, that citizens of his city hid some Jews to prevent their being sent away. "One soldier," he reports, "is said to have knocked on the door of a Jew and demanded, 'What are you?' The resident of the house answered truthfully, 'Tailor.' To which the not-too-bright soldier replied, 'Sorry to bother you, Mr. Taylor, but I'm looking for Jews.'")

As they prepared to leave their homes, Kaskel and several other Jews sent a telegram to President Abraham Lincoln describing their plight and pronouncing themselves "greatly insulted and outraged by this inhuman order, the carrying out of which would be the grossest violation of the Constitution, and our rights as good citizens under it."

Lincoln, in all likelihood, never saw that telegram, as he was busy preparing to issue the Emancipation Proclamation. The irony of his freeing the slaves while Grant was expelling the Jews was not lost on some contemporaries. The Memphis Daily Bulletin published the two documents one above the other. The juxtaposition of these events also shaped the responses of several Jewish leaders to Grant's order. They feared that Jews would replace blacks as the nation's stigmatized minority.

Fearing the worst, Kaskel wasted no time. "On my way to Washington, in order to get this most outrageous and inhuman order of Major General Grant countermanded," he announced to reporters. He begged the journalists to whom he told his story "to lend the powerful aid of the press to the suffering cause of outraged humanity" and "to blot out as quick as possible this stain on our national honor."

Arriving in the nation's capital just as the Jewish Sabbath was concluding on Jan. 3, Kaskel called at once upon Cincinnati's departing Republican congressman, John Addison Gurley, who enjoyed ready access to the White House. Together, they immediately went over to see President Lincoln.

Lincoln turned out to have no knowledge whatsoever of the order, for it had not reached Washington. According to an oft-quoted report, he resorted to biblical imagery in his interview with Kaskel, a reminder of how immersed he was in the Bible and how, like many 19th-century Americans, he linked Jews to Ancient Israel, and America to the Promised Land.

"And so," Lincoln is said to have drawled, "the children of Israel were driven from the happy land of Canaan?"

"Yes," Kaskel responded, "and that is why we have come unto Father Abraham's bosom, asking protection."

"And this protection," Lincoln declared, "they shall have at once."

Even if no such conversation actually took place, Lincoln did instantly instruct the general-in-chief of the Army, Henry Halleck, to countermand General Orders No. 11. Halleck seems to have had his doubts as to whether the order Kaskel has showed him was genuine, so in writing to Grant, he chose his words carefully. "If such an order has been issued," his telegram read, "it will be immediately revoked." Two days later, several urgent telegrams went out from Grant's headquarters in obedience to that demand: "By direction of the General in Chief of the Army at Washington," they read, "the General Order from these Head Quarters expelling Jews from this Department is hereby revoked."

In a follow-up meeting with Jewish leaders, Lincoln reaffirmed that he knew "of no distinction between Jew and Gentile." "To condemn a class," he emphatically declared, "is, to say the least, to wrong the good with the bad. I do not like to hear a class or nationality condemned on account of a few sinners."

The revocation of Grant's order by no means ended the controversy. Democrats in Congress sought, unsuccessfully, to censure Grant. The New York Times called upon its readers to remember that "All swindlers are not Jews. All Jews are not swindlers." Most of all, Jews discussed the matter among themselves, seeking to understand how, even in wartime, such an order could have been issued at all.

Grant himself never defended General Orders No. 11 and later omitted the episode from his "Personal Memoir." According to his son, Frederick, who assisted his father with those memoirs, the omission was deliberate. "That was a matter long past and best not referred to," he quoted his father as telling him. Julia, Grant's wife, proved far less circumspect. In her memoirs, she characterized General Orders No. 11 as nothing less than "obnoxious." The general, she recalled, felt that the severe reprimand he received for the order was deserved, for "he had no right to make an order against any special sect."

Had Grant himself expressed such sentiments in the wake of the order's revocation, his run for the presidency, in 1868, might not have proved so contentious. As it was, General Orders No. 11 became an important election year issue. For the first time, a controversy involving Jews stood front and center in a presidential campaign.

Grant's opponents insisted that a man who could expel "Jews as a class" for his war zone was unfit to be president. His supporters insisted that Grant was "steadfast" in his "adherence to the principles of American liberty and religious toleration," and that General Orders No. 11 was "directed simply against evil designing persons whose religion was in no way material to the issue."

When the votes were finally tallied, Grant emerged the winner by more than 300,000 votes and a healthy 134-electoral-vote margin. The Jewish vote, whose size pundits at the time greatly exaggerated, scarcely made much difference.

With the election behind him, so nobody could accuse him of pandering for votes, Grant released an unprecedented letter that told his supporters and nervous Jews just what they wanted to hear from the president-elect: "I have no prejudice against sect or race, but want each individual to be judged by his own merit. Order No. 11 does not sustain this statement, I admit, but then I do not sustain that order."

During his eight-year presidency, Grant went out of his way to prove just how unprejudiced he had become. He appointed more Jews to public office than all previous presidents combined, became the first president to attend a synagogue dedication and actively intervened on behalf of persecuted Jews in Russia and Romania. After he left office, he maintained friendships with many Jews, became the first president to visit the land of Israel and, in 1881, placed his name atop a call for a public meeting of protest when anti-Jewish violence broke out in Russia. One senses that whenever he interacted with Jews, and especially when he saw them persecuted, embarrassing memories of General Orders No. 11 flooded into Grant's mind.

As for Cesar Kaskel, he returned to Paducah after General Orders No. 11 was countermanded. He subsequently moved to New York, where he established an upscale clothing store at Broadway and Bleecker Street. In later years, he regaled customers with the story of his Civil War expulsion and its aftermath. He particularly recalled his vigorous and definitive response to the post commander who demanded to know by whose order he had returned to Paducah so soon after Grant had expelled him. It was, he replied, "by order of the president of the United States."

The Short Life of the Camel Corps
By KENNETH WEISBRODE

The Civil War featured many dazzling innovations: ironclads, hot-air balloons, the Gatling gun. But if armored warships and more powerful guns pointed to the future of warfare, another innovation, hailed at the time as a forerunner of combat to come, certainly did not: the United States Army's Camel Corps.

In 1836 an army officer from Georgia, George Crosman, first touted the idea of importing camels to America. The animals were perfect for making the long, grueling treks then being mapped out across the country. Still, not much came of the idea until about 15 years later when, thanks to some publicists like the well-known diplomat and writer George Perkins Marsh, the "Camel Transportation Company" was formed to operate a camel express between Texas and California and down to Panama, later to be called the "Dromedary Line." It wasn't alone: there was also an American Camel Company.

Both companies soon failed, but the idea had taken hold. Among its adherents was Jefferson Davis, the secretary of war under Franklin Pierce. A native of Mississippi, Davis was interested in the integration and development of the Southwest, perhaps with an eye toward expanding the Southern economy—and the slave system it relied on—toward the Pacific. But he and others struggled to find ways to overcome what in pre-railroad days was called the "tyranny of distance." Davis's belief that camels could be the solution was affirmed by a retired naval officer named Edward Beale, who had become something of a zealot on the subject of camels after reading about them in the French missionary Évariste R. Huc's "Recollections of a journey through Tartary, Thibet and China, during the years 1844, 1845 and 1846," a famous account of travels around Central Asia. In 1855 Davis had a ship outfitted and sent to North Africa and the Levant to purchase several camels "for army transportation and for other military purposes."

Overseeing the project for Davis was Maj. Henry Wayne, another camel advocate, who argued that the animals could have direct military uses in "speedy communication," and even as cavalry. He speculated that "Americans will be able to manage camels not only as well, but better than Arabs, as they will do it with more humanity and with far greater intelligence." Moreover, he added, the project would be "a legacy to posterity, of precisely the same character as the introduction of the horse and other domestic animals by the early settlers of America."

Joining Wayne on the voyage were his young son and Lt. David Porter, a naval officer and relative of Beale. Porter was also the brother-in-law of another camel enthusiast, the explorer and illustrator Gwinn Harris Heap, whose own father had been the American consul in Tunis. Together they formed a small but vocal American camel lobby.

The men sailed to Europe, where they stopped along the way to ask advice from experienced camel owners, including the grand duke of Tuscany, who had several on his estate. They also met zoological experts and scientists in England and France, some of whom discouraged them, partly on environmental grounds but also on financial ones, as the Crimean War had driven up the price of camels. But they proceeded onward after leaving Wayne's son behind in a French school, where he remained for three years before seeing his father again.

They traveled on to Tunis, Malta, Smyrna, Constantinople and Alexandria. They returned to Texas with about three dozen animals, including several Arabian (dromedary) and Bactrian camels, a "Tunis camel" and a Tulu, which was a mix of Bactrian and Arabian. A second trip, in 1856, resulted in another four dozen, as well as some camel handlers, Wayne's prediction about Americans' facility with the animals having proved too optimistic. (Among the handlers were two men who would become well-known figures around postwar Arizona and California: the Syrian Hadji Ali, a colorful, moderately successful businessman better known to Americans as "Hi Jolly"; and George Caralambo, a similarly colorful rancher who was renowned as "Greek George.")

The romance of camel-borne transportation took hold of the government's imagination in the late 1850s. Beale imported more dromedaries to California in 1857, and in 1860 some three dozen Bactrian camels were brought from Mongolia by a German entrepreneur, Otto Esche, also to California. Davis's successor, the Virginian John Floyd, was even more of a camel enthusiast, and he ordered a thousand camels to be bought and outfitted.

The camels began to prove their worth as pack animals. These "ships of the desert" could carry upwards of 300 pounds and could travel up to four miles an hour with few stops (certainly fewer than horses). They carried salt, dry goods and even the mail between Tucson and Los Angeles. Not only did they appear to be more economical than horses or mules, but also more self-sufficient: they ate Texas mountain cedar and creosote bush, plentiful plants that other pack animals wouldn't go near.

Camels also had disadvantages. They were known, with justification, for terrible tempers. Horses were prone to panic around them—a fact that the camel lobby tried to spin, arguing that marauding Indians would be less likely to attack their caravans as a result. But this did little to persuade soldiers, who wanted little to do with them. This included the man in command of Texas and therefore of most of the camels, Gen. David Twiggs. Twiggs' views were clear: "I prefer mules for packing."

On Feb. 28, 1861, Confederate forces took over Camp Verde, Tex., where many of the camels were based. With the lines to the Pacific suddenly cut and the impending war clouds concentrated in the East, nobody knew what to do with the animals. Commanders used them to give rides to local children. Some camels in Arkansas were taken by Federal troops, who sent them on to Iowa and then proposed that they be auctioned. Elsewhere Confederate soldiers pushed a camel off a cliff because they thought it was a nuisance. "They were like a wart on a stick. We had them and couldn't get rid of them," said one.

Beale did not give up. He wrote to the new Union secretary of war, Edwin M. Stanton, about devising new roles for the camels, but Stanton never replied. Eventually some were sold to the Ringling Brothers Circus. Others were made into jerky. Many were simply allowed to wander. In 1869 the first transcontinental railroad put an end to the "tyranny of distance"—and the need for camels.

A few of the camel handlers stayed on. Greek George changed his name to George Allen, got married and lived in what is now Hollywood. There were many rumors about his fate—that he had been killed by Apaches, or that he had committed suicide to avoid capture for a murder. In fact he died peacefully at Mission Viejo in 1913, at the age of 84.

Hi Jolly became a citizen around 1880 and became known as Philip Tedro. Like Greek George, he spoke better Spanish than English. He married in Tucson and had two daughters, Amelia and Herminia, and lived until 1902. Three decades later the state of Arizona built a monument to him: a stone pyramid with a camel on top.

As for the camels, there were sightings of their descendants throughout the Southwest until the middle of the 20th century.

Despite their exotic nature, the camels did prove useful and, even with the coming of the railroads, might have served a supporting role in the settlement of the American West. So why did the Camel Corps fail? Part of it was due to the inability of the lobbyists, who saw the camels' advantages in theory, to convince soldiers to overlook the many disadvantages that they saw in fact. But other innovations were successfully forced on military men. The camels, however, had the added misfortune of having Jefferson Davis as their lead advocate.

Still, why didn't the South make more use of the camels? Davis surely had other things on his mind during the war, and his commanders evidently failed to share his enthusiasm for the project. More decisive may have been the fact that so much of the war took place east of the Mississippi. The camels languished in the West.

We are left to wonder. What if the war had been fought differently? Would the camels have made a fine American cavalry? Would they have one day become as ubiquitous a symbol of the Wild West as the horse and cowboy?

LIST OF CONTRIBUTORS

AARON ASTOR is an assistant professor of history at Maryville College. He is the author of the forthcoming book "Rebels on the Border: Civil War, Emancipation and the Reconstruction of Kentucky and Missouri."

EDWARD L. AYERS is the president and a professor of history at the University of Richmond. He is author of several books about the Civil War, including "In the Presence of Mine Enemies: Civil War in the Heart of America."

THOM BASSETT is a lecturer at Bryant University and is at work on a novel.

RICK BEARD is an independent historian and coordinator of the Civil War Sesquicentennial for the American Association for State and Local History.

SVEN BECKERT is the Laird Bell professor of history at Harvard and the author of the forthcoming book "The Empire of Cotton: A Global History."

AMANDA BRICKELL BELLOWS is a doctoral candidate in history at the University of North Carolina.

DAVID W. BLIGHT is a professor of history at Yale. He is the author of "American Oracle: The Civil War in the Civil Rights Era" and is writing a biography of Frederick Douglass.

KEN BURNS is the director of the documentary series "The Civil War."

TOM CHAFFIN lives in Atlanta and is research professor of history at the University of Tennessee, Knoxville. His is author of, among other books, "Pathfinder: "John Frémont and the Course of American Empire." His book "Giant's Causeway: Frederick Douglass's Irish Odyssey and the Making of an American Visionary" will appear in early 2014.

BEN CLEARY is a writer and teacher in Mechanicsville, Va.

RONALD S. CODDINGTON is the author of "Faces of the Civil War," "Faces of the Confederacy" and "African American Faces of the Civil War." He writes "Faces of War," a column for the Civil War News.

MICHAEL DAVID COHEN, an assistant research professor of history at the University of Tennessee, Knoxville, is the author of "Reconstructing the Campus: Higher Education and the American Civil War" and a co-editor of "Correspondence of James K. Polk, volume 12, January–July 1847."

PETER COZZENS is the author of 16 books on the Civil War and the Indian Wars of the American West, including "Shenandoah 1862: Stonewall Jackson's Valley Campaign."

DANIEL W. CROFTS is a professor at the College of New Jersey. He is the author of "A Secession Crisis Enigma: William Henry Hurlbert and 'The Diary of a Public Man.'"

GREGORY P. DOWNS is an associate professor at the City College of New York. He is the author of "Declarations of Dependence: The Long Reconstruction of Popular Politics in the South, 1861-1908." He is also the author of the short story collection "Spit Baths."

Don H. Doyle, the McCausland professor of history at the University of South Carolina, is finishing a book on the international dimensions of America's Civil War.

Marc Egnal is a professor of history at York University, Toronto. He is the author of "Clash of Extremes: The Economic Origins of the Civil War."

David Eltis is a professor of history and the principal investigator for the Electronic Slave Trade Database Project at Emory University. He is the co-author, with David Richardson, of the "Atlas of the Transatlantic Slave Trade" and the author of "The Rise of African Slavery in the Americas."

Carole Emberton is an assistant professor of history at the University at Buffalo. She is the author of the forthcoming book "Beyond Redemption: Race, Violence, and the American South After the Civil War."

Nicole Etcheson is the Alexander M. Bracken professor of history at Ball State University and the author of "A Generation at War: The Civil War Era in a Northern Community."

Michael Fellman was professor emeritus of American history at Simon Fraser University, in Vancouver. He was the author, most recently, of "In the Name of God and Country: Reconsidering Terrorism in American History." He passed away in 2012.

Paul Finkelman is the President William McKinley Distinguished professor of law at Albany Law School and the author of numerous books on slavery, race and the Civil War.

Andre M. Fleche is associate professor of history at Castleton State College and the author of "The Revolution of 1861: The American Civil War in the Age of Nationalist Conflict."

Amanda Foreman is the author, most recently, of "A World on Fire: Britain's Crucial Role in the American Civil War."

William W. Freehling is a senior fellow emeritus at the Virginia Center for Humanities and the Singletary Professor Emeritus at the University of Kentucky. He is the author of "The Road to Disunion" and "Showdown in Virginia: The 1861 Convention and the Fate of the Union." He is currently writing a biography of Abraham Lincoln in his home study in Fredericksburg, Va.

Judith Giesberg, associate professor of history at Villanova University, is the author of three books on the Civil War: "Civil War Sisterhood: The United States Sanitary Commission and Women's Politics in Transition," "'Army at Home:' Women and the Civil War on the Northern Home Front," and "Keystone State In Crisis: Pennsylvania in the Civil War." She also directs the Memorable Days Project: The Emilie Davis Diaries.

David Goldfield is the Robert Lee Bailey professor of history at the University of North Carolina, Charlotte and the president of the Southern Historical Society. He is the author, most recently, of "America Aflame: How the Civil War Created a Nation."

Adam Goodheart is the author of the bestselling history "1861: The Civil War Awakening," and is at work on a new book on 1865, to be published in 2015.

JOHN GRADY is a former editor of Navy Times and a retired director of communications at the Association of the United States Army. He is completing a biography of Matthew Fontaine Maury. He is also a contributor to the Navy's Civil War Sesquicentennial blog.

MARK GREENBAUM is a writer and attorney in Washington.

JON GRINSPAN is a fellow at the National Endowment for the Humanities and the author of the forthcoming book "The Virgin Vote: Young Americans in the Age of Popular Politics."

WINSTON GROOM is the author, most recently, of "Shiloh, 1862."

GUY GUGLIOTTA is a former national reporter for The Washington Post. He is the author of "Freedom's Cap: The United States Capitol and the Coming of the Civil War."

STEVEN HAHN is a professor of history at the University of Pennsylvania. He is the author of "A Nation under Our Feet: Black Political Struggles in the Rural South from Slavery to the Great Migration" and "The Political Worlds of Slavery and Freedom."

MEREDITH HINDLEY is a historian and senior writer for Humanities, the magazine of the National Endowment for the Humanities.

HAROLD HOLZER is the chairman of the Abraham Lincoln Bicentennial Foundation. He is the author, co-author or editor of 44 books on Lincoln and the Civil War era, including "Lincoln: How Abraham Lincoln Ended Slavery in America," the young adult companion book to Spielberg's "Lincoln."

JEAN HUETS is the publisher of Circling Rivers, an independent press dedicated to historical fiction, nonfiction, poetry and drama.

MAYA JASANOFF is a professor of history at Harvard. She is the author of "Liberty's Exiles: American Loyalists in the Revolutionary World."

TERRY L. JONES is a professor of history at the University of Louisiana at Monroe. He has written a number of books on the Civil War, including "The American Civil War" and "Lee's Tigers: The Louisiana Infantry in the Army of Northern Virginia."

GEORGE B. KIRSCH is professor of history at Manhattan College. He is the author of "Baseball and Cricket: The Creation of American Team Sports, 1838-72" and "Baseball in Blue and Gray: The National Pastime During the Civil War."

ALBIN J. KOWALEWSKI is a public historian in Washington.

C. KAY LARSON serves on the board of the New York Military Affairs Symposium. She is the author of "Great Necessities: The Life, Times, and Writings of Anna Ella Carroll, 1815-1894" and the novel "South Under a Prairie Sky: The Journal of Nell Churchill, U. S. Army Nurse & Scout."

PHIL LEIGH is an armchair Civil War enthusiast and president of a market research company. He is preparing an illustrated and annotated version of the memoirs of Confederate Pvt. Sam Watkins entitled "Co. Aytch: Illustrated and Annotated."

PAT LEONARD is the editor and publisher of The Gold Cross, a magazine for volunteer emergency medical technicians in New Jersey. He has written two novels, "Proceed With Caution" and "Damned If You Do." His great-great-great uncle, Sgt. Jerome Leonard, served with the 55th Pennsylvania Infantry, was wounded at the Battle of Cold Harbor and later died at Bermuda Hundred hospital after his leg was amputated.

LOIS LEVEEN is the author of "The Secrets of Mary Bowser," a novel based on the life of the Richmond slave who became a spy for the Union Army.

CATE LINEBERRY was a staff writer and Europe editor for National Geographic Magazine and the web editor for Smithsonian Magazine. She is the author of "The Secret Rescue: An Untold Story of American Nurses and Medics Behind Enemy Lines."

PHILLIP W. MAGNESS is the academic program director at the Institute for Humane Studies, at George Mason University. He is the co-author, with Sebastian Page, of "Colonization After Emancipation: Lincoln and the Movement for Black Resettlement."

JAMIE MALANOWSKI was one of the original members of the Disunion project. He is working on a biography of the Civil war hero William Cushing.

KATE MASUR is a professor of history at Northwestern University. She is the author of "An Example for All the Land: Emancipation and the Struggle over Equality in Washington, D.C." and numerous articles on politics and emancipation in the Civil War era.

LOUIS P. MASUR is a professor of American studies and History at Rutgers University. He is the author of "Lincoln's Hundred Days: The Emancipation Proclamation and the War for the Union" and "The Civil War: A Concise History."

RUSSELL MCCLINTOCK is a history teacher at St. John's High School in Shrewsbury, Mass. He is the author of "Lincoln and the Decision for War: The Northern Response to Secession." He is writing a biography of Stephen A. Douglas.

MEGAN KATE NELSON is a lecturer in history and literature at Harvard University. She is the author of the forthcoming book "Ruin Nation: Destruction and the American Civil War."

KENNETH W. NOE is a professor of Southern history at Auburn University. He is the author, most recently, of "Reluctant Rebels: The Confederates Who Joined the Army After 1861."

SEBASTIAN PAGE is a junior research fellow at the Rothermere American Institute and Oxford University, co-author of "Colonization after Emancipation," and author of "Lincoln and Chiriquí Colonization Revisited."

RICHARD PARKER is a journalist and publisher in Texas and a regular contributor to McClatchy-Tribune Information Services.

CARLA L. PETERSON is a professor in the department of English at the University of Maryland, College Park. Her book "Black Gotham: A Family History of African Americans in Nineteenth-Century New York City," won the 2011 NYC Book Award in History from the New York Society Library and was a finalist for the 2012 Gilder-Lerhman Institute Frederick Douglass Prize.

CHRISTOPHER PHILLIPS is a professor of history at the University of Cincinnati. He is the author of six books on the Civil War era, including "Damned Yankee: The Life of Nathaniel Lyon" and the forthcoming "The Rivers Ran Backward: The Civil War on the Middle Border and the Making of American Regionalism."

NATALIE POSGATE is a graduate of Southern Methodist University in Dallas.

ELIZABETH BROWN PRYOR is the author of "Reading the Man: A Portrait of Robert E. Lee through His Private Letters."

DAVID RICHARDSON is a professor of economic history at the University of Hull and the founder and former director of the Wilberforce Institute for the study of Slavery and Emancipation. He is a co-author of the "Atlas of the Transatlantic Slave Trade" and is currently writing a book on the British slave trade and its abolition.

SETH ROCKMAN is a professor of history at Brown. He is the author of "Scraping By: Wage Labor, Slavery, and Survival in Early Baltimore." He is writing a book on plantation goods and the national economy of slavery.

ADAM ROTHMAN is an associate professor of history at Georgetown University. He is the author of "Slave Country: American Expansion and the Origins of the Deep South."

JONATHAN D. SARNA, the Joseph H. & Belle R. Braun Professor of American Jewish History at Brandeis University and the chief historian of the National Museum of American Jewish History, is the author of "When General Grant Expelled the Jews."

SUSAN SCHULTEN is a professor of history at the University of Denver and author of "Mapping the Nation: History and Cartography in Nineteenth-Century America" and "The Geographical Imagination in America, 1880-1950."

MICHAEL SHAPIRO is the assistant editor of the "Papers of Frederick Law Olmsted, Vol. 8" and the author of the forthcoming "Becoming Union Square: Struggles for Legitimacy in Nineteenth-Century New York."

DANIEL J. SHARFSTEIN, a professor of law at Vanderbilt University, won the 2012 J. Anthony Lukas Prize for his book "The Invisible Line: A Secret History of Race in America."

MANISHA SINHA is an associate professor of Afro-American studies at the University of Massachusetts, Amherst. She is the author of "The Counterrevolution of Slavery: Politics and Ideology in Antebellum South Carolina." She is writing a history of abolition.

RICHARD SLOTKIN is Olin professor of American studies emeritus at Wesleyan University. He is the author of "The Long Road to Antietam: How the Civil War Became a Revolution."

ADAM I. P. SMITH is the author of "No Party Now: Politics in the Civil War North."

DIANE MILLER SOMMERVILLE is an associate professor of history at Binghamton University. She is the author of the forthcoming "Aberration of Mind: Suicide, Civil War and the American South."

RON SOODALTER is the author of "Hanging Captain Gordon: The Life and Trial of an American Slave Trader" and co-author of "The Slave Next Door: Human Trafficking and Slavery in America Today." He has written more than 100 historically based articles for such magazines as Smithsonian, America's Civil War, Military History, Civil War Times and New York Archives. He is the recipient of the International and Regional Magazine Association's 2010 Gold Award for History and serves on the Board of Directors of the Abraham Lincoln Institute.

JOHN STAUFFER is a professor of English and African American Studies at Harvard. He is the author of "The Black Hearts of Men," "GIANTS: The Parallel Lives of Frederick Douglass and Abraham Lincoln" and with Edward Soskis "The Battle Hymn of the Republic."

RICHARD STRINER is a history professor at Washington College. He is the author of "Lincoln and Race."

MICHAEL O. VARHOLA is a freelance writer, author or co-author of 10 non-fiction books and two novels, editor of the America's Haunted Road Trip series of travel guides, and the founder of Skirmisher Publishing LLC's "Swords of Kos" shared-world fantasy fiction project.

CYNTHIA WACHTELL is a research associate professor of American studies and the director of the S. Daniel Abraham Honors Program at Yeshiva University. She is the author of "War No More: The Antiwar Impulse in American Literature, 1861-1914."

KENNETH WEISBRODE is a writer and historian. He is the author of "The Atlantic Century."

TED WIDMER is a historian at Brown University, where he is Assistant to the President for Special Projects. He has served as a senior adviser to Secretary of State Hillary Clinton, Director and Librarian of the John Carter Brown Library, and Director of the C.V. Starr Center for the Study of the American Experience at Washington College. He has written or edited many works of history, including, most recently, *Listening In: The Secret White House Recordings of John F. Kennedy.*

SEAN WILENTZ is the George Henry Davis 1886 Professor of American History at Princeton. He is the author of, among other books, "The Rise of American Democracy: Jefferson to Lincoln."

CHRISTIAN WOLMAR's latest book is "The Great Railroad Revolution: The History of Trains in America." He is currently writing a book about the Trans-Siberian railway.

INDEX

Illustrations are in BOLD

104th Ohio Volunteer Infantry, 153

114th Pennsylvania, 342

122nd Infantry regiment, New York Volunteers, Company F, 95

13th Amendment, 41, 394

13th Louisiana Volunteer Infantry Regiment, 139-140

1862, year in Civil War, 233-302; election of, 397-400

1st Louisiana Native Guards, **402**

21st Illinois Volunteers, 199

39th New York Volunteer Infantry Regiment, uniforms, 146

48th Pennsylvania Infantry, 114-115

5th Michigan Infantry Regiment, 342

6th Massachusetts, Boston, funeral procession of, 126-127

79th New York Volunteer Infantry, uniforms, 146

7th Louisiana Volunteers, 167

8th Wisconsin Regiment, Company C, eagle mascot, 152-155

9th Infantry Regiment, New York Volunteers, Company C, 94

Abolition, 11, 14-16, 22-26, 31, 45-48, 53-54, 86, 303, 382-387

Acoustic shadows, 101-103

Adams Jr., Charles Francis, 177, 323

Adams, Henry, 69, 317

Adams, John Quincy, 24

Africa, slave trade, 42-43, 62

African Americans, ix, xii, xii, xiii, 102, 355-359, 406-411; demographics, 19-22, 291-293, 290-294; free men at war, 401-405

African Civilization Society, 47

African male suffrage, 45-48

Alabama, xi, xiii, 1, 7, 60-64, 87, 96, 181, 182, 276, 295, 345, 395, 415; secession, 1, 61, 63; *See also* specific battles.

Albany Journal, 127

Alexander II, Czar of Russia, 75-79

American and Foreign Anti-Slavery Society, 46

American Anti-Slavery Society, 45, 46

American Colonization Society, 357

American Society for Promoting National Unity, 98

Ammunition, 370-373

Amputations in Civil War, 415-420

Anderson, Robert, 36, 38, 40, 99, 103-104, 202

Andersonville, 102

Andrews, James, 276-278

Anglo-African Magazine, 47

Antietam, Battle of, 12, 102, 280, 304, 338, 377-382, 389, 390, 399, 409; photos of, 381

Anti-Union sentiments, 111

Appomattox Court House, surrender at, vii, 102, 135, 227, 323

Arctic explorations, 287-290

Arkansas, 1, 7, 63, 268, 279, 295, 350, 437; secession, 1, 63

Army of Northern Virginia 226, 351, 377-379, 382, 397

Army of the Cumberland, 217, 220-221

Army of the Potomac, 225,234, 262, 309, 338-341, 378

Army of Virginia, 370, 378

Arnold, Isaac N., 384

Arp, Bill, 244

Ashby, Turner, 318-320

Associated Press, 246

Augusta Chronicle, 28

Bagby, Lucy, 22-23

Ball's Bluff, Battle of, 111, 160, 245

Balloon Corps, 171

Balloon reconnaissance, 163, 170-173

Baltimore Sun, 113

Baltimore, MD, 283; riots, 126-128, **129**, 130; Southern sympathizers, 113-115

Banks, Nathaniel P., 302, 404-405

Barton, Clara, 126

Baseball, 91-95; played in prisoner of war camps, **93**

Bates, Edward, 21, 251, **336**

Battle Cry of Freedom, x, xii, 102

Battle Hymn of the Republic (song), 193

Beauregard, Gustave Toutant, 185, 267, 272-274, 276, 306, 308

Beauregard, P.G.T., 1, 104, 166-169; note to Fort Sumter, 104, **105**

Beecher, Henry Ward, 47, 158

Bell, John, 24, 210

Belmont, August, 176

Benjamin, Judah P., 138

Benton, Thomas Hart, 196

Biddle, Nick, 112-115

Birney, James, 46

Bismarck, Otto von, 214-215

Black laws in Midwest, 210

Blair, Francis, 117

Blair, Frank, 196

Blair, Montgomery, **336**, 337, 387, 399

Blight, David, ix, 102

Blockade of Southern ports, 174-176, 180-183, 322, 362

Bloodlines, black vs white, 136-140

Blythe, David Gilmour, 393

Bohemians, 109-111

Bonham, Milledge Luke, 61

Boston, funeral procession of 6th Massachusetts, 126-127

Botts, John Minor, 39

Boys in Civil War, 215-219

Brady, Mathew B., 141-143, 381

Bragg, Braxton, 280, 394-397, 399

Brazil, slave trade, 42

Breckinridge, John C., 24, 60, 210

Brooklyn Excelsior baseball team, 95

Brooks Brothers, 134, 136

Brooks, Noah, 336-337

Brown, John, 48

Browning, Orville H., 197

Buchanan, Franklin, 364

Buchanan, James, 33-37, 39, 185, 210

Buckner, Simon B., 201

Buell, Don Carlos, 229-231, 268, 272, 276, 394-396

Bull Run, Battles of, 111, 159-231; correspondence about, 165; First, 66, 124, 159-170, 204, 209, 226-227, 229, 279 ; meaning of, 161-166; Second, 126, 280, 309, 338, 341, 369-370, 378, 399

Bullets, 371-373

Burns, Ken, xii

Burns, Ric, 102

Burnside, Ambrose E., 280, 381, 390

Burt, Armistead, 61

Business views of war, 97

Butler, Benjamin F., 66, 301, 402, 407

Butterfield, General, 46

Cady Stanton, Elizabeth, 86

Cairo, IL, 199-200

Calhoun, A.P., 61

Calhoun, John C., 60, 62, 138

California, Confederate plan to capture, 187-189

Camel Corps, 434-438

Cameron, Simon, 21, 122, 221, 264, **336**

Camp Chase, 217

Camp Parapet, LA, 300-301

Camps, card-playing in, 373-377; Union, 258-259, **260**, 261

Canada, escaped slaves in, 13-15, 23

Caprell, Madame (fortune-teller), 57-58

Card-playing in camps, 373-377

Carpenter, Francis Bicknell, 20-21, 333-337; painting of Lincoln, **335**

Cartoons of war, 241-244

Centennial, 102

Chadwick, Henry, 92

Charleston, IL, 48

Charleston, SC, vii, 1, 228, 33, 36, 48, 49, 51, 103-108, 131, 226, 231, 242, 247, 254, 261, 314, 413

Chase, Salmon P., 12, 21, 23, 217, 335, **336**, 378, 386

Chattanooga, TN, 275-278

Chesnut, Mary Boykin, 83-87

Chickamauga, GA, Battle of, 102, 216-217

Chimes of Freedom and Union: A Collection of Poems for the Times, 177

Chirquí, Latin America, emigration to, 355-359

Choiseul, Charles de, 167

Christmas (1860), 26-29

Cincinnati, commercial growth, 347-349

Civil liberties during Civil War, 391-394

Civil War, The (TV series), xiii, 102

Civil War and Abraham Lincoln, The, 9

Civil War and Politics, The 53-56

Civil War and Geography, The, 119-122

Civil War and Literature, The, 177-180

Civil War and Warfighting, The, 279-282

Civil War and the Foreign Context, The, 321-323

Civil War and Emancipation, The, 406-411

Clapp Jr., Henry, 110-111

Clark, Edward, 189

Clay, Henry, 23, 138

Clem, Johnny, **216**, 217, 218

Cleveland, OH, slave expectation in, 22-26

Clinch Rifles, GA, 147

Cobb, Thomas, 76

Cold Harbor, VA, 102

Columbus Daily Express, 217

Compromise of 1850, 32, 62

Confederate States of America, 1, 81-83, 159-230, 233-234, 241-244, 253-257, 266-275, 275-278, 279-282, 304, 394-397, 420-424; Congress, 71; doctors in, 223-226; flags, 166-170; hopes for US election of 1862, 397-400; plan to capture California, 187-189

Confiscation Act, 11; First, 159, 407; Second, 303, 327-333

Congress (ship), 366, 369

Congressional Medal of Honor, 278

Constitution, Thirteenth Amendment, 41, 394

Contraband (of slaves), 407, 411

Cooper Union, 48

Copperheads, 349, 398

Corinth, 307-308

Corps D'Afrique, 403

Corruption, 133-136

Crawford, Samuel W., 107

Cricket, 91-95

Crimean War, 214-215

Crittenden Compromise, 117

CSS Virginia (ship), 363-369

Cumberland (ship), 366, 369

Curtis, Samuel, 275

Davis, David Brion, 40

Davis, Garrett, 239

Davis, Jefferson, 25, 54, 71, 113, 187, 188, 189, 203, 271, 274, 350, 421, 435

Davis, Mrs. Jefferson (Varina Howell), 25

Debow's Review, 97

Delaware, 1, 10, 15, 160, 291, 292, 324, 407; abolition in, 235-237, 383

Democrats, 7-8, 46-47, 53-55, 149, 157, 197, 239, 296, 324, 327, 329, 383, 387, 393; in election of 1862, 397-400

Denmark and slave trade, 41

District of Columbia. *See* Washington, DC.

Divorce compared to secession, 83-87

Dix, Dorothea, 122-126

Doctors in Civil War, 282-287

Dodge, William E., 97-98

Dogs in Civil War, 152-155

Doolittle, James, 292-293

Doubleday, Abner, 107

Douglas, H. Ford, 23

Douglas, Stephen A.,7-8, 24, 32,

34, 69, 211, 397; debates with Lincoln, 211

Douglass Monthly, 30,

Douglass, Frederick, 27-28, 30-33, 44, 46, 74, 130-133, 205, 237, 356, 359, 406; critique of Lincoln, 130-133, 386

Dr. Smith's back room, 44-48

Dred Scott decision, 32, 45, 250-251

Drilling students, 314-315

Drought, 394-397

Drummer boys, 215-219

Drum-Taps, 111-112

Eagle in Civil War, 152-155

Early, Jubal A., 167-168

Eckels, Delana, 209, 210

Economic causes of Civil War, 95-98

Edwards Ferry. *See* Ball's Bluff, Battle of.

Election of 1862, 397-400

Emancipation Proclamation, xi, 12, 19, 20, 48, 56, 66, 79, 194, 237, 300, 303, 330, 389-438, 392, 406-411; coming of, 324-326; painting of Reading, **335**; Preliminary 385-387, 399, 409; Towards, 389-438

Emancipation, compensated, 324-326

Emerson, Ralph Waldo, viii, xii, 212

Emigration of African Americans, 47, 132, 237, 240-241, 291-293, 355-359

Ennals, Stehen & Maria, 14-16

Etheridge, Annie, 342

Europe, Union attitudes toward, 174-177; views on Civil War, 212-215, 321-323

Evangelicals, 155-158

Everett, Edward, x

Ewell, Richard S., 415-416

Fair Oaks Battle. *See* Seven Pines, Battle of.

Fallen Timbers, Battle of, 273

Faust, Drew Gilpin, ix

Female soldiers, 342-345

Fessenden, William P., 243, 332

First solder killed in Civil War, 127

Fitzhugh, George, 76, 298

Flags, Confederate, 166-170

Fletcher, William, 370-373

Florida, 7, 60, 87, 91, 188, 255, 278, 283; secession, 1, 61

Floyds, John B., 34

Foley, B.H., 37

Food shortages in South, 182-183

Foot, Solomon, 264-266

Forrest, Nathan Bedford, 273

Fort Blakely, 405

Fort Donelson, 152, 179, 231, 233, 253, 275, 280, 345

Fort Henry, 179, 345, 395

Fort McHenry, 113

Fort Monroe, VA, 66, 100, 172, 407

Fort Moultrie, 36

Fort Pillow, TN massacre, 102

Fort Sumter, SC, 1, 2, 33, 38, 63, 99, 103-108, 108, 130, 132, 148-149, 158, 159, 211

Fort Union, New Mexico, 188

Fort Wagner, 102

Fowler, Charles, 263-264

France, 160, 212-213

Fredericksburg, VA, Battle of, 12, 280, 418

Free men of color at war, 401-405

Free Soilers, 47, 156, 296, 386

Frémont, John C., 11, 65, 159, 200; Emancipation order in Missouri, 194-198, 407-408

Fugitive Slave Act, 15-16, 22-26, 45, 47, 48, 66, 131-133

Fulton, Robert, 252-253

Gamble, Hamilton, 195

Gambling in camps, 373-377

Gardner, Alexander, 381

Garibaldi Guard, **145**

Garibaldi, Giuseppe, 89, 214

Garnet, Henry Highland, 46-48

Garrett, Thomas, 15

Garrison, William Lloyd, 9, 45, 46, 96

Gaskins, Susan, 161-162

General Orders No. 11, 428-434

Geography and Civil war, 119-122

Georgia, 7, 87, 113, 182, 212, 219, 244, 395, 435 ; secession, 1, 60-63. *See also* specific battles.

German immigrants, 348-349

Germany, 212-215

Gettysburg, Address, x; Battle of, viii-ix, 216 ; before war, 3-5; 150th anniversary, vii; 1913 reenactment, vii

Gibson, Randall Lee, 136-140

Gladden, Adley H., 270

Glorieta Pass, Battle of, 190

Glory (movie), xii, 102

Go Down, Moses (song), 205, 207

Gorbachev, Mikhail, 79

Gordon, Nathaniel, 43

Goshorn, William, 22-23

Grant, Ulysses S., 3, 11, 29, 160,

198-202, 218, 219-, 223, 425; at Fort Donelson, 275; at Shiloh, 267-275; differences with Halleck, 305-308; expulsion of Jews from territories, 427-434; Mexican War, 199

Great Britain, 160, 212-213; and slave trade, 40-43; neutrality, 173-177, 322; views on Civil war, 321-323, 420-424

Greeley, Horace, 29, 47, 70, 78, 84, 159, 295, 296, 332, 383-384, 386

Green, Duff, 36

Greenhow, Rose O'Neal, 184-187

Gregg, William, 98

Habeas corpus, 149, 391-394

Haiti, emigration to, 47, 132, 356

Halleck, Henry W., 223, 229-231, 275, 305-308; as General-in-Chief, 308, 338, 341, 350, 432; countermanding expulsion of Jews, 432-433

Hamilton, Thomas, 47

Hammond, James Henry, 27

Hammond, William Alexander, 282-287

Hampton Roads, 364-369

Harper's Weekly, 134, 142

Harris, Wesley T., 258-259, 260

Harrison, William Henry, 69

Harvard University College Drill Club, 314

Harvey (dog mascot), **153**

Haupt, Herman, 204

Hayes, Isaac Israel, 287-290

Hays, Harry T., 167

Hays, John, 143, 386

Hemphill, Robert, 225

Henry, Joseph, 245

Herndon, William, 4, 52

Hill, A.P., 309-310, 381

Hill, Daniel H., 309

Hilton head, SC, Union tents, 258-259, **260**, 262

Hinckley, Caroline, 86

Hodgers, Jennie, 342

Hollandsworth Jr., James G., 403

Holmes Sr., Oliver Wendell, 128, 77

Homestead Act, 294-299

Homestead application by Daniel Freeman, **297**

Hooker, Joseph, 380-381

Horwitz, Tony, xiii

Houtze, Henry, 420-424

Howard, Joseph, 73

Hunnicutt, James W., 63

Hunt's Merchant Magazine, 97

Hunter, David, emancipation declaration in South Carolina, 325-326

Immigrants in Midwest, 346-349

Index (newspaper), 422-423

Indiana, 84; Confederate sympathies, 209-212; in election of 1862, 398-400

Inhuman Bondage, 40

Irish immigrants, 348-349

Ironclad ships, 362-369

Irving, Washington, 287

Italy, 160, 212

Ivanhoe, 316

Jackson, Andrew, 35, 62, **336**

Jackson, T.J. "Stonewall", 234, 309-312, 377-278, 418; Valley campaign, 309-310

Jarvis, Harry, 66

Jefferson, Thomas, 80

Jews expelled from Grant's territories, 427-434

Johnson, William H., 248-252

Johnston, Albert Sydney, at Shiloh, 267-272, 276, death, 178-179, 272, 274

Johnston, Joseph E., 167, 169

Jomini, Antoine-Henri, 228

Jordan, Thomas, 185

Kansas, 188, 211, 220, 238, 283

Kansas-Nebraska Bill, 7

Kaskel, Cesar, 438-434

Kearns Goodwin, Doris, xii

Kearny Cross, 342

Keckley, Elizabeth, 25-26

Kennedy, Anthony, 291

Kentucky, 1, 7, 10, 63, 195-197, 200-202, 220-223; abolition in, 383; commercial growth, 345-350

Kettell, Thomas Prentice, 97

Key, Francis Scott, 192

King, Dr. Martin Luther, Jr., vii, ix, xi, xii

Know-Nothing party, 56, 157

Korean War, ix

Ku Klux Klan, 102

Ladd, Luther C., 127

Lamon, Ward Hill, 73, 75

LaMontain, John, 172

Leaves of Grass, 109

Lee, Mary Custis, 115-119; letter regarding Robert E. Lee, **116**

Lee, Robert E., 3, 234, 280, 303, 304, 309-312, 338, 376, 378, 397; at

Antietam, 380-382; decision to resign Union Army, 115-119; in Maryland, 379-380, 385
Liberator, The, 86
Liberia, emigration to, 47, 356-357
Liberty Party, 46, 156
Library of Congress, 103
Lincoln & Herndon, 4
Lincoln (movie), ix
Lincoln Memorial, vii
Lincoln, Abraham, viii, ix, xiii, 5-8, 9-12, 16, 18-19, 39, 40, 48-52, 56, 63, 120-121, 220-221, 285-286, 313-314, 377-382, 400 ; and slaves, 20-22, 23-25, 32, 46, 48, 64-66, 194-198, 235-237, 237-241, 274, 324-326, 327-333, 355-359, 382-387, 389-390, 407-410 ; call for volunteers, 116, 148, 164, 279; cartoons of, **72, 393**; childhood, 50; Congressional speeches, 149-161, 409; correspondence with Czar Alexander II, 75-77; debates with Douglas, 211; election (1860), 1, 3-10, 25, 65, 69, 87-90, 111, 298; election campaign ticket (1860), **6**; generals and, 226-231; humor, 243-244; Inauguration (1st), 10; Inauguration (2nd), x; Jews and, 431-434; journey to Washington, 71-75; letters, xi, 87-90; Native Americans and, 359-362; overtures to South, 130-133; painting of, **333**; photographs of, 140, **141**, 142-144; problems with McClellan, 338-341, 378-381, 390; racial attitudes, 249-251; secession views, 81; war strategy, 230-231, 235-237 . *See also* Emancipation Proclamation.
Lincoln, Nancy Hanks, 50
Lincoln, Robert Todd, 179, 314
Lincoln, Sarah Bush Johnston, **49**, 50-52
Lincoln, Thomas, 50-51
Lincoln, Willie, 11
Literature and Civil War, 180
Little Crow, Chief, 359-360
Livermore, Mary, 123, 125, 342
London *Times*, 175
Longstreet, James, 309, 369
Lord, Daniel, 98
Louisiana, xiii, 3, 7, 58, 64, 136, 138-140, 147, 166, 188, 267, 279, 295, 301, 302, 307, 401-403, 419; secession, 1, 60, 61
Louisville, KY, commercial growth, 346-349
Lovejoy, Owen, 196, 334

Lowe, Thaddeus Sobieski Constantine, 170-173
Lumley, Arthur, 142
Lyon, Nathaniel, 199
Lyons, Lord Richard, 174-176, 321
Lyons, Maritcha, 44

MacKay, John, 208
Macon, GA, Christmas (1860), 26-29
Magruder, John Bankhead, 255
Mallory, Stephen, 253
Malvern Hill, VA, Battle of, 312
Manassas, VA, 161-162
Manning, J.M., 129-130
Manning, John L., 61
Manumission Society, 44, 46
Maps of Civil War, 246, **247**, 248
Marshall, Charles, 115
Martineau, Harriet, 176
Maryland, 1, 10, 13-14, 63, 307; abolition in, 383; Lee in, 379
Mason-Dixon Line, 13, 92
Maury, Matthew, 252-253
McCallum, Daniel, 203
McClellan, George B., 11, 74, 124-125, 199, 201, 229, 231, 256, 304 ; at Antietam, 377-382, 385;fired, 382, 390; headquarters, 245 ; questions about leadership, 338-341; Peninsula Campaign, 124, 172, 233-234, 247-248, 280, 303, 309-310, 363, 378, 395
McDowell, Irwvin, 166, 207
McGuire, Hunter, 415-416
McPherson, James, 102, 119
McPherson, James, x, xii
Medical and Surgical History of the War of the Rebellion, The, 283
Meigs, Montgomery, 11, 229, 262-265, 426
Melville, Herman, 16-19
Memphis, 230, 231, 274, 308, 345, 346, 429
Mental illness, 219-223
Mercier, Henri, 175
Merrimack (ship), 253, 363
Mexican War, 62, 213, 214, 229
Mexico, 212-213, 323
Miles, William Porcher, 168-169
Militia Act, 303, 332
Mills, Abraham G., 94
Mines (bombs), 252-258
Minié ball (bullet), 371-373, 416
Minnesota (ship), 366, 367
Mississippi, xi, 7, 25, 233, 295, 303, 306, 350, 390, 420, 428, 429, 435; secession, 1, 60- 63, 65

Missouri Compromise, 35
Missouri, 1, 10, 63, 160; slave confiscations, 160. *See also* specific battles.
Mitchel, Ormsby, 276-277
Mitchell, James, 355, 367
Moby Dick, 16-17
Monitor (ship), 364
Monroe Doctrine, 213
Monthly, newspaper, 130
Morill, Lot, xi
Morrill Land-Grant College Act, 174, 312-315
Morrill, Justin, 313
Morse, Samuel F.., 245
Morton, Oliver P., 211
Mumford, Lewis, 103
My Imprisonment and the First Year of Abolition Rule at Washington, 187
Myrick, Andrew Jackson, 360

Napoleon, 227-228
Nash, Thomas, 29
Nashville, TN, 228. 233
National Hymns: How They Are Written and How They Are Not Written, 193
Native Americans, 299, 359-362
Native Guards, New Orleans, 402-405
Naval blockade of South, 160
New Orleans Daily Picayune, 127-128, 149, 401
New Orleans, 57; capture of, 233; free men of color in, 401-405;Native Guards, 402-405; slaves in, 299-302; Union occupation, 300-302
New York City, draft riots, 55
New York *Herald*, 4, 29, 74, 135
New York Knickerbocker Base Ball Club, 92
New York State African American activism, 44-48
New York *Times*, xii, 6, 53, 54, 60, 69, 73, 78, 98, 110, 177, 192, 221, 286, 337
New York *Tribune*, 21, 29. 47, 70, 336, 383
Newspapers, 245-248
Nicholls, Francis T., 419
Nicolay, John, 123, 143
Nightingale, Florence, 123-124
North Carolina, 7, 53, 85, 137, 160, 233; secession, 1, 63
Nullification Crisis 1828-1832, 62
Nurses in Civil War, 122-126

O'Sullivan, John, 83
Obama, Barack, 71, 72
Official Records of the War of the Rebellion, The, x
Ohio River, 349
Ohio, commercial growth, 346-349
Olmsted, Frederick Law, 125-126
Opdyke, George, 135-136
Orr, James L., 61, 225

Paducah, KY, expulsion of Jews, 427-434
Palmito Ranch, 102
Parisen, Otto W., 94
Patriotic Gore, x
Pea Ridge, Ark, 275
Peabody, Everett, 270
Peace Conference, Washington, DC, 67, 70
Pearsall, A.T. (Aleck), 95
Perryville, KY, Battle of, 280, 390, 394, 397, 399
Pfaff's bar, 109-112
Phelps, John W., 300-301
Philadelphia Inquirer, 28
Phillips, Wendell, 9, 14, 86, 384
Photographic History of the Civil War, x
Photography, 140-144, 260-261
Pigeon Creek, Indiana, 50
Pinkerton, Allan, 72-74, 184-186
Pittsburg Landing, TN, Battle of, 268-272
Playing cards, 373-374, **375**, 376-377
Polk, Leonidas K., 200-201, 254-255, 268
Pope, John, 338, 360-361, 378
Port Hudson, 404-405
Porter, David Dixon, 256, 257
Pottsville, PA soldiers, 112-115
Potomac Creek Bridge, **203**, 204
Prang, Louis, 246-248
President Lincoln Reading the Emancipation Proclamation to His Cabinet (painting), **335**
Preston, John S., 63
Prisoners of war, **93**
Profiteering, 133-136
Preemption Act, 295

Radical Abolition Party, 24, 46
Radzinsky, Edvard, 79
Railroads, and the war, 202-205; chase to Chattanooga, 275-278; Federalization of, 203
Rains, Gabriel, 255-256, 258
Randolph, George Wythe, 81-83, 256

Randolph, Thomas Jefferson, 80, 82
Rebel yell, 163, 269
Redpath, James, 132
Regimental women, 341-345
Republican party, 155-158
Republics, 19th century, 99-90
Reserve Officers' Training Corps, 315
Revolutionary War comparison to Civil War, 126-129
Richmond Examiner, 67
Richmond, VA, 54, 253-, 255-256, 280-282, 338
Rights during Civil War, 391-394
Rip Van Winkle, 287-290
Robeson, Paul, 205
Robinson, James, 161-162
Romanticism, 318
Roosevelt, Franklin D., x
Roosevelt, Theodore, x
Roots (TV series), xii
Rosecrans, William S., 217
Ruffin, Edmund, 60
Russell, William Howard, 175, 299
Russia, Emancipation of the serfs, 75-79

Salisbury, NC prison camp, **93**
San Antonio, TX, 187-189
San Marino Republic, 87-90
Saulisbury, Willard, 291-292
Schools for soldiers, 312-315
Schwartz, Thomas F., 142
Scott, Sir Walter, 315-320
Scott, Winfield S., 34, 117, 171, 229-230
Secession, 1-98, 99-158
Seddon, James A., 2
Semaphore flags, 162
Seminole Wars, 255
Serfs in Russia, 75-79; songs of, 205-208
Seven Days Battles, 234, 280, 309-311
Seven Pines, Battle of, 234
Seward, William H., 9, 12, 21, 23, 76, 87, 89, 90, 157, 326, **336**, 341, 393; attitudes toward Europe, 174-177, 323
Seymour, Horatio, 55
Sherman, Ellen Ewing, 222
Sherman, William Tecumseh, 3, 256, 274-275; advice to Grant, 305-308; at Shiloh, 268-269, 273; depression, 219-223; March to the Sea, 204-205, 219, 226, 244
Shiloh Church, TN, Battle of, 11, 102, 215, 216, 223, 233, 266, **267**, 268-275, 306

Shropshire, John, 190
Sibley, Henry Hopkins, 187
Sioux Indians, 359-362; hanging of, 362
Six Months at the White House With Abraham Lincoln, 337
Slave ads, **13**
Slave auctions, 27-28
Slave trade, transatlantic, 40-43, 62
Slavery, 1, 30-33, 69-71, 99-100, 130-133, 138-140, 162, 165, 194, 327-333, 355-359, 382-387, 389-390; abolition in Delaware, 235-237, 338, 383; abolition in Kentucky, 383; abolition in Louisiana, 302; abolition in Maryland, 383; abolition in Washington, DC, 237-241, 290-294, 408;abolition in Western territory, 408; as contraband of war, 407-411; demographics, 19-20, **21**, 22-23; economic aspects, 95-98; in Russia, 75-79; in Border States, 324-326; in Virginia, 80-83; Mark Twain's views, 58-60; Thirteenth Amendment to Constitution, 41, 394; thoughts by Lincoln in 1860, 64-66
Slaves as servants on battlefields, 411-415
Smallpox, 250, 350-354
Smith, Andrew F., 181
Smith, Caleb, **336**
Smith, Edmund Kirby, 394, 399
Smith, Gerrit, 46
Smith, James McCune, 44-47
Social Civil and Statistical Association, 367
Soldiers, common, 106-107, 112-115; view of war, 281
Songs of slaves and serfs, 205
South Carolina, 85, 233; racial color lines, 137; secession of, 1, 9, 30-33, 60-63, 83-87. *See also* specific battles.
South, The, influence of Walter Scott on, 316-320
Southall Freeman, Douglas, 117
Southern Amaranth, The, 177
Southern Cross flag, 168-170
Southern Historical Society, x
Southern Literacy Messenger, 298
Southern Wealth and Northern Profits, 97
Spain, 213
Spanish American War, ix
Speciman Days, xiii
Speed, Joshua, 76

Spencer (servant), 411-415
Spirit of the Times, 94
Spotsylvania, VA, 225
Spratt, Leonidas W., 61
Spys, Southern, 184-187
St, Louis, MO, commercial growth, 346-349
Stampp, Kenneth M., 400
Stanton, Edwin M., 21, 44, 282, 284-285, **336**, 367, 378, 392, 402, 437
Star-Spangled Banner (song), 191
Starving the South: How the North Won the Civil War, 181
Stones River, battle of, 280
Stowe, Harriet Beecher, 158, 177
Strong, George Templeton, 191, 193, 378
Stuart, J.E.B., 168
Sumner, Charles, 96, 196, 238, 386
Surgeon General, 282-287

Taney, Roger Brooke, 391
Tappan, Arthur, 46-47
Tappan, Lewis, 46-47
Team of Rivals, xii
Telegraphs, 163, 171, 245-245
Tennessee, 7; secession, 1, 63. *See also* specific battles.
Tents, 258-259, **260**, 261
Texas, 7, 69, 180, 188-190, 279, 296, 435; secession, 1, 60-61
Thirteenth Amendment, 41, 394
Thompson, Jacob, 34
Thompson, John Reuben, 318-319
Thompson, John, 104
Ticknor, Francis Orray, 318
Toombs, Robert A., 15, 381
Tremont Temple, Boston, 32
Trent (ship), Affair, 176, 322
Trollope, Anthony, xi
Trumbull, Lyman, 330
Tubman, Harriet, 13-16, 24
Turner, Henry McNeal, 356
Turner, Nat, rebellion, 80
Twain, Mark, 56-60; views on slavery, 58-59
Tyler, John, 67-71, 295
Tyler, Robert, 71

U.S. Army Medical Department, 282
U.S. Capitol, construction, 261-266
U.S. Colored Infantry, 405
U.S. Congress, 327-333
U.S. Constitution, 11-12; Thirteenth Amendment, 41, 394
U.S. National anthem, 190-193
U.S. Sanitary Commission, 282, 352
U.S. Treasury Department, 249-250

U.S. War Department, 245
Uncle Tom's Cabin, 158
Underground Railroad, 13-16
Underwear, 424-427
Uniforms, cheaply made, 133-136; different colors, 144-148; fraud, 135-136
Union army, xiii, 66, 94, 96, 98, 99, 105, 111, 119, 164, 166, 180, 185, 209, 214, 215-219, 226-231, 233-234, 241-244, 266-275, 275-278, 279-282, 300-302, 402-405, 407-409
Union parties, 54-55
Union Square, New York, 99
United States Coast Survey, 19-20, **21**, 22-23

Van Dorn, Earl, 268
Vicksburg, MS, 154
Victor Emanuel II, King of Italy, 89
Victoria, Queen of Great Britain, 16
Vietnam War, ix
Virginia (ship). *See Merrimac* (ship).
Virginia Historical Society, 115
Virginia,7, 8, 19, 22, 23, 71, 76, 80, 97, 116-118, 127, 137, 159, 161-162, 166, 168, 169, 175, 225, 231, 248, 259, 301, 304, 308, 309, 327, 336, 338, 346, 377-379, 407, 408, 413; secession, 1, 37-40, 60, 62-66, 68, 69, 81-83; slavery in, 80-83. *See also* Richmond, VA and specific battles.
Virginians of the Valley, The, 318

Walter, Thomas U., 263
War of 1812, ix
War Telegram Marking Map, 247
Ward, Samuel, 46
Warne, Kate, 73
Warren, Robert Penn, ix
Washburne, Elihu B., 73
Washington Artillery, uniform, 147
Washington Star, 68
Washington, Booker T., 65
Washington, DC, abolition of slavery in, 11, 237-241, 290-294, 356, 408
Washington, George, 127
Wayne, Henry, 435-436
Webb, William, 65
Webster, Daniel, 39
Welles, Gideon, 326, **336**, 341, 364, 367, 387
West Point, 1, 218, 227
West Virginia, formation of, 2, 37-40
Western Department, 159

Western expansion, 294-299
Western territories, 120-121; Confederate plan to capture, 187-190
Wheeling Conventions, 1,
Wheeling Daily Intelligencer, 39
Whig party, 23, 24, 35, 46-47, 54-55, 62, 138, 198, 296, 328
Whistler, James McNeill, 223
Whistler, William McNeill, 223-226
White, John H., 135
Whitman, Walt, vii, xi, xiii, 99, 103, 108-112, 144, 179, 354, 418
Whittier, John Greenleaf, 177
Wide-Awakes political clubs, 157-158
Wilkerson, Samuel, 221
Wilkes, Charles, 176
Wilkes, May, 94
Willard's Hotel, Washington, DC, 67
William, T. Harry, 231
Willis, Edward, 350-351, 354
Wilson, Edmund, x
Wilson, Henry, 237-239
Wilson, Woodrow, viii
Wilson's Creek, MO, 124
Winsmith, John Christopher, 411-415
Wise, John, 171; cartoon, **242**
Women at war, 341-342, **343**, 344, 345
Wood, Fernando, 47, 98, 111, 393
Woolson, Albert, death, viii
Worth, Jonathan, 53
Wren, James, 112-113
Wright, John C., 68

Yale University, 138
Yorktown, VA, 255

Zouaves, 146, 148